Feeling, Thinking, and Talking

The way the brain, body, and mind interact with social structure to shape communication has so far not received the attention it deserves. This book addresses this gap by providing a novel account of communication as a social, biological, and neurological force. Combining theories from communication studies and psycholinguistics, and drawing on biological and evolutionary perspectives, it shows how communication is inherently both biological and social, and that language and the neural systems that support it have evolved in response to a complex social environment. It introduces a clear set of terms based on current research and illustrates key concepts using real-life examples from everyday conversation – speaking to a number of current debates around the evolutionary and biological basis of language and the relationship between language, cognition, and environment. Thought provoking and engaging, it will change the way we think about the relationship between communication and cognition.

L. DAVID RITCHIE is Professor of Communication at Portland State University. He is the author of four books, including three on metaphor theory, and has contributed extensively to journals and edited volumes.

Feeling, Thinking, and Talking
How the Embodied Brain Shapes Everyday Communication

L. David Ritchie

Portland State University

Shaftesbury Road, Cambridge CB2 8EA, United Kingdom

One Liberty Plaza, 20th Floor, New York, NY 10006, USA

477 Williamstown Road, Port Melbourne, VIC 3207, Australia

314–321, 3rd Floor, Plot 3, Splendor Forum, Jasola District Centre, New Delhi – 110025, India

103 Penang Road, #05–06/07, Visioncrest Commercial, Singapore 238467

Cambridge University Press is part of Cambridge University Press & Assessment, a department of the University of Cambridge.

We share the University's mission to contribute to society through the pursuit of education, learning and research at the highest international levels of excellence.

www.cambridge.org
Information on this title: www.cambridge.org/9781108969673

DOI: 10.1017/9781108979566

© L. David Ritchie 2022

This publication is in copyright. Subject to statutory exception and to the provisions of relevant collective licensing agreements, no reproduction of any part may take place without the written permission of Cambridge University Press & Assessment.

First published 2022
First paperback edition 2025

A catalogue record for this publication is available from the British Library

ISBN 978-1-108-83904-4 Hardback
ISBN 978-1-108-96967-3 Paperback

Cambridge University Press & Assessment has no responsibility for the persistence or accuracy of URLs for external or third-party internet websites referred to in this publication and does not guarantee that any content on such websites is, or will remain, accurate or appropriate.

To LaJean

Contents

List of Figures		*page* viii
Preface: The Genesis and Intentions of This Book		ix
1	The Embodiment Perspective	1
2	Homeostasis: Perception, Feelings, and Signaling	19
3	How Language and Conversation Evolved	46
4	Thinking: Using and Understanding Language	81
5	Emotion	101
6	Signals	123
7	Context	146
8	Relationships and Groups	163
9	Conversation	182
10	Play	207
11	Metaphor	223
12	Humor and Irony	246
13	Stories	264
14	Media Technology, Social Reality, and Discourse	279
15	Recap: Homeostasis and Communication	301
References		312
Index		333

Figures

2.1	Neuron and synapse	*page* 24
2.2	Motor and sensory regions of the cerebral cortex	31
2.3	The sensory homunculus above (a), motor homunculus below (b)	32
2.4	The sensory homunculus above (a), motor homunculus below (b) (repeated from Figure 2.3)	41
10.1	Lioness with her sister's cubs	209

Preface
The Genesis and Intentions of This Book

I entered graduate school in 1983 with an interest in the human mind/brain and how it interacts with other humans to construct and discover meaning. As I learned the theories and methods of the empirical/behavioral approach to communication taught at Stanford, I was repeatedly dismayed at the neglect of the cognitive processes through which messages are created and understood, a neglect that was then common to all the social sciences. At that time, the brain was still considered an impenetrable "*black box*": The proper conduct of inquiry was to study the relationship of "*inputs*" to "*outputs*,"[1] without futile speculation about what might happen between.

At that time, in the early 1980s, computation, and particularly artificial intelligence (AI), was entering its glory days. I had what now seems like the good fortune to enter the communication discipline without having ever taken a single course in the subject. This has allowed me to approach the subject matter innocent of the taken-for-granted assumptions and verities, to read the research and examine the data on their own terms. I was especially fascinated by theories that examine mind and its interaction with meaning. I had already become first enthusiastic, then disappointed by Freud, then by Jung. One by one I became intrigued by, adopted, then became disappointed by information theory, AI,[2] and other instantiations of what I have come to think of as "the *computer* metaphor." Like many other students and scholars of the era, I was deeply impressed with Shannon and Weaver's (1949) exposition of information theory, but I disregarded Wilbur Schramm's advice to "read Weaver first." When I finally did read Weaver, the contrast between his speculations and Shannon's elegant mathematics led me to disillusionment (and my first academic publication,[3] which later led to my first book[4]). I explored several

---

[1] Throughout the book I indicate metaphors, when their status as metaphors is relevant, by italics within quotation marks.

[2] In my first year at Stanford, I audited a course in Lisp, in which the ability to program a computer to respond to even the most simple verbal instructions was celebrated as a major achievement. My resulting skepticism was reinforced by reading Winograd and Flores's (1986) argument against conflating AI with cognitive theory.

[3] Ritchie (1986). [4] Ritchie (1991).

other simplifying (and mechanistic) models and computational methods, including various versions of co-orientation theory and "mental spaces."

I came to realize that all these approaches disregard the fact that messages are both originated and understood by evolved biological brains, though it took many more years of reading and study to realize the extent to which a biological brain is embedded in a biological body, how different a biological brain is from a computer, and how important that difference is. At about that same time, I encountered the idea of perceptual simulation in Shepard's[5] research on mental rotation and began to read all I could find on this and related topics. I also encountered Lakoff and Johnson's[6] theory of conceptual metaphors, though it would be over a decade before I was able to realize fully what could be done with it. Along the way, I also became deeply skeptical of one-variable explanations for human experience and behavior, communication in particular. Competition, power, sexuality all play a role, as do cooperation, curiosity, play, empathy, and imagination – among many other factors.

My dissertation, applying an abstract co-orientation model to social power, convinced me that the social and cultural context is central, not incidental. Working with mentors – especially Steve Chaffee, Don Roberts, and Mary Anne Fitzpatrick – convinced me that social interaction is a crucial component shaping both the origination and the interpretation of signals, a component none of the linear models I had found so intriguing could successfully incorporate. When Ray Gibbs introduced me to Lynne Cameron and Dynamic Discourse Analysis, the pieces began to fall into place. Robin Dunbar's[7] evidence that language is fundamentally about social relationships rather than ecological information provided the final catalyst.

The cover image reproduces a photograph of two golden monkeys grooming.[8] This activity, which is common to many mammal species, is a vital feature of primate social life, and primates of many species spend much of their waking hours grooming or being groomed. Grooming serves to recruit and sustain supportive relationships, appease higher-ranking individuals, or mollify a lower-ranking individual who has been defeated in a quarrel. Grooming (like sexual interaction) releases endorphins that lead to intense pleasure, even euphoria, which strengthens social bonds. Dunbar[9] claims that language/conversation developed primarily in response to the pressure of living in large and increasingly complex social structure. The use of language in conversation allows an individual to "groom" three others at one time,

---

[5] For example, Shepard and Metzler (1971).   [6] Lakoff and Johnson (1980).
[7] Dunbar (1996, 2003).
[8] I took this photo in Rwanda in 2019; it was the primary purpose of the visit to that lovely, tragic nation.
[9] Dunbar (1996, 2003).

thereby tripling the size of potential social networks. Primate grooming is not even remotely symbolic; it is physical and chemical. Likewise, the import of human talk is often only nominally symbolic; it is also primarily chemical (endorphins again), and much of the time it is physical, by way of physical proximity, direct touch, and synchronization.

While at Stanford, I also encountered Maturana and Varela's[10] theory of *autopoiesis*, but, like Conceptual Metaphor Theory, I did not yet know what to do with it. More recently, I encountered Damasio's recasting of very similar ideas in his theory of *homeostasis*, which incorporates several decades of additional neurological research, along with Damasio's own clinic-based research on the importance of emotion to reasoning. Damasio's explication of homeostasis and the contribution of chemical as well as neural signaling to homeostasis provides a large part of the framework for this book.

As I have read, studied, and conducted research into these phenomena, I have come to recognize that *cognition* is much more complex than I had ever imagined. It happens in the brain, but not just in the brain. It involves processes of neural activation that are based on waves of electromagnetic membrane depolarization (not the same as the electrical circuits in a typical digital computer), along with biochemical processes that affect various bodily organs directly even as they are enhancing or suppressing neural activity. It involves the entire body's interactions with the physical and social environment, and much of what constitutes cognition takes place *in* these interactions. All this – neural system, biochemical processes, social relationships, and interactions with both social and physical environment – is the result of biological evolution and, to an increasing extent, cultural evolution. The difference between *evolved* organisms and *designed* digital computers and electronic communications circuits is not incidental; it is vital to understanding both.

Dunbar convinced me that the "transmission" or "replication" of *information* is not central to communication. Although information has become increasingly important to human interactions with the physical and social environment, the primary function of communication continues to be *relationship*, the reproduction and elaboration of the social environment and each individual's negotiation of an identity within the social environment.

The Purpose of the Book

I first conceived of this project, early in graduate school, with the ambitious intention of constructing and presenting a theoretical perspective on human

---

[10] Maturana and Varela (1980).

communication based on biologically informed cognitive science. That initial project has inevitably expanded and transformed itself to the point that it scarcely bears any relation to the ideas and insights with which it began. Nonetheless, it still seems accurate to say that the purpose of this book is to propose a foundation for thinking about and studying human communication that is cognitive and biological as well as social.

During my graduate studies, I became aware how Communication, to an even greater extent than other social sciences, has grown and developed by the accretion of new concepts, new theories, and new research findings onto a relatively stable basic model. Hardly anyone in the social sciences cites Shannon and Weaver any more, but the source-channel-receiver model and the *"signal transmission"* metaphor it supports still underlie much of contemporary thinking about communication. This model, along with the *"computer"* metaphor for mind, permeates the technical language we use, and reinforces a model which I believe to be fundamentally obsolete – and misleading. As I have thought, written about, and taught some of these concepts over the years, I have concluded that introduction of a new way of thinking about communication based on contemporary neurological and social research requires that we clear away this metaphorical language and the old ideas embedded in it. Accordingly, a second purpose of the book is to critique this obsolete and misleading terminology and introduce a more objective and accurate, though austere, way of talking and writing about communication that is consistent with current biological and cognitive research.

The book begins, in Chapter 1, with a brief discussion of *embodiment* and *homeostasis* as a basis for a critique of terminology. The next seven chapters, constituting the first half of the book, present the concept of homeostasis and the neurological research supporting it, and develop it into an account of cognition (thought, emotion, and relationship). The second half of the book develops some of the implications of this account for basic communication processes, focusing in particular on conversation and figurative use of language in conversation.

I have acknowledged in passing several of the mentors and colleagues who have inspired and guided my thinking; I owe a deep debt of gratitude to all of them. I also owe a debt of gratitude to present and former students who have read and commented on this (and previous) books and articles; whenever I teach this material, I invariably feel that I learn as much from my students as they learn from me. I am fortunate to teach in a university with a somewhat older and more mature student population, most of whom work at least half time and many of whom have families as well as careers, and engage with the urban environment on a daily basis. They bring that "real world" with them into the classroom, and it provides an invaluable grounding for my theoretical as well as my practical thinking. I must mention two students in particular,

William Harvey, whose term paper on face-work greatly enriched my discussion of that topic, and Elise Stinnett, whose "student's eye view" of the book inspired wording changes and clarifications in several sections of the book during the final copyediting phase. My neurologist friend and hiking companion, Scott Emery, has generously explained basic concepts of neuroscience to me and corrected at least some of my more egregious errors of understanding.

Finally, I am as always indebted to my gracious and helpful editors, Helen Barton and Isabel Collins, and to the anonymous reviewers whose comments and suggestions have proven invaluable. The remaining errors and omissions are, of course, entirely my own responsibility.

1   The Embodiment Perspective

This chapter critiques the approaches to human communication and the conceptual language based on comparisons to digital computers that implicitly sustain assumptions of mind-body dualism. It introduces the embodiment perspective, the assumption that mind is a function of the evolved physical body, and proposes a neutral set of conceptual terms based on the actual observable physical processes that constitute communication.

In the past, communication theories[1] have generally been anchored in a story characterized by metaphors based on digital computers, codes, and signal transmission. All these are, in turn, shaped by the mind-body dualism that has haunted European and American thought at least since Plato, and based on the assumptions that thought is fundamentally rational, language is primarily a tool of logical thought, and communication is primarily a process of exchanging data, transmitting the output of one person's thought to serve as input to another person's thought. According to this story, ideas are consciously formed in the mind, using a "language of the brain," *mentalese*,[2] and encoded by the brain into language, which is then further encoded into sounds (or shapes for written language), then encoded into a message by activating appropriate muscle groups. This message, as if it were a physical object, is *"sent"*[3] to one or more *"receivers,"* listeners or readers who perform the opposite sequence of decoding, ending with a replica of a speaker or writer's thought. After *"decoding"* the message, a receiver may process the message using "mentalese" and formulate a reply, which is then encoded back into natural language to be *"sent,"* continuing the interaction.

---

[1] I use *theory* as it is defined in social science, not humanities, to denote a system of principled causal relations among concepts, subject to test, modification, and potential disconfirmation through evidence gained from systematic observation.
[2] Bergen (2012); Fodor (1975).
[3] I indicate metaphors (where their metaphoricity is important) by italicizing them and placing them within quotation marks.

The Embodiment Perspective

Over the past several decades, as new research tools have been developed, this classical account has been challenged on almost every front. Maturana and Varela[4] proposed the concept of *autopoiesis* as a systems-theory-based explanation of both life and mind as *autonomous, self-organizing*, and *self-generating*. Varela, Thompson, and Rosch[5] developed this into an account of "the *enactive* mind," in which the entire body is engaged in cognition. Damasio[6] showed that emotions are not separate from reason, as Plato insisted, but integral to reasoning and decision-making.[7] More recently, Damasio[8] developed the related concept of *homeostasis*, incorporating recent research on chemical and neural signaling.[9] Lawrence Barsalou[10] and other cognitive researchers[11] have demonstrated that mental activity, including using and understanding language, involves *perceptual simulations*, partial activation of perceptual and motor neural systems that would be fully activated by perceptions and muscular actions associated with the words, concepts, and grammatical structure. Other researchers in cognitive linguistics, testing and extending insights gained from Conceptual Metaphor Theory,[12] have shown that perceptual simulations associated with the literal meanings of words are partially activated even when the words are used metaphorically.

Research on consciousness has shown that most routine decisions are made, and actions initiated, before an individual is aware of having made the decision, and hence they cannot result from conscious thought.[13] Along similar lines, conversation researchers have found that it takes a second or longer to understand an utterance and more than a half second to formulate and initiate an utterance. However, the pause between speaking turns is usually considerably less than a half second, and the next speaker often begins speaking before the previous speaker has finished. This indicates that listeners are able to anticipate accurately when the speaker will finish, and that they have begun to prepare their own utterance well in advance of beginning a speaking turn, contradicting traditional assumptions about the role of consciousness in originating and interpreting messages. The assumption that language exists primarily to serve rational thought by exchange of truth-conditional propositions[14] has been challenged by research suggesting that language (and the

---

[4] Maturana and Varela (1980).
[5] Varela, Thompson, and Rosch (1991); see also Di Paolo, Rohde, and De Jaegher (2010).
[6] Damasio (1999).   [7] See also Seligman et al. (2016).   [8] Damasio (2018).
[9] See Chapter 2 for a more complete discussion.
[10] Barsalou (1999, 2008); Seligman et al. (2016).
[11] See Bergen (2012) for a comprehensive review.   [12] Lakoff and Johnson (1980, 1999).
[13] For a review and discussion, see Baumeister and Masicampo (2010).
[14] For example, Bickerton (2009).

brain systems that support language) evolved primarily in response not to ecological pressures but to the pressures of living in a complex social structure,[15] and that maintaining social relationships through "grooming" and exchanging news about other people's relationships ("gossip") is still the primary function of language.

The primacy of formal logic is also challenged by research on how ordinary people reason about causality. For example, Deanna Kuhn[16] tested the ability of successful practitioners in several professions to engage in reasoning about causal relations according to the standard model of scientific logic (in which alternative hypotheses are tested against each other) and discovered that only advanced doctoral students in philosophy could perform these logical tasks correctly. Most of the other subjects preferred to synthesize ideas from the alternative theories into a comprehensive account rather than test them against one another. Kuhn argued that this indicates a need for better logic training in professional schools, but reexamination of Kuhn's evidence suggests the opposite conclusion, that people, even well-educated people, do not find formal scientific logic useful in their everyday lives, and that it is actually very difficult to learn to use formal logic.[17] If formal logic is that difficult to learn and use, and if experienced and well-educated reasoners resist using it, it is probably not part of the brain's natural functioning.[18]

Extensive research by Kahneman and Tversky[19] established that people routinely fall back on simple heuristics in their reasoning, even about important issues like financial investments and public policy preferences. Greene[20] shows that even highly influential moral philosophers tend to be guided by moral heuristics and adapt their highly trained logical reasoning skills to support the conclusions drawn from their moral beliefs, rather than examining or revising these moral beliefs. More generally, researchers have recently shown that people routinely engage in "motivated reasoning": They selectively focus on evidence that supports their prior beliefs and discredit or reinterpret evidence that contradicts their prior beliefs. Again, even highly educated people are susceptible[21] to this kind of bias in reasoning – and it is quite difficult to avoid.[22]

---

[15] See, for example, Dessalles (2014); Dunbar (1996, 2003, 2014). [16] Kuhn (1991).
[17] Ritchie (2003c).
[18] Seligman et al. (2016). On the other hand, it appears that the brain does something that can be described by natural language statistics, but that doesn't mean that it actually does the same computations that a statistician would use (Chapter 3).
[19] Kahneman and Tversky (1982). [20] Greene (2014).
[21] The fact that biased processing and motivated reasoning are so widespread – effectively universal – suggests that "susceptible" may not be the right word: In computer science jargon, perhaps it is "a feature, not a bug."
[22] It should be obvious from recent science news that social and physical scientists are not immune from the effects of motivated reasoning and confirmation bias.

Most of these ideas have found their way in a piecemeal fashion into recent communication theory and research, but many of the rationalist and computational assumptions linger on in research methodology[23] as well as theoretical writing, often embodied in unchallenged metaphorical language. Toward the end of this chapter, I will briefly examine the assumptions implicit in some of this metaphorical language and propose alternative terminology that is less likely to reinforce inaccurate and obsolete beliefs; a more detailed discussion can be found in Chapter 6.

The central, motivating purpose of this book is to rethink the foundations of communication theory, how we think and talk about human communication, in a way that acknowledges and incorporates this accumulating evidence and recognizes communicating subjects as evolved biological organisms. I will organize the discussion around several interrelated conceptual frameworks and core concepts, which will serve as a foundation for challenging and examining previously taken-for-granted assumptions.

First, the evolved biological body is the focal center of it all. Both thinking and communicating are biologically evolved social processes, engaging the entire body. They engage biologically evolved neural processes that primarily serve to maintain the reproductive fitness of biological organisms within a complex and ever-changing environment, in particular the social environment.[24] The capabilities that produce sophisticated philosophical arguments, profound religious insights, and stunning works of art are all happy but incidental extensions of fitness-related processes.[25]

Second, consistent with systems theory thinking, the ongoing dynamic responses and adjustments that Damasio summarizes as "homeostasis" constitute a process at multiple levels, from the individual cell through tissues and organs to individual persons and on to groups, cultures, and societies. Within an individual body, each organ's output is input to other organs, and all organs strive to maintain homeostasis by responding to the other organs; the net result is the much more complex homeostasis of the body as a whole. Similarly, each individual in a social group takes and responds to input from others; the net process of these interactions is the homeostasis of the group. This is why Damasio uses the term *homeostasis* rather than *balance*: A dynamic system is never in balance; it is always in the process of perceiving and adjusting to both internal and external units, each a complex system in its own right, that are also constantly perceiving and responding to each other and to themselves.

---

[23] For example, Thorson, Wicks, and Leshner (2012). [24] Barrett (2020).
[25] Writing in the summer of 2020, I can't help adding that the ability to produce horrific weapons, environment-destroying pollutants, and so forth, is also an (un)happy but incidental extension of the same processes – consistent with meme theory (Chapter 3).

Signaling systems, including the body's neural and chemical signals as well as language and other social signals, also evolved in support of individual and social group homeostasis. Unlike computers and transmission systems, neither the brain nor language is *designed*. The parts, including the perceptual and signal production systems, coevolved with each other – and with other constraints. Evolution is messy and rarely leads to *optimal* results: *Adequate* is far more common.[26] Motivated reasoning, susceptibility to perceptual illusion, and the development and spread of useless and even pernicious memes as well as useless or pernicious physiological characteristics and other apparently suboptimal features must be understood in this context. We communicate with the body we have, not the body that a priori reasoning or clever engineering principles would lead us to believe we must, surely, have.

Third, humans have evolved as social animals, and human signaling, particularly language, evolved and developed in response to the pressures of living in large complex social groups, and probably also in response to the mutual dependence of individuals on their primary groups and of the dependence of the group itself on the complex homeostatic relationships among humans. As fundamentally social creatures, humans are also deeply dependent on culture, the transmission of learned practices (social as well as ecological) across generations. A unique and crucial contribution of a flexible and powerful language is to facilitate relatively rapid cultural and social change in response to a fluctuating environment[27] through both imitation and intentional instruction, a process sometimes theorized as *cultural evolution*.[28]

A fourth consideration in the structure of this book is the importance of language itself in all these processes, in the homeostasis-maintaining processes of individuals, social groups, and cultures. As such, understanding how language evolves and adapts and is used in conversation is important to understanding the complex nature of human communication. That includes "indirect" communication forms such as language play, metaphor, humor, and storytelling, each of which will get its own chapter.

A fifth consideration follows from the importance of language itself. In particular, metaphorical terms often carry unacknowledged assumptions and constraints on theory development and understanding, and sometimes on

---

[26] It is intellectually and emotionally satisfying (and spiritually useful) to marvel at the subtle and complex intricacies of evolved biological systems, which are truly amazing and beautiful. However, we must not allow our justifiable awe to blind us to their fundamentally unplanned, *un*-designed, and ad hoc features. See Chapter 2 for a more complete discussion.

[27] Writing in 2019 and 2020, I cannot help commenting on the irony that these very cultural transmission and adaptation tools that have enabled us to adapt to almost every environment on Earth have apparently also enabled us to despoil and possibly destroy the environment of the entire planet.

[28] For example, see Heyes et al. (2020); Dennett (2017).

evidence-gathering and analysis. Accordingly, beginning in this chapter, and then throughout most of the book, I will explicate and critique terminology that has come to be taken for granted but that implies unjustified and misleading assumptions about both cognition and communication. Communication theorists have adopted and reified seductive *"machine," "computer,"* and *"telecommunication"* metaphors, which obstruct our ability to see how people actually communicate (and how people use metaphors[29]).

Reified metaphors and other fallacies have sprung in part from the understandable desire of social scientists to achieve something like the kind of rigor achieved in the physical sciences, especially in physics and engineering disciplines based on physics. Because computers, like brains, process data, and (in the early days of artificial intelligence (AI) research) we were able to describe precisely how computers process data, the computer became a popular, if highly misleading, model for the brain. Along the same lines, because our research methods, including computer modeling as well as many of our statistical methods, require us to classify both perceptual stimuli and behavioral responses into discrete categories, and because the *"code"* metaphor assumes digitization, we concluded that these digitized categories represented something real about human cognition and communication. However, as my mentor, Steve Chaffee, used to admonish, "never give a methodological answer to a theoretical question." The fact that a manageable research design requires that we digitize behavior does not mean behavior is digital, and the fact that certain aspects of human perception and response can be simplified and modeled on a digital computer does not imply that human cognition is either simple or digital.

The foundational perspective of the book is that human communication is *embodied* in a *biological* sense, as well as in a *social* and *cultural* sense. The *biologically embodied* perspective includes the role of communication in the body's processes of maintaining *homeostasis*[30] as well as the engagement in language use and comprehension of neural systems primarily associated with perception and muscular action.[31] The biologically embodied perspective also requires continual attention to the processes of evolution, especially biological evolution but also cultural evolution.

The *social* perspective includes the recognition that social relationships and social structure are themselves fundamentally biological and coevolved with the physiological features that support them. The social perspective also involves recognizing that the function of communication as a medium for developing and maintaining the social relationships is essential to our *biological* survival, what Dunbar[32] refers to as the "grooming" and "gossip"

---

[29] Chapter 11.   [30] See Chapter 2.   [31] See Chapters 3 and 7.
[32] Dunbar (1996, 2003); see Chapter 5.

functions of language use. The *cultural* dimension of communication includes recognizing that culture is also fundamentally biological, an outgrowth and expression of biologically evolved processes. Culture also includes the contextual background of ideas, behaviors, and norms (including what Dawkins[33] and Dennett[34] call *memes*[35]) that are transmitted by communication and form much of the content of communication. Finally, at a *conceptual* level, communication is characterized by fundamental ambiguity[36] and the ubiquitous use of heuristics[37] rather than formal logic.

Communication as a discipline has arisen as an amalgam of theories and concepts from several other, more traditional, disciplines, including Rhetoric, English, Linguistics, Psychology, Sociology, and Anthropology; in many ways, Communication is still largely interdisciplinary in theory and method as well as in practice. This eclectic interdisciplinarity is both a strength and a liability. It is a strength because it affords the opportunity to cross boundaries that often prevent workers in one discipline from recognizing and benefiting from discoveries that are so well-known in another discipline that they are taken for granted.[38] It is a liability because central concepts, often originally based on obscure theories, are defined and explained in eclectic and sometimes mutually contradictory ways, in many cases based on obsolete or a priori reasoning or infelicitous metaphors. In order to achieve the core objectives of this book, it will be necessary to clear away some of the metaphorical underbrush that clutters theoretical writings about communication, and propose a conceptual language that is free of archaic "*machine*" and "*digital computer*" metaphors and more consistent with an embodied, biological perspective.

Communication Is Biological. Life requires constant action and change, interacting with an unpredictable and constantly changing environment. All organisms *perceive* and *react* to features of the external environment that are necessary to their survival – for example, by moving toward and ingesting nutrients, moving away from and avoiding poisons and predators. Most organisms also perceive and react to *signals* from other organisms. Multicelled organisms, including humans, have quite complex interactions with the external environment; the tissues and cells of multicelled organisms also have complex interactions with each other. Communication, within our bodies and with other humans, as well as with other organisms, is essential to our lives. Communication is one of the most important functions of living organisms,

---

[33] Dawkins (1976). [34] Dennett (2017). [35] See Chapter 3 for a more detailed discussion.
[36] Sperber and Wilson (1986). [37] Kahneman and Tversky (1982).
[38] An example I recently encountered is Petty and Cacioppo's (1981) Elaboration Likelihood Model, which neatly solves some long-standing problems in metaphor theory – but is largely unknown to linguists, philosophers, and even many psychologists who study metaphor.

and the complex ways we communicate are generally regarded as defining features of what it means to be human. Language is commonly mentioned in this regard, but other modes of communication are no less important to our distinctive humanity.

On the other hand, it is also important to avoid the fallacy of assuming a crisp dividing line between the communication behaviors of humans and those of other organisms. Research in the past few decades has produced convincing evidence that our human modes of communication are continuous with those of other species, especially other primates but also other mammals – and even birds. Although human language vastly exceeds the signaling behavior of any other species[39] in its richness and complexity, anyone who would fully understand human communication cannot afford to neglect the study of the communication behavior of other primates as well as many other species of mammals, birds, and even less complex organisms.

Because of the conceptual sophistication and complexity of human language, and because language is the medium in which both science and philosophy are conducted, most of the discussion of human communication has focused intensively on language. Other modes of signaling are often misleadingly labeled as, for example, "body *language*."[40] The indisputable role of language in both abstract thought and discourse about abstract ideas has also led to an intensive focus on the use of language to express ideas. Ironically, until recently, the role of the brain and central nervous system in language use has been largely neglected.

When I began my own academic study of communication, in the 1980s, the brain was dismissed as a "*black box*,"[41] a mysterious and complicated organ that, because we had no way to "*peer into* it," was out of bounds for theorizing, much less researching, communication. As a result, theorists fell back on a metaphor popularized by the midcentury progress in computational science:[42] The brain is a "*computer*" and communication is a process of "*encoding*" ideas into signals that are "*sent to* a *receiver*" where they are "*decoded*" into the same ideas. This theoretical language went hand in hand with the rapid development of research in "AI," which was often described as the *only* available avenue for empirical research into how communication "*messages*" are created, "*transmitted*," and understood. The prevailing doctrine was that, if you could not express

---

[39] Perhaps excepting the cetaceans; at this writing, we know that the signals of whales, for example, are very complex; we do not know whether they accomplish communication in any sense comparable to human communication.
[40] "Body *signals*" is a more accurate, hence preferred, term.
[41] **Notation**: Where metaphors are relevant to the discussion, I will mark metaphorical words and phrases by placing metaphorical elements in italics and the entire phrase within quotation marks (e.g. "body *language*" and "*black box*").
[42] Ritchie (1991).

your theory in a functioning computer algorithm, you did not have a valid theory.[43] This approach tacitly implies that body, brain, mind, and language are in some sense *designed* and *engineered*, which in turn implies an *engineer*, a creator or creative process with *agency* and *intentionality*.

Metaphors of Communication. This approach to research and theorizing about human communication, which Damasio[44] calls the "Boolean logic" approach, is consistent with the "*computer*" metaphor of mind, popularized in the 1950s and still advocated by some theorists. However, it is inconsistent with a growing body of research that challenges the implicit separation of mind from body as well as the implicit separation of thinking from communicating. It also implies a degree of precision in the everyday use of language that is not supported by analysis of actual conversations. Michael Reddy,[45] an early critic of the computer/algorithm approach, called it the CONTAINER/CONDUIT metaphor. Reddy pointed out that we speak and write of messages "*containing*" information, that are "*put into a message*" by a "*source*" and "*sent to*" a "*receiver*," who "*extracts*" the "*information out of*" the message. Reddy's primary criticism of this metaphorical language was that it constrains how we understand language, and encourages a view in which misunderstanding is the result of inept "*encoding*" or "*decoding*," either "*putting* ideas *into the wrong containers*" or "*getting the wrong ideas out of the containers*." All this implies that "*messages are objects*" that must be "*sent*" and "*received*." Reddy proposed an alternate view, in which interlocutors do not have access to each other's "*codes*." A person creates a message by trying to anticipate how other interlocutors will understand certain utterances or gestures; other interlocutors interpret the message by drawing inferences about what the source must have intended – all without any access to what others intend or mean by the signals they produce.

Reddy's critique has been the center of continued controversy. Krzeszowski[46] defends the use of the CONDUIT metaphor on the basis that it is difficult or impossible to discuss communication without using metaphors, and the overwhelming preponderance of discourse about communication uses one or all of them. He acknowledges that "the early, crude version of the CONDUIT metaphor ... is based on the false assumption that meanings are stable and permanent and do not change, very much like concrete things in the containers" and that "there is no such thing as stability of meaning."[47]

---

[43] For example, Feldman (2006), but for an early contrary view, see also Winograd and Flores (1986). See also Goatly (2007).
[44] Damasio (1999, 2018).   [45] Reddy (1993). See Chapter 6.   [46] Krzeszowski (2020).
[47] Krzeszowski suggests an alternative phases of matter metaphor (i.e. "*solid,*" "*liquid,*" "*gas,*" and "*plasma*") to describe this instability of meaning. However, this scheme would introduce its own confusion – and it is unlikely that many Communication students understand the underlying physics.

Krzeszowski complains that arguing "about meanings of particular linguistic expressions [comes] at the expense of concentrating on what really matters." However, Krippendorff argues that the continued use of these metaphors effectively obscures "what really matters." Krippendorff[48] argues that the language we used to develop and describe our theories shapes how these theories are understood and applied, "and has a good chance of affecting how the stakeholders of our scholarship subsequently communicate." The use of object/container metaphors makes it difficult "to reflect on the implications of our own discourse." Because they objectify the message, these metaphors obscure the fact that people frequently disagree about both the intention and the meaning of communication acts. Use of these metaphors "celebrates animistic conceptions of texts speaking to us, ... and renders incomprehensible the dynamic world of communication of which we are a part."

Krippendorff suggests we use human-centered language that acknowledges imagination and creativity of ordinary discourse, such as "interpreting, articulating, inferring, narrating, conversing, collaborating, negotiating, and interacting." I endorse use of human-centered words, and in this and subsequent chapters, I will suggest a more austere foundational terminology based on an examination of the actual physical events that constitute communication: A person alters the physical environment to create a pattern that another person can perceive, infer that it is intended as a signal, and interpret. The core terms are not *send* a *message* but *create* or *enact* a *signal* to *express* an idea, not *"receive"* a *"message"* (passively) but *perceive* and *interpret* a *signal* (actively). Signaling behavior (including perceiving and interpreting or responding) is grounded in biology, and all the rest, including all the human-centered terms Krippendorff proposes, builds on this fundamentally biological basis, vastly elaborated through social interaction and cultural transmission.

In sum, even as a metaphor, *"send* a message" makes sense if, and only if, you agree that messages are *objects*, that words and gestures have precise meanings, and that they are understood in the same way by everyone who has an adequate knowledge of the language. I agree with Krippendorff that use of these terms in scientific discourse (and in teaching) can only serve to sustain and propagate the epistemological errors from which they derive – just as use of terms derived from the Ptolemaic model of the solar system (e.g. *sunrise* and *sunset*) sustain and propagate a geocentric model, and use of terms derived from a creationist account of evolution (e.g. *design*, natural *selection*) sustain and propagate a creationist model. So, I accept Krippendorff's challenge:

---

[48] Krippendorff (2017, p. 98).

"Critically examining the social implications of our discourse and revising its vocabulary accordingly should be a continuous project of communication scholarship."[49] That is one of the primary objectives of this book.

Communication Is Cognitive. Lakoff and Johnson[50] used linguistic data to develop a theory of Conceptual Metaphors and argued that our experience of abstract concepts is grounded in our actual physical experience of the world. They demonstrated that metaphorical expressions in spoken and written language (and by extension in visual images and other perceptual interaction) express these underlying conceptual metaphor. Using Reddy's examples, "*empty* rhetoric" and "*put your* ideas *into* words" and "*send* a message" express the conceptual metaphors IDEAS ARE OBJECTS and WORDS ARE CONTAINERS.[51]

Barsalou[52] demonstrated that abstract ideas can in principle be expressed completely by means of *perceptual simulations*, the partial activation of neural systems associated with perception and with activation of muscle systems. Barsalou concedes that some thinking occurs by way of abstract symbols, but argues that complex thought requires perceptual simulations. Zwaan[53] argues that both "embodied" cognition using "modal[54]" symbols and abstract ("amodal") symbols are involved in cognition, including language use and interpretation. A large body of research supports the claim that perceptual simulations are routinely, if only briefly, activated while comprehending language,[55] including metaphors,[56] although it is still unclear to what extent simulations are necessary to comprehension.

In brief, the beliefs about the relationship between communication and the body that were formerly expressed by the dismissive "*black box*" metaphor and the doctrine of mind-body separation have been challenged and undermined by a growing body of research on human cognition, neurology, human language use, animal communication, and evolution. Much of this evidence points to a view of mind, communication, and language as a function of the entire body, not just the cerebral cortex. Although some of this research has found its way into recent research and theorizing about human communication, the field is still burdened by an obsolete set of metaphors and metaphor-based terms that anchor our thinking about communication in a rationalist,

---

[49] Krippendorff (2017, p. 98). [50] Lakoff and Johnson (1980); see Chapter 10.
[51] **Notation**: Where the discussion requires it, I will designate conceptual metaphors by placing them in small capital letters – for example, "IDEAS ARE OBJECTS" and "WORDS ARE CONTAINERS." See Chapter 11.
[52] Barsalou (1999). [53] Zwaan (2014).
[54] That is, related to *modes* of perception; *amodal* is, conversely, *not* related to modes of perception.
[55] See Chapter 4; for a detailed review, see Bergen (2012).
[56] Gibbs (2006, 2008); Gibbs and Matlock (2008); Chapters 4 and 10.

computational model of mind – and make it more difficult to understand the fundamentally biological foundations of communication.

Communication Is Social. Communication is commonly explained as being primarily about transmitting precise information such as facts, requests, intentions, and so forth. However, researchers have consistently found that only about one-third of communication is about transmitting this kind of objective information: two-thirds is about social relationships.[57] Some communication about relationship is what Dunbar calls "gossip," information about relationships, but much of it is what he calls "grooming," nontelic chatter about topics that are of little or no consequence, with the primary purpose of building and maintaining harmonious relationships. (Gossip also serves a "grooming" function.) Language is constantly in flux, and it is inherently complex and ambiguous. Conversation is the basic use of language, and storytelling is a fundamental part of conversation. Language use also incorporates metaphor, humor, and other forms of playfulness.

The accumulating evidence suggests that conversation and language evolved together, in response to living in a large and complex social structure. Researchers have also found that about two-thirds of the relationship work of communication is accomplished by what is often called "nonverbal" signals, signals that are not recognized as lexical units (words) in spoken or written language. Conversely, these "nonverbal" signals, including gesture, facial expression, and vocal qualities are consistently used as part of language, to qualify, extend, and substitute for both the lexical and the syntactic features of language[58]. For this reason, as well as to include sign language in the discussion, I prefer a term like "nonlexical" signals.

Communication Is Cultural. Culture is a set of practices, beliefs, and assumptions that influence how people act and how they interact with other people. Culture centrally includes signaling behavior, how people create, use, understand, and respond to signals. Culture is transmitted both by observation and by communication, including formal instruction (e.g. by parents) as well as responses that either encourage or discourage repetition of a behavior. Although culture is distinct from genetically determined (innate) behavior, it is strongly influenced by innate traits. Genetically determined traits that increase an individual's ability to acquire the local culture, including language, will increase the individual's reproductive fitness, and will be transmitted to future generations. Conversely, cultural traits that are easier and more rewarding to acquire and reproduce are more likely to be successfully

---

[57] For example, see Dessalles (2014); Dunbar (1996, 2003); Enfield (2017).

[58] McNeill (2000, 2005). Following McNeill's argument, I argue that these signals should properly be considered, researched, and taught as part of language, certainly not as *separate* languages. See Chapters 6 and 9.

transmitted. Accordingly, the process of transmission itself will tend to reshape the culture. Perversely, the same processes that lead to transmission and reshaping of desirable cultural beliefs and practices are also responsible for transmission and reshaping of *undesirable* beliefs and practices[59].

Concepts and Metaphorical Terms

Theories and research about human communication have developed from several different disciplines, reflecting a wide range of perspectives. This eclectic background has led to the accretion of metaphors, concepts, and metaphor-based concepts that often obscure as much as they illuminate. Clear thinking about any complex phenomenon requires a foundation of clearly specified terms that distinguish among relevant concepts and processes. It is difficult to discuss abstract concepts without some recourse to metaphors, and a good metaphor or metaphorical story can often facilitate understanding. However, when metaphors have misleading implications that contradict well-established empirical evidence, it is time to replace or at least carefully qualify them.

The concept of communication itself has been defined in scores, possibly hundreds, of ways. The broadest of these definitions derives from the oft-repeated (and unfortunately just as often decontextualized) phrase "You cannot not communicate," which apparently originated in research on schizophrenia by Watzlawick, Beavin Bavelas, and Jackson[60]. In the particular social context of schizophrenics and their families, these researchers discovered that family members interpret and assign meaning to virtually everything others do, even when they do nothing at all. Unfortunately, that context-specific observation has been overgeneralized and applied to all situations, even situations in which there are no detectable social relationships. The result is that *communication* has often been treated as a synonym for *behavior*, a conflation that is valid only within narrowly specified contexts – such as treatment of troubled relationships. I have even had students, probably under the influence of popular culture writings about nonverbal communication, claim that a rock lying in a remote part of a desert "communicates" – by which logic *communication* is made out to be a synonym not merely for *behavior* but also for *existence*.

Defining communication as coextensive with existence or even with behavior leaves us with two words for one concept, where only one is needed, and no word for a separate concept where at least one is needed. If *communication* = *existence* (or *behavior*), then what term do we use for a behavior enacted with the purpose or intention that someone else perceive it, recognize it as

---

[59] Dennett (2017); Heyes et al. (2020); see Chapter 3 for a detailed discussion.
[60] Watzlawick, Beavin Bavelas, and Jackson (1967/2011).

intentional, interpret it, and respond to it? Accordingly, if I find the concept necessary, I will use only one term, *exist*, for the condition of being present in the universe. I will use another term, *behavior*, for any action performed by a living organism, intentional or not. I will reserve the term *communication* for behavior performed with the purpose or intention to mean something for another organism, to be perceived by and influence in some way another organism's action in the world. I will distinguish between *signals*, which are intentional or at least serve a primary function of communication, and *cues* or *signs*, which are neither intended nor primarily evolved for purposes of communication, but may provide a basis for valid attributions and inferences.[61]

Another common source of confusion is the *"code"* metaphor and the closely related *"computer"* metaphor, both of which often imply an unrealistic degree of precision. In general, much of what is communicated cannot be succinctly expressed; how does one *"decode"* a gentle touch on the shoulder or a slight alteration in voice tone? Too much of the communication literature implies a degree of precision in signals that is difficult, if not impossible, to justify empirically. Even language, which is often regarded as the epitome of code-like precision, is often quite ambiguous, and can almost always be altered across a wide spectrum of feeling and response by subtle differences in vocal inflection, facial expression, gesture, and other signals[62].

Similarly, communication scholars often refer to the person who enacts a gesture or other signal as a *source* who *sends a message* to one or more *receivers*. This is also misleading: Except in the case of *"snail* mail" (messages written on paper and stuffed into envelopes), *nothing is sent or received*. What happens is that originators alter the perceptible environment in some way (generate sound waves, alter the shape of their face or arms, generate patterns on a computer screen) which others observe, notice, and interpret. In vocal communication, sound waves are propagated across a space; the molecules themselves move only slightly back and forth as the compression wave passes through. In visual communication, light waves are propagated. Even if light is considered in its particle phase, as photons, it's not the photons that comprise the message; it is the pattern of photons, as they reflect the pattern of the signal, an object, or action that does *not* move across the space.

These terms are widely used in communication textbooks and even in scholarly articles, usually without any thought given to their entailments, the implicit assumptions they convey or the ways they can mislead readers about the actual nature of communication. Because of their central importance to a clear understanding of the topic, these terms will be discussed in more detail in

---

[61] Chapter 6. I adopt the word *cues* somewhat hesitantly, since cues in the context of a theatrical performance are themselves *signals* of a certain type.

[62] Chapters 4, 6, and 8.

Chapter 6, and in other chapters as they are relevant. Other useful terms, such as *meme* and *metaphor*, will be defined as they appear.

Homeostasis, Representation, and Communication

Throughout, this book is based on the insight that communication is a function of both mind and body. Mind is a function of the brain as an integral part of body. The brain, hence the mind, is shaped by evolution, the body interacting with the environment. Mental processes, including use of language and signaling in general, involve the entire brain, including neural circuits primarily devoted to perception and muscular control.

The nervous system, including the brain, evolved primarily to regulate internal body functions (maintaining homeostasis) and the interaction of body with the external environment in service of homeostasis[63] and reproductive fitness. The brain maintains a representation of the current state of the body in its environment and, in humans, a representation of the self in its social environment. The interoceptive nervous system transmits information about the state of bodily tissues and organs, and the exteroceptive nervous system (the "five senses") transmits information about relevant aspects of the external environment. This, plus the ability to call up a representation of past states of the body and the environment from long-term memory, allows the brain to forward-project representations of self-in-environment.[64] Among modern Homo sapiens, these representations include short-term representation of how a situation is likely to develop (essential for coherent social interaction, including conversation) as well as projected scenarios of how different courses of action might affect the longer-term development of the current situation – a major function of consciousness.[65] At least in modern humans, cognitive representations incorporate perceptual, emotional, and motor simulations (partial activation of associated neural circuits) as well as neural links to related concepts and expressive language.[66]

Language and the supportive physiology of the brain, face, hands, vocal tract, and sense organs evolved initially (along with music, dance, and gesture) to cope with the pressures of living in a large and complex social structure, by supporting building and maintaining social support networks (allies and friends). Language use in conversation, play, storytelling, humor (and, of course, flirting) releases endorphins that contribute to developing and strengthening social bonds. Thus, language enables its users to bond with at least three times as many people through an extension of grooming behavior.[67]

---

[63] Damasio (2018).   [64] Seligman et al. (2016).
[65] Baumeister and Masicampo (2010); Seligman et al. (2016).
[66] Barsalou (2008); Bergen (2012); Barrett (2017).   [67] Dunbar (1996).

Language also enables its users to recruit allies and friends by displaying desirable qualities such as the ability to recognize and resolve incongruencies.[68] As language developed and coevolved with the supportive physiology of the brain, face, hands, and vocal tract, it also extended social and ecological surveillance through gossip about other group members and their relationships and reporting on changes in the physical environment.

In parallel with the development of the abstract conceptualizing capabilities associated with advanced language use, early hominids began to develop *theory of mind*, the ability to represent (imagine) another person's thought processes. As *second-order theory of mind* developed, providing the ability to represent how another person represents one's own thought processes, it became possible for individuals to become an object to themselves, which may have been an essential step in the development of reflexive self-awareness, a key component of consciousness. Baron-Cohen identifies theory of mind as one of two types of empathy, along with the ability to experience a vivid representation of another person's affective state and to express an appropriate emotional response. He argues that the development of these two types of empathy – about 70,000 to 100,000 years ago – led both to the elaboration of social relationships and culture and to the rapid acceleration of toolmaking and artistic expression, beginning about 40,000 years ago.[69] Advanced levels of theory of mind also contributed to more effective collaboration; as a result, group members actively encouraged metacognition and metacommunication, the ability to reflect on and communicate about one's own thought processes, which increased the importance of cultural development in the evolution of both mind and language.[70]

Theory of mind and reflexive self-consciousness led to the ability to represent relationships and social groups as independent entities subject to homeostasis. To the extent that a relationship or social network is important to individual homeostasis, the homeostasis of the group is also important. Relational and group homeostasis is maintained through gossip and metadiscourse about relationships. Group culture and norms are expressed, transmitted, and reinforced through storytelling, humor,[71] and gossip. Group homeostasis is also maintained through the "punishment imperative," the expectation that members of a group will punish violations of norms such as fairness.[72]

A basic punishment for violating relational expectations or group norms is weakening of the relationship or reduced status within the group (loss of "*face*"); At the extreme, continued violation of norms and expectations can lead to termination of relationships and exclusion from the group. Because

---

[68] Dessalles (2014).   [69] Baron-Cohen (2020a, 2020b).   [70] Heyes et al. (2020).
[71] Billig (2005); Norrick (1993, 1997, 2010); Fine and DeSoucey (2005).
[72] See, for example, Lakoff and Kövecses (1987).

most humans are highly dependent on strong social ties and frequent social interactions, maintaining one's own social status or "face" is an important part of every interaction, and apparent attacks on one's social status are taken as seriously as an attack on one's body or possessions. Consequently, "facework," conducting interactions in such a way to minimize unintended threats to one's own or others' social status, is integral to all social interaction.

Language use and other forms of complex social interaction also accelerate the development, refinement, and spread of *memes*, new behavior patterns (including signaling and language), often including memes that are potentially harmful or even fatal to individuals[73] and memes that are detrimental to the group. The dissemination of these behavior patterns is influenced by how easy and rewarding it is to repeat and imitate them; as they spread, they tend to "evolve" as they are modified to fit the capabilities and motivations of cultural groups, so they become ever easier and more rewarding. This process of learning, modifying, and repeating behaviors accounts for a substantial amount of the development of both language and culture more generally.

Curiosity and play (both solitary and social) are observed in many species, and apparently rewarded with endorphins. Together, they contribute to innovation, and social play contributes to social bonding. Among humans, both play and curiosity are influenced and shaped by culture and facilitated by language use. Language play includes various forms of metaphor, humor, and narration, and contributes to the expansion of vocabulary, hence of the expressive power of language. Play, sparked by curiosity, has been a major force driving the development and elaboration of culture and invention.

An important focus of invention is communication. New media, beginning with language, extend, reinforce, and elaborate both cognitive capabilities and social structure.

Language amplified and extended the possibilities for social relationships as well as for abstract thought about both the physical and the social environment. Visual depiction put representations of significant animals in a shared, public form. Writing objectified language, enabling users to perceive their language and their expressions of experiences and ideas as independent objects; it also extended the reach of language in both time and space. Other media – print, telegraph, radio, television, and, most recently, the computer with its many manifestations – have amplified, diversified, and complexified communication and the cultures it supports.

Communication, using language and an array of other signal systems, initially evolved in support of the brain's homeostasis-maintenance functions.

---

[73] Dennett (2017).

As the brain and language coevolved, they supported an increasingly complex social structure and culture. Human cognition and communication can only be understood as the interaction of body, mind, relationship, and culture. I will begin with homeostasis and the embodied mind in Chapter 2. I will end the book with a necessarily brief account of communication media, the way they interact with all these processes, and their effect on discourse.

Summary

In this chapter, I argued that the conceptual language used in traditional approaches to communication rely on metaphors that implicitly sustain assumptions of mind-body dualism consistent with a *"computer"* metaphor of mind and *"signal transmission"* and *"object"* metaphor for communication and messages. I briefly reviewed evidence that contradicts these assumptions and support an *embodiment* approach, based on the assumptions that mind and communication are functions of the entire physical body, and evolved in support of reproductive fitness. I proposed an alternative set of conceptual terms based on the actual physical processes of communication. I briefly introduced three concepts that are of central importance to the argument advanced throughout the book, *homeostasis*, *representation*, and *simulations*. Chapter 2 provides a more detailed account of these concepts, based on a summary account of key features of the nervous system, including the brain, and of the signaling processes both internal and external to the body.

2 Homeostasis
Perception, Feelings, and Signaling

Traditional theories of language use and communication are implicitly based on the assumptions that mind is separate from body, that ideas and thoughts are objects, independent of both mind and language, that ideas move through space from one mind to another, and that two or more minds can share exactly the same ideas and thoughts. Nineteenth-century metaphors of the body as a "*machine*" have been overlaid with computer and electronic transmission[1] metaphors: The brain is a "*computer*" and mind is "*software*"; the body is a "*vehicle*" for the mind, a "*tool*" by which the mind "*sends*" and "*receives*" messages.[2] According to the logic of these metaphors, communication is successful only if the "*receiver*" ends up with a thought ("an *object*") that is identical to the thought that was "*sent*." All these implications are inconsistent with recent and current research. This chapter provides a more detailed account of central concept of homeostasis and the embodiment perspective. It focuses on the most relevant features of the organization and functions of the brain and nervous system, detailing crucial differences between neural activity and the processes of a digital computer, and provides the foundation for a more detailed treatment of language and cognition in subsequent chapters.

Embodied Cognition

Until recently the body itself has been of little interest for theorizing about either cognition or communication. However, recent research has focused on mind as a function of the biological body, with implications that are important for understanding communication as both biological and cognitive. Signals, including language, are created, comprehended, and responded to by the body. This entire process evolved in response to the interaction between organism

---

[1] Reddy (1993).
[2] Along with "*tool*," "*send*," and "*receive*," the "*machine*"/"*object*" metaphor persists in metaphors like "*input*," "*output*," and "number *crunching*," all of which reify abstract concepts like *information*.

and environment,[3] particularly the social environment, in the service of optimizing the organism's reproductive fitness in a constantly changing environment. The brain is part of the central nervous system, which in turn is thoroughly integrated into the body and interacts constantly with the entire body. According to the *embodiment* perspective, *mind* is an abstract summary of the integrative and coordinating functions of the central nervous system, which evolved and functions in service to the body and its reproductive fitness, the "prime mover." This new focus on the biological body implies attention to evolution, both as a means of tracing precursors of mental functions in less complex (and earlier) life-forms and as a means of understanding how the organs and processes of thinking and communicating developed in the form that we encounter and use. Accordingly, an account of the embodiment perspective must begin with evolution.

Evolutionary Perspective. The term *reproductive fitness* blends two concepts that are easily (and commonly) misunderstood. *Reproduction* refers to the ability of the organism itself, the body, to have offspring and thereby to project itself into the future. Reproduction *also* refers to each gene's projection into the future as part of the body's reproduction of itself.[4] The concept of *fitness* is also easily misconstrued. The word is often used, as in "physical fitness," to imply an *optimal* state of health and strength. But this is not how evolution works: The organisms that survive and reproduce are rarely optimally fit; merely *adequately fit* will suffice.[5]

In this sense, *fitness* refers to how well an organism is "*fitted* to" its environment.[6] Specifically, *reproductive fitness* refers to whether the composite of all the organism's features fits its environment sufficiently well that it can survive long enough to have offspring that will also survive to reproductive age. Many of an organism's features are likely to be suboptimal, and some may be detrimental to the welfare of the organism; all that matters is that the composite of all the features is *adequate* for survival and reproduction. The conventional phrase "survival of the fittest" implies a constant state of competition and strife, something like a marathon, in which success means achieving an

---

[3] Damasio (2018).
[4] Dawkins (1976). As Dawkins also demonstrated, an individual gene need not make a positive contribution to the overall reproductive fitness of the organism in order to be projected forward into the next generation. To the contrary, humans carry many genes that are associated with traits that are quite detrimental to the overall health of the organism. As long as these traits are not lethal (prior to sexual maturity), they may continue to propagate (and to cause misery for their carriers). Some implications of this idea for communication will be discussed in Chapter 3.
[5] It would be hard to maintain *optimal* fitness in an environment that keeps changing.
[6] For humans and other social species, the environment to which the organism must be adequately fit includes the social environment. As a result, as social organization becomes more complex, social interaction comes to play an increasingly important role in both cultural and biological evolution (Heyes et al., 2020).

optimal level of fitness and crossing the finish line *first*. A more accurate phrase would be "survival of the adequately fit,"[7] a marathon in which merely crossing the finish line, managing to have viable offspring, constitutes success.

Homeostasis

Within a complex multicellular organism, every unit, every organ, tissue, and cell, survives by maintaining a dynamic balance of energy, nutrients, and wastes, responding to perturbations from other units as well as from external sources. Each unit's responses affect other units in a continuous process, each within the constraints of its own chemistry and its physical environment. All this is dynamic and constantly changing; no organism can ever achieve and sustain an optimal internal or external balance. Maturana, Varela, and Rosch refer to this process as *autopoiesis*, a "continuous material regeneration of a self-bounded, self-constructing network of molecular transformations in a far from-equilibrium situation."[8] Damasio summarizes the process of constant interaction and adaptation as *homeostasis*.[9] Because Damasio explicitly incorporates signaling both within the organism and externally, I will use his term.

Perception, behavioral response, and the signaling that connects perception and behavioral response are driven by the need to maintain homeostasis, a dynamic balance of chemical and physical conditions optimal for sustained life and future reproductive success. Communicative signaling within and between organisms is driven by the same needs, fundamental to all organisms. This signaling within humans (and other animals) includes both the electrochemical signaling associated with neural systems and the chemical signals emitted by many bodily tissues and organs, as well as by the bacteria, viruses, and other independent organisms that inhabit our digestive tract, tissues, and organs. These signals operate with varying degrees of specificity in complex ways that biologists are barely beginning to understand.

Homeostasis at every level is "forward-projecting." Long-term survival and reproductive success within the organism's ecological environment requires projecting past experiences and present perceptions as a basis for future

---

[7] At times of scarcity or other heightened risk, the bar may be raised: What constitutes a "sufficiently good fit" will vary according to the ecological conditions that, in most ecosystems, tend to swing in a cycle between abundance and scarcity, good times and hard times. Chance also plays a role; for example, if an otherwise "fit" organism is killed by fire, flood, or accident before reproducing, its genes die with it, no matter how "fit" they were.

[8] Di Paolo, Rohde, and De Jaegher (2010, p. 48); see also Maturana and Varela (1980); Varela, Thompson, and Rosch (1991/2016).

[9] Damasio (2018).

actions.[10] Reproductive units that are "forward-looking" in this sense are more likely to reproduce; more precisely, genes that code for "forward-looking" behavior are more likely to reproduce and spread. For all organisms, the external environment includes other organisms trying to maintain *their* homeostasis: No organism can achieve and maintain a perfect balance, and every organism must continually adjust and adapt to a constantly changing environment.[11] For humans and other social species, the environment includes the social and cultural environment that helps organize and regulate access to nutrients, shelter, and reproductive opportunities. The ability to perceive and predict changes in the physical and social environment, including other organisms' actions, greatly increases an organism's ability to project the current homeostatic conditions forward in time: This is one of the factors driving neural and brain evolution.

The ability to form, simulate, and recall perceptions is an important part of the central nervous system's contribution to overall homeostasis. Damasio argues that mind is based on the ability to synthesize multisensory perceptions; both consciousness and feelings are in turn based on the simulations that constitute mind. These images coalesce into internal representations of both the internal state of the body and relevant features of the external environment and generate actions based on dynamic predictive representations of the world: To a large extent, thinking *is* sensory perception processing.[12] Crucially for communication, that includes the thinking involved in recognizing, interpreting, and originating language and other forms of interaction.

The Brain and Central Nervous System

The central nervous system includes two classes of perceptual systems that help maintain a current representation of the state of the body in its environment. *Exteroception*, the famous "five senses," reports on relevant features of the external environment, and *interoception* reports on relevant features of the internal environment. The brain maintains a representation of the body in its environment, updated continuously by signals from these systems, and a forward-projected representation of possible future states, based on a

---

[10] "Sense-making," in the *Enactive mind* tradition (Di Paolo, Rohde, and De Jaegher, 2010); see also Damasio (2018); Seligman et al. (2016).

[11] The ability to adapt to a constantly changing environment is one important element of fitness. Note that organisms may cooperate or compete; either way, they will affect each other's homeostasis.

[12] Barrett (2017, 2020); Barsalou (1999, 2008); Damasio (2017). Di Paolo, Rohde, and De Jaegher (2010) criticize the concept of internal representation, but from their discussion, it appears they have in mind a computational form, which is separable and distinct from the body and its neural signaling. It must also be noted that people differ in the balance of perceptual simulation and flow of silent language they experience. I will return to this topic later in this chapter.

representation of past and current states. The brain responds to current or projected future threats to homeostasis with signals that instigate corrective actions, chemical as well as muscular. These representations include time (sequential change and causality): Elementary *stories*[13] are intrinsic to cognitive processes.

Neural Function. The human brain is estimated to include something like 100 billion neurons.[14] In addition to perhaps as many as a thousand different types of neurons, the brain is also infused with smaller cells called glia, which were once thought to have no function other than supporting and maintaining the neurons. There are about ten times as many glial cells as neurons in the brain, and recent research suggests that the glial cells also contribute to cognitive functions, although exactly what they do is not well understood. Most neurons are sheathed in myelin, which acts as an insulator, limiting the "*leakage*" of electromagnetic charge from the axon, thus preserving signal strength and reducing secondary excitation of neighboring neurons. However, not all neurons are fully sheathed; Damasio[15] speculates that the resultant cross-excitation between unshielded or partially shielded neurons may itself contribute in subtle ways to neural functioning.

Each neuron has a bulbous cell body (the *soma*) containing the nucleus and mitochondria. Thousands of dendrites (long filaments) feed into the soma, and a single axon with thousands of branches extends outward, often thousands of times the length of the soma, contacting other neurons at *synapses*. Figure 2.1[16] provides a stylized diagram; in an actual neuron, there would be many more dendrites and axon branches, most of them much longer relative to the size of the soma. Note the nucleus in the soma; recent research suggests that DNA, far from merely specifying the form and organization of neurons, is actively engaged in ongoing cell processes, with various genes being activated or suppressed in response to external signals. How this affects neural transmission and what role it might play in cognitive functions such as memory or signal processing is uncertain. In terms of the computer metaphor, this would be like individual transistors in a digital computer having the capacity to change their own logic functions and thereby actively alter the logical structure of the computation processes.[17]

---

[13] Chapter 13.
[14] Estimates of the exact number range from around 86 billion to over 120 billion.
[15] Damasio (2018).
[16] Drawing illustrating the process of synaptic transmission in neurons, cropped from original in an NIA brochure. User: Looie496 created file, US National Institutes of Health, National Institute on Aging created original. Creative Commons. Public domain. www.commons.wikimedia.org/wiki/File:Chemical_synapse_schema_cropped.jpg. Converted to gray scale.
[17] Learning programs do something like this, but the actual physical process is entirely different.

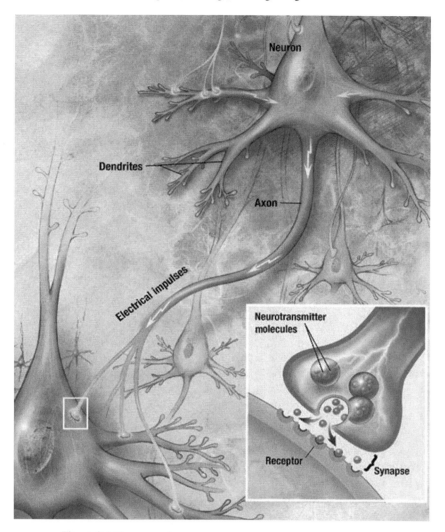

Figure 2.1 Neuron and synapse

Each axon branch terminates at a synaptic gap, a very narrow space separating it from the next neuron, usually at a dendrite but occasionally directly at another neuron's soma (Figure 2.1). Each neuron is connected via synapses to around 10,000 other neurons (neurons in the brain stem are connected to many more than that), totaling upward of 1,000 trillion synaptic connections. A typical neuron *"fires"* five to fifty times per second, with each pulse lasting less than a thousandth of a second: A wave of membrane depolarization propagates rapidly along the axon and its extensions, releasing neurotransmitters at each synapse that indirectly affect the electrochemical potential of the receiving neuron.[18] Some synapses increase the probability that the receiving neuron will in turn fire; others inhibit or prevent it from firing. The process of learning includes generating new connections between neurons as well as strengthening existing connections according to the Hebbian principle that "those that fire together wire together."[19] (Conversely, unused connections weaken over time and eventually disappear: "Use it or lose it.")

Neural transmission is *electrochemical*, based on waves of membrane depolarization leading to the release of ions at the synapses. Electronic computers are purely electrical, based on the movement of electrons through the system. Although neural transmission is remarkably fast, it is much slower than the electrical transmission in a digital computer, and the process of neural excitation and firing is even slower compared to the action of transistor "logic gates" in an electronic computer.

The functioning of synapses is also affected by at least 100 different chemicals that infuse the surrounding space, with complex effects on neural functioning, including changing the threshold of excitation required for the neuron to fire. These chemicals originate throughout the body, and they vary in concentration in an analog rather than digital fashion. Both the effects of these chemicals and the difference in transmission and processing speed have important implications for perception, emotional response, language processing, reasoning, and consciousness. They also play an important role in the brain's "reward system," which facilitates and encourages social bonding and affects learning and memory. Dopamine and serotonin, for example, are both stimulated by social affiliation. Dopamine affects the ability to feel pleasure, to think, plan, and experience interest. Serotonin affects mood, sexual desire, appetite, sleep, and memory.[20]

Hawkins observes that the neocortex is "the organ of intelligence," planning, and reasoning. It is organized in 150,000 neural columns, each consisting of about 100,000 neurons, clustered in minicolumns of about 100 neurons each; the minicolumns can be distinguished physically, but there is no visible separation among columns, which can be distinguished only by function.

---

[18] In terms of homeostasis, these neurotransmitters stimulate and disrupt the internal homeostasis of the receiving neuron; the "*firing*" and resultant wave of depolarization is how the receiving neuron restores its own homeostasis – by perturbing the homeostasis of the *next* neuron, and so on (Maturana and Varela, 1980).

[19] Much of this is accomplished and consolidated during sleep.

[20] Barrett (2017). Researchers are barely beginning to understand the influence of this complex chemical bath on communication processes. They apparently affect interpretation as well as attention, emotion, and mood.

Although there are dozens of types of neuron in the neocortex, each column consists of more or less the same set of neurons, organized in a similar way across all regions (visual, language, etc.) and across mammalian species, with minor variations. Most of the synaptic connections are local and run vertically, but some have longer-distance connections with other brain regions. In every region, some cells project to some part of the brain related to movement as well as senses.

About 10 percent of the synapses feeding into a neuron are located sufficiently close to the soma to activate a wave of depolarization; the synapses located further from the soma affect (decrease or increase) the neuron's level of activation for a brief time. These prime the neuron (when twenty or so of them are stimulated at once) but do not cause it to spike; they serve as predictions. The synapses closer to the soma confirm the prediction if they cause the neuron to fire; if they don't, the activation subsides.

Every column is a basic circuit, similar to those of other mammals. Each column operates as a quasi-independent information processor, performing parallel operations on separate perceptual input representing distinct features of the same object or experience. Each column represents a predictive model, compares incoming stimuli to expected stimuli, then refines the prediction by adding or deleting synaptic connections. The net result of all these individual representations is a predictive model of the overall physical and social environment, the "forward projection" described by Damasio. Humans are constantly learning models and forget most of them quickly (short-term or "working" memory).

Prediction includes sequence and location, what will be seen next, where will it be seen, what will be seen if eyes, head, or body moves, and so forth. This requires that the column must have neurons that represent reference frames (spatial or conceptual) that allow an object to be manipulated as a whole, or its features manipulated with reference to it; they serve to plan and create motion and action. This aggregate process of prediction and (dis)confirmation requires physical or attentional motion. Thousands of reference frames are activated simultaneously. Knowledge is established by a preponderance of output from the many cortical columns ("*voting*"). Long-distance connections transmit their guesses to many but not all the other relevant columns until the entire network settles on an answer. It is apparent that language and other relevant conceptual knowledge contribute to the "voting" through signals that increase or decrease the sensitization of neurons in relevant columns.

Every column has cells specialized to locate the animal in space, and where it will be when it moves, both absolutely and with respect to a frame of reference. (A commonplace example of this process is when athletes project the location of a ball and their body, both in real space and in relation to each other.) Every column has similar cells, allowing the neocortex to keep track of thousands of objects at once. Associative memory allows the neocortex to search several location "maps" at once.

The neocortex has many complementary models of any particular object – for example, tactile, visual, motor, conceptual. Even a complex sense like vision is processed by many discrete columns that process different aspects of visual information. Knowledge about any object or idea is distributed among thousands of columns, and each column stores and processes information about many objects, though the capacity of each column is finite and limited by the type of input it receives. As the athlete example illustrates, expertise entails having well-elaborated reference frames and the ability to find a good reference frame to arrange facts, predictions, and observations.

The Computer Metaphor for Mind. Aside from differences in speed and complexity and the analog influence of chemicals, the "all or none firing" aspect of neural function would be generally consistent with the "*computer*" model of the brain that dominated cognitive science from the 1950s until quite recently. According to the "*computer*" metaphor, neurons (or synapses) can be construed as "logic gates," equivalent to transistors. Like the transmission of electrical signals through the transistors in a digital computer, the propagation of depolarization pulses along the brain's neural paths through the synaptic logic gates can be modeled using Boolean algebra. Some neurons increase the probability that the next neuron will fire (= 1); other neurons inhibit firing (= 0). According to the computer metaphor, the brain's "*machine-level*" (so-called "*wet-ware*") operations, like those of a digital computer, use a code that can be described in binary as a string of 0s and 1s (excites or inhibits), and memory is also represented by *something* that can be described in binary digits.[21]

Modern general-purpose digital computers have an operating system and one or more programming "*languages*," higher-level logic codes loosely analogous to natural language (but very precise by design, compared to the ambiguity of natural languages), with nouns (logical "*objects*") and verbs (operations performed on these "*objects*"). Although these programs can be "hard-wired" into the circuits of a special-purpose computer, in a general-purpose computer they are stored as patterns of electromagnetic potential on "*memory* chips" separate from the hardware. The computer model of mind posits that the brain *also* has a logical language, *mentalese*,[22] consisting of a set of abstract symbols in which actual thinking is conducted.[23]

---

[21] Researchers have yet to arrive at a convincing account of where or how this is done – although we can be fairly certain it is fundamentally different from the "storage and access" operations of computer memory.

[22] Bergen (2012); Fodor (1975).

[23] Presumably these abstract symbols would take the form of arbitrary patterns of neural or synaptic activity with an arbitrary relationship to the ideas, perceptions, or activities they signify.

28   Homeostasis: Perception, Feelings, and Signaling

Three interesting claims follow from the digital computer model. The first is that any valid theory of cognition, including memory and consciousness as well as reasoning and language use, must be stated in a way that it can be represented in an algorithm, formulated as a computer program, and tested by running the program on a sufficiently powerful digital computer.[24] Second, it would in principle be possible, given a sufficiently powerful digital computer with a sufficiently large memory capacity, to encode the entire contents of a human brain into a suitable programming language and upload it all into a digital computer. At that point, the computer would *become* the person, with the prospect of living forever[25] – or as long as somebody can be convinced to maintain and supply power to the host computer.

Third, and of the greatest interest here, the computer model implies that all communication signals must be first translated or *"encoded"* from mentalese into natural language, transmitted or *"sent,"* then translated or *"decoded"* back into mentalese. Mentalese is assumed to be wholly abstract and symbolic, even more so than natural language (which does include onomatopoeic words like "cuckoo" and "sizzle," and is intertwined with intonation, gesture, and other analog signaling systems).[26] A corollary is that communication follows a linear sequence of steps, beginning with forming an idea (in "mentalese"), encoding the idea into a natural language phrase or sentence, encoding the phrase or sentence into the physical actions necessary to utter that phrase, then executing the actions.

The computer model of the brain came to dominate cognitive science in the 1950s, when computer science and the emerging science of artificial intelligence (AI) were accomplishing feats that still seem little short of miraculous,[27] and when very little was known about the actual physiology and functioning of neurons or the biological brains they constitute. Since that time, powerful tools like fMRI and the electron microscope enabled neurologists to investigate both individual neurons and assemblies of neurons, both in the incomprehensibly complex human brain and in the much simpler brains of organisms like the

---

[24] For example, Feldman (2006). Thus far, "sufficiently powerful" continues to be a goal rather than a realization.

[25] This claim, associated with Ray Kurzweil in particular, will not be of further interest to this book.

[26] As far as I have been able to determine, no evidence has as yet been found to support the existence of anything like "mentalese." Although many "computer metaphor" theorists dismiss it as an epiphenomenon, most people experience conscious thought, at least, largely in their primary language – and thus requiring no translation. See also Dor (2014); for a more general discussion and critique of the computer metaphor, see Everett (2017) and Goatly (2007). A more detailed discussion of signaling will be found in Chapter 6.

[27] Understanding natural language was not one of the "miraculous" accomplishments of algorithm-based AI research; eventually, an entirely different approach was developed, based on natural language statistics, that has become successful for a steadily growing range of language tasks (see Chapters 3 and 4).

nematode *caenorhabditis elegans*. In parallel, cognitive psychologists and psycholinguists have developed more sophisticated experimental designs to observe and measure how humans (and other organisms) perceive, recall, and respond to stimuli, including signals from other organisms, with an astonishing degree of precision. Coupled with similar advances in genetics and biochemistry, these research tools have developed a picture of the brain and its functions that is more complex, and largely incompatible with the digital computer metaphor.[28]

In particular, the actual activity of neurons is much more complex than the simple *"computer"* metaphor implies. As previously noted, the sensitivity of synapses is modulated along an analog continuum by an ever-changing brew of chemicals, some of which originate in other parts of the nervous system and throughout the body in both glands and tissues. Neurons can communicate directly with other neurons without using the synapses, in a process called *ephapsis*, based on extracellular electromagnetic fields. Neurons also interact with the glia, and their activity can be affected by chemicals originating in the cells they connect with, all of which modulates the neuron circuits. These interactions and effects have yet to be adequately researched, but based on what is already known, the operation of neurons "can no longer conform to the simple on/off schema and cannot be accounted for by the simple digital design."[29] In brief, the operation of the nervous system, including the brain, is a complex blend of electrical and chemical processes, distributed throughout the body and not restricted to the brain. Although these complex interactions could, in principle, be modeled by a Boolean algorithm, they are more consistent with a model based on a complex array of semi-independent, nested, and continuously interacting analog subsystems, some of which also participate in digital (all or nothing) interactions, each responding to the activity of other subsystems, all within and contributing to the overall system.[30]

In summary, although in principle all these complex electrochemical and chemical interactions could be described in a binary code, the code would have to be many times more complex than the *"computer/software"* metaphor suggests. It is becoming increasingly evident that the *"digital computer"* metaphor, supported by a computational model based on Boolean algebra, is marginally relevant (at best) to how the human nervous system functions. Although some aspects of neural functioning seem to be digital, consistent with Boolean algebra and the *"computer/software"* metaphor, overall the brain/nervous system is more analog than digital.[31] Far from being a discrete

---

[28] Dor (2014); Everett (2017); Goatly (2007).   [29] Damasio (2018, p. 64).
[30] In principle, with enough computing power, any object or process can be digitized to within any specified degree of accuracy. That doesn't mean the process itself is digital.
[31] Chapters 4 and 6.

organ, the brain is massively interconnected and fully integrated with the entire body. Understanding either body or brain requires that they be considered as a unitary system. Every aspect of communication, including originating, producing, recognizing, and interpreting signals as well as emotional responses and intellectual deliberation, is distributed across many areas of the brain and influenced by the conditions and processes of many parts of the body.[32]

Structure of the Brain

Research based on autopsies of patients suffering brain damage from injuries, strokes, and disease have provided a crude map of brain areas that are involved in processing signals, including external and internal perceptions, memory storage and recall, initiating and coordinating muscular action, and maintaining homeostasis throughout the body. More recently, experiments performed during surgical treatment for brain injuries, diseases, and malfunctions such as epilepsy have provided an even finer-grained "map" of the brain and its connections, by way of the central nervous system, to the rest of the body. Tools like the fMRI have enabled neuroscientists to detect which regions of the brain are activated during (hence, presumably, involved in) specific processes such as perception, signal processing, emotional processing, language creation and interpretation, and other communication activities.

As Figure 2.2[33] shows, each of the primary senses is processed in a separate region of the brain; these regions are further segregated and specialized for different aspects of perception, as discussed in the following sections. Vision, for example, is quite complex: The representation of the world that we experience includes form, edges, colors, light/dark, and motion, each processed separately; this "what" aspect of the image is itself processed separately from the location, the "where" of an image. Figure (the object of attention) and background are also processed separately. To achieve a coherent representation, the visual image must also coordinate with information from other senses, particularly hearing and interoception about the body's location and orientation. Since these senses are processed at different speeds, some of the information is delayed (one function of "reentry circuits"), so that we experience the world as a single coherent whole. We have the impression that we are experiencing the world directly, as it is, but what we actually experience is an image constructed from what the brain *expects* to perceive, based on its current representation of the situation, all modulated by the complex interaction of

---

[32] Seligman et al. (2016).
[33] Blausen.com staff (2014). "Medical gallery of Blausen Medical 2014." *WikiJournal of Medicine* 1(2). doi:10.15347/wjm/2014.010. ISSN 2002-4436. - Own work. Downloaded from Creative Commons: Public domain. Image converted to gray scale.

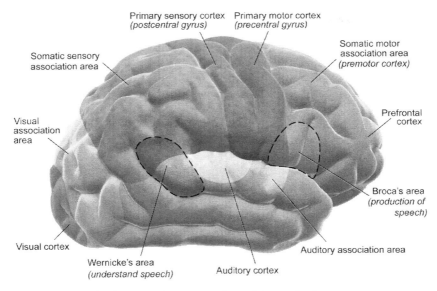

Figure 2.2 Motor and sensory regions of the cerebral cortex

sensory signals.[34] What we experience as "the present" is actually a composite of perceptions that originated at various times in the very recent past and predictions based on past experience.[35]

Figure 2.2 shows, stretched across the top if the brain, two parallel regions, the Primary Motor Cortex, where the "motor control" activities of the muscles are coordinated, and the Primary Sensory Cortex, where information from the senses is coordinated. These two regions also coordinate directly with each other in various ways, including language comprehension and response (Chapter 4). Both motor and sensory cortices roughly map onto the shape of the body itself, as shown in Figure 2.3.

Physiology of Communication. It is evident that language and the sophisticated communication it affords must make a major contribution to reproductive fitness. The human brain consumes between 12 and 25 percent of the body's total energy consumption (depending on factors like the level of concentration, how "*hard*" one is thinking). Our large brains require humans to be born at an early stage of development and remain dependent on parental

---

[34] A consequence of this is that we do not actually "live in the present." Rather, we live in the (very) recent past; what is experienced as "present" happened about a half second ago. "Action in the present" is always action in the (near) future; as a consequence, all perception is memory, and all action is based on prediction.

[35] Seligman et al. (2016).

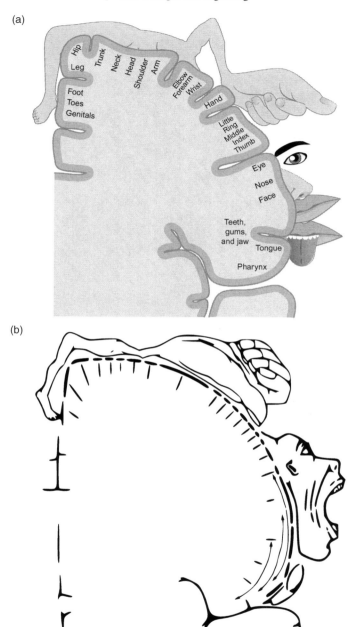

Figure 2.3 The sensory homunculus above (a), motor homunculus below (b)

care for several years; even so, childbirth requires large hips that impede mobility, and childbirth constitutes significant risk to the mother. The arrangement of the vocal tract for speech, particularly the location of the larynx, causes further difficulties, including the risk of choking to death.[36]

The brain is not specialized for language any more than it is for toolmaking, but both activities have influenced the evolution of the brain and neural systems. For example, the gene FOXP2, necessary for language, also facilitates cognition and control of muscles beyond those used for speech. "Every part of the vocal apparatus has a non-speech-related function that is more basic from an evolutionary perspective and that is found in other species of primates. Language and speech came later and exploited human bodies and brains ... altering them over time."[37] The ease with which other primates as well as humans learn sign languages and the universal use of gesture as an accompaniment of speech suggests that human brains are equipped to create and process signals in multiple modalities. The large number of neural connections to hands and mouth that render them as efficient ways to produce symbolic signals have evolved in response to the importance of complex and finely nuanced signaling.

Once the ability to use and recognize abstract symbols developed, it is likely that languages evolved relatively rapidly. As the benefits of expanded communication grew, evolutionary pressures sharpened the ability to produce clearer sounds and engage in longer and more involved conversations.[38] All this required the parallel development of culture, expanding both the contexts and the topics of talk.

Early research with patients who had suffered brain damage from strokes or injuries identified Wernicke's area as the location of speech comprehension and Broca's area as the location of speech production. More recent research, using fMRI and other brain-scanning technologies, has shown that the actual picture is much more complex. Wernicke's area is necessary but not sufficient for speech comprehension, and Broca's area is necessary but not sufficient for speech production. If Wernicke's area is damaged, speech comprehension will be impaired or lost entirely. Similarly, if Broca's area is damaged, speech production will be impaired or lost entirely. However, both Wernicke's and Broca's areas are involved in a much broader range of processes[39] – and several areas of the brain are engaged in both comprehension and production of speech (Chapters 3 and 4).

Everett argues that *Homo erectus* very likely had some degree of language ability, although they may have had less precise, more slurred, slower and less subtle speech compared to modern humans. Nor could they have discriminated the same range of speech sounds as modern humans. However, they very

---

[36] Everett (2017). [37] Everett (2017, p.89). [38] Everett (2017). [39] Everett (2017).

likely had sufficient memory to support thousands of symbols, and their material culture suggests that they possessed at least rudimentary language. According to the Baldwin effect, the more important speech became, the more refined physiology suitable for clarity and precision would be selected for.[40] These refinements in turn supported more complex language and conversation, leading to more refined physiology, and so forth, in a spiral of coevolution.

Perception. Humans famously have five senses – vision, hearing, smell, taste, and touch – each with its own specialized receptors. In addition to these exteroceptive senses, we also have *interoceptive* senses, including muscle awareness, pain, and balance, as well as heartbeat, nausea, and other epigastric sensations, and *introspective* awareness of our own thought processes.[41] All these contribute to the brain's dynamic representation of the current state of body-in-environment.

The senses map onto the body in the primary sensory cortex. Figure 2.3[42] illustrates how the neural receptors are mapped onto this region of the brain with a "homunculus," an image of a human body distorted so that the relative size of each body part represents the relative density of neural signals originating in that body part. About half of the signals come from the face and hands, reflecting their importance in communication.

Of the five exteroceptive senses, vision (which accounts for as much as 80 percent of our sensory input) is possibly the most complex, involving several stages of processing, beginning at the retina, and supported by connections to muscular systems that control the direction of gaze, focus of the lens and width of the pupil, the light-admitting aperture, as well as by short- and long-term memory. Most of the processing required to present a coherent image to conscious awareness happens well below the level of consciousness, with separate neural pathways processing edges, shapes, motion, color, and lighting: The visual experience itself arises 150 to 350 milliseconds after light strikes the retina.

Much of what we "see" does not reflect the actual pattern of photons on the retina but what the brain expects to see, based on general knowledge about the physical setting, memory, and the objects that have been identified.[43] The visual system continually updates, fills in details, and corrects this image by comparing it with the most relevant parts of the actual visual image, the patterns it computes based on the patterns of neural impulses originating from

---

[40] Everett (2017).
[41] Interoception and introspection play a key role in Barsalou's account of how abstract reasoning can be accomplished purely by means of perceptual simulations: See Chapter 4.
[42] **Sensory Homunculus-en.svg** Illustration from Anatomy & Physiology, Connexions Web site. www.cnx.org/content/col11496/1.6/, June 19, 2013. Downloaded from Creative Commons. Public domain.
[43] Barrett (2020); Seligman et al. (2016).

the light-sensitive cells that line the retina. This is nicely illustrated by the famous "gorilla in the basketball game" experiment in which subjects are shown a video of a basketball practice and instructed to count the number of passes between players wearing dark uniforms.[44] Partway through the video, a person wearing a gorilla suit walks across the floor and waves at the camera. Consistently, over half the subjects in the experiment do not report having seen the gorilla.

As the gorilla experiment demonstrates, this process of updating and correcting is strongly influenced by both expectations and attention – based on what is most relevant to the current situation. Less relevant information is often filtered out long before the image is incorporated into the representation that forms part of conscious experience. Perception is an active process, constructing a model of the world (which is sometimes wildly inaccurate). "Perception is a construction of precisely those features that are useful in our struggle to survive...."[45] This selectivity also applies to communication: What we think, hear, and see is strongly influenced by what we expect to hear and see; when the actual stream of language deviates from expectation, it may not be noticed, and if it is noticed, it may require effortful reframing to make sense of it.[46]

The retina is made up of a dense layer of photoreceptor cells. When looking at an object, light passes through the lens of the eye, which focuses it onto the retina. Photons strike the layer of photoreceptor cells, which vary in sensitivity to wavelengths and intensity. When enough photons strike a particular photoreceptor cell, the cell "*fires*," generates a wave of electrochemical depolarization that excites other neurons behind the retina. Each of these secondary neurons receives pulses from thousands of retinal cells, aggregate and transmit information about color and brightness to other sets of neurons, which further aggregate and transfer the information, and so on. At each stage of processing, detailed information is lost, consolidated and sacrificed to the overall pattern.

Aggregated information from the retinal cells is transmitted in parallel through separate channels that detect edges, masses, colors, textures, and motion. These separate patterns are aggregated and recombined as representations of objects (what), still separated from representations of their locations (where)[47], then separately transmitted to the primary sensory cortex, where they are finally merged into a single image of an object and its location relative to other objects in the visual field. This is the earliest point in the processing at which an individual can ordinarily be consciously aware of any of the sensory data – but usually it is also merged with sounds (aggregated through a similar and parallel process from information transmitted by the sonic receptors in the ear) and experienced as a single coherent *object* in *space* and *time*.

---

[44] Furley, Memmert, and Heller (2010). [45] Koch (2019, p. 16). [46] Chapters 6, 7, and 9.
[47] Ungerleider and Mishkin (1982; Mishkin, Ungerleider, and Macko, 1983).

Hearing is only slightly less complex than vision. The physiology of the ear is such that receptors in different locations within the ear are sensitive to different pitches. Loudness, duration, and tempo are also separately detected, and, as with vision, these separate features of the sound stream are aggregated at a higher level into a single unified sensation of sound. Like the visual system, the hearing centers of the brain determine the directional source of sound by comparing the timing of the signal detected by each ear, through a complex set of interactions that incorporate interoceptive information about the position and orientation of the head.

The third of the "five senses" relevant to communication is *touch*, which includes pressure, texture, and warmth. Touch (and pain) sensors are located all over the external skin as well as in many interior parts of the body; they are concentrated in particularly important regions, including the genitals, face, and fingers. Touch sensations are transmitted to the brain where they are registered on a region of the brain that resembles a distorted analog map of the body itself (Figure 2.3). The various aspects of touch are also part of many conceptual schemas[48], and tactile simulations, along with simulations of associated emotions, may be activated by priming a concept (sometimes quite strongly, as in post-traumatic stress disorder).

Taste and scent are localized in the mouth and nose; they figure less prominently in human communication (unlike dogs, for which scent is a major medium of communication). Nonetheless, like tactile sensations, taste and scent are part of many conceptual schemas. Simulations of a powerful taste or scent associated with a concept may be experienced when the concept is activated and conversely, as Proust's famous ruminations on the taste of a madeleine illustrate, a taste or scent can activate an associated schema, along with simulations of a complex set of other associated sensations.

Although they are rarely considered part of the "five senses," the *interoceptive* senses are also important to phenomenal awareness. Just a few examples: Sensors in our inner ear interact with vision and sensations from muscles and joints to provide composite senses of balance and inertia (experienced as weight). Sensors in muscles and joints also provide information about resistance (also experienced as weight). Epigastric sensors provide sensations of nausea, fullness, hunger, and so on. These sensations all contribute to the brain's continuously updated representation of the body-in-environment.

"Phenomenal awareness," our conscious experience of the world, is never just "seeing what is in plain sight." Rather, our moment-to-moment experiences of the external environment and our body interacting with the external environment are the product of extensive interpretive work, originating with

---

[48] Chapters 4 and 7.

the brain's representation of what it *expects* to perceive. This predictive representation, based on background knowledge and memory, selectively filters and makes sense of the stream of sensory data,[49] both exteroceptive and interoceptive, according to the predicted relevance to the demands of the current situation.[50] Complex memories as well as imagined future or alternative experiences, constructed from various recalled elements, can be activated by any of the associated sensory images, and by simulations activated by language.[51] All this continues during conversation, including awareness of the conversation itself.[52]

Experience. Each of the three associated senses (vision, hearing, and touch) has a location where eyes, ears, and body are perceived. The self, the subjective *I*, is located at a singular point,[53] which is also the focus of behaviors. Having a perspective is a result of the interaction of sensation and muscular action. Enteroception, particularly heartbeat and breathing, tends to pull this point of perspective, the location of ego, downward into the area of the chest, while vision and hearing pull it upward into the skull. The location of *I* may vary somewhat as the balance of senses and muscular action varies, according to the demands of the current situation, influenced by cultural norms and expectations.

Experience and consciousness reside in the cortex, with about ten billion pyramidal neurons intermixed with interneurons that only form local connections. The pyramidal neurons, involved in coordinating attention and responses to stimuli, transmit outputs to and receive inputs from other cortical sites, including in the opposite cerebral hemisphere. The highly organized neocortical tissues are associated with subjective experience.[54] The prefrontal cortex is involved in metacognition (what Barsalou[55] calls *introspection*), but the sensorimotor experiences such as listening to music, dreaming or daydreaming, riding a bicycle, planting a garden, all generated by the "posterior hot zone," account for most of our daily experiences.[56]

Memory. Humans have several distinct types of memory. *Sensory* memory endures for less than a second after the sensation has ceased. Short-term or *working* memory is biased toward sound, and endures for a minute or less, although it can be extended through a rehearsal loop, as we do when dialing a long telephone number. Capacity of working memory is limited to about five to seven distinct ideas or facts, although this capacity can be considerably increased by "chunking" discrete facts together in some way. Long-term memory, which can last a lifetime, includes several subtypes. Implicit

---

[49] Baumeister and Masicampo (2010); Edelman (2004).   [50] Chapter 4.
[51] These may be fleeting simulations of a sensation or stories – sometimes quite complex.
[52] Chapter 9.   [53] Koch (2019, p. 9).   [54] Koch (2019)   [55] Barsalou (1999, 2008).
[56] Koch (2019, p. 58–63).

memory, largely unconscious, includes procedural memories – skills like walking or riding a bicycle and tasks like washing, drying, and stacking dishes, which we do with little or no conscious thought, are based on procedural memory. *Declarative* memory includes our memory of events and experiences (*episodic* memory) and our memory of facts and concepts (*semantic* memory).[57]

Memories are initially consolidated within a few hours after the experience (episodic) or learning (semantic); at this point the memories are still dependent on the hippocampus. The hippocampus is also involved in emotion processing and response; not surprisingly, emotions can have a strong effect on the consolidation and retention of memories. Memories are more permanently consolidated (during deep sleep) over an extended period of weeks to years. Especially during the initial phase of consolidation, memories are susceptible to reconstruction, both under the influence of communication and in accordance with prior knowledge and beliefs. Because of the limitations of perception and attention, our episodic memories are full of gaps, which are often filled in from background knowledge and beliefs but can also be filled in from simulations formed via communication. This is part of why it is so easy to implant a false memory, as often occurs (intentionally or not) when a police officer's "helpful" remarks while questioning a witness induce the witness to recall events that never occurred and participants who were not present.

Factual and conceptual (semantic) knowledge is organized, via associative links, into *frames* or *schemas*.[58] Many of these schemas, representing frequently encountered activities, experiences, and ideas, can be quite complex, and may also be interconnected with procedural knowledge. Encountering one part of a schema – a word or symbol, or even a sound or smell – will usually activate other, closely connected parts of the same schema, including associated emotional responses, so that they are more readily recalled (the phenomenon measured by word association tests).

Memories are not stored in any discrete part of the brain but are scattered throughout the brain; recalling an event or concept involves reconstructing the memory from these scattered parts, although under some circumstances (usually involving strong emotion), a memory may be stored, and subject to recall, as a whole.

Hemispheric Specialization. The cerebrum is divided into two lobes or hemispheres, which differ somewhat in their function. These differences, however, are much less pronounced and more subtle than was once believed (and is still claimed in pop psychology and self-help books). Wernicke's and Broca's areas are usually located in the side opposite the dominant hand, the

---

[57] Everett (2017).   [58] Chapters 4 and 7.

left hemisphere for most people. Word production and grammar are more strongly associated with the left (dominant for right-handed people) hemisphere, intonation and emphasis with the right. Most communication functions involve both hemispheres. Previous speculations about the specialization of the right and left hemispheres (left-handed/"right-brained" people are more creative; right-handed/"left-brained" people are more rational) have not been borne out by research; as with most commonly held beliefs about the brain and its functioning, the story is much more complicated than that.

Survival Circuits. LeDoux[59] claims that all mammal species, including humans, have some form of neural "survival circuits" that coordinate actions related to basic needs: defense, maintenance of energy and nutrition, fluid balance, regulation of warmth, and reproduction. Like Damasio, LeDoux argues that these circuits can be traced back to mechanisms in primordial organisms. The general survival circuits are continuous across all mammal species, but the associated behaviors are unique to each species. Different animals respond to different unconditioned stimuli but can generalize these responses through conditioning to other stimuli. For example, rats respond to the smells of predators but can learn through conditioning to associate these with and react to conditioned stimuli that would be neutral without conditioning. In humans and other primates, the sight of a snake or spider activates a defense circuit, as do fearful and aggressive faces of conspecifics. Mating is likely to involve circuits for aggression against competitors, for display and mate selection, for copulation, and so on, according to species-specific characteristics.

Survival circuits detect information relevant to particular body-environment interactions and control external and internal responses to maintain homeostasis, based on innate and learned stimulus-response patterns. Survival circuits respond to challenges and opportunities, often experienced as emotional or motivated situations. They activate innate behavioral responses, including release of chemicals such as adrenaline, cortisol, testosterone, and other chemicals that prepare the body for action. They enhance attention to relevant stimuli (e.g. the orienting response to sudden loud noises) and retrieve relevant information and behavioral responses from memory. They increase the probability that relevant instrumental actions will be learned, and activate both specific and generalized physiological arousal. Neurons that synthesize and release norepinephrine, dopamine, serotonin, and so forth, contribute to brain arousal, with particular effects on information processing (stimulated by the amygdala). Peripheral systems also release hormones such as cortisol, epinephrine, norepinephrine, and so on. Effects of central modulators are rapid,

---

[59] LeDoux (2012).

and peripheral hormones are slower; this can prolong the state of arousal and attention.

Survival circuits interact closely. For example, in the presence of a threat to survival, other activities such as eating and sex are suppressed. But eventually, as defense or other high-priority behaviors exhaust energy resources, hunger will become increasingly important. Even within functions such as reproduction, there may be several distinct circuits; for example, the reproductive function is served by circuits for courtship, for competition, for copulation itself. Moreover, although some circuits like defense stimulate immediate action, circuits like those for sex or nutrition may alter information processing if immediate action toward the goal is not possible. For example, a lioness who spots a warthog downwind of her must work out a route to circle around to a downwind position and get close enough for a successful attack without being detected.[60]

Coordinating Representations and Actions. Signals from various parts of the body are assembled into a single coherent representation in the cortical sensory area, which lies in a strip across the top of the brain, organized in analog fashion, in a map of the body as illustrated in Figure 2.4.[61] Muscular activity is coordinated in a cortical muscular area adjacent to and closely parallel to the cortical perceptual area. The neural connections for both perception and fine muscular control are most dense for hands and facial muscles, particularly the mouth. Not surprisingly, these are also the muscles that figure most prominently in communication. This pattern reflects the coevolution of the brain and nervous system with language and communication practices in general. Both cortical coordination areas are engaged during language comprehension and production.[62]

Physiological Adaptations for Communication

The concentration of muscular control neurons in bodily areas associated with communication corresponds to changes, particularly in the hands and face, that facilitate language use and comprehension. The pronounced flexibility and fine motor control of the hands is already apparent in other primates, supporting Everett's contention that adaptations suited to language use almost all

---

[60] Observed in Botswana in 2016. As previously noted, this forward projection often takes the form of stories that provide the basis for deciding which approach is most likely to be successful. The relationship of survival circuits to human emotions will be discussed in Chapter 5.

[61] By mailto: ralf@ark.in-berlin.de - File: Homunculus-ja.png Translated from Image: Homunculus-de.svg by CC BY-SA 4.0, www.commons.wikimedia.org/w/index.php, Public domain. Figure 2.4 is identical to Figure 2.3; it is repeated here for readers' convenience.

[62] Chapters 3, 4, and 9.

Physiological Adaptations for Communication 41

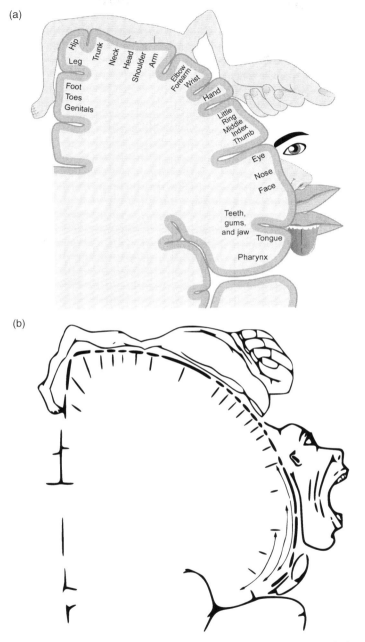

Figure 2.4 The sensory homunculus above (a), motor homunculus below (b) (repeated from Figure 2.3)

originated with other functions,[63] with the one exception of fine control over the tongue, essential for articulating a wide range of phonemes.

Another implication of this diagram is the distance between neural processing regions of the body, which parallels the actual relative location of the areas to which the signals are directed. Several areas of the brain are involved in both processing and producing language; these include both sensory and motor (muscle control) areas that would be activated by actually performing actions associated with words, and motor areas (mouth, larynx, and tongue) that would be activated by actually speaking associated words. Processing "he kicked the football" and responding to a question about the sentence partially activates the neural systems associated with leg and foot as well as those associated with the speech organs. Processing "he bit the apple" similarly activates neural systems associated with biting – jaw and mouth. Because the neural signals from the foot must travel farther, responding to a sentence involving "kick" takes longer than to a sentence involving "bite."[64]

Several other features of human anatomy are particularly well suited to language use, and very likely precipitated further coevolution with the development of language. The larynx, for example, is essential to human speech sounds and the use of intonation and pitch to qualify the meaning of utterances. Fine control over breathing is essential for many aspects of speech, including shaping the sounds and maintaining prosody, organizing speech into comprehensible segments, and singing operatic arias. Autonomous control over breathing also permits us to produce speech while engaging in other activities. The shape of the mouth and nasal cavity contributes to the range of phonemes we can produce as well as to our ability to project sound over relatively large distances. A typical human produces 135–185 words per minute, which requires rapid and precise movement of tongue, lips, and larynx as well as precise control over exhaling. To understand this rate of speech requires equivalent precision in the detection and interpretation of sound, for which our ear canals are exquisitely well adapted.

Both hands and face are finely adapted for complex communication. The face has about thirty distinct muscles; in combination these can display at least 20,000 distinguishable expressions.[65] More than 7,777 distinct gestures have been identified in a classroom setting and 5,000 in a clinic setting.[66] Pei estimates that, combining all the fine movements of the entire body, humans can display as many as 700,000 distinguishable physical signs.[67] These abilities to generate distinguishable shadings of gesture and expression are matched by the acuity of our perceptual systems: Human observers can distinguish movements as brief as 1/50th of a second, and the brain can register

---

[63] Everett (2017).　[64] Bergen (2012).　[65] Birdwhistell (1970).
[66] Burgoon, Guerrero, and Floyd (2016); Krout (1954a, 1954b).　[67] (Pei, 1965).

facial expressions and body movements as brief as 125 microseconds, even when they elude conscious awareness.[68] These gestural capabilities are matched by similar ability to produce and detect fine distinctions in speech. They also argue strongly against a digital code model of gesture, facial expression, and vocalics[69]: When these analog signals are digitized, it is very likely that each individual does it somewhat differently, partly under the influence of local cultural practices and partly under the influence of personal history and communication context.[70]

Everett acknowledges that *Homo erectus*, lacking many of these anatomical adaptations, could not have produced or discriminated the range of speech sounds typical of modern languages, but claims that *erectus* would nonetheless have been capable of a less refined but still serviceable spoken language. According to the Baldwin effect, as spoken language became more important, physiological features suitable for greater clarity and precision would be more adaptive, hence more likely to be passed along to future generations. Like many other features, language and its physiological substrate coevolved over thousands, possibly hundreds of thousands of years.

Reward Systems: Why Solving Puzzles, Eating, and Sex Are Fun

An animal that has ready access to nutrients, avoids predators and other hazards, resolves ambiguous situations, and engages in sexual intercourse is more likely to propagate its genes. Put the other way around, genes that code for traits that improve the animal's access to nutrients, decrease its exposure to hazards, and increases the probability that it will engage in sexual intercourse are more likely to appear in future generations. For animals like humans and most other primates that live in complex social environments, genes that code for traits that lead to higher status within the primary group, more stable social relationships and a more cohesive primary group are also more likely to appear in future generations, because they are directly related to primary needs.

A secondary implication of these facts is the evolution of reward systems. If behaviors that improve access to nutrients, improve social status, and lead to sexual intercourse are experienced as pleasurable, these behaviors are more likely to occur. Conversely, if behavior that exposes the animal to hazards or decreases its access to nutrients and sexual opportunities are experienced as

---

[68] Burgoon, Guerrero, and Floyd (2016); McLeod and Rosenthal (1983).
[69] As Burgoon et al. point out, several researchers have proposed systems to categorize these paralinguistic signals, but, useful as these categories are to researchers, there is little evidence that individuals use them in routine communication.
[70] An example of differential digitization of speech is the "r"/"l" distinction, important in English. Japanese speakers are able to produce both sounds but do not differentiate them. See Chapters 5 and 9 for a more detailed discussion.

painful or otherwise aversive, they are less likely to occur. Consequently, genes that code for endorphins and other pleasure-producing hormones (and for discomfort-producing "punishment" systems) that enhance reproductive fitness are also more likely to appear in future generations.[71]

Among primates, including humans, social behaviors such as grooming (and, in humans, conversation) releases endorphins that produce a relaxed, pleasurable state. Enjoying a good meal, solving a difficult puzzle, and sexual interaction at any level – even mild flirting – are all experienced as pleasurable. Social interaction also releases dopamine, a neurotransmitter that plays a role in how we feel pleasure, as well as in thinking, planning, focusing on a topic or task, and even in our ability to find things interesting. Conversely, interaction with more powerful or hostile members of a social structure is experienced as uncomfortable, even aversive, as is exposure to physical hazards. Encounter with hostile persons or physical risk releases chemicals such as adrenaline and cortisol that prepare the body for action. Once the action is completed and the threat overcome, cortisol levels return to normal. However, if effective action is impossible (the hostile person is one's immediate supervisor or a schoolyard bully), the cortisol level remains high, leading to anxiety, depression, sustained high blood pressure, heart disease, and other negative consequences.

The story is complicated by the fact that exposure to threat or danger also releases adrenaline and norepinephrine, which produce a state of heightened arousal that can sometimes be pleasurable.[72] This entire complex system is even further complicated by the existence of external chemicals, notably alcohol, hallucinogens, opium derivatives, and other alkaloids that interact with the neural sensors ordinarily associated with the body's internally generated regulatory chemicals. In effect, these "*hijack*" the body's homeostasis-maintaining system, in much the same way that seductive but destructive "memes" like suicide subvert the social homeostasis processes of communicative systems.[73]

Summary

In this chapter, I gave a more detailed account of homeostasis. I briefly summarized key features of the evolutionary perspective as a basis for explaining how key features of both internal and external signaling systems have evolved in support of homeostasis. I described the most relevant features of

---

[71] Hurley, Dennett, and Adams (2011) extend this basic idea to humor, arguing that the enjoyment we get from understanding a joke is based on the reward for resolving the incongruity of the punch line.
[72] This may account for the popularity of horror movies and amusement park rides.
[73] Dennett (2017); Chapters 3 and 5.

brain organization and neural functioning, including the neural mechanisms hypothesized to maintain and update a detailed representation of the body in its social and physical environment, a crucial contribution of the neural system to homeostasis. The chapter closes with a brief discussion of the chemical "reward system" that has evolved to encourage adaptive behavior and discourage maladaptive behavior. Chapter 3 provides a summary account of language evolution based on its contribution of homeostasis.

3 How Language and Conversation Evolved

Language is one of the defining traits that distinguish humans from all other species. Although the boundary between human communication and that of other species has come in recent years to be seen as somewhat blurred,[1] it is still evident that human language, like human communication generally, is far more complex than the signaling of any other species. However, research into the signaling and communication of other species can provide useful insights into human communication, and research in philology provides clues as to the development of and relationships among modern languages. This chapter provides an account of how the pressures of living in an increasingly large and complex social group contributed to homeostasis and the evolution of language and discusses the implications of a social account of language for understanding communication.

Language, prior to the development of durable written symbols, left no physical trace. Some of the physiological features of human anatomy that facilitate both spoken and gesture language do leave a physical trace that can provide some clues, for example, in the shape of the skull cavity. Artifacts like tools, artwork, jewelry, and cosmetics provide more clues. However, the nature of language at any stage in human history prior to the invention of writing can only be inferred from secondary evidence. Theories of language origins reflect the contemporary culture of social science and contemporary views about what it is to be human, supported by whatever secondary evidence is available, including comparative linguistics and evidence from research on other species' signaling systems and attempts to teach natural or invented human languages to members of other species. Theories of language also reflect (and contribute to) our shared sense of collective identity, who we are as humans and how we are related to other animal species, notably to other primates and to all the hominids that preceded, coexisted with, and interbred with Homo sapiens. Inevitably, this shared but rapidly changing sense of collective identity influences theories of language, language evolution, and the development of conversation.

---

[1] See, for example, Seyfarth and Cheney (2018).

What Is Language?

There is no one clear definition of language. Dediu and Levinson describe language as a *"fuzzy cloud,"* shaped by the intrinsic requirements of communication, properties and constraints of the human brain, perceptual, vocal and auditory systems, and the contingencies of biological and cultural evolution. The beginnings of language are shrouded in the mists of time; some theorists argue for a beginning as recently as 40,000 years ago, but others argue that spoken language in some form must have emerged between 1.5 and 0.6 million years ago. In any case, modern languages are shaped by both cultural evolution and coevolution of supporting brain and muscular systems over the past half million years.[2]

It is generally accepted that a true language includes a *lexicon* and *syntax*. A lexicon is a set of abstract symbolic signals (words) that have generally accepted meanings. Syntax is a system for organizing words into meaning units (e.g. clauses and sentences). Classically, speech has been regarded as the paradigmatic form of language, so *word* initially refers to a sound or combination of sounds (*phonemes*) that members of a speech community regularly use and recognize.[3] Syntax includes word order, extensions (prefixes and suffixes), modification of the typical sound of a word or shape of a sign, and combinations with syntactic *"helper"* words (e.g. *swim* to *swam* to *have swum*) as well as conjunctions and articles that have no independent meaning. Recently sign languages have been recognized as true languages, so "words" must also be understood to include movements (gestures and facial expressions) with generally accepted meanings. Since gestures, facial expressions, and intonations can radically alter the meaning and interpretation of both spoken and signed utterances, these so-called nonverbal signals might also be considered as part of language.[4]

Syntax may, but does not always, include complex ways of ordering signals[5]: For example, in English, one can say either "Jane threw the stone at Dick" or "Dick threw the stone at Jane," but they have very different meanings. Syntax also often includes transformations of words that alter their reference ("Jane throws the stone," "Jane threw the stone," "Jane has thrown the stone") as well as words that have no meaning independent of the utterance in which they appear ("Jane threw the stone at Dick but missed him").

Everett observes that language engages interwoven patterns of symbols, structure (*syntax*), qualifiers, and emphasizers such as gestures and pitch, all

---

[2] Dediu and Levinson (2014); Everett (2017).
[3] However, the concept of words as distinct from intonation units may be a product of literacy (Chafe. 1004; Ong, 2002).
[4] See Chapter 6.   [5] Everett (2017).

shaped according to cultural context. Language involves the physical properties of signals (sounds and gestures, e.g. *phonetics*), meanings or interpretations (*semantics*), sound and word structure (*phonology* and *morphology*), word order and other features of syntax or grammar, customs of usage (*pragmatics*), and principles for structuring conversation. However, a fully functional language can have a very simple syntax[6]; Everett argues that languages develop only the vocabulary and syntax that is needed for a culture's ecological niche. Intricate syntactic structures are added for cultural reasons, and are not essential to language.

Everett claims that the earliest languages originated a million years ago (well before the appearance of *Homo sapiens*) with a simple Type 1 grammar, a linear word order with no recursion, and a vocabulary of at most a few thousand symbolic signals (probably a combination of gestures and sounds).[7] This would have expanded as the ecological niche became more complex, but only to the extent supported by the evolving complexity of the perceptual and neural systems. According to Everett, syntax plays a relatively minor role in human language; it primarily serves to filter out irrelevant associations and guide the hearer toward the intended interpretation.[8] Syntax is important for complex arguments and storytelling, but not for ordinary, everyday activities.

Nonsymbolic gestures, intonation, and other signals can radically change the meaning of an utterance, and are often regarded as part of language. These so-called nonverbal signals are themselves culturally embedded and informed. Language use engages the entire body and mind, the intellect, emotions, hands, mouth, tongue, brain, and perceptual systems, and it also requires extensive unspoken cultural and contextual knowledge.[9] The most common forms of human language are speech and gesture, both of which require rapid production (and perception) of symbolic actions. This in turn relies on physiological features that have coevolved with complex spoken and gestural communication.

Evidence from contemporary research supports the claim that communication, not reasoning, is the primary function of language, but use of language for thinking and communication are mutually enhancing.[10] Language is primarily for and about conversation and interaction; all other uses of language are secondary.[11] Using language for decision-making also involves metacommunication, describing and evaluating one's own thought processes.[12]

---

[6] Everett (2017).
[7] Everett's claims about the early origin of language are highly controversial; to some extent, it depends on how "language" is defined.
[8] This claim is consistent with research reported by Landauer and Dumais (1997).
[9] Everett (2017); Kendon (2014).   [10] Everett (2017).
[11] Clark (1996); Everett (2017); Ginsburg and Jablonka (2014).   [12] Heyes et al. (2020).

Language apparently originated in response to the pressures of living in large complex social structures.[13] The grooming and bonding functions of language require only minimal linguistic skills, suggesting that interpersonal interaction may have been a primary original context and function for language. These functions influenced the coevolution of language with neurological and physiological language systems from the outset. However, chorusing and swaying (music and dance), involving the entire group, may also have contributed to the evolution of language. Everett claims that building communities, cultures, and societies is "the ultimate purpose and accomplishment of language."[14] The meshing of these two functions, interpersonal bonding and cultural development, contributes to the complexity of language. Further complexity comes from the extension of language to coordinating activities such as foraging and toolmaking. Coordination is an obvious extension of social bonding, and probably influenced language evolution from the outset.

Simpler systems of signaling can provide or indicate objects and actions for others to experience either directly or vicariously, for example, through cries of pain or physical contact. Dor proposes that language works by providing instructions that allow others to construct a representation of the experience in their own imagination. This affords a means of communicating inner as well as outer experience.[15] Experience is *private* and *variable* across individuals; this leads to *experiential gaps*, the inability to access others' private experience. Consequently, interlocutors can only reconstruct each other's experience by way of signals that are unavoidably ambiguous.[16]

Dor suggests that language may have begun with experiential communication, direct indication, which can accomplish a lot in terms of social interaction, bonding, and coordinated action. Then some of this developed into instructive communication, which over time developed into a language to fulfill the instructive function more efficiently – with more categories and more refined subcategories, coevolving with the capacity of the brain to process and the hands and vocal organs to produce and perceive ever more complex and subtle signals. "Humans had to reach the limits of experiential communication, and build communities complex enough, dependent enough on communication, and sophisticated enough in terms of collective innovation" to begin to develop ways to bridge the communicative gap.[17]

Language has a symbolic landscape, a lexicon plus a semantic web (symbols and strings of symbols that express various features of experience), a simplified model of the experiential world, a socially developed normative worldview, and

---

[13] Dunbar (1996, 2003); see also Bruner (1983).
[14] This claim is consistent with Dunbar (1996) and Dessalles (2014).   [15] Dor (2014).
[16] Dor (2014), but also see Tabossi (1981).   [17] Dor (2014, p. 118).

a communication protocol – procedures for communication that include syntax and conversation structure. Language use requires three representations: The *private intentional meaning*, the private representation of experience, is represented in *semantics*, the symbolic forms of collective meaning, then these symbols are expressed in observable signals as an *utterance*. The addressee employs the reverse of each step: recognizing perceived signals as an utterance, constructing the symbolic representation, then constructing a mental representation of the apparent intended experience.[18]

The meshing of interpersonal with societal and cultural functions may also help explain the ambiguity, which is a common feature of language. Ambiguity is partially alleviated by extensive background knowledge, commonly taken for granted within a speech community but, in a more general context, often requires explanation. Everett points to a trade-off between the size of a vocabulary, which facilitates precision and elaboration, and ease of acquiring and fluency of using a language. Ambiguity, polysemy, and metaphor help to expand potential expressiveness for a given-size vocabulary by increasing the role of contextual knowledge. Clarity is also promoted by phonology, which organizes sounds to make them easier to recognize, and prosody, which breaks utterances into parts and makes the logic of an utterance easier to follow. Both phonology and prosody are supplemented and reinforced by gestures, vocal qualities, and so forth, which qualify and refine representations. During the process of language acquisition in early childhood, brain areas that control speech production and recognition adapt to the features of the language or languages regularly encountered by the child. This process is initially governed by social-interaction needs[19]; acquisition of grammar, perspective-taking, and conversation structure are driven by imitation and instruction.[20]

The typical (traditional and functionalist) account of both brain evolution and language evolution starts with an individual brain, computing and reasoning about information concerning the external environment as a basis for planning and reasoned action. Emotional responses and feelings are often neglected in functionalist accounts of language evolution or included almost as an afterthought. Similarly, the use of language in social interaction usually figures in conventional accounts of language evolution primarily in terms of planning, deciding, and executing group actions such as food gathering or defense against enemies and predators. Emotional expression and routine nontelic social interactions (such as play or gossip) rarely figure in conventional accounts.

---

[18] Dor (2014). See also Arundale (2010), discussed in Chapter 9. [19] Bruner (1983).
[20] Heyes et al. (2020).

A growing number of cognition and language theorists are taking a different approach. Damasio[21] argues that cognition is fundamentally about maintaining a representation of the state of the organism, threats and opportunities, and responding to the situation. Dunbar[22] and Dessalles[23] focus on the social functions of language as a means of coping with a larger and more complex social hierarchy, arguing that language enabled early hominids to maintain social homeostasis by building social relationships to cope with threatening social interactions (aggression) and improve predictability, thereby helping to control stress and anxiety. Before I develop an account of cognitive and language evolution combining these insights, I will begin with a summary of the standard account, the basis for many traditional communication theories, which is still defended by many theorists.

Language Evolution as a Response to Ecological Pressure

The standard account of language evolution focuses on "information" in the restricted telic sense of "information theory,"[24] primarily focused on direct survival needs, including surveillance, gaining information about the external environment, and coordinating responses to this information with a larger group. According to this account, the driving forces behind development of language were ecological pressures in the form of increased risk from predators, scarcity of food or other resources, and competition for resources. These pressures would lend additional value to the language-supported capacity for displaced reference – communicating (and thinking) about objects (resources, predators, or competing groups) in a different location and about both objects and events that were encountered in the past or might be encountered in the future (displacement in both space and time). They would also lend additional value to the language-supported capacity for describing, considering, and evaluating alternative courses of action, devising a plan, then coordinating a group effort to implement the plan. According to these accounts, only serious, telic, referential, and propositional communication are bona fide [25] language use; paratelic uses, including play and casual chatter, are peripheral.

Contrary to conventional accounts, most conversation is about relatively trivial matters[26]; exchange of serious telic information accounts for very little language use. The size of the cerebral cortex, essential for complex social

---

[21] Damasio (1996, 2018).   [22] Dunbar (1996, 2003, 2014).   [23] Dessalles (2014).
[24] Information theory defines the information value of a signal in terms of the statistical probability of observing that particular signal relative to the distribution of possible signals; attempts to apply this definition to language and other forms of human signaling have been consistently unproductive (Ritchie, 1986, 1991).
[25] For example, Raskin (1985; Attardo, 2001; Raskin & Attardo, 1994).
[26] Dessalles (2014). I will return to this topic in Chapter 4.

interaction and language use, is correlated with the size and complexity of a species' typical social group but not with any measure of ecological challenges.[27] A third problem is how to get from no language to a complete, complex language sufficient for ecological surveillance, planning, and coordination. In addressing ecological pressures through bona fide language use, how useful would it be to have, say, a dozen abstract words? What use would a handful of abstract words be to one member of a group if no one else in the group could understand or reproduce them? In sum, the accumulated evidence is not consistent with the conventional claim that language evolved in response to resource and predation pressures.

Animal Communication

Since the early development of the standard account of language evolution, animal research has blurred the distinction between animals and humans, demonstrating both greater complexity in animal communication systems and a surprising ability of some animals to learn and use language-like signal systems. Cetaceans, including whales and dolphins, use complex and prolonged sequences of sounds that apparently have a communicative function, although it is still only poorly understood. Language-training experiments have shown that many species, including other primates, can learn to associate an impressive number of abstract symbols, including words in a human language, with simple concepts. Some are capable of combining two or even three symbols in a simple string, and of adapting the symbols to use them in novel ways, for example, metaphorically and humorously. However, they use them only to communicating with human trainers and keepers, do not teach them to juveniles, and rarely if ever use them with conspecifics.[28] Alex the African gray parrot has an English vocabulary of over 500 words and can combine them in simple sentences to make requests and comments and respond to questions. Alex can label objects, shapes, and small quantities and use these labels to identify, categorize, quantify, request, or refuse about 100 different objects.[29] Other experiments have shown that some animals are capable of understanding that a conspecific, or one of the human trainers, has a different visual perspective and different knowledge than the subject, which implies at least basic theory of mind (ToM).[30] These are important, if limited, steps along the way to the evolution of language.

---

[27] Dunbar (1996, 2003).
[28] To be sure, these experiments create an artificial "language" in an artificial environment: The possible utterances have to do with satisfying needs in the environment of an animal research laboratory, and do not necessarily have anything to do with any other of the animal's needs or motivations.
[29] Pepperberg (2006).   [30] Chapter 4.

All social species have signal systems, although few are as complex as that of cetaceans. All social birds and mammals have alarm calls.[31] Vervet monkeys give distinct alarm calls, each of which leads to distinct escape responses, to carnivores, eagles, baboons, unfamiliar humans, and snakes,[32] and the colobus monkey has distinct alarm calls associated with threats from the air, on the ground, and on the ground but able to climb trees. However, these signals are usually only weakly subject to autonomous control, and even their status as signals is subject to dispute, since the monkeys typically continue emitting the alarm call after all other members of the troop have responded by scrambling to safety.

Most social animals also have a repertoire of social-interaction signals, usually including threat, dominance, submission, and signals of sexual interest and receptivity. These vary in the degree of voluntary control.[33] Most social animals engage in social play, which requires signals of playful intention. Most primate species and many other social species engage in grooming, also initiated by signals. Alarm and sexual interest are among the earliest forms of animal signals, and, among animals with complex social organization, social signals are important.

Modern apes have better voluntary control over hand motions than vocalization, so it is easier to teach them gesture-based than vocal language. This, plus the ease with which humans develop and use sign language and the fact that human infants use gestures for language-like activity before they use sounds, suggests that a gesture language may have developed first.[34] However, in some primate species, voluntary mouth actions and vocalizations play a role in communication. Baboons use a range of grunts, and gelada baboons and several other primate species engage in chorusing and adapt vocal patterns to each other. In general, more complex social interactions lead to more complex vocalization, and there is a correlation between the amount of time spent grooming and vocal repertoire. Actions involved in speaking and gesturing build on oral–manual actions employed in other practical actions, particularly eating; these appear to be adapted and repurposed for communication.[35]

Both chimps and bonobos have a variety of vocal call types. Screams and barks potentially convey social information; changes in acoustic structure (vocalics) can express the animal's identity, social role in a fight, and the intensity of an attack. Both chimps and bonobos appear to be able to control

---

[31] Until recently, use of "culture" with respect to nonhumans was discouraged, but evidence of cultural transmission among many other species is accumulating to the point that it is difficult to ignore (Seligman et al., 2016; Whiten, 2021).
[32] Cheyney and Seyfarth (1985). [33] Kendon (2014); Tomasello (2008).
[34] Kendon (2014). [35] Kendon (2014).

and modify vocal signals in response to social variables.[36] Both chimps and bonobos sometimes combine vocalizations into sequences that convey information such as the quality of a food source or the nature of a fight, in a range of contexts. Females seem to be aware of the effect of sexual vocalizations on others and exercise some control – for example, inhibiting sexual vocalization in the presence of a high-ranking female. There is also evidence that chimpanzees sometimes take account of what listeners already know – for example, in threat calls.[37] Large-brain species forage or hunt strategically rather than opportunistically, taking account of the habits of prey or typical location of food.[38] In order to do this, they must have something like a narrative representation of the prey or food item and of the foraging or hunting activities.

At least some monkeys have rudimentary perspective-taking skills, based on "mirror neurons" dedicated to imitating perceived actions.[39] These include neurons for observing and executing hand actions such as grasping and manipulating and communication-associated mouth gestures such as lip-smacking and lips and tongue protrusion. Although there is only limited direct evidence of mirror neurons in humans, there is considerable indirect evidence from brain imaging and behavioral studies.[40] These mirror neurons contribute to the ability to understand that another person has a mind independent of one's own and to recognize that the other person may not perceive or be aware of something that is apparent and obvious to oneself. They also play an important role in communication.

In sum, it appears that the range and complexity of animal thought, culture, and communication greatly exceeds what was formerly believed, and the integration of (more flexible and better controlled) gesture with vocalization (less flexible, but still subject to some autonomous control) is relatively common, at least among other primates. All this is consistent with parallel development of gestures and vocalization in the early evolution of human language.[41] It also appears that the ability to develop and use tools may have developed in tandem with language. Developing a tool, using one object to act on another object, requires at least a minimal ability to blend a representation of affordances (hard and heavy or something termites might want to climb) with a representation of an objective (break open a nut or extract termites from their nest). More elaborate tools, such as stone flakes for skinning a prey animal or cutting its flesh, require acting on an object to change its affordances. This requires a more complex representation of the ultimate objective, the

---

[36] Clay and Zuberbuhler (2014). [37] Clay and Zuberbuhler (2014). [38] Everett (2017).
[39] di Pellegrino et al. (1992); Gallese et al. (1996); Gallese and Goldman (1998).
[40] Cook et al. (2014).
[41] Whiten (2021) describes evidence that cultural transmission of both signaling and tool use (including self-decoration) is widespread among animal species, contrary to long-held beliefs that only humans possess culture.

immediate objective (design of the tool), and the effects of striking one rock with another. These forward-representation skills are similar in type to those required for language use.[42]

Language as a Social Tool

Damasio[43] argues that cognition is fundamentally about maintaining a representation of the state of the organism, threats and opportunities, and responding to the situation. *Feelings* represent a qualitative, analog summary of neural signals about homeostasis, central to the activities of the body's neural system, including the brain, and thus an important dimension of cognition. Language facilitates extension of homeostasis maintenance to the social world, so feelings, as a representation of homeostasis, are basic to language and social interaction as well as to thought. As with theory of mind (ToM), the ability to communicate about feelings and emotions is crucial to social cooperation, and its development is socially transmitted and controlled.

Dunbar argues that complex cognition and language evolved in response to the pressures of living in a complex social order[44] – at first, as an extension of grooming but also to keep track of others' relationships. Just as patting and stroking can elicit a rewarding pleasure response and increased bonding, if certain vocalizations (or gestures) are pleasurable to others, or otherwise affect others' behavior, they may be intentionally performed. Once language becomes a source of pleasure or other rewards, an individual can "groom" three people at once by using language, potentially tripling the maximum size of a primary social group.[45] Supporting these claims, the relative size of the cerebral cortex correlates with the size and social complexity of typical primary groups, and not with signs of ecological stress such as food scarcity or risk of predators.[46]

Dessalles[47] argues that grooming alone can't be the full explanation, because it requires only a limited vocabulary and little or no syntax. He proposes that language use in conversation served to advertise one's desirable attributes as a friend and companion. Language typically does not deal with important matters; most talk is trivial (and the actual content soon forgotten). Dessalles argues that the invention of weapons reduced the importance of size and strength and increased the importance of mutual support relationships. In this environment, important qualities of friends include the ability to

---

[42] The importance of fine motor skills and tactile sensitivity in the fingers and hands for both tool use and communication is reflected in the neural maps in Figures 2.3 and 2.4.
[43] Damasio (1996, 2018).   [44] Dunbar (2003).
[45] Technologies like oratory, writing, print, and electronic media, which extend the range and audience for communication, may also extend the potential size and complexity of primary social groups (Chapter 14).
[46] Dunbar (1996).   [47] Dessalles (2014).

anticipate danger and avoid surprise (detect and resolve inconsistencies), as well as companionability and willingness to spend time together. This goes beyond Dunbar's claims by adding components of cognitive ability (detect and resolve inconsistencies) and communication skill. Thus, conversation evolved first and foremost to display desirable cognitive, social, and communication attributes in order to recruit friends and expand social support networks.

Everett proposes a *"sign progression* theory" of language origin, arguing that the symbolic signals of language emerge gradually from indexes (e.g. pointing, beckoning, miming) and that grammar came later. Everett identifies three levels of complexity in language, all three of which are evident in at least one contemporary language. In a Type 1 language, symbols are arranged in a sequence, like beads on a string. In a Type 2 language, symbolic signals are arranged both linearly and hierarchically, so that symbols are combined inside other symbols – for example, in complex phrases. A Type 3 language adds the property of recursion, the ability to put one thing inside another thing of the same type without limit.[48]

Tools demonstrate and reinforce displacement, the ability to separate meaning (hunting, food gathering, eating) from referent (an actual hunt, actual consumption of food). Manufacturing and carrying a tool from one location to another requires the ability to simulate how the tool will be used.[49] Tools may have been discovered by serendipity, as a result of playing with objects in a way that revealed their affordances.[50] While clinking two rocks together (perhaps just to hear the sound they make), an early hominid may have knocked a sharp-edged flake off one of them, and noticed its ability to cut. Even the chimpanzee trick of "fishing" for termites with a slender stick or grass stem may have its origin in play-based serendipity, when a chimp playing with a small stick poked it into the opening of a termite mound.

Given the slow onset of tool invention and use, it seems likely that initial tool use predated the *concept* of tools by millions of years. Everett argues that true culture can be said to exist only when the tools used by one group display features that distinguish them from those of another group.[51] Deliberately inventing a tool for a particular purpose is a sign of an advanced level of conceptual thinking and the ability to project a simulation of a desired reality into the future.[52] Teaching another member of the group how to manufacture and use a tool is a sign that culture has progressed beyond simple observation and imitation, and an indication that a species has at least begun to master the

---

[48] Everett (2017). [49] Everett (2017). [50] Chapter 10.
[51] Although deliberately *teaching* others to use tools is unusual, it appears that many species have "culture" at least to the extent of observing and adopting innovative behaviors, including playful and self-decorative behavior as well as utilitarian behaviors such as foraging and hunting (Whiten, 2021).
[52] Seligman et al. (2016).

concept of tools. Tools may not be symbols for chimpanzees, but they are likely to have taken on cultural and symbolic importance for early hominids. Like language, the culture of tool invention and use is likely to have developed incrementally and gradually.

Communication requires intentionality, volitionally directing attention toward something, and shared intentionality, inducing others to direct their attention toward the same thing (or idea).[53] Everett claims that all animals have some degree of intentionality. Primates have been observed to carry objects that have some resemblance to a significant object (e.g. treating a stick as an infant) and even to modify its shape or appearance, which demonstrates a rudimentary merger of intentionality and representation, basic to all human language.[54] Indexes are a form of metonymy, use of some aspect of nature to represent (and eventually communicate with) nature. Visual icons have been collected by hominins for over three million years, which suggests an indexical function, an external representation of what they resemble and represent, both for individual thought and for communication with others.[55]

The next step is to combine intentionality and representation with symbol creation and the beginning of language. The core of language is the symbolic signal or signal stream – for example, a word, intonation unit, or gesture, combining a commonly recognized form with a consistent and predictable response or set of responses (meaning). The constraints of human production, perception, and cognitive abilities guided the process, but as cultures developed in complexity, cultural forces would have an increased influence on the development and use of symbolic signals.[56] Neural and physiological features that facilitate use and recognition of signals would confer significant survival and reproductive benefits, leading to sustained coevolution of language with the neural, perceptual, and motor control systems, and with the shape and configuration of signal-producing body features such as hands and lips. As communication came to confer more benefits to reproductive fitness, evolutionary pressures also led to improved ability to produce clear sounds in long and more involved conversations.

Word or phrase-based communication entails a word-based episodic recall, including the ability to reconstruct and imagine novel experiences without relying on experiential cues, so past episodes and others' experiences become readily accessible to communicating instructions for imaginative reconstruction and invention. This applies to both internal communication (language-stream thought) and external communication with others.[57] The growing importance of language-based communication also drove improvements in memory, supporting the ability to remember signals as symbols rather than

---

[53] Searle (1995); Tomasello (2008).   [54] Everett (2017).   [55] Everett (2017).
[56] Everett (2017).   [57] Ginsburg and Jablonka (2014).

merely parts of a specific situation.[58] This leads to conscious awareness and increased autonomous control over learning. The importance of these processes to social interaction and cooperation likewise led to increasing cultural transmission and cultivation of these skills.

Play. Social play probably contributed to language development in several ways, including complex vocalization and the recall and reenactment of past events, imitation of animals and other natural phenomena as well as imitation of other group members. Coordination of movements and orientations with cooperative intentions establishes a shared attentional frame, a necessary basis for developing shared reference.[59] Linguistic creativity, rooted in play, contributes to both vocabulary and syntax development.[60] Metaphorical thinking is manifest in the representational play in prelinguistic children and young bonobos and the play behavior of gorillas.[61] Incorporating imitation of observed activities into play uncouples the imitated activities from any particular situation and allows them to acquire a general abstract meaning. Pretend-play includes counterfactuals and distinction between the imagined and the actual, and between sign and the signified.[62] It is very likely that language and play developed in tandem, interacting with each other in ever-more complex configurations.[63]

Theory of Mind (ToM) and Signaling. At the most fundamental level, the phenomenal universe is neatly divided between *me* (the individual organism with its homeostasis needs) and *other* (everything else). *Other*, in turn, is divided into *resources*, *threats*, and *irrelevant*, then into *objects*, *animals*, and *other people*. Obtaining resources and avoiding threats is greatly facilitated by the ability to predict the conditions of the external environment, which is, in turn, facilitated by the ability to recognize and predict the actions of other organisms. The realization that other organisms also have needs and intentions and that their actions are also driven by homeostatic needs, and the ability to form a representation of the other organisms in the environment that includes motivated behavior, can greatly improve one's ability to predict their behavior and respond appropriately. This in turn contributes to one's own homeostasis, particularly for a species with a complex social hierarchy.

The ability to recognize and simulate or model another person's perceptions, behavior, and thought processes has been identified with many labels; *theory of mind* (ToM) was initially proposed by Premack and Woodruff.[64] The initial concept has been developed in several directions, and expanded to distinguish affective ToM from cognitive ToM. It has long been recognized that perspective-taking, the ability to recognize that another person may experience

---

[58] Ginsburg and Jablonka (2014).   [59] Kendon (2014).   [60] Knight and Lewis (2014).
[61] Ginsburg and Jablonka (2014).   [62] Ginsburg and Jablonka (2014).
[63] See Chapter 10 for a more complete discussion.   [64] Premack and Woodruff (1978).

both perceptions and thoughts different from one's own, is only gradually developed during childhood.[65] Research in child development has identified five stages of ToM development:[66] recognition of differences in desires, beliefs, knowledge, false beliefs, and hidden emotions.

At the point when animals begin to develop even one degree of ToM, the ability to model/imagine how another animal will perceive – and react – to a signal (or cue), the potential arises for intentional utterance. Rather than emit signals only in response to a visual stimulus, animals may perform signals (honestly or deceptively) to elicit a desired response. This is the first level at which signaling can be considered fully intentional communication, the beginning of language.

First-order ToM refers to the ability to represent what another person may be perceiving and thinking from the perspective of the other person ("I *know* he can't see what's behind his chair") and has been demonstrated in several other primates. Cognitive first-order ToM is usually achieved by human children by age five; affective first-order ToM has been observed in infants within the first six months.[67] First-order ToM enables an individual to represent the other's reaction to a signal – an alarm call or invitation to groom or play.[68] If ToM is accompanied by some degree of control over the signal, the way is open to reproduce the signal *deceptively*. What would ordinarily serve as a cue alerting other animals to the presence of a predator or a signal of playful intention is deployed to alter the other animal's mental state, to induce the belief that a predator is approaching or that one has playful intention, whether or not it is true.

Second-order ToM refers to the ability to represent how another person represents one's own mind ("I *think* he *knows* I can't see what's behind my chair"). Second-order ToM develops by age ten and sometimes as early as six or seven.[69] Third-order ToM refers to the ability to represent how other people represent how one represents their minds. ("I *think* he *knows* I *know* he can't see what's behind his chair"; "She probably *doesn't realize* that I *think* she is *lying*.") Even human adults find it difficult to go beyond third-order ToM on a regular basis,[70] and adults often fail to apply theory-of-mind skills even when they are readily available.[71]

---

[65] For example, Fodor (1989); Frith and Frith (1999); Piaget and Inhelder (1967).
[66] Wellman, Fang, and Peterson (2011). Among humans, it is evident that ToM and the language used to communicate about mental states and experiences are learned both by imitation and by intentional instruction; Heyes et al. (2020) claim that cultural transmission is involved in the development of ToM among both humans and other species.
[67] Westby and Robinson (2014).   [68] Arbib (2012); Kendon (2014).
[69] Perner and Wimmer (1985); Westby and Robinson (2014).
[70] ToM is marvelously lampooned by Wallace Shawn in the famous poison scene in *The Princess Bride*.
[71] Keysar, Lin, and Barr (2003).

Theory of mind is crucial for many communication activities, including social cooperation, and will be discussed again in the later chapters. Third-order ToM facilitates the development of what is often called "common ground," the sense of what knowledge, beliefs, and perceptions are held in common by oneself and others. This is an essential basis for ordinary conversation, and a central element in culture. ToM may also be a factor in the origin of certain religious beliefs, including animism, the belief that spirits inhabit other animals, trees, and even rivers and storm clouds, and may play a role in forming a personal identity and sense of self.

Like language, ToM activates various regions of the brain. An individual may represent own or other's cognitive processes or affective state; each of these four activities engages different brain areas.[72] Thinking about another person's emotions and imaginatively simulating the other person's emotions activate different areas of the brain.[73] Thinking about emotional and perceptual experiences also activate the regions of the brain that are associated with the experience itself.[74]

Social Knowledge. Seyfarth and Cheney[75] report evidence that several nonhuman primate species have detailed and extensive knowledge of social structure, and combine this knowledge with evidence from other animals' vocalizations to draw inferences about the social structure of their group. Baboons know individual identities, dominance ranks, matrilineal kin membership, and use of different calls. Baboon vocalizations are individually distinctive, and recognized by others, and they are associated with predictable types of calls, so listeners can derive social information from calls they hear. Moreover their response to vocalizations is affected by the social context. For example, after losing a fight, a female baboon will respond as if a threat grunt is directed at her, but otherwise, she is likely to respond as if it is directed at someone else.

Godfrey-Smith,[76] in a response to Seyfarth and Cheney, argues that communication must be understood as simultaneously expressive and interpretive, and points out that baboons have a very small and uncomplicated array of signals; the complexity is all in the audience's thought processes. Seyfarth and Cheney concede the point, but argue that the ability of baboons to integrate complex social knowledge with information gleaned from others' vocalization demonstrates a potential avenue for the early evolution of language. Progovac[77] observes that several animals in language acquisition experiments have acquired the ability to create two-word phrases using a simple verb–noun syntax. She compares these calls to two-word colloquialisms that appear in many languages, such as "cry-baby" and "kill-joy." Many of these formulaic

---

[72] Shanton and Goldman (2010). [73] Lucariello et al. (2007). [74] Cabeza et al. (2004).
[75] Seyfarth and Cheney (2018). [76] Godfrey-Smith (2018). [77] Progovac (2018).

phrases have an insulting meaning, which Progovac relates to the status competition and sexual aggression universal among mammal species. All these social uses of a limited repertoire of signals point toward an answer to "what use is a limited vocabulary?" They collectively suggest how a vocabulary could begin with a small range of signals and then gradually expand.[78]

Second-order ToM, the ability to represent the other animal's representation of one's *own* state of mind, leads to the ability for both animals to represent the other animal's possible intentions when emitting a cue. Once both animals recognize this common ground, this shared level of ToM, they can use the signal as a *symbol* to refer to something (such as a predator or food source) that is not present or an offer (e.g. to groom or to play) that is not presently intended.[79] These developments greatly expand the potential for social cooperation, and provide a scaffold for the development of intentional instruction and cultural transmission.

Thus, a rudimentary vocabulary might develop as reflexive cues are transformed to intentional signals, which activate simulations of the situation plus response, with the response partially suppressed. This would include cue/signals of aggression, invitations to groom, warning of predator, and so forth. Given early primates' weak control over vocalization, this may have begun with gesture[80] or perhaps with a combination of gesture and vocalization. However, vocal signals have many advantages, including the possibility of using them while engaged in other activities and without needing to be in sight of one another, so vocalization is likely to have developed at a fairly early stage.

These abilities, to anticipate others' responses to a signal, produce a signal voluntarily in order to elicit an expected response, then use a signal to communicate about an object (a predator or food source) or activity (grooming or sex), would likely confer an increase in homeostasis and reproductive fitness.[81] Once this happened, the brain and other systems associated with producing, perceiving, and using vocal and visual signals would begin to adapt through ordinary evolutionary processes. Individuals with greater facility to use symbolic communication would cooperate more effectively with other members of the group, survive longer, and leave more offspring.

Dennett argues that the symbolic behaviors themselves, which he calls *memes*, and behavior sequences (*memeplexes*)[82] are likely to have undergone independent evolutionary development, as they were transformed in ways that

---

[78] Everett (2017).
[79] This would represent a large additional step, requiring evolution of additional neural capacity.
[80] Corballis (2004); McNeill (2012); Rizzolatti and Arbib (1998); Tomasello (2008).
[81] For example, Dennett (2017).
[82] Both the terms and the concepts were introduced by Dawkins (1976).

rendered them easier and more rewarding to notice, remember, and reproduce.[83] The ability to originate, acquire, and produce memes would confer at least a social advantage, leading to coevolution of related brain areas with the elaboration of meme use. Finally, Dennett points out that, once coevolution of memes and brains became established, *some* of the memes (cultural practices) are likely to have been useless or even detrimental to the humans who adopted them. If they are easy to imitate and rewarding to perform, even otherwise detrimental memes will spread through a population. Heyes et al. show that the social transmission of advantageous memes also increases the success of groups, and they argue that cultural processes are the primary factors in the evolution of cultural activities, language and conversation in particular.[84]

Everett claims that language must have developed one million or more years ago, based on evidence of complex tool development and use, and of coordinated social action (e.g. migrating across a wide strait to colonize new lands, such as Australia.) This language, according to Everett, was probably a Type 1 grammar, simple word order without recursion. Initially it need not have included a particularly large vocabulary; a vocabulary need be just large enough to serve the group's ecological niche.[85]

Many theorists have objected to gradualist accounts of language evolution by pointing out that having the ability to communicate linguistically about abstract concepts is pointless unless others acquire the same ability at the same time. But the account proposed here avoids this objection. The baboons described by Seyfarth and Cheney interpret signals in a rich and cognitively complex way, and the two-word phrases described by Progovac provide a ready bridge from the "sparse signal/complex interpretation" condition decried by Godfrey-Smith to a fully interactive communication, initially based on a limited vocabulary. Once ToM has developed sufficiently for individuals to anticipate and simulate others' responses to even a handful of signals, and these signals begin to be used intentionally to influence others' behaviors, it is a plausible next step for others to acquire a second-order ToM and the ability to recognize intentionality, from which recognition the concept of conversation, as a sequence of chained signal-response actions, might gradually emerge. There is no need to posit some sudden evolutionary leap from no language abilities at all to full-blown human language with thousands of

---

[83] Following an idea initially proposed by Dawkins, Dennett assigns independent *agency* and the personality trait of *selfishness* to memes. However, as I have elsewhere argued (Ritchie, 2019), this extension of "meme theory" is neither necessary nor empirically justified. I will discuss and critique Dennett's arguments in greater detail later in this chapter.
[84] Heyes et al. (2020). They do not address the cultural transmission of adverse behaviors, physical or conceptual.
[85] Everett (2017): Everett's claims are interesting but quite controversial.

symbols, a complex syntax, displaced reference, orderly turn-taking, and all the other trappings of modern language use.[86]

Several researchers have suggested that language initially developed through bodily gestures rather than vocal speech.[87] Corballis points out that other primates have sophisticated control over gestures and suggests that the physiological changes needed for fully modern human speech developed gradually. Initially, facial expressions accompanied and amplified gestures and body posture; as these came to be supplemented by sounds (hisses, grunts, tongue-clicks, etc.), they moved inside the mouth, precipitating the gradual evolution of the ability to produce increasingly complex vocalization. The pragmatic advantages of speech over gesture precipitated physiological changes that render vocal signals more versatile and more efficient, and contributed to a gradual transition from gesture to speech.

Corballis argues the shift from gesture to autonomous vocal speech was an essential step toward the development of fully human culture.[88] As Corballis points out, present-day speech still involves a system of facial gestures, many of which are internal to the mouth and only partially visible. Corballis supports this proposal by pointing out that gestural language, requiring extensive use of hands and arms, would support complex social organization, but would also explain why, after an initial explosion of innovation, tool manufacture underwent only minor further development for nearly two million years, until the development of spoken language freed up the hands for other uses and supported conversation *about* tools while making or using them.

The Gradual Development of Language

The ability to interpret and draw complex inferences from others' signals, even if they are not intentionally produced, is functional even if it is possessed by only one member of a social group, since it confers considerable advantage in negotiating a complex social order. Conversely, the initial ability to produce alarm calls or other cues as signals at will to alter another animal's state of mind is also functional even if it is possessed by only one member of a social group, since it also confers potential advantages in competing for food and sex and in recruiting allies. As the ability spreads, through normal evolutionary processes, brains will begin to evolve in ways that bring these separate abilities together and make it easier to recognize and use symbols. As soon as a single member of the species develops the ability to recognize the intentionality of false signals (second-order ToM), this will confer advantages by enabling that individual to resist manipulation by others. This ability will also spread

---

[86] Everett (2017).   [87] For example, Corballis (2004); Rizzolatti and Arbib (1998).
[88] Corballis (2004).

through normal reproductive processes and induce further evolution of the brain's ability both to create and to recognize these emerging signals.

To elaborate: If Alpha discovers that uttering a low-pitched grunt will elicit a desired response from Beta, Alpha's use of this discovery is not contingent on Beta's understanding. Once Beta makes the same discovery, Alpha's discovery may become less useful as a deception strategy, but it opens up possibilities for enhanced social interaction by using the grunt[89] as a *symbol* referring to the predator or food source or whatever evoked the sound. A rudimentary vocabulary will eventually form, conferring advantages that cause the ability to spread throughout the group, along with supporting neural circuits. As it becomes possible to use the faked cue or associated vocalization or gesture for deception and other social purposes, it will become a communicative *signal*. In sum, social information such as that gleaned by Seyfarth and Cheney's baboons will be even more useful once individuals can relate this information to other members of her kinship group, the next step in the evolution of language.

The ability to imitate others' gestures, facilitated by mirror neurons, provides a ready scaffold for the development of language.[90] An initial vocabulary could grow incrementally, one cue-based signal at a time. At some point, playful or serendipitous invention of sounds and gestures kick in, adding to the small but expanding vocabulary. These might develop from sounds emitted during play, grooming, and sex, which would enhance the value of the proto language as an extension of grooming. Second-order ToM: Once Beta achieves the ability to recognize the relationship between Alpha's signal and Beta's own response, particularly if Beta has the ability to control her own response, then the foundation is laid for symbolic communication: The signal can be used to *indicate* a response without *performing* the response. This can easily enough be generalized to include a signal Alpha emits upon encountering an object (another person, food, or a predator) or upon performing or witnessing a particular action (grooming or play). In this way, a vocabulary could grow within a group, gradually at first, then accelerate as brain and muscular physiology evolve to accommodate signal use and recognition, and intentional instruction replaced imitation as a means of transmission. The ability to acquire and use this vocabulary would increase homeostasis and confer survival advantages for the individual, so that the cognitive ability to acquire and use these signals would coevolve with the ability to produce and interpret them and the development of language would begin to accelerate. The

---

[89] It is more likely that a different but serendipitously associated gesture or vocalization would develop for use in communicating about the referent, leaving the original warning value of the screech intact.

[90] Rizzolatti and Arbib (1998).

ability to communicate about one's own mental state would improve cooperation and increase group homeostasis, indirectly contributing to individual-level reproductive fitness, further accelerating the development and elaboration of ToM and metacognition.[91]

To the extent that these cue-based signals are useful, they will themselves come to be stored in long-term memory in association with the expected responses and simulations of the associated perceptual and motor control neural activity. These stored "words" will come to be associated with memories of typical (frequently occurring) situations in which they are used. These associated situation memories will come to be part of the "meaning," along with the initial referent.[92] As this rudimentary vocabulary develops and spreads through the group,[93] perception/brain/production systems able to create, process, and understand these signals will confer a survival advantage, leading to further evolution of signaling ability. Language and associated cognitive and vocal capabilities must have coevolved in interaction with each other.

Elaborating the Signal System. Many of the initial symbols are likely to have been social – for example, threaten, mollify, request, excuse, persuade, invite, play, and groom, or deceptive use of ecological signals such as predator warnings. Useful environmental information is present from the outset in the form of alarm calls and feeding sounds, but if the primary force driving the development of advanced cognitive and communicative capabilities was social, the development of ecological signaling probably lagged behind social signals. However, the ability to extend surveillance by providing information is one of the characteristics of a useful friend,[94] and promotes cooperation on ecological (environment-related) tasks as well as social interactions. Ecological signaling in service of cooperation as well as deception is likely to have developed in tandem with social conversation, or perhaps with a slight delay. The structure of conversation, including turn-taking, is likely to have developed along with the growth of a vocabulary and syntax, since the logic of any exchange beyond brief utterances requires it.[95]

The ability to indicate persons, signals for *I*, "you," "she/he," and eventually "us" and "them," probably developed quite early, along with very rudimentary syntax ("I groom you"/"you groom me"), promoted by a gradually expanding range of language uses and communication contexts. Even a few dozen "words," plus a simple S-V-O grammar, would serve immediate purposes

---

[91] Heyes et al. (2020).
[92] This is approximately the same mechanism by which humans, especially in a literate society, acquire most of our vocabulary (Landauer and Dumais, 1997).
[93] The intentional use of cues as signals qualify as what Dennett calls a "meme."
[94] Dessalles (2014). [95] Enfield (2017); Enfield and Sidnell (2014).

and drive further evolution of language capabilities, including alterations to the vocal tract and hearing as well as to various areas in the brain. We know from several language acquisition experiments that at least a few other species are capable of acquiring hundreds of words and combining them in two- and occasionally three-word sequences; it is reasonable to assume that early ancestors of humans also had at least this capability. All these capabilities may have developed by expanding and diversifying existing neural circuits and capabilities. Early on, vocal qualities and facial expressions as well as gesture and body stance will form part of the grammar, applying the expressive qualities of these behaviors to emphasize or qualify the vocalizations or gestured signs.[96] Like simple conversation structure, nonlexical signals were probably part of language from the beginning. Given the origin of language in negotiating and representing (to self and others) the complex relationships that constitute the social structure of the group, politeness (and intentional impoliteness) probably developed very near the beginning.[97]

This rudimentary situation might have lasted for some time before subsequent elaboration occurred. One step toward a more abstract level of signaling might follow from (and promote) further expansion of ToM. If Jane recognizes that Tom has a representation of Jane's mental state (second-order ToM), then it is only one further step for Jane to form a representation of how Tom represents her own mental state (third-order ToM: Jane thinks Tom believes that she is deceiving him.) The development of metacommunication to improve cooperation also requires awareness of one's own mental state, so at this point, Jane's mental state will become an object to herself, independent of her body, as she is able to represent her own thought processes and motivations from an external perspective. Part of this accomplishment would involve the ability to represent her own use of signals as vocabulary. It would also allow her to represent words as objects independent of their "meanings," the responses they evoke, which in turn allows for words to be manipulated in Jane's "inner speech." This would allow Jane to present her "self," her emotions and thought processes, as she wishes Tom to perceive her. It would also facilitate a quantum leap in the power and range of thought – and eventually provide a scaffold for the development of reasoning, argumentation, and logic (as well as poetry and theology).

As third-order ToM develops and expands, both the language system itself and the associated cognitive states and activities will gradually become objects to language users, as will the ability to impart knowledge by means of symbolic communication – that is, to teach and inform as well as to gossip about others and about one's own introspective thoughts. At this point, telic

---

[96] Arnold (2018).   [97] Grice (1975); Leech (1983); Chapters 7 and 8.

uses of language (for exchange and discussion of ecological information and plans of action) must have begun a rapid expansion. Like the vocabulary itself, "common ground," the mutual knowledge of a shared repertoire of communicative signals and knowledge of the social and physical environment, developed in a gradual but inevitably expanding way.

Expanding Vocabulary. McNeill claims that gesture came first, mainly because other primates do not have the voluntary control over vocalization required for language, and do have fine control over arms and fingers.[98] Everett (and others) disputes this. I see no reason why both might not have developed simultaneously and gradually, until vocalization eventually became dominant in response to the ecological and cultural situation.

Both gesture and sounds are used to induce grooming and may have become associated with simulations of responses. These may both have provided the grounding for generalized signals, at first used to evoke the response, then to evoke a simulation of the response. Gesture, sounds, vocal qualities, and facial expressions also figure in other social interactions, including signaling playful intentions, aggressive intention (dominance) and submission. Many species use sounds to maintain contact with the group, and most use alarm calls to signal threat. Many of these gestures and sounds are associated with responses that can be represented and eventually simulated (once at least some members of the species achieve at least minimal control over the signal), thus becoming part of a nascent vocabulary.

Totemic Imitation. Some primates engage in dance-like movements and group vocalization.[99] As emotional empathy and ToM developed, synchronous movement and vocalization sessions may have incorporated imitations of significant animals, both their behavior and the sounds they make, in a ritual way. The concept of using gesture and sound to elicit a desired effect in social interactions with other members of the group might in time be generalized to parasocial interactions, intended to summon, dominate, or propitiate the spirit of a prey animal or a predator. Cave paintings of animals that date back at least 35,000 years may reflect a similar or related focus on simulation of significant animals, thereby objectifying the internal visual simulation of these animals and making them social as well as private.

Theory of mind may also have been extended to natural events, so that imitations of forces such as water, wind, and fire may also have been incorporated into ritual song and dance. The mirror system for body movement is activated by dance; the auditory cortex is also activated, even when watching silent videos of dance.[100] All these imitative sounds and gestures, capable of activating perceptual simulations, "summoning the spirit" of an animal or

---

[98] McNeill (2012); see also Corballis, (2004); Rizzolatti and Arbib (1998). [99] Arbib (2013).
[100] Whitehead (2014).

weather phenomenon, would become part of an incipient vocabulary. As meta-simulation developed through introspection, increasing the ability to simulate the simulation process itself and communicate one's own simulations to others, these imitations became more stylized. Then the ability to string two or more stylized signals together, blending them into a phrase, could develop culturally, providing the basis for a genuine language – as well as more sophisticated and formalized genres of music and dance.

The four major language areas – Broca's, Wernicke's, temporal pole and superior temporal sulcus – are all activated by pretend play. Three are activated by dance, but only one is activated by general body movements.[101] A similar activation occurs during role play, narrative, and daydreaming. Humans appear to have as many as six distinct mirror systems. Two of these, reading body actions and affect, are also present in monkeys. The others represent song and dance, mimetic and pretend play, role play, and a language system.[102] All these coevolved with and contributed to the development of language and complex culture.

Elaborating Syntax. Syntax poses greater difficulties, if only because it requires a more abstract level of thought. Once Jane can use and manipulate words, even if her vocabulary consists of only a few dozen signals, the potential exists for a low level of abstract thought, which in turn provides the basis for a rudimentary grammar. Once a rudimentary vocabulary includes signals for objects and actions, logic indicators become useful: Affirmation/negation and existence/not existence would be early candidates, along with time (past, future) and more complex forms such as conditionals and imperatives. The development of an introspective vocabulary for metacognition and metacommunication would lead to even more complex syntactic forms. All this depends to a great extent on what is useful in the group's ecological niche,[103] but it may also depend on what members of a culture find interesting and rewarding – that is, on the elaboration of curiosity and play.

According to McWhorter,[104] newly formed languages such as creoles usually have a simple straightforward grammar; complexity is added as succeeding generations of children learn the language (and play with it). However, Everett argues that more abstract concepts like past, future, and so forth, are likely to develop only when changes in the social or ecological situation render them useful.[105] Here's where the developing ability to represent mental states (ToM) might make an additional contribution. Higher-order ToM, the ability to represent how someone else represents one's own mental state and thought processes, implicitly enables one to represent and reflect on one's own thought

---

[101] This is an additional argument against the use of the phrase "body language."
[102] Whitehead (2014).   [103] Everett (2017).   [104] McWhorter (2018).
[105] Everett (2017).

processes. This also implies the ability to *recall* and form a representation of one's *previous* thought processes and perceptions, which would lead to a conscious representation of the *past*. From there it is a short step to representing what one might experience and one's potential thought processes in the *future*,[106] and the possible future thoughts and actions of others (including, perhaps, the personified "other" of prey, predator animals, or natural forces).[107] As language develops and becomes detached from the here and now and a group's ecological niche rewards the ability to represent past and future, syntax will develop to support communicating about past and future – and about real versus imaginary.

Halliday[108] observes that grammatical and conversational structures that reflect new structures of knowledge are precipitated by major changes in human culture, which require new forms of communication. One such change was beginning to live in settled communities, followed by transition from a hunter-gatherer to an agricultural economy. In hunter-gatherer societies subject to large predators, males speak quietly to preserve stealth and mimic animal sounds to aid in hunting. Females, while gathering in the forest, speak loudly or sing in choruses to demonstrate group size and discourage predators.[109] They also speak and sing in ritualistic choruses, metaphorically imitating and satirizing male sexuality as a strategy to inhibit outbreaks of male sexual aggression. As men yielded to women's sexual strategies, principles of childhood play were extended to adult rituals.[110] Gendered mimicry drives both vocabulary and norms. Mimetic sounds develop into words for what is imitated,[111] and these are incorporated into ritual, play, and language.

Metaphor. Metaphor[112] entered the picture early, and may have contributed to expanding both vocabulary and syntax. As simulations become richer and more complex, and corresponding mental schemas (patterns of densely interconnected neural representations) become richer and more complex, the ability

---

[106] According to Koch (2019), the causal interaction of past, present, and future within a neural system is the qualifying foundation for consciousness.

[107] Humans have always had at least an implicit social relationship with animals, particularly predator and prey animals, often deifying them or treating them as symbolic kin. This social relationship continues in our encounters with the supposedly "wild" animals in wildernesses and game preserves.

[108] Halliday (1998).

[109] Lewis (2014). More recent research has produced evidence that women were also sometimes hunters, and men sometimes gatherers. However, this does not change the central thread of Lewis's argument.

[110] Knight and Lewis (2014).   [111] Lewis (2014).

[112] Here, consistent with Lakoff and Johnson (1980), I define metaphor as experiencing an abstract concept as, or understanding in terms of, a less abstract, more direct type of experience. For example, many common expressions in English are based on PASSION IS FIRE, in which strong emotions are experienced *as* fire (e.g. hot and destructive). See Chapter 10 for more detailed discussion.

to use and interpret metaphors by activating only a part of the simulation schema could develop in several ways. What is probably required is at least a sufficiently complex ToM to represent the simulation-activation process itself, to simulate and represent the others' responses to a signal.[113] The advantage of developing accurate predictions about others' (and one's own) behavior[114] will also drive this development. Conceptual metaphors[115] develop quite naturally through extension of the network of experiences (as simulations) associated with the primary signals, which also extends vocabulary.[116]

Metaphor may have developed originally as metonymic representation of animals by imitating characteristic sounds and movements. Once people gained the ability to simulate others' mental states and others' perceptual simulations, utterances – words and gestures – may have been used to evoke a situation-relevant part of their associated simulations. The social use of and reaction to this kind of representation contributed to expansion and further refinement of vocabulary. Conceptual metaphors based on extending the neural responses activated by commonplace experiences probably figured in the development of language from very early in the process.[117]

Abstraction and Ambiguity. The process of abstraction and development of truly arbitrary abstract symbols probably developed in much the same way that Kanji and other pictogram written languages developed – a representation slowly abstracted away from the grounding, applied metaphorically, then even further abstracted until the grounding became almost unrecognizable.[118] Semantic meanings, relations of words to other words, developed as language elaborated beyond the initial simulation/experience grounding.

Language was probably *never* precise or code-like.[119] Certain calls and gestures may have initially had a code-like precision, but as soon as signals began to be used to evoke/activate simulations outside the original grounded context, and the activation became less than full, or blended with other simulations, ambiguity and generality would creep in. Precision is not needed for the social functions of language, although it may be desirable for some aspects of social control and coordinated action. It is unclear exactly what forces may have led to the earliest attempts to establish precise meanings. The development of agriculture and large-scale social organization may have been a major contributor. The early development of writing systems in service of extended social control would certainly have motivated attempts to

---

[113] The role of simulation and semantic connections in language use and comprehension is treated in more detail in Chapter 4.
[114] Heyes et al. (2020). [115] Lakoff and Johnson (1980, 1999).
[116] Gibbs (2006); Jamrozik et al. (2016).
[117] Lakoff and Nunez (2000) argue that mathematics developed out of a similar process of metaphorical extension.
[118] Everett (2017). [119] Everett (2017).

stabilize meanings,[120] because written language is more permanent than speech or gesture.

Use of language as a cognitive tool may have developed early and in tandem with the development of signal systems to include more abstract simulations. As early humans learned to use signals to activate their own simulations, and to use a sequence of signals to activate a complex representation, mentally recalling the signals would activate mental simulations of the represented objects or narratives: The "inner flow" of language might emerge gradually, contributing to the development of full consciousness and sense of self. Beyond a certain level, both a sense of self and elaboration of abstract thought require social interaction, which in turn provides the basis for an "inner dialog" of language, interacting with, reflecting, and contributing to the "outer dialog" of actual conversation.

Everett argues that language and culture, manifest in the use of symbols, grammar, and associated visual and vocalic signals, were probably among the strongest contributors to evolution of human intelligence. At a sufficient level of abstraction, language is useful both for private reflection and for collective thought through communication. Complex thinking may be favored by evolution, especially cultural evolution, because it supports complex planning. Indirection and politeness (*facework*) may have developed later: "A *neanderthalensis* could have just grunted and demanded a piece of meat ... because they might not have had request forms as well developed as our own ...."[121] However, as ToM developed sufficiently to represent how others represent oneself, facework and politeness would be needed to maintain social bonds and reduce conflict.

Language for Coordinating Action. Dunbar suggests that the initial impetus for language evolution was the pressure of complex social structure rather than ecological pressures and the need to coordinate activities like foraging and defense, but that does not rule out an early adaptation of language for coordinating action. Coordination is improved by social bonds and by synchronized movements, and many other mammals coordinate activities such as hunting. Some, like wild dogs, engage in a dance-like series of rhythmic movements prior to commencing a hunt. As language developed and was used for social interaction and coordination, it would be readily adapted to coordinating survival activities like hunting, foraging, and encounters with other groups. These coordinative uses of language increased the usefulness of language, and further contributed to the evolution of vocabulary, syntax, and the associated perceptual and neural systems.

---

[120] Halliday (1998).   [121] Everett (2017, p. 258).

Implications for Our Understanding of Contemporary Language

As Dunbar points out, language still plays a key role in both "grooming" and "gossip" – learning about others' social relationships and one's own place in social order. In his data, about 65 percent of all conversation is focused on social relationships, not on the telic "information" that is the central focus of many theories of communication. The other 35 percent of language use is accounted for by persuasive as well as informative roles of language, and the informative role is often both general and abstract. In my own data, storytelling and language play are more frequent than telic (informative) language uses. Code-like precision is important for some informative and coordinating functions, but expressive power is more important for most language uses.

Language is almost always ambiguous[122] – and ambiguity, the nuances of meaning associated with ordinary words and phrases, is a major contributor to its expressive power. This is not just strategic ambiguity, although that plays a role. Landauer and Dumais[123] provide convincing evidence that an individual's understanding of a word, its meaning, is largely a factor of its relationships with the contexts in which it has previously been observed, and thus changes subtly each time the word is encountered in a new context.[124] Because of this, any word or phrase can have a diverse array of meanings to any one individual, depending on the context, and will have slightly different meanings to any two individuals.[125]

Language elements – words and syntax – have some code-like features (i.e. dictionary representations or definitions), but these are mostly imprecise, because dictionary definitions are themselves assembled from observed usage, which varies across time, space, and culture. Even when a technical term is carefully defined – for example, in a scientific paper – its meaning often undergoes a process of "*drift*," which then requires a subsequent writer to undertake a concept explication to restore some semblance of precision to the term. Most language elements are connected through cooccurrence in similar contexts with other language elements (words, phrases, and utterance contexts), present as neural linkages in the brain, which accounts for phenomena like word association. Most language elements activate some degree of perceptual simulations,[126] both directly and by way of associated words. For example, "vulture" activates simulations of the bird both flying and on the ground, and also activates associated emotions, including disgust and fear along with simulations associated with metaphorical uses and interpretations. "Vulture" is also likely to activate semantic links to words and phrases like

---

[122] Everett (2017); Wilson and Sperber (2004). [123] Landauer and Dumais (1997).
[124] This parallels the subtle changes in a memory every time it is recalled. [125] Lyons (1977).
[126] Bergen (2012).

"dead animal" and "rotten meat," which also activate links to the perceptual simulations associated with these related words. Finally, "vulture" activates associations with explanations and general knowledge, possibly including scientific knowledge – for example, about the role of vultures in the ecosystem, their mating behaviors, and so forth. This indeterminate and imprecisely bounded set of associations doesn't constitute a unique meaning so much as it provides a field of potential meanings.[127]

Memes: Units of Cultural Practice

Theologians have struggled for centuries to explain why an omnipotent creator would allow the existence of genetically transmitted diseases like multiple sclerosis, and why good people do bad things. These same paradoxes confront genetic scientists (how can "survival of the fittest" allow the continuation of multiple sclerosis, sickle cell anemia, and color blindness?) and culture theorists (how do useless and even harmful practices like self-mutilation and suicide endure and spread through society?)

To address the apparent contradiction in evolution theory, Dawkins[128] proposed that the gene, not the organism, is the unit of evolution, and genes act solely to perpetuate themselves, without regard for the welfare of organisms that carry them, summarized in his metaphor of "the *selfish* gene." By personifying genes, assigning independent agency and intentionality to them, Dawkins dramatized the fact that an individual's genetic heritage is not necessarily all benign, not even from the limited perspective of reproductive fitness. A gene that codes for a trait that is *eventually* disabling or leads to misery or early death can propagate without limit, if only it allows the organism to live long enough to reproduce. Even genes that code for potentially fatal traits can propagate if they are not always fatal, especially if they are associated with genes that code for traits that increase overall reproductive fitness. Personifying these genes as "*selfish*" dramatizes the fact that their propagation often detracts from the welfare of the carrier. However, it also implies that genes are capable of having a *self* with *needs* and *intentions*, and of *devising actions* to achieve those intentions – which implies both *agency*, the capacity for purposive action, and a decidedly sophisticated level of mental activity. This is contrary to the fundamental principle that evolution has no direction or purpose but is entirely driven by the organism's interactions with its environment and by random alterations in its genome (a thoroughly *passive* process, in contrast to the *active* process implied by "*selfish*").[129]

---

[127] Chapter 11.   [128] Dawkins (1976).
[129] For a detailed discussion and critique of the PERSONIFICATION metaphor, see Ritchie (2020).

Addressing the apparent contradiction in culture theory, Dawkins extended the "*selfish*" metaphor to culture. He coined the word "*meme*," a blend of *gene* and *mime*, to indicate any minimally coherent unit of meaning, ideation, or cultural practice, and argued that these *memes* (behavior and thought patterns) are also "*selfish*," in the metaphorical sense that they are often learned, expressed, and propagated (like "*selfish*" genes) independently of whether they contribute to or detract from the welfare of the those who learn and express them. To cite one of Dawkins's examples, the *celibacy* meme, a central feature of Roman Catholic doctrine, is directly detrimental to the reproductive fitness of its carriers. In Roman Catholic doctrine and practice, the *celibacy* meme is combined with and supported by an array of memes, including *saints, sexual shame, guilt, repentance, redemption*, and an array of rituals and ceremonies. These memes fit together in a *memeplex*, an array of memes that tend to be recalled and enacted as a coherent whole. Consequently, the celibacy meme has been propagated for nearly 2,000 years.

Dennett extends the metaphor to characterize memes as "*infectious*" like viruses, and to argue that memes, like genes, are subject to evolutionary processes that increase their "*virulence*" and enable them to spread like viruses through a human culture. I have elsewhere[130] criticized the metaphorical language used by Dennett, Dawkins, and other meme theorists on the grounds that the metaphor "*selfish*" misleadingly assigns both agency and personhood to genes and to memes, neither of which possesses the ability to have *intentions* or a *self* with *interests*. However, stripped of the metaphorical language, the underlying idea is useful: Memes and the behaviors they constitute often spread rapidly through society even when they are detrimental both to the individuals who learn and repeat them and to society in general. Two particularly deadly examples of "*selfish*" memes that sometimes spread rapidly in spite of their harmfulness are *suicide* and *mass murder*. These spread through the same processes of cultural transmission and learning that also spread useful memes[131] and contribute to the development of language and culture.

Memes are "cultural *items*," a "*way of behaving* (roughly) that can be copied, transmitted, remembered, taught … *memes are ways*: ways of doing something, or making something, but not *instincts* … memes are transmitted perceptually, not genetically."[132] A word or phrase is a kind of meme, as are pronunciations and ways of creating a plural or organizing words into

---

[130] Ritchie (2020).
[131] Phillips (1980). Note that the common phrase "natural *selection*" similarly personifies nature in a way that contradicts a basic tenet of evolution theory, that evolution has neither purpose nor goal. The popularity of this phrase is, of course, itself an example of a "*selfish*" (i.e. perversely propagated) meme, in that its use is detrimental to the audience's understanding of evolution theory.
[132] Dennett (2017, p. 206, italics in original).

meaningful sequences. A dance step is a meme, as are flower arrangements, waving "goodbye," and making an obscene gesture. Thus far, *meme* is a useful term: As Dennett claims, we have no other word to express this idea.

Just as the evolution of genes is driven by characteristics that will lead to the propagation of the gene, whether they are beneficial or detrimental to the organism as a whole, the "*evolution*"[133] of memes is driven by characteristics that make particular memes easier and more rewarding to learn and imitate, regardless of whether they benefit the welfare of individuals or groups who adopt them. However, contrary to Dennett's dramatic language, memes do not "compete for brain space," they have no intentions, and they do not "*invade*" minds. To reproduce a meme, an individual observes a phrase, gesture, obscene joke, or dance step, remembers it, and subsequently repeats it. In some cases (like a complex dance step), humans may work quite hard to acquire a meme (which the choreographer worked hard to develop). In other cases (like advertising jingles or the gestures and phrases of social interaction), memes may be easily, almost automatically, acquired and stored in memory – without the individual even being aware of it. This is true of harmful memes like self-mutilation and smoking cigarettes as well as to misleading semantic habits like referring to the nonpurposive effect of differences in reproductive fitness as "*selection*," with the unintended implication that a conscious agent is responsible for evolution. The nonpurposive nature of meme acquisition applies equally to pointless memes such as wearing a baseball cap backward and to beneficial memes such as saying "thank you" or opening the door for a companion.

The Meme Theory Account of Culture and Brain Evolution. Dennett's model of cultural evolution starts with the idea that memes are independent of the individuals who acquire, retain, and enact them. People do intentionally evaluate behavioral patterns and, sometimes, ways of speaking ("*memes*") and choose to acquire and produce them, often with considerable effort. Group members also instruct new members in the performance and use of memes that benefit the group, such as the metacognition and metacommunication associated with evaluating and reporting confidence in one's decision-making.[134]

Many hours of practice are required to acquire the *memeplex* for playing the violin or making a sushi roll. However, as Dennett claims, most memes are developed spontaneously and acquired automatically, with little or no

---

[133] Compare to Heyes et al. (2020). The usage here is metaphorical, at least in the sense that biological evolution requires a physical substrate (e.g. DNA) that shapes the developing organism and is susceptible to random modification. No such substrate has been found for memes.

[134] Heyes et al. (2020).

conscious attention. Young children acquire new words (and syntax) automatically, day after day[135] – including new words their parents would prefer they not acquire. Not only is this routine, everyday meme acquisition nonintentional, but it is also difficult to control – to the greater glory of advertising professionals.

Dennett proposes that language may have begun with a handful of memes – cultural behaviors, including rudimentary language units, sounds and/or gestures that were acquired (observed and retained) then propagated (produced and imitated) until they became a common feature within a group. If some of the early memes provided an advantage (led to improved social interaction, stronger peer bonds, and higher status in the group[136] or to greater success in mating or food gathering[137]), then they would become more or less *obligatory*, necessary to survival and reproductive fitness. Once memes began to improve reproductive success, the human brain evolved to accommodate the process of meme acquisition. This led to a cycle of coevolution – meme-receptive brains acquire memes more readily, which provides the capacity to develop and propagate more memes with an even greater effect on reproductive success, and so on.

As with genes, Dennett argues that the fundamental mechanism of meme "*evolution*" is suited to the development and dissemination of helpful memes that contribute to individual reproductive fitness and group success, and to neutral memes that have no effect on reproductive fitness. Unfortunately, the same processes are also suited to memes that detract from reproductive fitness or group success. Rephrased in terms of learning theory, these claims seem almost obvious: people often learn and imitate ideas and behaviors that lead them to refrain from reproducing themselves, mutilate or starve their bodies, risk their lives in foolish ways, disrupt valued relationships, or even commit suicide. Behaviors of this sort, harmful memes, have probably been a part of human culture from the beginning.

What makes Dennett's argument interesting is that he shows how the transmission of neutral and detrimental behavior patterns can be explained as *part of* the process of culture change and transmission, not an exception to it. There is no need to invent "just so stories" to account for every quirk of human behavior. However, he develops the metaphorical implications of the idea that memes are independent of the people who learn, retain, and produce them in ways that are misleading and obfuscating as well as entertaining. To take just the example of self-harm and suicide, extensive research has shown how factors such as imitation and parasocial identification with a suicidal hero (e.g. Kurt Cobain) can contribute to the spread of the pernicious suicide

---

[135] Landauer and Dumais (1997).   [136] Dunbar (1996).   [137] Bickerton (2009).

meme.[138] There is no need to ascribe intentionality or agency to the suicide meme in order to explain its pernicious spread,[139] and doing so has the potential to confuse more than to enlighten. Dennett's metaphor system is itself a good example: It is useful insofar as it renders his ideas more memorable, but it is, at the same time, harmful insofar as it contributes to an erroneous teleological concept of evolution and a reified personification of cognitive processes.

The Elaboration Likelihood Model[140] is helpful: Memes are more likely to be learned, remembered, and reproduced if an individual has the *ability* and *motivation* to do so. This locates the "selective principle" neither in a personified meme nor in the rational decision-making of an individual, but in the interaction between perceptual and performative characteristics of a meme and the capabilities and motivations of humans who encounter the meme – whether these motivations are accessible to conscious thought or not. A meme will spread through a population if its characteristics fit[141] the capabilities and motivations of a significant portion of the population (the cultural environment), whether it is beneficial to them or not. Any alteration (random or intentionally introduced by an advertising agency) that improves the meme's fit to the cultural environment will increase the probability that the meme will spread.

The process of recall and repetition shapes, streamlines, dramatizes, and revises the memes in ways that make them more likely to be retained and repeated.[142] Thus, memes will develop characteristics that are increasingly well-fitted to the capabilities and motivations of members of a culture. There is no need to assign personhood, intentionality, or agency to the meme, *or* to assign rational assessment and decision-making to individual members of the culture. Memes, including pernicious memes, are not independent of embodied human psychology, social interaction, and culture; they are part of it, a logical consequence of the interaction of psychology, communication, and culture. Imitation, intentional instruction, and repetition are themselves useful memes;

---

[138] For example, Phillips (1980); Phillips, Lesyna, and Paight (1992); Bould, Jamieson, and Romer (2003).

[139] As I write this, in late 2020, a dozen examples of pernicious conspiracy theory memes also come to mind. Many of them, like QAnon, seem to be spreading not only by way of the learning devices associated with Dennett's meme theory but also through deliberate and malicious dissemination.

[140] Petty and Cacioppo (1991).

[141] This is the actual meaning of "reproductive fitness" with respect to memes.

[142] Alport and Postman (1947). This is most often unintentional, a result of how memory and recall functions. However, as the QAnon example illustrates, pernicious memes are sometimes deliberately honed and reshaped to make them easier and more rewarding to imitate and reproduce.

it is unsurprising that memes spread so quickly, even destructive memes like conspiracy theories (QAnon) and self-mutilation.

In his list of insights provided by meme theory, Dennett introduces another useful insight wrapped in a biological metaphor, *"the fitness of memes." Reproductive fitness* has a relatively precise meaning in biology and can be applied to cultural practices only metaphorically: Cultural practices have no physical existence and no way to reproduce themselves. The underlying idea can easily be rephrased in language that is slightly more cumbersome but lacks the misleading metaphorical implicatures as "the ease with which memes can be learned and imitated and the psychological and social rewards for doing so." Memes do *"evolve"* in the sense that, as they are observed, remembered, and repeated, they become easier and more rewarding to learn and repeat.[143] This *"evolution"* has been extensively researched by persuasion,[144] communication, and marketing researchers – and exploited by advertising professionals and other agents of meme propagation.

The *meme* concept, recognizing that ideas and practices have an existence independent of any individual person and often spread through society in ways that are independent of individual intentions, has several advantages. The first of the three insights conveyed by the *meme* concept listed by Dennett, *"competence without comprehension"* (p. 210), emphasizes that cultural practices often appear to be designed, even when they were not the product of any identifiable author. Young children acquire social practices like "thank you" and "please" long before they understand their function in social interactions. (But their acquisition of these practices is encouraged by intentional instruction from their parents and others.) Much of the conversational behavior even of mature adults, such as turn-taking and face-management, is skillfully executed by people who are often unaware they are doing it.[145] Even when a lexical unit is the product of deliberate design, such as Freud's term "complex," it is often transformed through nonauthored cultural processes.[146] Someone, somewhere, must have been the first person to wear a baseball cap backward, and someone, somewhere, must have been the first person to say "I was, like, ..." or "the thing is, is that . . . ." We will never know who, where, or why. The *meme* concept can also help explain the spread of "malignant, useless, burdensome, fitness-reducing elements of a culture"[147] – not as a substitute for, but in combination with continued

---

[143] Alport and Postman (1947).
[144] For comprehensive reviews of classical persuasion research relevant to the learning and reproduction of memes, see Petty and Cacioppo (1981); Moyer-Gusé (2008).
[145] Enfield (2017).   [146] See Moscovici (2004) for a fascinating account.
[147] Dennett (2017, p. 215). Unfortunately, Dennett ignores the trenchant critique of rational actor assumptions by Kahneman (2013; Tversky and Kahneman, 1992), for which Kahneman won a Nobel Prize. (See also Gilovich, Griffin, and Kahneman, (Eds.), 2002.)

Summary 79

research on the social, cultural, and psychological processes in persuasion, learning, recall, and performance.

Language continues to evolve – indeed, in the age of electronic communication, it seems to evolve and change ever faster.[148] Along with lexical units that are defined in a dictionary, language includes sound particles like "uh" and "um"[149] as well as variations in voice quality, facial expression, and gesture that qualify, extend, contradict, and substitute for the lexical units traditionally considered to constitute language. Figurative speech, especially wordplay (Chapter 10) and metaphor (Chapter 11), are common vehicles of language extension and evolution. Language evolution is constrained by the capabilities of human signal use and detection, as well as by the many contexts of language use (Chapter 9).

Language and Homeostasis

We may never have a definitive account of what precipitated the complex physiological and cognitive changes necessary for modern human language. The evidence seems convincing that these changes were in large part responsive to the pressures of living in large complex social groups, then responded to changes in the social environment that language use itself shaped. Initially, the contribution of language to homeostasis may have been primarily a matter of recruiting and maintaining social relationships. However, it is also apparent that social surveillance (monitoring the activities and relationships of other group members) played an important role, probably from the beginning. Language, both as a tool for abstract cognitive representation (including *memes*) and as a tool for secondary surveillance ("gossip"), would certainly have contributed to individuals' ability to maintain an increasingly accurate representation of alternative social futures as a way to predict the consequences of interactions in the present. In the form of storytelling and other group activities, it contributes to social-level homeostasis, maintaining and strengthening the cohesion and vitality of groups. Storytelling, in particular, facilitates shared representation of potential future conditions, which in turn serves both group homeostasis and the quality of individual forward projections in service of individual homeostasis.[150] These functions of language-based communication will be developed in more detail in the last half of the book.

Summary

In this chapter, I reviewed research suggesting that language evolved, not in response to information-exchange needs associated with ecological pressures

---

[148] Chapter 14. [149] Following Enfield (2017). [150] Chapter 14.

but as a means of developing and maintaining supportive relationships in response to living in a large, complex social hierarchy. I explored the contribution of perspective-taking (ToM, abetted by mirror neurons) to the further development of language. I described "meme" theory as a useful tool for understanding the spread of ideas and behaviors, including useless and even harmful ideas and behaviors. All these aspects of language evolution are important for understanding contemporary communication behavior, because they redirect attention away from rational and telic communication toward social and paratelic communication. The implications of these factors for cognition (including reasoning) will be developed in Chapter 4; the implications for ordinary conversation and discourse will be developed in the last half of the book.

4 Thinking
Using and Understanding Language

The human brain does some amazing things. The routine everyday activities of getting out of bed, dressing, feeding ourselves, interacting with other people, and generally getting by are remarkable in themselves; what we can learn to do with a little effort is even more amazing. How do we do it? How do we plan and build complex structures, invent and play complex games, solve crossword puzzles, and debate theories about how our marvelous minds work? What is the role of consciousness in this mental activity? How do we learn, use, and understand language and other complex systems of communication, and how do they contribute to cognition?

These are not new questions; they have been debated by philosophers and scientists for centuries. In this chapter, I will begin with a brief discussion of mind and consciousness, followed by a more extended discussion of perceptual and motor simulation. I will introduce conceptual metaphors, which receive a more extensive treatment later in the book. I will briefly discuss scripts, schemas, and frames, and the role they play in both thinking and language use. Then I will turn to the question of how the mind processes language.

Mind

There is something almost miraculous about the experience of mind – a topic that would be impossible to discuss without the equally miraculous experiences of *self* and *consciousness*. This sense of the miraculous may account for the belief, widely held among both philosophers and laypersons, that mind must be something else, not only separate from our bodies but also even different in substance. Yet, just as there is little evidence of the "mentalese" required by the computer model of the brain, there is no evidence beyond the purely anecdotal of anything like a nonbiological "mind-substance." On the other hand, there *is* a growing body of evidence supporting the claims that the phenomena associated with "mind" can be accounted for by purely biological processes associated with homeostasis, and that these processes involve the entire body, not just the brain.

Until recently, the standard view of thinking was based on logical reasoning. However, recent research supports a very different view, in which thought and action are implicit, intuitive, and intertwined with emotion rather than explicit, deliberate, and "objective." Most people experience a constant stream of thoughts, often on apparently random topics. These thoughts have perceptual and evaluative as well as verbal components, sometimes in the form of an internal dialog, but with a succession of foci. Usually the thoughts focus on ideas and representations of events, physical and emotional states (feelings), and social interactions.[1] People can imagine rich and detailed episodic and narrative representations of the past or future, complete with spatial and objective details, actions, and emotional responses. These projected representations include partial activation of associated perceptual and motor neural circuits, and reuse episodic and evaluative information from memory. They form a large part of our mind-wandering and play a role in deliberation and planning. In the more chaotic form of dreams, they invade our sleep. Psychologists are coming to believe that the constant flow of thoughts, "mind-wandering," serves the purpose of planning; it also supplies material for creative imagination, and for otherwise abstract reasoning. Deliberative planning is effortful, but mind-wandering is not.[2]

Identity and the Self. A concept of oneself as an entity distinct from other people requires an understanding that other people are distinct from oneself – first-order theory of mind (ToM).[3] But with second-order ToM, once it is possible to represent how others represent oneself, then it is also possible to form a *representation* of a distinct *self*. To "see ourselves as others see us"[4] is to see ourselves as *objects*. To form an objective representation of oneself as a thinking entity – to engage in *introspection* and form a complete *introspective awareness* of one's own thought processes – requires not only second-order ToM ("I *know* what my mind is *thinking*") but also third-order ToM ("I *know* what my mind *thinks* I *want*"). We form a composite representation of how others represent us and our introspective awareness of our own thoughts and feelings, and this becomes our sense of self, our *identity*, which we spend a lot of time and effort attempting to represent accurately (or deceptively, in some cases) to others.

We often have a sense that "other people don't really know me." This is probably because, through interoception and introspection, we observe ourselves, our actions as well as our feelings, and form representations of the various aspects of *self* from these observations. Then we attempt to explain these representations to others, who have their own observations and representations of us. All this is only possible once we have achieved at least

---

[1] Chafe (2012).   [2] Seligman et al. (2016). See also Damasio (1996, 1999).   [3] Chapter 3.
[4] Robert Burns, "To A Louse, On Seeing One on a Lady's Bonnet at Church."

second-order ToM, the ability to see one's self as an object. It is only *fully* possible with third-order ToM, blending self-perception (interoception and introspection) with feelings. Thus, we each have a social self, the composite of how we think others perceive us,[5] and a private self, the amalgamation of feelings (perceptions and independent thoughts plus emotional responses) about ourselves as experiencing and thinking agents. Third-order ToM, the perception of self as a thinking agent, is probably also the source of the homunculus illusion, the sense of an "inner person" to whom the senses report and from whom decisions and actions originate.

Consciousness

Part of the experience of being human and having a self is the experience of consciousness, and not just in the sense of being phenomenally aware of our surroundings, of the threats to homeostasis and opportunities for enhancing homeostasis. Most people believe we have conscious control over both experiences and actions, that "I am the captain of my soul,"[6] in the words of a Victorian poet. This is usually accompanied (at least in European and American cultures) by a belief that one has a unique "inner self," the "real me" that cannot be known by anyone else. These beliefs have been shaken by a battery of research findings. First, the idea of a private subjective "inner self" was assailed by research demonstrating that others can predict our behavior in a given situation as well as we; Bem[7] argues that we have no privileged access to our attitudes or motives but judge ourselves and infer our attitudes and our motives in exactly the same way as others do – by observing our own behavior.

What Does Consciousness Do? Extensive research has shown that conscious explanations for our actions are often demonstrably wrong, drawn from folk theories. Reliance on misleading cues can convince the conscious mind to report erroneously that it has acted. Research using brain scanning shows that neural processes associated with initiating action begin at least a half second before a research subject reports having decided to act. Conversely, nonconscious reminders of a goal can lead to action as effectively as conscious reminders. In sum, whatever consciousness does, it is apparently not important for knowing our own attitudes or initiating action.[8] On the basis of these and similar findings, many researchers have argued that consciousness is an epiphenomenon, a coincidental product of other brain processes that contributes nothing to reproductive fitness.

---

[5] Mead (1934).   [6] William Ernest Henley (1988), *A Book of Verses*.   [7] Bem (1972).
[8] Baumeister and Masicampo (2010); Libit (1985); Nisbett and Wilson (1977); Wegner (2002).

Baumeister and Masicampo[9] argue that deciding and directing action in the present moment is the wrong focus: consciousness performs a complex set of functions that might be summarized as maintaining a representation of the self in time, space, and social relationships[10] and projecting it forward in alternative (and often fanciful) scenarios. Consciousness consolidates information from the present physical and social environment, memory, and general knowledge; projects alternative futures based on alternative courses of action; resolves contradictory needs and impulses, including needs based on social and cultural expectations; weighs alternative actions; formulates and updates plans. At least in casual conversation, the details of carrying out these plans (including formulating words and sentences) are executed by preconscious automated routines that are not always under conscious control, although they are usually monitored and often corrected or repaired by conscious action.[11] Consciousness is engaged in deliberating on how to express a complex idea and monitoring, evaluating, and correcting utterances. These and other communication functions of consciousness will be discussed in more detail in later chapters.

Metacognition. An important function of consciousness entails metacognition, the ability to monitor, represent, and, to some extent, control our cognitive processes. Metacognition is highly adaptive, and it is found in other species as well as humans; Heyes et al. argue that metacognition is transmitted both genetically and culturally.[12] Metacognition is subject to communication at a gross level through signals, including posture (Rodin's *The Thinker* comes to mind), facial expression, and vocal qualities. Language enables humans to describe and label our mental state and cognitive processes to ourselves as well as to others. This in turn provides the means to influence the thought processes of others, to deliberate both privately and collectively about our thought processes, and to make explicit plans regarding our own thought processes. Metacognition provides a means for evaluating and communicating the degree of uncertainty or confidence in perceptions and judgments, recognizing and correcting errors, off-loading and sharing cognitive processes, and synthesizing the separate experiences and insights of multiple people.

Memory. It is commonly believed that memory is both accurate and permanent, but, in fact, it is neither. Human memory is dynamic, subject to constant alteration as it interacts with fresh experience. When a memory is recalled into working memory in a new context, new information is often inserted seamlessly into the memory as it is stored again. Emotions, plans, and goals affect how memory is interpreted, elaborated or even deleted, and

---

[9] Baumeister and Masicampo (2010).
[10] That is, in service of homeostasis (Chapter 2); Seligman et al. (2016). [11] Chapter 8.
[12] Heyes et al. (2020).

connected with other memories. The function of memory is not to provide a permanent, accurate representation of the past, but to serve the present needs of homeostasis, including social homeostasis. Both past (memory) and future (forward projection) are to a large part socially constructed, subject to and in part shaped by the matrix of conversations in which we live.[13]

Elements of episodic memory (what, when, where, who) appear to be separately maintained; when an episode is recalled, these elements are fused to create a complex representation. This repository of episodic memories provides the raw material for projecting representations into the future as well as for processing and understanding present experience through prediction, testing, and updating.[14] The hippocampus plays a central role in this process – in particular, in the ability to recall that the various events cooccurred.[15]

Perception, Understanding, and Language

What I have been calling "the conventional story," the computer/signal transmission metaphor for communication, dates from the beginnings of the digital age, when the exponential growth in computational power and sophistication foregrounded the digital computer and the complex algorithms it supported as an obvious model for any process that detects and processes information (in effect, virtually everything). With the publication of Shannon's elegant treatise on "the mathematical theory of communication,"[16] and its enthusiastic overgeneralization in Weaver's[17] interpretive essay, the digital computer became the model for almost everything. The universe is a computer, society is a computer, DNA is a computer, and the human brain is a computer.

The Conventional Story: The Digital Mind. Boroditsky and Prinz[18] trace the origins of cognitive science to the confluence of Chomsky's critique of behaviorism and the rise of artificial intelligence (AI) research, which itself became possible only when computer memory and processing had developed to a certain level. From the early successes of AI, it seemed obvious that information processing, including human thought, must require a language-like system of abstract symbols combined through syntax-like algorithms. Chomsky's program of linguistic research suggested that abstract symbols

---

[13] Seligman et al. (2016).
[14] Hawkins (2021); see Chapter 2. Children become capable of formulating episodic thoughts about the future only when they have gained the ability to recall personal experiences from the past.
[15] Seligman et al. (2016).   [16] Shannon (1948); Shannon and Weaver (1949).
[17] Weaver (1949); for a detailed critique, see Ritchie (1986, 1991).
[18] Boroditsky and Prinz (2008).

and syntax are innate features of the brain itself.[19] Because the symbols and syntax are innate, they are distinct from natural languages like English or Chinese: According to this perspective, we think in an innate language of thought, *mentalese*[20]. Boroditsky and Prinz observe that this proposition is often treated as an unarticulated background of cognitive science, a default assumption against which alternative proposals must be measured.

As Boroditsky and Prinz[21] note, there are several problems with the conventional account. In particular, *mentalese*, an abstract "language of the brain," is merely an assumption, based on how digital computers work, with no evidence that it actually exists. As Boroditsky and Prinz point out, a feature list, as predicated by conventional computer-based theories of language comprehension, is meaningless without some underlying representation of the features: "Ducks do not just have feet, they have *duck* feet."[22] Admittedly, a feature list could conceivably be sufficiently long and detailed to account for at least the most common variations on each feature, but there is no evidence of this, and the processing requirements would be horrendous. (How many sublistings would be needed just for "feet"?)

There is also the question of how a brain organized according to digital logic might evolve. Brains, like other parts of organisms, evolve by adapting and expanding whatever already exists. If primitive neural systems initially developed as extensions of perception/reaction systems, then evolved the ability to predict future states and assess the potential outcomes of alternative reactions, as Damasio claims,[23] how would a proposition-based "language of the brain" develop in the first place? In response to these issues, at least two alternatives to the digital brain/mentalese account have been proposed; each is supported by extensive evidence, but each poses its own problems and limitations.[24]

Perceptual Symbols. Barsalou[25] argues that thinking is done through *perceptual simulations*, partial activation of neural systems associated with perception, muscular action, and introspection. As we interact with an object (or process or action) on multiple occasions, we gradually form a composite neural representation of the muscular actions and perceptions that are typically engaged by those interactions. These *perceptual symbols*, partial

---

[19] These are not the words and syntax of the natural language we speak and write, but the symbols of "mentalese" and the "deep structure" that underlies the syntax of all spoken/written languages.
[20] Fodor (1975); for a more detailed discussion of the conventional account, see Chapter 2.
[21] Boroditsky and Prinz (2008); see also Sampson (2005).
[22] Boroditsky and Prinz (2008, p. 100).
[23] See Chapter 2 for a detailed discussion.
[24] Boroditsky and Prinz (2008).
[25] Barsalou (1999, 2008); see also Bergen (2012); Boroditsky and Prinz (2008); Gibbs (2006, 2008); Chapter 3.

activations of neural systems, are manipulated as we think about objects, processes, and actions.

Gibbs[26] argues that language interpretation in particular involves embodied simulation, the active construction of a simulation in which we imagine performing the actions and perceiving the objects identified by the language. Thus, when one reads an account of a ball game, one will experience partial activation of the neuron groups that would become activated while witnessing or performing the plays, accompanied by partial activation of the neuron groups associated with the muscular actions of the players, as well as their thoughts and emotions, their disappointments, frustrations, and surges of elation.

Barsalou[27] begins with the perceptual neural system, the "five senses" (sight, hearing, smell, taste, and touch), *interoception* (awareness of one's own internal body states, such as hunger or exhaustion), and *introspection* (awareness of one's thought processes, including assessment, evaluation, and confidence).[28] Conceptual thought uses either the same circuits as perception and motor control or parallel circuits; concepts are represented by only partial activation of the associated neural systems – those that are relevant to the current context of communication and action. When reading about a zebra, the simulation will include the animal's shape (in the most familiar orientation) and the characteristic stripes – but not in enough detail to count the stripes or even locate them with respect to other visual features.

When one encounters a word or phrase, neural groups associated with perceptual features of the named concept and with muscular responses associated with the concept are partially activated, and experienced as a *simulation* of the associated objects and events that are relevant in context. *Eagle* might activate partial simulations of the bird's typical shape and color, how it sits on a tree limb or soars in the sky. (The shape that is simulated, for example, sitting or soaring, depends on the context, as will be discussed in a later section.) *Hammer* might activate simulations of the ringing sound of a hammer on a nail, the feeling of swinging a hammer, or the shape of a familiar type of hammer – again, the simulated details will be largely determined by the context and previous experience.[29]

A persistent objection to the perceptual symbol systems hypothesis is that it cannot account for how we think about abstract concepts. However, Barsalou[30] demonstrated that, in principle, perceptual simulations suffice for abstract

---

[26] Gibbs (2006, p. 434). [27] Barsalou (1999, 2008).
[28] Introspection is approximately what Heyes et al. (2020) describe as metacognition, the representation of one's own thought processes.
[29] The neural systems involved in these processes are discussed in Chapter 2.
[30] Barsalou (1999).

thought, including logical inference. Even abstract ideas like *equality* can be represented by simulating our own introspective experience of like or unlike objects, or of stories about fair or unfair actions, and *negation* can be represented by simulating the disappearance or removal of an object, or, again, a story about denial or refusal.

Evidence for Perceptual Simulations

Over the past few decades, hundreds of research studies have demonstrated that perceptual and motor simulations are activated during language use and comprehension[31] as well as during certain abstract reasoning tasks. Experiments using fMRI to identify which areas of the brain are activated during either an actual task (clenching one's fist or listening to a sound) or imagining performing the task have shown that the same part of the brain that is active when hearing a sound is also active when imagining the sound.[32] Similarly, the same part of the brain that is active while performing a muscular action such as clenching one's fist is also active when imagining the action, or reading or hearing a sentence about oneself or another person performing the action.[33]

In one of the earliest studies to challenge the computational account, Shepard[34] presented subjects with a spatial visualization task similar to those often used in intelligence and aptitude tests. A geometric figure, drawn to imply three dimensions, is shown in a particular position alongside a similar figure in a different position, and the subject is asked whether the two images represent the same "object" or a mirror image. The second object is rotated through different angles, for example, either 30 or 100 degrees. If the computational model of cognition is correct, the subjects solve the problem the same way a computer would solve it, by using trigonometry, in which case it would take exactly the same amount of time to compute the 30 and 100 degrees rotations. However, Shepard found that the time required to identify the correct figure increased in proportion to the number of degrees through which it had to be rotated, supporting the conclusion that subjects use simulations of the rotation.

Several convergent research programs have supported the claim that perceptual simulations are activated by language. Studies using techniques such as fMRI have demonstrated activation of perceptual and motor control regions of the brain consistent with the language being processed.[35]

---

[31] See Bergen (2012) for a review.
[32] Halpern and Zatorre (1999); Wheeler, Petersen, and Buckner (2000).
[33] Ehrsson, Geyer, and Naito (2003).
[34] Shepard and Metzler (1971); Cooper and Shepard (1973).   [35] Seligman et al. (2016).

Eye-tracking experiments have demonstrated eye movements consistent with the direction of motion implied by a spoken or written account. Experiments using response latency demonstrate facilitation or interference effects consistent with partial activation of topic-relevant regions of the brain.[36]

Simulating Visual Experience. A series of experiments by Zwaan's research group is illustrative. First, he had the subjects read one of two sentences that imply a different orientation of the same object – for example, the subjects in stimulus condition one would read "The carpenter hammered the nail into the floor," implying a vertical nail. In condition two, the subjects would read a sentence that is identical, except it ended with "... into the wall," implying a horizontal nail. Immediately after the sentence, the subjects were shown a picture of an object and asked to decide whether the object was mentioned in the sentence. In half the trials, the image showed an unrelated object such as an elephant, in which case the correct answer is "no." In the other half of the cases, the image showed a nail; in half of *these* trials (25 percent of the total trials), the nail was shown in a vertical position, matching the position implied by "... into the floor" but not the position implied by "... into the wall." In the other 25 percent of the total trials, the nail was depicted in a horizontal position. Thus, in half the trials for which "yes" was the correct response, the image matched the orientation implied by the sentence, and in half the trials for which "yes" was the correct response, the image did not match the orientation implied by the sentence. The subjects in the matching image condition (image of a vertical nail after hearing "... into the floor") took less time to give the correct answer than the subjects in the mismatch condition, implying that the subjects in the mismatch condition had to rotate a simulation of a nail through 90 degrees before deciding that it matched the visual image[37] – consistent with Shepard's findings.

In another experiment based on the same design, the subjects read either "The ranger saw the eagle in the nest," implying a bird standing up with folded wings, or "The ranger saw the eagle in the sky," implying a horizontal bird with outstretched wings. As in the nail experiment, the subjects correctly identified an image of an eagle that matched what the sentence implied more quickly than an image of an eagle that did not match.[38]

Spivey[39] had subjects listen to a story while an unobtrusive camera recorded their eye movements. Half the stories did not involve motion, but the other half did imply motion upward, downward, to the right, or to the left. He found that the subjects' eyes moved in the direction implied by the story as they listened to it, supporting the conclusion that they were mentally simulating the movements of the person in the story.

---

[36] Bergen (2012). [37] Stanfield and Zwaan (2001).
[38] Zwaan, Stanfield, and Yaxley (2002). [39] Spivey and Geng (2001).

Another series of experiments by Zwaan demonstrated that syntax (e.g. word order) influences how we simulate motion.[40] In one experiment, the subjects listened to sentences that imply motion – for example, "The pitcher hurled the softball to you" (motion toward the observer) or "You hurled the softball to the pitcher" (motion away). He then showed the subjects two images in rapid succession, each on screen for a half second, and asked them to decide whether the images depict the same object. The images might be of unrelated objects (a softball and a watermelon), or they might be an image of a softball followed by another image of a softball, either slightly larger than the first image (as it would appear if moving toward the observer, matching the first sentence) or slightly smaller (as it would appear if moving away, matching the second sentence). When the second image was smaller than the first, the subjects who had just heard the sentence implying motion away responded more rapidly than those who had heard the sentence implying motion toward; conversely, when the second image was larger, the subjects who had just heard the sentence implying motion toward responded more rapidly than those who had heard the sentence implying motion away.

In a related experiment conducted by Bergen,[41] the subjects heard either a participant version (e.g. "You threw the baseball to the catcher," implying motion away (the image will get smaller)) or an observer version (e.g. "The pitcher threw the baseball to the catcher," implying lateral displacement). If the second image was slightly smaller but in the same location, the subjects correctly identified it as the same object more quickly for "You threw the baseball" than for "The pitcher threw the baseball." If the second image was the same size but displaced slightly to the right, the subjects correctly identified it as the same object more quickly for "The pitcher threw the baseball."

Perceptual simulations are always partial, at least for familiar objects and actions about which we have detailed knowledge. Working memory is not adequate to represent everything most of us know about an automobile, for example; simulations will include features relevant to the current situation or salient from recent experience. To test this, Borghi[42] had subjects read sentences implying a perspective either inside or outside a familiar object – for example, "You are driving a car" versus "You are washing a car." Subjects then saw a word or phrase that identifies an object found inside the car (for example, "gas pedal") or outside the car (for example, "tires" or "antenna"). Subjects responded more quickly to phrases naming objects consistent with the perspective implied by the sentence: "Gas pedal" and "steering wheel" are recognized more quickly for "driving" than for "washing" a car; "tires" and "antenna" are recognized more quickly for "washing" than for "driving."

---

[40] Zwaan, et al. (2004).   [41] Bergen (2012, ch. 5, p. 111).
[42] Borghi, Glenberg, and Kaschak (2004).

More striking evidence that people tend to simulate "being there," putting themselves into the situation described by a sentence, comes from an experiment by Yaxley and Zwaan.[43] In one example, subjects read "Through the clean goggles, the skier could easily identify the moose" or "Through the fogged goggles, the skier could hardly identify the moose." They found that subjects in the "fogged goggles" condition more rapidly identified an image of a moose as having been mentioned if the image was low resolution (blurred) than if it was high resolution. We not only simulate ("see") the object that was mentioned, in the disposition and detail implied by the communicative context, the described situation; we also "see" it in the manner that is implied by the described situation, including blurred by fog.

Simulating Muscular Experience. Hundreds of experiments have demonstrated that, in addition to perceptions, we also simulate muscular actions by partially activating associated neural systems. One experimental design focuses on the action-sequence compatibility effect.[44] Glenberg and Kaschak asked subjects to read a series of sentences and decide whether each sentence makes sense. They presented subjects with a bank of three buttons in a line; when the middle (gray) button is pressed, a sentence is presented on a screen above the buttons (and a timer is started). The white button ("Yes, it makes sense") and the black button ("No, it does not make sense") were located, one close to the subject, in front of the gray button and one farther from the subject, behind the gray button; their positions were reversed for half the trials. Of the sentences that were written to make sense, half implied motion toward the subject (e.g. "Katie handed the puppy to you") and half implied motion away from the subject ("You handed the puppy to Katie"). They found that when the implied motion and the motion required to provide a "yes" answer were in the same direction (compatible action sequences), the response was faster than if the motions were inconsistent. These findings imply that the motor control systems for moving the arm forward or backward were partially engaged in simulating the motion implied by the sentence. If the response required a compatible motion, the simulation will facilitate and speed the response motion; if it requires an incompatible motion, it will interfere with and slow the response motion.

As we process utterances, we seem to experience brief and weak simulations of perceptual and muscular features of each word, starting when we begin to expect it, then replaced with a simulation of the next word. At the end of an expressive unit, a sentence or complete clause, we experience a simulation of

---

[43] Yaxley and Zwaan (2007).
[44] Glenberg and Kaschak (2002); see also Bergen and Wheeler (2005); Borregine and Kashack (2006); Glenberg et al. (2008); Kaschak and Borregine (2008); Tseng and Bergen (2005); Zwaan and Taylor (2006).

the situation expressed by the expressive unit as a whole.[45] As I will discuss in more detail in the chapter on metaphor, there is also considerable experimental evidence that we experience perceptual simulations of the metaphor vehicle as well as of the apparent meaning of the metaphor in context, although the results from brain-scanning research using fMRI have been more equivocal, suggesting that the simulations are strongest for novel or engaging metaphors and weaker for familiar, partially lexicalized metaphors.[46]

Negation also engages simulations. Kaup and her colleagues[47] presented people with negated sentences, such as "There was not an eagle in the sky" or "There was not an eagle in the nest." After a 250 millisecond delay, an image of the same object in one of the two positions was presented, as in Zwaan's experiment described earlier. Just as an image (an eagle standing upright with folded wings) elicited a faster response when it matched an affirmative sentence ("The ranger saw an eagle in the nest") than when it did not match, an image also elicited a faster response when it matched a negated sentence ("There was not an eagle in the nest"). Kaup, Lüdtke, and Zwaan[48] extended this basic design, varying the interval between presenting the sentence and the image. When they presented the image after 750 milliseconds, there was no significant difference in response time to the factual and the counterfactual image. After 1,500 milliseconds, the subjects responded slightly faster to the factual image than to the counterfactual image: When we encounter a negated sentence, we first simulate the counterfactual scene, then negate it and process the factual scene.

Using semantic priming, Giora and her colleagues found similar results.[49] Subjects were presented with an affirmative sentence (e.g. "This instrument is sharp"), negation sentence ("... is not sharp"), or antonym ("... is blunt"). Subjects were then presented with a string of letters and asked to decide whether they form a word; the string might be nonsensical, related to the prime (e.g. "piercing") or unrelated (e.g. "glowing.") Consistent with a long tradition of semantic priming research, the related word ("piercing") was recognized faster than an unrelated word in response to both the affirmative sentence ("... is sharp") and for the negated version ("... is not sharp") but not for the antonym ("blunt").

Objections to the PSS (Perceptual Symbols Systems) Account. As an argument against the proposal that perceptual symbols (simulations) are the primary medium of thought, Boroditsky and Prinz note that some concepts are associated with a large number of perceptual features, often in several modalities. This seems like a bit of a straw man, since no one claims that *all* features

---

[45] Bergen (2012).   [46] Littlemore (2019).   [47] Kaup et al. (2007).
[48] Kaup, Lüdtke, and Zwaan (2006).
[49] Giora et al. (2004). The original research was conducted in Hebrew.

of a concept are activated at the same time. Barsalou, for example, posits that simulations are always partial and incomplete. For example, when one thinks of a zebra, the shape, color, and pattern of stripes will usually be only partly simulated; it is impossible to count the stripes. As the research on driving versus washing a car demonstrated, the features that are simulated are dependent on the context and perspective (and, one might add, on the subject's unique past experience with the concept).

A second argument is that some concepts are complex or extended in space and/or time, hence might incur excessive processing costs. However, perceptual simulation theories posit only that relevant features are simulated – and there is evidence that extension over time or space *is* simulated in some contexts. Barsalou has shown that perceptual symbols can, in principle, provide the basis for formal inference and certain other reasoning processes; Lakoff and Nuñez[50] argue that even mathematical reasoning is based on embodied experience of quantity and quantitative relationships.[51]

Boroditsky and Prinz's third and fourth objections to PSS as an exclusive mode of thought seem more convincing. At least some kinds of reasoning, including mathematics, are heavily dependent on symbols, more efficient, and, at least for most of us, considerably easier to accomplish by using abstract language and symbols. Finally, although perceptual simulations appear to play an important part of communication,[52] perceptual simulations must be converted to language to be communicated, and much of the complex communication that is done with language would be quite awkward using only perceptual simulations.

Boroditsky and Prinz argue that the shortcomings of perceptual simulations as a medium of thought and communication can be overcome by combining them with natural language, including conceptual metaphors, scripts and scenarios, and emotional expression.[53] Perceptions and perceptual simulations readily activate language, including stories,[54] and most language activates perceptual simulations, often including simulated stories. In turn, language is itself understood both in terms of perceptual symbols and in terms of its connection to other language.[55] This is also consistent with Zwaan's argument that cognition includes both simulations and amodal symbols.[56]

Metaphor. Lakoff and Johnson[57] argue that abstract concepts like *time*, *life*, and *power* are experienced by "conceptual metaphors." Time is

---

[50] Lakoff and Nuñez (2000).
[51] Children often learn to count with their fingers, and to add and subtract using piles of blocks; trivially, even adults use their fingers, for example, while enumerating reasons for or objections to doing something.
[52] Bergen (2012).   [53] See also Barsalou (2008); Zwaan (2014, 2015).   [54] Ritchie (2017).
[55] Landauer and Dumais (1997).   [56] Zwaan (2014, 2015).
[57] Lakoff and Johnson (1980, 1999). For a detailed discussion, see Chapter 11.

experienced as (MOTION THROUGH) SPACE, as expressed in common phrases like "A *long* time ago" and "Their marriage *came to an end*." LIFE IS A JOURNEY, which has "a *beginning*" and "an *end*." POWER IS UP, according to "*higher* authority." Most familiar concepts are expressed and experienced as one or more of several different conceptual metaphors, each of which expresses a particular aspect of the concept. Like literal language, metaphor also activates perceptual simulations associated with the vehicle topic, the word or phrase that is used metaphorically. However, metaphors don't always strongly activate perceptual simulations, and the more familiar the metaphor is, the weaker the simulation.[58]

Schemas, Scripts, and Scenarios. We organize much of our conceptual knowledge in categories, based on relevant qualities that objects or events seem to have in common; for example, "activities undertaken for fun, often involving competition" might define a category of *games*. We also organize our knowledge in *schemas*. A schema associates objects or actions according to common activities or purposes rather than shared characteristics: *Scissors*, *needle*, and *cloth* have no common properties, but they are used in a common activity, *sewing*. Once one element of a familiar schema has been encountered and the schema is activated, the related elements will be more readily recognized – for example, the *sewing* schema will also activate words and concepts like *fabric* and *button*. A particular type of schema, a *script*, involves a time and sequence dimension as well. A common example is a *restaurant* script; most of us have several variations – for example, one for a fast-food restaurant and another for "fine dining." These scripts tell us what to expect and how to behave; we usually follow them with little or no thought. An unfamiliar situation, for which one does not have a detailed script, can greatly increase cognitive load (and anxiety), because it entails increased uncertainty and requires detailed attention to social cues.

Many abstract concepts are represented by scripts or scenarios: Boroditsky and Prinz[59] cite *democracy* as an example. Associated concepts include *debate*, *voting*, *ballot*, and *election*. Other familiar concepts understood by scripts include *wedding*, *graduation*, and *contest*. Each of these is associated with a variety of scripts, most of which are readily recognizable by members of the same culture.

Frames. Some psychologists use the word *frame* as a synonym for *schema*, but communication researchers have generally used it to refer to a way of understanding a situation and the kind of response and behavior it calls for. Metaphorically, "*frame*" can refer either to a *structure* or the boundaries of an

---

[58] Littlemore (2019); see Chapter 11.   [59] Boroditsky and Prinz (2008).

image, as in *picture frame*. In journalism and discourse analysis, the "*framing*" of a news story or conversation may refer to how it is organized ("*structured*") or how certain features are made more salient and others are excluded or downplayed, "what's in the picture and what's out of the picture." Gamson[60] argued that journalists present issues within *story frames* according to news values and audience expectations; Iyengar[61] argued that news media emphasize *episodic* rather than *thematic* frames, especially in covering crime and poverty, emphasizing particular episodes rather than underlying societal themes. Price, Tewksbury, and Powers[62] demonstrated that framing a story about a retiring accountant as human interest versus finances can strongly influence what readers attend to and recall as well as their subsequent opinions about the topic. Tracy[63] found that when interlocutors in 911 emergency calls frame the interaction in divergent or contradictory ways, these frame conflicts can lead to miscommunication and failure of a communicative interaction. In a series of studies, Boroditsky and her colleagues have shown that incidental features of language can frame a described episode in a way that influences how much responsibility is assigned to a person who causes an accident[64] or how to think about an increase in crime rates and what kind of public response is most appropriate.[65]

Hawkins[66] argues that frames (including place and situation) are represented in the neural columns that process perceptual features, and play a role in confirming or disconfirming predictions. Presumably something like this is also involved in assessing the relevance of perceptions to particular schemas or scripts. The interaction of language and other signals with framing will be discussed in more detail in later chapters.

Emotion. Emotions, which represent in part values-based responses to events and thoughts (including representations of past and future), affects attention, perception, memory, cognition (including motivation and interpretation of experiences), and action. Emotions prepare the body for action and coordinates responses to a variety of challenges and opportunities. Emotion also has a strong effect on memory, what is stored, how it is stored, and how it is recalled and reshaped. Emotion serves as a comprehensive analog information-processing system, crucial for our ability to function effectively in our social and physical environment, and close to one-fifth of our thoughts about the future involve emotions.[67]

---

[60] Gamson (1992).   [61] Iyengar (1991).   [62] Price, Tewksbury, and Powers (1997).
[63] Tracy (1997).   [64] Fausey and Boroditsky (2010, 2011).
[65] Thibodeau and Boroditsky (2011).
[66] Hawkins (2021); see Chapter 2 for an extended discussion.
[67] Seligman et al. (2016). See also Damasio (1996, 1999).

Instances of behavior that is evaluated as morally good or bad evoke emotional responses, which may be the basis for moral concepts.[68] Inducing a negative emotional state can increase subjects' tendency to judge an act as immoral, even when it would ordinarily be considered benign.[69] Conversely, inducing a positive emotional state can lead subjects to switch from a rule-based to a consequence-based framework for moral judgments; after watching a comedy sketch, subjects were three times as likely to offer consequence-based responses to moral dilemmas.[70]

Researchers have also found that emotional responses vary according to the nature of the violation. Crimes against persons elicit anger from observers and guilt from malefactors, crimes against community elicit contempt, and violations of sexual or other norms associated with "sacred" or "natural" law elicit disgust from observers, shame from malefactors.[71] The proposal that emotions provide a basis for moral concepts and moral reasoning is consistent with either an innate or a socially constructed view of emotional experience.[72] It is also consistent with Damasio's claim that emotion is important for reasoning and decision-making. Finally, it is consistent with the claim that perceptual simulations play a central role in thinking and language processing. Just as we can perceive our own emotional arousal through interoception and our emotional evaluations through introspection, we can also simulate these perceptions, and those simulations can be manipulated, compared to, and combined with other perceptual simulations.

Natural Language Statistics (Semantic Connections). Landauer and Dumais[73] point out that children learn an average of about twelve new words a day, few of which are defined or explained for them; most are learned through contextual information. Landauer and Dumais claim that the contexts in which we encounter words provide most of our understanding of their meanings. Each time we encounter a word in a new context, its meaning changes, if only very slightly. Their research group developed a language analysis program, Latent Semantic Analysis (LSA),[74] based on how frequently a word occurs in the same context as all other words from a particular vocabulary (e.g. general English or biological texts). By using this procedure, the LSA algorithm has achieved a grade equivalent to a C (passing) on language vocabulary tests. When the cooccurrence matrix is developed from a sample of textbooks for a subject like history or chemistry, the LSA algorithm is able to achieve a passing grade on content-specific multiple-choice tests. By comparing an expert's response to an

---

[68] Boroditsky and Prinz (2008); Haidt (2001); Prinz (2007); for a more nuanced account, see Greene (2014).
[69] Wheatley and Haidt (2005). [70] Valedesolo and DeSteno (2016).
[71] (Rozin et al., 1999); Prinz (2007). [72] See Chapter 5 for a more detailed discussion.
[73] Landauer and Dumais (1997).
[74] This is but one of many programs that do much the same thing, using similar mathematics.

essay question to students' responses, the LSA algorithm has assigned grades that correlate as well with human graders' scores as the human graders correlate with each other.

LSA uses only cooccurrence of words and passages ("natural language statistics"), and does not account for how syntax contributes to meaning. LSA has also been criticized because words are not "grounded" in the actual world to which they refer. Kintsch[75] points out that the brain's store of accumulated experience, as well as syntactic constructions, could be connected in a semantic network in the brain, although incorporating these into a computer algorithm poses daunting challenges. Neither Kintsch nor Landauer and Dumais claim that our brains calculate a cooccurrence matrix every time we encounter a new word or use language, but the LSA algorithm seems to approximate, at an abstract level, the networks of neural connections among words (and concepts) that become partially activated as we encounter and use language. These connections have also been documented in research on "lexical priming,"[76] the phenomenon in which encountering one word or concept increases the salience and accessibility of related words and concepts. As early as the first year of life, infants use cooccurrence information to resolve the meaning of words.[77]

Humans can extract a substantial amount of meaning from the internal relations among symbols, even when they are invented and totally ungrounded. Boroditsky and Ramscar[78] invented a set of novel words and constructed a stream of words in which each critical word appeared with the same frequency, but with unique patterns of cooccurrence. Subjects were asked to learn as much as they could about the meanings of words by listening to the stream. When asked to rate how similar pairs of words were in meaning, they assigned greater similarity to words that more frequently cooccurred in the same contexts. In a follow-up study, Boroditsky and Ramscar assigned made-up words to novel objects and had subjects listen to "alien conversations" about these objects. When asked to rate the similarity of the objects, the subjects rated the similarity of objects according to how frequently their names appeared in similar contexts. These studies confirm that people do use cooccurrence to inform their judgment about both words and the objects named by words.

Synthesis: Context-Limited Simulation Theory[79] Extended

Boroditsky and Prinz conclude from their review of the research that the human conceptual system benefits from a combination of emotions, perceptual

---

[75] Kintsch (1998).   [76] Hoey (2005); Tabossi (1989).
[77] Smith and Yu (2007), cited in Seligman et al. (2016).   [78] Boroditsky and Ramscar (2003).
[79] Ritchie (2006, 2017).

and motor simulation (including simulation of emotional arousal and evaluation), conceptual metaphor, and abstract language; narrative also seems to be important. Other researchers have reached similar conclusions, often focusing on a narrower range of social phenomena. Petty and Cacioppo,[80] based on a review of persuasion research, formulated the *Elaboration Likelihood Model* to help explain the circumstances in which people are more likely to be persuaded by peripheral cues (such as source attractiveness), which they call the *"peripheral route,"* and when they are more likely to elaborate a message, engage in elaborate reasoning about a topic, and be persuaded by the quality of arguments (the *"central route"*). They concluded that, to engage in message elaboration and attend to the quality of reasoning (the central route), people must have both the *ability* and the *motivation* to think more deeply about a topic. *Ability* includes background knowledge and intellectual acuity as well as freedom from distraction. *Motivation* can be provided by the personal relevance of a topic or intrinsic interest.

Sperber and Wilson[81] argue that humans are intrinsically disposed to seek *relevance*. According to Relevance Theory, communication is based on a *mutual cognitive environment*, the set of *cognitive contexts* that the interlocutors believe to be known and salient to everyone engaged in discourse. These apparently include concepts, schemas, scripts, and frames, as well as memories and simulations of past events and projected simulations of future potential outcomes. The *relevance* of a communicative act (utterance, gesture, etc.) is defined as the effect on the mutual cognitive environment achieved by a given effort. Sperber and Wilson further stipulate that all communicative acts, including language, are inherently ambiguous, and susceptible to multiple interpretations; the search for relevance includes a search for context(s) to which an act may be relevant as well as interpreting the act by broadening and/or narrowing its reference and customary meaning as needed to fit one or more known and salient contexts.

In my own previous research on metaphor use and comprehension, I have proposed that the degree to which perceptual and motor simulations of metaphor vehicles are activated is subject to contextual constraints.[82] Consistent with the Elaboration Likelihood Model, people must have the ability as well as the interest to elaborate the potential simulations associated with a metaphor vehicle. Consistent with Relevance Theory, *ability* includes knowledge and salience of relevant contexts; interest may be affected by either relevance or the intrinsic interest of a metaphor – which helps explain the finding that novel metaphors are more likely to activate detailed perceptual simulations.

---

[80] Petty and Cacioppo (1981).
[81] Sperber and Wilson (1986/1995); Wilson and Sperber (2004).
[82] Ritchie (2013); for detailed discussion, see the chapter on Metaphor.

Zwaan[83] argues that both abstract symbols and perceptual simulations contribute to language use and comprehension. Even familiar words are likely to activate links to other words (including definitions) and associated perceptual and motor simulations; syntax guides the assembly of these simulations and semantic links into complex propositions *and* simulations. Zwaan also emphasizes the importance of the broader social and cultural context of language use. Language itself exists within a matrix of ideas, persons, cultural norms and expectations, and so on; every utterance both draws on and contributes to this social and cultural background.

Summary

There is no evidence of an independent "language of the mind," but there is substantial evidence that people use natural language in combination with emotional responses, perceptual and motor simulations, scenarios and stories, in thinking, reasoning, and deciding. Words allow us to name and objectify concepts – experiences, actions, states, qualities, and so forth – at different levels of abstraction, and thus to treat our experiences as well as our thoughts as independent objects. Syntax helps us establish, think about, and communicate about our past, present, and potential experiences as if they existed, somewhere in the phenomenal world, independent of us. Metacognition and metacommunication allow us to use abstract language to represent and explain our thought processes to each other, as a basis for improved cooperation.

Most words weakly activate neural systems (schemas and frames) associated with their reference, experienced as perceptual and motor simulations, and syntax shapes these simulations. Conversely, perceptions and perceptual simulations also activate associated language – and words will usually activate at least some associated words. This combination of syntax with words and simulations allows us to think about and experience relations among concepts at almost any level of abstraction – for example, from "My neighbor's toy poodle" to "dogs" to "animals" to "objects." These relationships might be causal, comparative, relational, and so on. With a little training, we can engage in more formal, rule-bound reasoning about relationships among objects using one or another system of logic.[84]

All this is powered by the brain-in-body and its homeostasis-maintaining processes of perception, emotional response, representation, and forward-projection. We think our representation of our body-in-environment situation is reality, but both perception and action are based on prediction, which is in turn based on what LeDoux calls our body's "survival circuits." As I write,

---

[83] Zwaan (2014, 2015). [84] Chapter 9.

sitting on a bluff above the Willamette River, I have the illusion that I am seeing the actual river, a scene refreshed several times a second as my visual cortex processes the firing of retinal cells in response to the photons entering my eyes. What I am actually seeing is a representation of the familiar scene, with the currently relevant or otherwise salient parts of the scene being updated and corrected according to the sensory input.[85] That is also true of the sounds and smells, and the feeling of the breeze on my skin and the bench under my thighs. We experience what the brain has predicted, partially updated according to the most salient perceptual information.

As one reads or listens to language, the brain is also continually predicting what comes next, the end of the word, the rest of the sentence, the entire passage. These predictions enable us to process linguistic input in real time, fast enough and just accurately enough to participate coherently in a conversation.[86] Conversely, as I write, my brain is also predicting what I will write next, the overall direction of this chapter, the rest of this sentence, and the next few words, thereby facilitating the smooth actions of my fingers on the keys and a smooth flow of language.[87] Related ideas and alternative phrasing appear into consciousness, and may bring the entire process to a halt while I consider them. Chafe likens this process to the words appearing, one thought unit at a time, as if from behind a curtain.[88] Exactly what goes on "behind the curtain" is not altogether clear, but it most likely involves perceptual symbols (abstracted from perceptual simulations) in some blend with natural emotions, language words and phrases, and the conceptual metaphors and perceptual simulations activated by *these* words and phrases.

These ideas have interesting implications for conversation and for communication in general, which I will take up in Chapters 7–12, as well as for the nature of consciousness and reason.

---

[85] If a scene is entirely new, such as a previously unvisited cathedral or national park, it may take much longer, several minutes, for the brain to construct a representation.

[86] Enfield (2017); see Chapter 8 for a more detailed discussion.

[87] I was fortunate to have learned touch typing in high school; writers who have not learned touch typing may not experience this as a smooth flow.

[88] Chafe (1994); Chapter 9.

5 Emotion

Theorists generally agree that emotions are important both to mental functioning and to social interaction, but the nature of emotions is still subject to vigorous debate.[1] Adherents to the "natural kind" approach argue that emotion categories such as anger, sadness, and fear are biologically given categories that have evolved as behavioral adaptations and cannot be reduced to more basic psychological concepts. Some natural kind theorists further argue that each basic emotion category (e.g. anger or fear) is associated with a particular locale or network in the brain and with a particular set of facial muscles that combine to express it. Much of the research on display and recognition of nonverbal emotional expression[2] assumes that all humans experience, express, and perceive the same basic set of emotions, although emotional display in certain contexts is influenced by cultural norms.

In contrast, psychological constructionist approaches assume that emotion categories such as anger, fear, happiness, and sadness are socially learned categories, based on a set of basic psychological operations common to all mental states.[3] Sensory signals from the body are experienced as "core affect," a mental representation of changes in the current state of the body that are sometimes experienced as pleasure or displeasure (e.g. pain or discomfort), and associated with some degree of arousal. Core affect is interpreted – made meaningful – through a process of conceptual categorization based on culturally learned concepts and on knowledge and memories of past experiences. In this chapter, I begin with a discussion of the classic view of "basic emotions" as innate and universal, which still dominates the discussion of emotion in communication, then review some recent critiques of the classic view and several alternative views that have been recently advanced. I discuss the role of emotion in reasoning and communication, and end with a discussion of terminology used to communicate about emotions.

---

[1] Lindquist et al. (2012); Colombetti (2014).
[2] For example, Ekman (1993); Ekman and Friesen (1971); Ekman and Cordaro (2011).
[3] Lindquist et al. (2012).

The Classic View: Basic Emotions

The standard account of emotions, which has dominated both communication textbooks and popular discussion of emotions for several decades, holds that all humans experience a set of innate basic emotions, express these emotions using the same combinations of facial muscles ("facial Action Units" or AUs[4]), and can readily identify the emotions others are experiencing from their facial expressions. The initial research began with a list of six emotions – anger, fear, surprise, sadness, disgust/contempt, and happiness – which the researchers identified intuitively as basic emotions.[5] Professional actors were hired and carefully coached to produce each of these six "basic" emotions for still photos, deliberately exaggerating the facial expression for each.[6] The result was several images for each "basic" emotion, which have been used in hundreds of studies, and which have consistently shown that members of every culture tested can accurately associate each image with the correct emotion label or, in another research design, with the appropriate brief story about an emotional experience.[7]

In the canonical research design, each image is presented along with the list of six emotion labels (for cross-culture studies, translated into the subject's native tongue). The subject is asked to select the label that best described the emotion. In a slightly different version, the subject reads or hears a brief, one-sentence story, such as "Her mother recently passed away," shown only two photos, and asked to choose the photo that best fits the story. Using these two methods, researchers have found that people all over the world can match the photos with emotion terms with accuracy consistently above 80 percent. These results are commonly taught in classes in nonverbal communication and interpersonal communication. Typically, the facial expressions associated with emotions are called "codes," implying a one-to-one relationship between each "basic" emotion and a particular facial expression (as represented in the six photographs). According to this view of emotion, the brain has a discrete neural circuit for each emotion. Each emotion circuit causes a characteristic pattern of contractions in a particular subset of the forty-two small muscles in each side of the face, an emotion "*fingerprint*"[8] that yields a universal, easily recognized and "*decoded*" facial expression. According to the standard

---

[4] Ekman and Friesen (1978).
[5] Burgoon et al. (2016); In Ekman and Cordaro (2011), Ekman separates *disgust* from *contempt*, yielding a list of seven basic emotions.
[6] Barrett (2017).
[7] Replications using spontaneously produced emotion expressions have produced similar, although slightly less accurate, results.
[8] Barrett (2017).

account, these facial expressions are artifacts of evolution, and can be identified in many other mammals.

Further support for the "basic emotion" view comes from other evidence, including research that demonstrates similar emotion expressions produced by congenitally blind children, who could not have learned facial expressions by observation.[9] However, Rinn[10] videotaped congenitally blind and sighted participants while they posed expressions of fear, anger, surprise, disgust, and humor and found that, except for humor, the blind participants did not consistently use the facial Action Units predicted by Ekman and Friesen,[11] and they produced portrayals significantly less easily detected by sighted subjects than those produced by sighted participants. In another study, using both sighted and congenitally blind participants, Galati et al.[12] used cluster analysis to compare the similarity of AUs with the similarity of emotions for both sighted and blind participants. For both groups, the first axis appears to express level of activation, explaining about 43 percent of the variance for both sighted and blind participants. The second axis, which accounted for 20.6 and 28 percent of the variance for the two groups, appears to represent a hedonic dimension, with joy widely separated from negative emotions. Moreover, the AUs associated with particular emotions were not always those that were theoretically predicted, and there were no specific patterns of AUs for the studied emotions for either group, sighted or blind, suggesting that the same groups of facial muscles may be used to express different emotions.

The Expanding List of Emotion Categories. Observational research has shown that each emotion, like fear or anger, is associated with a diversity of facial expressions and vocalics, which vary according to the context. Each emotion category can produce and be identified by a variety of signals. For example, when people are angry, they may frown, scowl, shout, glower, exhibit an "*icy* calm," and so on. In response, Ekman[13] has extended the basic emotions theory by redefining basic emotions as emotion *categories* that can be expressed by a range of physiological responses according to different triggering events or experiences. Subsequent researchers have expanded the list of basic emotions and emotion categories to include interest, shame, distress, pride, love, warmth, and guilt.[14] Ekman additionally suggests sensory pleasures, amusement, relief, excitement, wonder, and ecstasy.[15] With these additions alone, the list of basic emotions has expanded to over twenty and counting, lending a decidedly ad hoc air to the theory. Moreover, cultures vary

---

[9] For example, Fulcher (1942); Eibl-Eibesfeldt (1970); Ortega et al. (1983).
[10] Rinn (1999); for a slightly different view, see Galati, Scherer, and Ricci-Bitti (1997).
[11] Ekman and Friesen (1978).   [12] Galati, Scherer, and Ricci-Bitti (1997).
[13] in Ekman and Cordaro (2011).   [14] Burgoon et al. (2016)
[15] in Ekman and Cordaro (2011).

in the emotions that fit each category: For example, *fear* includes alarm, anxiety, dread, fright, horror, panic, scare, terror, and trepidation, along with milder emotions like concern, dismay, and worry – and this is just a partial list of related words in English. This proliferation of "basic" emotions seems more consistent with socially learned cultural categories, conditioned by individual experiences and the degree of arousal and hedonic value associated with various experiences.

Methodological Issues. Barrett[16] argues that the canonical studies present several methodological problems. The initial list was derived from the researchers' intuition rather than empirical research, and most of the recognition research has relied on photos of professional actors rather than on spontaneously produced expressions. Furnishing subjects with a list of "basic" emotions primes the relevant concepts; even the word "emotion" can influence how subjects respond. Some of the procedures used to cope with the difficulty of research in non-Western cultures have undermined the rigor of even the basic study design. For example, in a study conducted in New Guinea, Ekman and Friesen had to try several standard procedures that failed before the researchers devised an innovative narrative-based procedure that worked. Ekman and Friesen ascribe this to the subjects' culturally based discomfort with the research process, but Barrett argues that it could also have resulted from cultural differences in the process of recognizing and interpreting facial expressions.

In another classic study cited by Barrett as evidence of priming, Sauter et al. gave feedback to subjects, and had them listen to a story as many times as needed until they could explain the emotion in their own words.[17] Replications using different methods to reduce the risk of priming have produced accuracy considerably lower than was observed using the original study design, although the results are usually still significantly greater than chance.[18] Gendron et al.[19] demonstrated that members of the Himba ethnic group from Namibia were able to recognize posed facial expressions only when cues to emotion concepts were embedded in the experiments. When people are shown contextual information, such as body posture and vocalic qualities, their interpretations often contradict those based on the facial photo alone.[20]

Tassinary and Cacioppo[21] used facial electromyography (EMG) to identify the facial muscles that moved when subjects were induced to experience various emotions. The results showed that muscle movements do not match the movements implied by the posed photos, and do not reliably indicate the emotion reported by subjects. At best, the recorded muscle movements were

---

[16] Barrett (2017).   [17] (16 Sauter et al., 2015, p. 355; Gendron et al., 2014a).
[18] Widen et al. (2011); cited by Barrett (2017). Again, the results were still above chance.
[19] Gendron et al. (2014).   [20] Avieser et al. (2008).   [21] Tassinary and Cacioppo (1992).

able to distinguish between negative and positive affect, more consistent with a constructionist than with an innate emotion perspective.

Newborns make distinctive facial movements, recognizable – for example, as interest, puzzlement, pain, and distaste[22] – but they do not show differentiated expressions like the canonical photographs from the basic emotion method, and they do not have a distinctive cry for each emotion.[23] Children quickly learn to express, identify, and label emotions through communication with parents and caregivers, who label other people's emotions and suggest labels for the child's own emotions. In sum, Barrett[24] argues that the "basic" emotions are European American emotion concepts, culturally transmitted through mass media and, in much of the research conducted in non-Western contexts, inadvertently taught to research subjects by the research procedures.

Survival Circuits

LeDoux[25] criticizes previous theorists for starting with human concepts of emotion and looking backward to find them in other animals. He suggests instead that we start with functions present in animals and then see how they extend to humans, and how they might be related to emotions and feelings. LeDoux argues that all mammal species, including humans, have neural *survival circuits* for basic needs: defense, maintaining energy, nutrition, fluid balance, regulation of warmth, and reproduction.[26] These circuits can be traced back to mechanisms in primordial organisms and are found in all mammal species, although they are realized in each species according to its ecological niche.

LeDoux proposes that humans experience associated feelings when we perceive the heightened states of arousal and other physiological changes produced by survival circuits.[27] We then appraise and label the interoceptive experience, drawing on our linguistic knowledge. LeDoux warns against attributing any of our linguistically mediated emotional responses to other species, since we have no way of knowing how they might experience either the physiological adaptations (e.g. states of heightened arousal) or the external conditions that activated the survival circuit and precipitated these adaptations. The social emotions such as guilt, shame, envy, pride, and love that we experience are not associated with survival circuits at all, but rather with processes related to social interaction, and indirectly with homeostasis maintenance.

---

[22] At least three of these – interest, pain, and distaste – are also observed in animals.
[23] 13 Oster (2005).   [24] Barrett (2017).   [25] LeDoux (2012).   [26] See Chapter 2.
[27] It might seem more straightforward simply to state that we experience the adaptations as feelings, and interpret them according to personal experience and cultural/linguistic categories.

The survival circuits overlap with each other in the neural systems they engage, although current imaging techniques are not sufficiently precise to isolate specific systems. For example, areas within the amygdala are engaged by both fear and learned cues about food, including food aversion. In the fear circuit, perception of a threat goes directly to the amygdala, then the hypothalamus, to the midbrain, then to the motor system and innate defense circuit. Thus, the physiological response to fear is often well underway before the individual has become conscious of the threat.[28]

Survival circuits do not align well with Ekman's basic emotions or emotion categories. For example, there is no "anger" or "happiness" circuit. Aggression is specific to the context – for example, defense against conspecifics or predators, aggression against prey, competition for mates, protection of offspring. Pleasure and happiness are specific to the circuits for energy and nutrition, fluid balance, heat balance, sex, grooming, and play; the subjective feelings experienced when any of these needs are fulfilled are likely to be interpreted and labeled as pleasure, happiness, or joy. Moreover, it appears there are multiple neural circuits for different functions – for example, for defense in various threat contexts; what we label "fear" may result in either freeze or flee, depending on whether escape is a possibility. Reflexive reactions to stimuli, including interest, pain, distaste, play, and grooming, appear to be common at least across primates, but these do not align well with Ekman's concept of basic emotions.

Cultural Construction of Emotion

Barrett and her colleagues[29] argue that emotions are not innate, but culturally constructed and learned as emotion concepts based on emotion categories. Specialized brain regions assign categories to events and experiences based on prior experience, including communication.[30] Changes in core affect in one's own body, or affective cues such as facial expression, vocal qualities, and so forth, are assigned in a context-sensitive way to emotion categories such as anger, disgust, fear, and so forth. These emotion categories are socially constructed and represented by emotion words that label and communicate about the inferred emotion and guide culturally appropriate and often scripted responses.[31]

Barrett and her colleagues claim that emotional experience is grounded in two dimensions of our interoceptive experience, *affect* (hedonic valence) and

---

[28] See also Griffiths and Scarantino (2009). [29] Barrett (2017); Lindquist et al. (2012).
[30] Lindquist et al. (2012); see also Barsalou (2003, 2008); Barsalou and Wiemer-Hastings (2005).
[31] Barrett's account of emotional experience and communication is consistent with the metacognition theory advanced by Heyes et al. (2020); detailed communication of and about emotion is as important to cooperation as communication about one's confidence about perceptions and judgments.

arousal.[32] Affect and arousal summarize the interoceptive reports of the body's current state, what Barrett calls the "body *budget*" and Damasio calls *homeostasis*. Projected forward, affect is "your brain's best guess about the state of your body budget."[33] These dimensions of experience, affective valence and arousal, are biological and evolved, and they are evident in other animal species and in human infants from birth.

Self-Attribution. Evidence in support of a constructionist account of emotion has been accumulating for decades. One controversial research paradigm has used induced arousal to explore the process through which people make sense of affective experience. In the classic study, Schachter and Singer[34] injected subjects with either epinephrine or a saline solution control and then staged a social interaction designed to elicit either euphoria or anger. Some subjects in each condition were informed about the actual nature of the injection, and others were deceived. Consistent with Schachter and Singer's hypothesis, subjects who were administered epinephrine but led to believe it was neutral reported a more intense experience of the target emotions than subjects who were not deceived. Marshall and Zimbardo[35] replicated the original study for the euphoria condition only, using several methodological improvements. Their subjects in the heightened arousal conditions showed heightened negative rather than positive affect; Marshall and Zimbardo concluded that the experienced state of heightened arousal produced a negative affective bias.

An implication of self-perception is that people's attributions about the emotional import of physiological arousal should vary according to the context. Dutton and Aron[36] had an attractive female experimenter approach male subjects on a high and potentially fear-inducing suspension bridge or on a lower, subjectively safer bridge. After administering a questionnaire that included a Thematic Apperception Test (TAT), she provided a business card that included a phone number (not her own number), "in case you have any questions about the study." Those who approached on the high bridge (fear/arousal condition) gave more sexually oriented responses to TAT pictures and were more likely to attempt to contact the experimenter later than males who approached on the low bridge (neutral condition).

Excitation Transfer. In several experiments, Zillman and his colleagues have confirmed that a state of arousal associated with one emotion can be

---

[32] These in turn are strongly influenced by the release of chemicals, including endorphins, dopamine, serotonin, adrenaline, cortisol, and so on.
[33] Barrett (2017, p. 82).
[34] For example, Schachter and Singer (1962); see also Barrett and Russell (2015); Lacey and Lacey (1962); Mezzacappa, Katkin, and Palmer (1999).
[35] Marshall and Zimbardo (1979).
[36] Dutton and Aron (1974); see also Cantor, Zillmann, and Bryant (1975).

"*transferred*" to (reinterpreted as) a completely different emotion category. For example, half of a group of subjects were exposed to a series of sexually explicit photographs and half to a series of nonsexual photographs and then half of the subjects in each group were insulted by a confederate. In a subsequent "conditioned learning experiment," the subjects had the opportunity to administer what they believed to be painful shocks to the confederate. The subjects who had seen the sexually arousing photographs prior to being insulted by the confederate administered consistently longer and more painful shocks to the confederate than those in the neutral condition.[37]

Cantor, Zillmann, and Bryant[38] used an exercise routine to raise the subjects' level of arousal, then exposed the subjects to an erotic film either immediately after exercise, when they recognized that their level of arousal was due to the exercise, after partial recovery, when their arousal state was still high, but they incorrectly believed they had fully recovered, or after they had returned to baseline, and they correctly believe they had fully recovered. Subjects who viewed the film during the second phase, when they were still in a state of heightened arousal but did not recognize their residual state of heightened arousal, rated the film as more sexually arousing than subjects who viewed the film in either the first or third phase of recovery. This supports the claim that residual arousal from an activity (physical exercise) enhances emotional responses to an unrelated stimulus only if it cannot be attributed to the actual cause and is thus misattributed to the proximate stimulus.

Cantor, Bryant, and Zillmann[39] had undergraduate research subjects read one of four written passages, selected to be either positive or negative in hedonic tone and either high or low in arousal. They were then asked to read and rate a series of cartoons and jokes. For both positive and negative hedonic tone, subjects who read the high arousal passages rated the cartoons and jokes as significantly funnier than subjects who read the low arousal passages.

In sum, in response to situations that potentially affect their homeostasis, humans, like other animals, experience both arousal and affective valence, which may trigger contextually relevant survival circuits. Unlike other animals, humans attempt to explain and give meaning to these experiences by attributing both the affect and the arousal to a salient element of the present context and assigning the experience to a relevant emotion category. "I feel aroused. I am watching a comedy skit. The skit must be really funny." "I feel aroused. I am in the presence of an attractive potential romantic partner. I must be in love." "I feel aroused. Someone just insulted me. I must be angry." The ease with which sexual arousal can be transformed/transferred to anger

---

[37] Cantor et al. (1975); Zillmann et al. (1974); see also Tannenbaum and Zillmann (1975).
[38] Cantor, Zillmann, and Bryant (1975).
[39] Cantor, Bryant, and Zillmann, (1974); see also Cantor and Zillmann (1973).

and vice versa is highly consistent with the cultural construction model, which holds that emotion consists of affective valence, arousal level, and cognitive appraisal or attribution.

The Facial Feedback Effect. Conversely, in the *facial efference*[40] or *facial feedback* effect, merely shaping the face in the form of an emotional expression such as smiling (happiness) or scowling (anger) triggers an experience of the emotion. These findings are commonly cited in support of the claim that emotion expression is biologically innate. In one study, Strack et al.[41] asked subjects to rate how funny cartoons are while either holding a pen between their lips, which simulates the muscular configuration of a frown, or between their teeth, which simulates the muscular configuration of a smile; those who simulated a smile found the cartoons funnier than those who simulated a frown. However, after reviewing the accumulated research in this area, Cappella[42] concluded that only a "weaker version" of the facial feedback or facial efference hypothesis can be supported (feedback from the configuration of facial muscles influences hedonic valence but not necessarily the category of emotion experienced), and the effects are generally weak.[43]

Emotion and Homeostasis

In animals, sensory input that represents an opportunity or resource (e.g. to ingest food or engage in sexual activity) will trigger a heightened state of arousal along with the activation of reward systems, release of endorphins and other hormones that motivate appropriate action (eating or copulating). Conversely, input that represents a threat (e.g. aggression by a more powerful conspecific) will also trigger a heightened state of arousal, accompanied by activation of avoidance systems, release of stress hormones, including cortisol that motivate a different kind of action (retreat, hide, or fight). The degree and quality of arousal and the specific nature of associated actions will depend on the context, the nature of the opportunity, resource, or threat, and the survival circuit it activates.

In humans the situation is considerably more complex. Humans have much the same set of reflexive responses, based on similar survival circuits, and if a stimulus, particularly a perceived threat, produces an extremely high degree of arousal, the response may be reflexive, entirely under control of the survival circuit. If the degree of arousal is moderate, consciousness and culture will

---

[40] Adelman and Zajonc (1989).
[41] Strack et al. (1988); see also Rutledge and Hupka (1985); Zajonc et al. (1989).
[42] Cappella (1993).
[43] Buck (1984) argues that the facial feedback effect is merely due to learned stimulus-response patterns in which activation of facial muscles for whatever reason activates a previously learned set of responses, including affect.

intervene. At this point, the brain will interpret the information to update its representation and forward projection of homeostasis, and construct forward projections of one or more alternative responses, influenced by cultural norms, the current social context, and situationally relevant scripts. Part of this interpretive process involves assigning the feeling to an emotion category and lexical label according to the context; the label itself will contribute to constructing and selecting among alternative forward projections. The culturally constructed emotion labels interact with the visceral (arousal plus hedonic valence) response to shape the reaction.

The situation of humans is different in another and even more important respect. Our homeostasis is affected by our primary group, our perceived social status, and perceived threats to that status ("face threats"). Thus, in addition to the basic biological imperatives present in the survival circuits (e.g. nutrition, defense, sex), we experience secondary social and cultural imperatives of relationship, social status and obligations, cultural norms (e.g. pride and shame), all tied up with *face*.[44] These may account at least in part for the mismatch LeDoux notes between animal survival circuits and human emotions: Most of our complex emotions are responses to social and cultural opportunities and threats, which only indirectly implicate the basic biological needs implicated in survival circuits. It is also worth noting that even cultural emotions like shame can become associated with particular stimuli (e.g. an image of sex organs or sexualized body parts) so that the experience of shame and other social emotions, just like intense fear or aggression, may be transmitted to the amygdala even before the stimulus itself is processed and enters consciousness. The cultural associations greatly complicate the experience of the blend of emotion with sensation Damasio calls *feelings*.[45]

Some of the facial expressions classically associated with Ekman's basic emotions appear to be based on reflexive biological responses. Disgust in response to a substance such as rotten food is mostly physiological, as is the elevated posture, bared teeth, and low vocal tones associated with aggression. But anger itself is a social emotion, often a response to a perceived social offense or face threat. The transfer of disgust from spoiled food or poisonous substances to violations of social norms seems metaphorical,[46] as does the expression of *fear* in response to a potential loss of social status or having to give a speech in front of a group of strangers, or *aggression* (as *anger*) in response to opposition or a perceived face threat. Both animals and humans will experience an impulse to flee or otherwise avoid a larger, more aggressive animal ("fear"), but only humans will also "fear" being socially humiliated for

---

[44] Chapter 8. [45] Damasio (2018).
[46] Violations of social norms also constitute a threat to homeostasis, just as contact with spoiled food does.

Emotion and Homeostasis

running away from danger. Only humans respond emotionally to purely symbolic stimuli (like a KKK hood, a school mascot, or a religious ikon).

The brain's representation and forward projection of the current state of the *person* (the body as well as the social identity and *face*) includes social resources and threats, and are expressed as simulations (perceptual, motor, and narrative) as well as language. Social resources and threats are much more complex and seem to be at least as important as physical resources and threats to our sense of well-being. Thus, we can think of emotion as a response to an actual or potential change in homeostasis. Emotions include situation-relevant physiological arousal and valence as well as social and culturally informed interpretation of the state of arousal, based on the context. The intensity of the response may be a function of the individual's social status as well as of the scale of the threat or resource.

Mirror neurons produce a simulation of others' physical response, and this is at least part of how we understand others' emotional expression.[47] Interfering with this mirroring reduces the ability to identify others' emotional responses, and conversely inducing a similar configuration of facial muscles increases the ability to identify others' emotional expression.[48] This effect also helps explain the phenomenon of "social contagion," the tendency of strong emotional expression and even moods to influence others to experience a similar emotion or mood.

Strategic Emotional Expression. Griffiths and Scarantino[49] argue that emotions are designed to function in a social context, and provide means for skillful engagement with the world, not necessarily mediated by conceptual thought. Emotions are often part of strategic signaling to achieve a reconfiguration of the relationship. Sulking, for example, is a strategy for seeking a better deal. While conceding that "many emotional expressions have a nonarbitrary relation to the organism's motivational states,"[50] they argue that emotional expressions are also frequently part of a negotiation with an open-ended outcome.

Several observations support these claims. When people behave inappropriately, others evaluate them more favorably if they display embarrassment. Apparently embarrassment is a signal of recognizing and accepting the violated norms. Athletes such as bowlers who have scored well are more likely to smile after they turn to face their companions. Individual appraisal of a situation is often linked to others' reactions – a tactless remark or off-color joke is evaluated according to others' reactions, and a child, after falling, will often look toward its parent before crying. Emotional expression

---

[47] Enticott et al. (2008).   [48] Oberman, Winkielman, and Vilayanur (2007).
[49] Griffiths and Scarantino (2009); see also Crivelli and Fridlund (2018).
[50] Griffiths 7 Scarantino (2009, p. 446).

is scaffolded, both in acquisition and in performance, by physical as well as social contexts. Emotional expressions are associated with social contexts such as weddings, funerals, and graduations as well as with physical contexts such as churches and athletic stadiums. Crivelli and Fridlund[51] report that Trobriand Islanders understand the classic photographic representation of "fear," not as fear but as a threat produced by witches in an attempt to frighten villagers in order to steal food.

The Enactive View

Colombetti rejects Barrett's conclusion that meta-analysis of past research indicates a lack of emotion specificity, although she allows that the Basic Emotion Theory has an ad hoc flavor as a result of successively adding new "basic emotions" and weakening or adjusting its assumptions to accommodate new findings.[52] Her own primary criticism of Basic Emotion Theory is its insistence that certain basic emotions are experienced and recognized across cultures, and that several other culture-specific emotions are also experienced, in many cases as blends or combinations of the "basic" emotions. She concludes that the entire notion of "basic" emotions is redundant, misleading, and unnecessary.

In place of an innate affect program, Colombetti argues that "emotional episodes should be understood as self-organizing patterns of the organism."[53] In response to a "triggering event," various neural systems that control attention, evaluation, arousal, and so forth, interact in a dynamic process of reciprocal influences. Colombetti is not specific about the nature of the "triggering event," but presumably it could be a present experience, a remembered experience, or even an imagined future experience. The activation and mutually constraining interactions among these neural systems result from and are shaped by genetic and developmental factors that interact over time. Observations of interactions between infants and their mothers show that their interactions are dependent on each other, suggesting that the dyad should be considered a "coupled system." We know from other research that adults also entrain with each other's emotional expressions as well as vocal qualities and other signals while engaged in conversation, which generally supports Colombetti's claim that "emotional episodes can span two or even more organisms."[54]

Because the neural processes involved can organize themselves in various ways, presumably in response to specific aspects of the "triggering event" (Colombetti is vague about this), emotional episodes are potentially highly

---

[51] Crivelli and Fridlund (2018). [52] Colombetti (2014, p. 36).
[53] Colombetti (2014, p. 53). [54] Colombetti (2014, p. 68).

variable. All emotional experiences (and expressions), including Ekman's "basic emotions," are open, flexible, and sensitive to the context in which they occur. For this reason, Colombetti argues that it is not necessary to posit cultural display rules to explain deviations from the prototypical emotion expressions (but she does not dispute that cultures do have display rules, e.g. "Boys don't cry").

Colombetti characterizes *moods* as longer-lasting conditions, which can make consistent emotions more likely than inconsistent emotions. She explains this in mathematical terms as "altering the topology space" (an infusion of a math concept that strikes me as rather ad hoc) but ignores the probably more relevant effect of body chemistry on neural functions, including sensation. This is a potentially important topic, since both moods (extended over time) and emotions (short-lived) can strongly affect how people generate, interpret, and respond to signals.

Colombetti also introduces an interesting discussion of sensory experience, distinguishing between senses as "transparent" and as "intentional objects." For example, the tactile sense can be relatively "transparent" when the attention is focused on the object being touched, but the experience of touching the object can itself be the focus of attention, as an "intentional object." Listening to music is similar: The listener may experience the music itself, with no awareness of *listening* to it, or may experience *listening to music* as an activity. Similar considerations apply to the interoceptive perception of muscular activities. A skilled tennis player may simply experience playing the game, or may experience her body's engagement with the racquet, ball, and net. Even walking or riding a bicycle can yield the same distinction: One's legs may be almost transparent media of motion, or they may be intentional objects, sources of pleasure, pain, or both. "The performative body is neither transparent nor an intentional object of awareness; it is the body as experienced during the skillful performance of a specific activity, when one need not attend to one's body but is nevertheless very much aware."[55]

Similar considerations apply to emotional experience. Colombetti compares the interoceptive awareness of background bodily feelings to "*colored window glasses*," which are transparent to the perception of the world, but "*color*" it with affective tones. Each emotion affects the body ("*colors the glass*") in a unique way, leading to a unique affective perception. Even when attention focuses on the external situation and not on the bodily state, the bodily state contributes to ("*colors*") the emotional experience. Colombetti provides the example of worrying about missing a flight while on a slow train or caught up in traffic on the way to the airport. The individual may not attend to the tensed

---

[55] Colombetti (2014, p. 117).

shoulder and neck muscles, but they are still part of the emotional experience – and may enter attention once she has arrived on time and begins to relax. Colombetti denies that any form of representation plays a role in the experience of emotion, but her explanation here is completely consistent with Damasio's claim that the brain maintains an up-to-date and forward-projecting representation of the state of body in its environment.[56]

Synthesis: Affect, Arousal, and Emotion

We know that other social mammals display positive and negative affect, which may not qualify as *emotions* of happiness, pleasure, fear, or aggression, but must at least be continuous with the physiological bases for these emotions. They also display playful intentions (the "play face") and exhibit evidence of positive affect while engaged in play or grooming. We know that other mammals display negative affect in ways that map onto *fear* (e.g. avoidance and submissive postures) and *aggressive intention*, which, as LeDoux points out, is not the same as the socially charged emotion of *anger*. Other mammals avoid noxious odors and eject bad-tasting substances, which is similar to but not necessarily the same as *disgust*. Domesticated animals that are treated as pets display something like attachment and dependency – negative affect when familiar humans are absent, positive affect in response to their humans' presence and to being touched and petted. However, as LeDoux points out, these physiological responses correspond only poorly to categories identified as emotions.

Barrett argues that these behaviors are not *emotions*. This is true at least in part by definition, because she and her colleagues have defined *emotion* as a language-based concept, from which it naturally follows that animals lacking language do not experience emotion. Positive affect is associated, in other mammals as well as humans, with increased levels of pleasure-enhancing endorphins in the bloodstream, and shared positive affect leads to social bonding in all social species. The presence of a threat (an aggressive member of the same species or a predator) induces a particular set of biochemical and physiological responses in other mammals as well as humans, the basis for *fear*, and the presence of a rival for sex or status induces the response basis for aggression – and for the socially and culturally conditioned emotion of *anger*. The response to either a threat or a rival can be readily detected in other mammals as well as in humans. At least to this degree, consistent with the research of Ekman and his colleagues, it appears that some basic physiological responses, and overt signs (face, body disposition, vocalics, and actions), result

---

[56] See Chapter 2.

at least in part from genetically inherited neural systems common to social mammals. However, as Ekman more recently acknowledges, the experiences English speakers include within the categories labeled *fear* or *anger*, for example, include a variety of context-specific responses, each represented by a variety of facial expressions (and other signals), and most or all of which are routinely produced for strategic reasons related to social interactions.

When it comes to the elaboration of emotional categories – for example, the many faces of anger or happiness – Barrett's case for language-based emotion concepts seems quite strong. Among other results of language use, *introspection*[57] allows us to perceive, think about, analyze, and communicate with others about our responses, including our feelings, physiological responses and emotions, whether they are in some sense innate or entirely culturally constructed. We can parse any given feeling endlessly. (Barrett cites evidence that people who learn to identify a wider range of emotions in themselves are happier and mentally healthier.) We also extend our concepts metaphorically: Unlike other mammals, a human can be even more *disgusted* by a moral transgression than by the rotting corpse of a dead sheep,[58] and we can *fear* a failing grade on an exam or a drop in the stock market as readily as we fear an aggressive animal or a high cliff. The *fear* of a failing grade or drop in the stock market may be viscerally experienced, complete with a full range of physiological changes, or it may be purely abstract. Language also extends the range of emotion-producing stimuli to include spoken threats, insults, praise, endearments, vulgarities, and so on.

The case for biologically based universality of responses to threat (*fear*), rivalry (*aggression*), satisfaction of a bodily need (*pleasure*), and a distasteful substance or object (*disgust*) seems quite solid, whether these are called *emotions* or merely *affect*. However, the claim that emotion *categories* are the product of culture and language, interacting with the biology of affective valence and arousal and with individual experiences accumulated over a lifetime also seems quite convincing. The ease with which a particular emotion can become activated by context-based interpretation, or a state of arousal induced as negative affect can be transformed into a positive emotional experience (anger to sexual arousal, sexual arousal to anger, pain to aesthetic appreciation, etc.) suggests a strong cultural and experiential component. The varieties and nuances of experience all assigned a common label like *fear* or *anger* also suggests a strong cultural component. Moreover, people often spend considerable time ruminating on an emotional experience, both privately

---

[57] See Barsalou, (1999, 2008).
[58] Humans are unique among animals in the ability to exhibit a *disgust* response to a sexually arousing image.

and in conversation with friends and close associates, in order to understand and express the exact nature of the emotion.[59]

The behavior of humans as well as other animals is shaped in part by genetic heritage but is largely constrained – and shaped – by the circumstances of the organism's ecological niche. It is likely that people who live in an arid desert will develop an "emotion" that might be labeled "joy at finding fresh water," and share this emotion, or at least the underlying physiological responses, with other desert-dwelling people – and animals. The (often quite intense) emotion activated by solving a difficult mathematical problem or a complex crossword puzzle is unique to humans who have a history of a particular kind of symbolic communication. The ecological niche of humans emphatically includes complex social organizations and practices, including language and mathematics, with all their subtleties and affordances. Complex social organization greatly expands the range and variety of emotional experience, and discussing these experiences with others expands the range and nuances of emotion labels. The expanded range of both experience and labels is likely to be accompanied by an expanded range of perceivable combinations of facial muscle contractions and vocal inflections (i.e. of emotional expression). Emotion is not merely biological and cultural; it is also social and introspective.

Emotion and Reason

Damasio[60] observed that patients with damage to areas in the prefrontal cortex related to emotional experience exhibited difficulty making even simple personal and social decisions. In most of these cases, the ability to describe and consider alternative courses of action was unimpaired, but they were unable to use this information to make a choice, and when they did make a choice, it often turned out disastrously. According to Damasio's somatic marker hypothesis, people mentally simulate the future events that would result from each choice, and experience at least a simulation of the feelings associated with each potential future. These bodily feelings (the somatic markers) and associated emotions provide an analog synthesis of the body's complex responses to a potential outcome that influences, motivates, and often dominates the decision-making process. Damasio[61] argued that these somatic markers increase the accuracy, efficiency, and quality of decision-making by incorporating more information than is possible with a more systematic and abstract form of reasoning.[62]

---

[59] Chapter 11. [60] Damasio (1996, 1999). [61] Damasio (1999).
[62] Bechara et al. (2005), but also see Dunn, Dalgleish, and Lawrence (2006).

Communicating Emotion

Physiological arousal prepares the body for potential action, and affective valence is both innate and a function of conditioned learning (in the future, seek *this* and avoid *that*). According to LeDoux, the physiological responses to unconditioned stimuli are instigated by specialized neural *survival circuits* that are genetically linked to relevant stimuli – for example, defense circuits triggered by perception of a snake or spider, feeding circuit by perceptions associated with food, and so forth. These circuits can be easily conditioned to respond to certain other stimuli (conditioned learning). The physiological changes triggered by the survival circuit are also influenced by context: if escape is possible, a perceived threat activates changes that prepare for flight; if not, the response may be to hide or to "*freeze*," remain as still and quiet as possible, often both. Depending on the circumstances, the heart rate may increase and blood rush to the surface of the skin, producing an increase in body temperature and flushing, or blood may be routed to the viscera and drained away from the skin, producing decreased external temperature and a pallid appearance. These conditions describe very different experiences, and differ radically in the details, but they are all routinely lumped together within the single unitary concept of *fear*. Either threat or surprise (including a very pleasant surprise like an unexpectedly generous gift) leads to widened eyes and orienting toward the relevant stimulus, leading an observer or an experimental subject to label the resulting expression as fear, surprise, or joy according to the context.

Emotion Cues and Signals. These changes in preparation for action happen automatically and are at most only partially subject to volitional control; they may be perceived by others and interpreted as *cues* to the individual's state. However, other physiological changes appear to have evolved as signals, at least partially subject to volitional control. Many mammals respond to threats from a more powerful or dominant conspecific (the defense circuit) by assuming a lowered profile and displaying other evidence of submission.[63] A similar posture is used to signal playful intent – but accompanied by different facial configuration and different vocalization. Conversely, if the threat originates with a less powerful or subordinate conspecific, the animal may assume an elevated profile and display signs of aggressive capability and intentions such as bared teeth or claws or (in humans) doubled-up fists. Like the expressions of guilt and shame discussed by Griffiths and Scarantino, these displays can be understood and are often volitionally displayed as part of a complex negotiation over social status, relational outcomes, and situational interaction outcomes.

---

[63] In humans, this is expressed in various degrees of bowing, lowered eyes, and so forth.

Humans (and a few other primates) can perform, deliberately, a passable imitation of some of the preparatory changes and most of the response signals. Few humans are capable of intentionally altering heart rate or blood flow to the skin, but widened eyes, orienting toward a stimulus, altered breathing rate and pattern, *"freezing*," or assuming a posture of preparation to flee are easily – and frequently – imitated. Biologically evolved signals like the lowered or elevated posture, changes in vocal pitch and loudness, displaying a "play face," and so on, are easily and commonly produced. (More than one courtier has muttered an obscenity under his breath while bowing deeply before the king.) To the extent that the "common emotion expressions" reflect biologically universal survival circuits and ecological stimuli common to most or all human societies (snakes, spiders, high cliffs, fast-moving streams, and things that make loud noises are all dangerous regardless of where one lives), people will be able to produce an exaggerated and easily identified imitation of stereotypical responses to these common stimuli and use these volitional imitated responses as communicative signals. They will also be able to produce the stereotypical emotional responses with a range of alterations to express nuances of emotional meaning.

The evidence from research by Ekman and others that people all over the world can match carefully posed facial expressions with emotion words has been cited as support for the claim that facial expressions have a coded relationship to these emotions. Virtually all textbooks (and popular books) treating nonverbal communication refer to these expressions as *"encoding"* and *"decoding"* emotions. However, the evidence from studies using naturally produced emotions and asking subjects to explain what the depicted person is experiencing, without mentioning the word *emotion* or providing any emotion words, shows both a higher degree of complexity and a much lower degree of accuracy. Apparently, the relationship between emotions and facial expressions is code-like only if the facial expressions are produced, in a deliberately exaggerated way, by a skilled *"encoder"* (e.g. a trained actor or an accomplished liar). Ironically, an emotional expression that is deliberately produced is usually considered insincere, which suggests that emotional expression is code-like only when it is insincere – or when it is staged as part of a theatrical performance.[64]

Feelings. Damasio distinguishes *emotions* from *feelings*, which he defines as "the result of a cooperative partnership of body and brain, interacting by way of free-ranging chemical molecules and nerve pathways."[65] These "free-ranging chemical molecules" include the adrenaline and epinephrine used in

---

[64] Actors portraying Willie Loman or Othello in serious productions are certainly *sincere*, but they are sincere in a sense very different from the sincerity of the characters they portray.
[65] Damasio (2018, p. 12).

excitation-transfer and other emotion-related experiments, as well as oxytocin, cortisol, testosterone, and many other chemicals that affect tissues, skin, genital areas, brain regions, internal organs, and, in short, the entire body.[66] Sensations, including touch, pain, hunger, and nausea, interact with each other and with the various chemicals and neural activity. Touch in the genital area or other sexualized (erogenous) zones is quite different in effect from other touch; mild muscular pain after vigorous exercise is different in effect from intense pain of a muscle cramp. The effects and qualitative experience of these and most other sensations are strongly influenced by social and cultural context. The result is a constantly changing analog blend of emotion and sensation that is part of the "stream of consciousness," the flow of thoughts discussed in Chapter 4. Emotions are often discussed as if they are binary (either one feels angry or one does not) and independent of sensation, but more often emotions are experienced as an analog blend of arousal, sensation, and valence – that is, as a component of *feelings* – that constantly change both in quality and in intensity.

Emotion Categories and Terms. The forward-projected model of body-in-environment maintained by our extended brains incorporates information from interoception (e.g. arousal, affective valence, sexual sensitization, hunger, thirst, tiredness, and other sensations) and introspection (perception of one's own thought processes, memories, plans, and so forth) along with information from external perception, the present context, and cultural norms. Natural kind theorists argue that the six basic emotions (at least) are experienced through interoception, perception of a biological response. Social constructionists like Barrett argue that interoception provides information about the body's state of arousal and affective valence; this information is combined with exteroception, information about the external environment, and information about how these conditions match up with plans and desires (introspection). On the basis of the introspective information, the experienced state of arousal and valence is assigned to a culturally determined category. LeDoux's concept of survival circuits suggests a qualification to the constructionist view, in that the interoceptive information will include information about how the body's response is mediated by relevant survival circuits. The process of assigning the response to culturally acquired emotion categories according to the perceived context is basically the same. Griffiths and Scarantino carry these lines of thinking further, emphasizing that observable expressions of cultural emotion categories are frequently produced within ongoing social interaction, for the purpose of negotiating relational and situational outcomes.[67]

---

[66] Damasio (2018); Epstein (2018).
[67] They are also produced to enhance storytelling, express irony, and, in general, support or qualify vocal communication.

As Colombetti argues, the accumulated evidence supports the claim that emotional experience and expression are the products of lifelong interaction between innate (genetically inherited) responses to ecological opportunities and threats and culturally conditioned experience. Many emotion expressions are somewhat similar across all cultures and can be recognized and identified by members of even quite different cultures with accuracy well above chance, but they are strongly influenced by the social context and may be interpreted quite differently by members of different cultures, and in different situations. Most of us become quite adept not only at *recognizing* and *interpreting* emotional expressions but also at *simulating* – or concealing – them quite early in childhood: These are clearly important social skills.

In sum, it is apparent that much of our emotional experience and expression are based on the interaction of many neural systems, and it is socially originated and culturally defined. A typical human language has hundreds of words for emotional experience, each of which can be used to express a distinct nuance of experience. At the same time, the exact quality of experience described by a particular term may differ, at times radically, among speakers of the same language and members of the same social group. Is it timidity, shyness, reserve, or aloofness? Is it anger, resentment, annoyance, impatience – or concentration?

Communicating about Emotions

Feelings are expressed as they are experienced through nonlexical signals that include vocalic qualities, gestures, and posture as well as the facial expressions researched by Ekman and others. However, we do not always consciously attend to our feelings unless they become salient (for whatever reason). We do not just express feelings as we experience them; we also describe, analyze, and discuss them. When they seem inappropriate or sanctioned, we suppress them as well as we can; when they seem particularly relevant to the current context, we express them, sometimes in a deliberate and exaggerated form, and often explain them. Our emotional lives form a large part of the relationship talk that constitutes around two-thirds of our conversation, and we have an extensive repertoire of emotion concepts and terms that we use both in explaining our emotional experiences to others and in thinking about them.

Lakoff and Johnson[68] argue that abstract concepts, including emotion concepts, are understood and expressed through conceptual metaphors, relationships with less abstract, more directly (and, usually, physically) experienced concepts. Many of our emotion terms and concepts have a metaphorical basis.

---

[68] Lakoff and Johnson (1980, 1999); see Chapter 11.

Thus, we understand *anger* (and *passion* in general) as HEAT ("*boiling mad*"), PRESSURE ("*erupted*" or "*exploded*"; "*outburst*"; "*contained*"), or TEXTURE ("*irritation*," "*grated on*"). *Affection* can be "*tender*" (TEXTURE), "*close*" (PROXIMITY), "*warm*" (TEMPERATURE), or "*sweet*" (NOURISHMENT). Each of these terms activates partial simulations, neural systems associated with the literal experience, which may influence as well as express how the emotion is experienced.

Since Lakoff and Johnson's initial analysis of conceptual metaphors, there has been a series of attempts to elaborate and build a systematic science around the insights of Conceptual Metaphor Theory.[69] Many of the attempts to render a precise account of conceptual metaphors imply a code-like and deterministic relationship, consistent with the use of "is" in examples like ANGER IS HEAT. Some theorists have gone even further, proposing conceptual structures that blend basic metaphors in ways that produce, for example, ANGER IS HOT FLUID IN A CONTAINER UNDER PRESSURE.[70] These elaborated conceptual structures are sometimes posited as both culturally shared and neurologically real, then used to analyze metaphors in textual discussions of emotional experience.[71] However, their ontological status is still very much up for debate.

Like the metacognition about confidence in one's judgments that are central to the metacognition arguments of Heyes et al.,[72] nuanced communication about emotional experience is crucial to social cooperation. Direct expression of feelings increases one's predictability, and the ability to interpret others' emotional expressions is an important component of social competence.[73] The ability to identify and think clearly about one's own feelings as well as to communicate accurately is important to personal homeostasis as well as to successful relationships, as demonstrated by the importance of a large vocabulary of emotion terms.[74] Physiological arousal is both a direct response to stimuli, mediated by survival circuits, and a result of context-mediated evaluations of stimuli; these in turn are largely the result of socially acquired concepts and scripts. In sum, emotional experience and expression have a basis in biologically evolved responses, but they are largely cultural and social.

Summary

The case is quite strong that humans, like other animals, experience physiological arousal with a hedonic valence blended with an array of sensations in response to potential contributions to homeostasis (opportunities) and threats

---

[69] Ritchie (2021). [70] For example, Lakoff and Kövecses (1987); Kövecses (1990).
[71] For example, Esmaeili, Akhavan, and Amjad (2015); see Chapter 11.
[72] Heyes et al. (2020). [73] Burgoon et al. (2016). [74] Barrett (2017).

to homeostasis. Some of these experiences (pleasure, play, dominance, and submission) are associated with perceptible physiological responses in humans that resemble those of other primates (at least); others (sexual interest and receptivity) are more species-specific. Whether these physiological experiences and responses constitute *emotions* is largely a matter of definition.

It is also true that humans experience and express a much wider range of responses than any other animal, especially to social situations (including but not restricted to opportunities and threats). These are certainly cultural in origin and acquisition and social in purpose, although, like the more basic physiological responses, they can have powerful and unanticipated effects on an individual's mental state and physical actions. On the other hand, even the more basic experiences that humans share with other mammals (pleasure, play, dominance, submission, and sexual interest) are subject to intentional imitation and expression.

Even if there is a set of innate and universally recognized basic emotions, communicating them and communicating about them is culturally mediated and part of social interaction. Feelings are analog, ranging from barely detectable to overwhelming, and often blended in complex ways, none of which is conducive to "encoding." The experience of arousal and hedonic valence and the more complex experience of feelings that results from identifying and labeling the arousal as a particular "emotion" are central to both individual and socially collaborative deliberation and planning. The physiological states of arousal and valence motivate and shape the behavioral responses of all animals. Because humans are uniquely capable of labeling even the finest nuances of arousal plus valence and communicating these nuanced labels to each other, the resulting "emotions" play a powerful role in both individual and collective cognitive processes, planning, and action.

6 Signals

Unlike most other animals, humans have volitional control over a very wide range of both sounds and muscular activities, and most of it is used at one time or another as a signal. Even reflexive actions like blinking, coughing, or sneezing, which are only weakly subject to autonomous control, can be imitated with communicative intent. With forty-two independently controllable muscles on each side of the face,[1] humans are capable of an estimated 20,000 distinguishable facial expression. Our hands can produce an estimated 5,000–8,000 distinguishable gestures.[2] Our vocal range is equally expressive. Most humans can hear frequencies ranging from about 16 to 20,000 Hz. and produce a range of several octaves, with volumes ranging from barely audible to painfully loud. Our bodies have evolved to produce, recognize, and interpret language, and to express a wide range of ideas and feelings using gestures, facial expressions, and vocal intonations. As if that is not enough, we also express our ideas, identities, and feelings by painting, modifying, rearranging, and otherwise decorating both our bodies and our physical surroundings.

In terms of the evolutionary pressures discussed in previous chapters, it is obviously important to the propagation of our genes that we be able to express and understand a wide range of ideas and feelings, as well as "facts" and justifications for claiming that they are facts, and to make fine and subtle distinctions throughout that range of expression. All this contributes to our brain's ability to maintain a representation of the body's internal and external homeostasis, and to project the representation forward into the future in the form of predicted changes in the physical and social environment and predicted responses to alternative courses of action. It also contributes to our ability to collaborate with others to maintain representations of our relationships, primary groups, extended groups, nations, and even all of humanity, to project them forward in multiple alternative narratives, and to maintain the homeostasis of our relationships and our social contexts. As Dunbar and others have pointed out, for human beings the most important feature of our

---

[1] Barrett (2017).   [2] Burgoon et al. (2010).

environment is other people, our relationships with them, and their relationships with each other. The use, recognition, and interpretation of expressive signals are the primary means by which we maintain and project forward a representation of these relationships.

It has become customary to distinguish the vocal signals, the words (and gestures) that are lexicalized as part of formal language[3] from all other signals, which are lumped together, along with behaviors and features that have no communicative intention at all, as "nonverbal." The result is a conceptually and theoretically incoherent mishmash of ideas.[4] Many of the signals typically designated as "nonverbal" are part of language use, both in conversation and in more formal discourse such as public speaking.[5] Other behaviors and features that are typically discussed as "nonverbal communication" are not intentional in any sense, although some of them may provide cues from which it is possible to infer something about another person's attributes or current frame of mind. Still others, like the now fully discredited "science" of "phrenology" and the various features associated with the equally discredited concept of "race," do not provide any valid cues.[6] In between these extremes lie the diverse array of signals by which we express emotions, moods, identities, and intentions. Any perceptible object, substance, or action that can be volitionally controlled can be converted to and used as a signal.

In this chapter, I take a more functional approach. I begin by expanding the discussion of signals as intentional behavior introduced in Chapter 1, followed by a discussion of language, including the audial and visual signals that are produced and understood as language substitutes, extensions, and support. Finally, I will discuss signals intentionally produced to express emotions, moods, or personal identity. Architectural features, furnishings, decorations, and other aspects of the physical environment, which are also frequently included in discussions of "nonverbal communication," are sometimes produced as signals (e.g. symbols of wealth, power, piety, etc.), but, in general, they are more accurately considered as part of the physical context, and will be discussed in Chapter 7.

---

[3] Until recently, this meant *vocal* or *written*; only recently have sign languages been generally accepted as true languages.

[4] It appears that this situation partially reflects the neglect of (and sometimes disdain for) all signals outside of formally defined language that prevailed in social science disciplines until relatively recently. By the time "non-verbal communication" had ceased to be treated as a dumping ground for unacknowledged and underrated aspects of communication, it had become a vigorously defended territory – arguably an equally unsatisfactory situation from the perspective of conceptual and theoretical clarity.

[5] Enfield (2017); Calvert and Campbell (2003); Cornballis (2004); Gibbs (2006); Rizzolatti and Arbib (1998). This is a staple of rhetoric and has been well recognized at least since Aristotle.

[6] "Body type" is another popular but highly questionable "*code*"; even its value as a cue is limited at best.

Signaling

The most obvious and uniquely human signal system is spoken (or signed) language, but language interacts with other signals, and meanings of linguistic utterances can be altered, sometimes even reversed, by a visible physical action such as a wink or a shrug of the shoulders, or by subtle shifts in vocal qualities. After a brief discussion of signaling as a form of intentional behavior, I will begin this discussion with language, because it is the most complex and structured form of communicative signaling, and forms a core part of almost any extended communicative exchange. The discussion of language will also provide a basis for discussing the rich array of other signal systems that are commonly used in conjunction with and often as part of language.

Intentionality. In Chapter 1, I gave a provisional definition of *communication* as behavior performed with the intention or function to mean something for another organism, to influence in some way another organism's understanding, representation, and behavior in the world. This provisional definition requires attention to some other concepts, beginning with *intention*, which in turn implies *mind*. According to the homeostasis perspective mind is a function of the neural system and its representation of the state of the body in its environment, both present and projected forward into possible future states. Evaluation of possible future states and the associated feelings and actions may then produce an *intention* to act in a way that will maintain or improve homeostasis. Admittedly, it is often difficult to determine whether an action was intentional,[7] or how others were intended to interpret and respond to a signal. This difficulty should not excuse researchers from acknowledging and grappling with the concept.

Another useful concept is *affordance*, how one might interact with an object or another organism – including an object or action's potential as a signal. Affordances are based on physical characteristics but may also include cultural characteristics. Affordances of human-created objects most obviously include the purposes for which they were created, fostered, and maintained, but they also include other ways in which one might interact with the object. For example, a hammer has a long, rigid handle that fits most human hands well; it has a heavy (typically iron) "*head*," which has a flat surface on one end and may have curved "*claws*" on the other. The immediate affordances of a hammer include striking or breaking other objects, prying and lifting nails or staples, but it may also be used to prop open a door or window or anchor a light object in a windy place, or it may be left in a conspicuous place as a signal.

---

[7] Burgoon et al. (2016).

A third useful concept is *relevance*. At the basic organism level, a state or action of an object or another organism is relevant to an organism if its affordances affect homeostasis (a potential threat or resource).[8] The *relevant* features of an object such as a hammer depend on the *context* and a user's present needs. From the perspective of communication, affordances include possibilities such as being positioned, altered, or manipulated in a way that attracts others' attention and encourages them to infer communicative intent. The relevance of the resulting signal then refers to its potential effects on the mutual cognitive environment.

Much of what organisms, including humans, encounter is not relevant to them, and much of what organisms do is not relevant to other organisms. The rock in the desert is relevant to hikers only if they have need of (or concern about) its affordances – it is hard, heavy, and a certain shape. These features are *cues* to its possible affordances; for example, it might help hold a tent in place during a windstorm, or might help pound the tent stakes into hard soil, or someone might trip over it, or it might fall on someone's head. *Cues* do not require or imply intentionality in any sense. The rock has potential uses and potential effects, but it has no intentions and communicates nothing. If it is intentionally placed next to a trail, atop a stack of other rocks, the rock serves as a *signal*, created by a human who arranged the rocks with the intention to communicate something that *may be* relevant to another human; for example, it may indicate where a trail leads. Similarly, my neighbor's dog has long shaggy hair, a feature that is of no interest to me. If I were in the business of dog-grooming, the dog's hair might serve as a *cue* to a potential commercial relationship with the dog's owner, but since I am not in that business, the affordance of being long enough to trim or comb out has no perceptible bearing on my own homeostasis. The dog's hair is a feature of its genetics, and not in any sense intentional. If it was bred to have long shaggy hair or its owner has had it combed or trimmed, *that* expresses an intention of the breeder or of the owner, but not of the dog. Whether it constitutes *communication* depends on the breeder's or owner's intention.

An interesting case is presented by the poison arrow frog. This species has evolved two features that protect it against predators. Its skin exudes a potent toxin, which is relevant to the homeostasis of potential predators. Fortunately for local predators, the poison arrow frog has also evolved a distinctive pattern of bright colors – and local predator species have coevolved a healthy aversion to frogs with this pattern of colors. The coloration has evolved for (or in response to) the *purpose* or *function* of warning predators about the poison, but the frog has no control over its skin composition or coloration and no

---

[8] *Relevance* is an important concept in itself, and will receive a more detailed treatment in later chapters.

awareness of how it benefits from the poison and the warning coloration. The habit of avoiding frogs with this coloration has also evolved for the purpose of avoiding the poison. Local natives, however, having discovered the effects of the poison, gather the poison and treat their arrow tips with it, an action that is fully intentional – but this is not communication, since a user's intention is to use the arrow to kill other organisms, not for it to be perceived and interpreted by them. Leaving a poisoned arrow outside a rival's residence, however, might be intended as a signal, a deliberate act of communication. The arrow may be interpreted as either a threat (hostile) or an offer to go hunting together (friendly); the ambiguity does not detract from its status as a deliberate signal, although it may detract from its effectiveness.

A *signal* is an action or state that is performed or displayed with the intention, purpose, or function that it be perceived and interpreted or responded to by another organism. Here we might usefully distinguish at least two degrees of intentionality in addition to the *purpose* or *function* that led to coevolution of the frog's poison and coloration with the predator's aversion to that pattern of color. Much of human communication, including speech and gesture, takes place too rapidly to permit detailed planning and control by conscious thought. In my conversation with my wife about what to have for dinner, or in my conversation with my neurologist friend about Damasio's latest book, I certainly *intend* every phrase I speak, even though the pace of normal conversation does not permit conscious deliberation about each word before it is spoken. If I realize I just said something that does not express the idea I intended, or might be offensive to a listener, I correct it. But if one were to hesitate long enough for conscious deliberation over every word choice, the conversation would take on a halting quality that would be uncomfortable for everyone.[9] Much of one's use of language in these conversations is *non-deliberated intentionality*. In my conversation with my wife about the dinner menu, I *deliberate* about the options, but not about how to express my responses to them. Part of the conversation is *deliberate*; all of it is *intentional*. If we are merely chatting about our day's activities, the entire conversation is intentional, but little of it is deliberate.

When I have a new idea or an idea that is difficult to express for some other reason, I may pause, consider different ways to express the thought, *deliberate* about the best word to use, select one, possibly recall or invent a metaphor to express the idea, then continue with the conversation or writing task. Like my expression of a dinner menu preference, this utterance results from conscious *deliberation*, and it is an example of *deliberate intentionality*. These distinctions are important for a clear understanding of communication.

---

[9] Enfield (2017); see Chapter 9.

To summarize, interactions among organisms regularly involve a process of perception and response, sometimes but not always mediated by some process of interpretation, inference, or attribution. Perception is always partial and purposive: The perceptual environment has often been characterized as a "blooming, buzzing, confusion,"[10] presenting a virtually unlimited array of stimuli, including light, sound, touch, and chemicals. Perceptual sensors are tuned, first by evolution then by processes of attention, then by culture and social interactions, to respond to a very narrow range of these stimuli. This "perceptual world" corresponds to objects and events relevant to each organism's ecological niche, what it needs to maintain homeostasis. Senses are tuned to detect *patterns*, nonrandom arrangements of stimuli (e.g. objects, events, and motions).[11]

Many of the patterns we detect are irrelevant, at most objects of curiosity (e.g. finding a shape resembling an elephant in the clouds or a "face" on the moon). A subset of patterns we detect are *cues*, which may support inferences about an object or organism even though they are not produced with any purpose or intention to be perceived or interpreted by others. Humans are disposed, both evolutionarily and culturally, to find and interpret patterns, to interpret these patterns as cues, and to invent stories to explain them and derive inferences from them. Humans look for patterns even in random events, contributing to superstitions and conspiracy theories. Another set of patterns is *signals*. A *signal* can be defined as a patterned alteration of the perceivable environment that is produced with the purpose, function, or intention that one or more other organism(s) perceive it and interpret or at least respond to it. In this age of responsive computers and robots, we might want to change the word "organism" to "entity," since people frequently generate signals for these nonorganic entities – and respond to signals they generate.

Communication, then, can be more precisely defined as a process in which one entity generates signals with the purpose or intention that other entities perceive them and recognize or respond to them as signals, resulting in some change in the others' actions, cognitive states, or both. Under some circumstances, as observed by Watzlavik, Beavin, and Jackson,[12] *intentionally* and *obtrusively* ignoring a signal can itself be interpreted as a signal, hence qualify as communication. However, not all behavior or lack of behavior provides

---

[10] For example, James (1890/1981).
[11] As Wilson (2017) points out, we have the capability of perceiving only a small portion of the potentially informative features of our involvement, and we attend to only a small portion of what we can perceive. Subsonic sound and radiation in the infrared and ultraviolet spectrum, for example, might provide very useful information if we had evolved the capability to detect them. Conversely, humans also tend to detect patterns that are not present, even in random stimuli, a factor in perceptual illusions and conspiracy theories.
[12] See Chapter 1.

meaningful cues and an even smaller subset of behavior (and nonbehavior) generates intentional signals; one certainly *can* "not communicate" – without having any purpose or intention not to communicate. Unfortunately, in what seems to have become a culture of intrusive snooping, what one *cannot* do is prevent others from making attributions based on involuntary cues or completely random events or even on wholly irrelevant incidental behaviors or characteristics[13] – or absence of certain behaviors or characteristics.

In the human realm, some behaviors that are not under volitional control provide a basis for inferences or attributions: People generally have no direct control over pupil dilation (which may result from arousal, interest, or attraction – or from light conditions or ingestion of certain drugs) or blushing (which may result from embarrassment or arousal – or from exertion or various medical conditions). We also often make attributions on the basis of actions and conditions over which people may have volitional control – for example, the way they sit, stand, or dress, the direction of their eye gaze, and so on. Sometimes these actions and conditions are intended as signals; sometimes they are not. We also make attributions based on effectively random actions, such as a muscle twitch or spasm caused by a random neural impulse, or an orienting response to a distant noise or a flash of light reflected from the windshield of a passing auto. Thus, although the definitions of incidental behaviors, cues, and signals/communication are clear in principle, in practice these distinctions often blur. Taking the example of pupil dilation, few, if any, people can voluntarily cause their pupils to dilate (or not dilate), but we can take actions – like entering a dimly lighted room (or taking certain drugs or wearing colored contact lenses) – that will lead pupils to dilate or appear to dilate. Hence the romantic effects of candlelight dining, which leads to dilated pupils and may result in attributions of interpersonal attraction. If this effect is intended, or if it occurs in response to the presence of an attractive other, then the dilated pupils, or the action that led to the dilation, can be reasonably classified as a signal, an instance of communication.

To summarize, it is useful to distinguish at least three levels of intentionality and relevance.

- *Incidental* stimuli. Most of the stimuli we are physiologically able to detect are incidental and nonintentional, with no apparent relevance. Our perceptual systems often filter these out.

---

[13] It is even more unfortunate that so many authors of popular books on "nonverbal communication" encourage both the propensity to pry into others' private thoughts and the belief that it is possible to "read minds" through attention to nonintentional behaviors. To my knowledge, no researcher has as yet investigated the ethical and interpersonal communication problems that result from this kind of intrusive overinterpretation: the topic is overdue for research.

- *Cues.* A cue is a stimulus or a pattern of stimuli that indicate a resource, a threat, or an otherwise relevant situation. With respect to communication, a cue provides a basis for drawing inferences about or attributing qualities or intentions to another organism. A cue is not intentional, may or may not be relevant to the current situation, and may or may not be within the control of the observed entity.[14]
- *Signals.* A signal is a stimulus or pattern of stimuli that is produced by a living organism *with the intention* (e.g. human speech), or *for the purpose* (arrow frog coloration and monkeys' warning shrieks), of being detected by another living organism and eliciting a particular response.

There has been much confusion around these three categories, especially in the extensive literature on "nonverbal" communication. The confusion is partly understandable, since the three categories sometimes blur together. A tear rolling down a cheek may result from grit in the eye, in which case it is a cue but not a signal. It may be a signal of strong emotion, at best weakly subject to volitional control, or it may be produced to elicit a particular response, a deliberate signal. Most of the piles of rocks we encounter when hiking in the wilderness are the result of gravity acting on loose rocks, merely *incidental*. However, sometimes rocks are deliberately stacked up, in a pattern unlikely to have resulted from random rockfall, to serve as trail markers, property boundaries, or for other reasons, in which case they are correctly interpreted as *signals*.

A final caveat about intentionality: in many cases, observers, including researchers, have no way to decide whether an action is intended as a signal or not. This has led many theorists to propose doing away with the concept of intentionality – but that would be a clear case of "throwing the baby out with the bathwater," since our very ability to communicate depends on our ability to recognize and distinguish intentional behaviors as communicative signals. Both the practice and the study of communication are inherently constrained by existential uncertainty about what a speaker means or intends and what a hearer understands. Admitting that we can never be *certain* whether an action had a communicative purpose or was intended as communication, or what it was intended to express, does not imply that the distinction is of no interest; indeed, signals often include features (such as exaggerated emphasis) that have the express intention of marking them as having been produced with the intention to communicate. We are always in the position of making inferences based on appearances – and often of correcting our inferences according to

---

[14] As an ethical point, I would further argue that others should not be held accountable for cues over which they have no control. In most cases, considerations of privacy should require that such cues be disregarded.

Signaling

apparently disconfirming subsequent evidence.[15] As researchers, we cannot excuse ourselves from this universal human condition, or pretend to have risen above it.

Signals. Communication begins with a *signal*, a pattern created in the perceptible physical environment with the intention, purpose, or function that it will be perceived by another organism, recognized as a signal, and responded to or interpreted in such a way that it affects the perceiving organism's behavior or its representation of the current situation. A signal must be perceived, and it must be recognized as a signal – that is, it must be readily differentiated from random or incidental objects and events.[16] If signals are biological in origin or part of cultural system such as language, they carry a presumption of intentionality. If an ordinarily nonintentional action or object is used as a signal, it must be set apart or emphasized in some way that marks it as ostensive, a meta-signal to communicate "this is a signal."

The evolutionary earliest signals derive from stimulus-response systems. A condition or action that produces a beneficial response (one that contributes to homeostasis) will be repeated. Conversely, a response to a stimulus that either produces a continuation of a beneficial stimulus or discontinuation of a detrimental stimulus will also be repeated – and will itself in time become a signal. Organisms that produce this kind of signaling behavior are more likely to reproduce; this is the basis for innate signaling systems, including those between cells and tissues within any multicellular organism (Chapter 2). Most signaling behavior has this character. However, humans (and possibly a handful of other animal species) also use a wide range of volitional signals, signals that are not biologically innate, but are more or less intentionally and often deliberately produced within the context of social interaction. The most obvious of these occur as part of or in conjunction with language. Human emotional expression is also largely volitional, and most readily identified when it is deliberately enacted (Chapter 5); although, ironically, it is more trusted when it appears to be nonvolitional.

Spoken languages use a range of sounds distinct from other vocalizations, and their distinct qualities identify them as intentional signals (although language elements – words – are sometimes uttered reflexively, as in response to pain or surprise). Sign languages also use a range of gestures, stylized to distinguish them from other body movements and identify them as intentional. All cultures use and recognize an array of emotional expressions (e.g. fear, anger, sadness, happiness, surprise, disgust, shame, gratitude), as well as conventionalized actions (vocalizations, gestures, facial expressions) that are

---

[15] Chapter 9.
[16] This requirement implies that signal production capabilities must coevolve in tandem with systems for perceiving, recognizing, and understanding signals.

produced in a stylized way that identifies them as intentional signals. Any behavior that is subject to volitional control can be used as a signal by producing it ostensibly, in an exaggerated or stylized manner that marks it as intentional. Signals are often produced in combination with each other, separately or as part of the flow of language.

Language

Conversation is the basic form of language use, and conversation includes a wide range of signals. The discussion in this section will focus primarily on language as it appears in conversation, supplemented by comments about written language where needed.

The basic components of a language are vocabulary (a set of conventional signals) and syntax (a set of conventions for organizing and qualifying signals).[17] At the intersection of vocabulary with syntax are signals that add meaning to phrases but have little or no meaning independent of the context in which they appear. These include prepositions (at, in), articles (the, a), intensifiers (very), and other accompanying signals. Enfield[18] argues that we need to include *uh, um, huh?* and similar sound particles in this group as part of language. Even though these particles have no independent meaning, they appear frequently in conversation (close to once per minute) and play a distinct, regular role in language use. Intonations, gestures, and facial expressions regulate turn-taking, and the flow of language and subtle qualities of intonation can change the interpretation of a word, sentence, or even a complete utterance.[19] A strong case can also be made for including all these signals as part of language.

While speaking, people tend to move their bodies in ways that reinforce (or sometimes qualify) the spoken message. Posture, gestures, and facial expressions influence how people understand the spoken message and provide supplementary contextual and relational information. Under difficult listening conditions, listeners are aided in comprehending what is spoken by attention to lip movements; Cantonese speakers can distinguish between intonations that mark the difference between two otherwise identical words by face shape alone[20], and neuroimaging studies show that both Broca's and Wernicke's areas are active when people interpret facial gestures.[21]

Word Meaning. We tend to think of meaning in terms of dictionary definitions, but both dictionaries and definitions are artifacts of written language. Even in literate, book-based cultures, most word meanings are learned, not by memorizing their definitions but by observing their co-occurrence with

---

[17] Chapter 3. [18] Enfield (2017). [19] Chapter 3. [20] Corballis (2004); Gibbs (2006).
[21] Calvert and Campbell (2003).

other words and their association with contexts (surrounding language and social situations) in which they appear.[22] Conversely, dictionary definitions are derived from observing how words are used in actual discourse.

A long tradition of word association research has demonstrated that words (and their references) are organized in semantic memory in *schemas*, networks of coactivation based on association with a common set of concepts and practices, reinforced by the frequency with which two words or actions are encountered within the same communicative interaction.[23] When any word or phrase is encountered, spreading activation increases the salience of other words and phrases that belong to the same schema(s). As a result, the neural representation of related words and phrases become more activated (more *salient*), thus more likely to be recalled or produced in a free association test. As words are encountered in discourse, closely related words and phrases will be at least weakly activated, potentially contributing to meaning.

There is also a growing body of evidence that, as words are encountered, the neural systems that would be active if the referent were actually perceived, as well as those that would be activated if associated actions were actually performed, are partially activated as weak perceptual simulations of the referenced object, action, or state. These perceptual simulations include emotions that might be experienced in association with the referent of the word: If a word refers to an object or action that is associated with sadness or happiness, encountering that word is likely to produce at least a weak and brief feeling of sadness or happiness.[24] The associations need not be from direct personal experience: Both word-word associations and perceptual simulations are often acquired culturally, for example, through storytelling.

Word-play, metaphor, irony, and other figurative uses of language also affect how we use and understand words and phrases. Most common words have a metaphor somewhere in their history, although in many cases the metaphorical origins are lost in time and culture. However, extensive research evidence has shown that even when a metaphor has been encountered so frequently that the metaphorical meaning has come to be accepted as a secondary "literal" meaning of the word,[25] perceptual simulations associated with the basic, original meaning are often weakly activated.[26] Figurative language is an important feature of language use and will be discussed in more detail in later chapters.

---

[22] Hoey (2005); Landauer and Dumais (1997); Tabossi (1989). [23] Chapter 4.
[24] Bergen (2012). See Chapter 4 for a more complete discussion.
[25] Here it must be noted that dictionary definitions are derived from how a word is used, so after a metaphor has become widespread, dictionary publishers will present the metaphorical interpretation as part of the word's "meaning," whether or not ordinary users recognize it as a metaphor.
[26] Gibbs (2006, 2008; Gibbs and Matlock, 2008). See Chapter 11 for a more detailed discussion.

Because we learn these components of meaning through unique individual life experiences, each person will understand words and phrases somewhat differently. The communicative context will influence which meanings become activated, but different participants in a conversation will not necessarily activate similar meanings.[27] There is, in short, a fundamental ambiguity to language,[28] which may not always be apparent within a communication interaction: the ambiguity usually becomes apparent only if it causes a relevant misunderstanding. This ambiguity is rarely apparent in ordinary conversations, when precise meanings are often unimportant to the social purpose of the interaction and redundant features of the context guide interpretation and narrow the range of plausible interpretations.[29]

Word Form (Morphology). Although I have argued elsewhere in this book against characterizing communication, including language, as digital and code-like, there is an important sense in which language *can be* described as a digital code. Every spoken language is composed of a finite set of *phonemes*, discrete sounds (*phones*) that are assembled into the sound units (*morphemes*) typical of that language. Similarly, alphabet-based print languages are composed of a finite set of discrete symbols (*letters*) that bear a loose relationship to the phonemes recognized in the language. Letters can be assembled into small discrete clusters (*syllables*) that correspond more or less closely to the morphemes of the spoken language.[30] In the sense that words in all spoken languages are composed of discrete sounds and that the phonemes of spoken words are (more or less) deterministically matched with letters or groups of letters, morphemes are matched with syllables composed of letters in an alphabetical language, and words are matched with particular sequences of syllables, language is a code. By extension, producing language is a process of encoding into phonemes, syllables, and letters, and understanding language is a process of decoding these letters, syllables, and phonemes, all according to relationships that are learned (and maintained) primarily through observation and practice.

However, the story is not quite that simple. Different people do not pronounce phonemes exactly the same way, and even one individual may pronounce a word differently on various occasions, depending on mood, health, energy level, and so on. The range of acceptable sounds (*phones*) that will be recognized as representing a given phoneme is characteristic of each language,

---

[27] Lyons (1977).   [28] Wilson and Sperber (2004); Chapters 3, 4, and 7.
[29] Chapters 7 and 9.
[30] The ideograms or pictographic characters in such languages as Chinese and Japanese are also decomposable into a semantically related characteristic set of marks, but they bear a very different (and more complex) relation to the spoken languages. [I am indebted to Min Zhu and Xuede Zhao for the wording of this footnote.]

but often differs among dialects of the language, and it can be quite ambiguous.

Handwriting differs at least as much as pronunciation – and printed materials (paper or electronic) use hundreds of different fonts. In both spoken and visual communication, we are presented with analog signals, which our perceptual systems have been trained to digitize by assigning them into categories, using various clues to decide – for example, whether a written symbol is *r*, *h*, *n*, or perhaps something else altogether. Our perceptual and language recognition systems are similarly capable of correcting pronunciation, spelling, and even grammatical errors, including dropped phonemes and syllables, "on the fly." This is commonly done in an automated way that may not even be noticed unless something calls attention to it.[31] However, it is nowhere near as deterministic as the word *code* implies, and the categorization process often draws on the context in which the sound or shape is encountered, which introduces a kind of "*circularity*" into the process: The signal is assigned to one or another category and interpreted as one or another phoneme or letter based on the apparent meaning of the utterance, which itself depends on how the signal and the word it helps form is interpreted. Subsequent processing frequently forces the listener or reader to "*go back*" and correct an initial interpretation of the signal.[32] What one hears another person say is often a function of what one expected to hear them say, and it is often subject to post hoc correction.

Emblems (Code-Like Gestures). Spoken language is also accompanied by culture-specific gestures (*emblems*) that can be and often are substituted for spoken words. The head nod (yes) and head shake (no) are common examples. Other visual emblems in English include "V for Victory" (or, since the 1960s, "peace"), shrugged shoulders ("I don't know" or "I'm indifferent"), and hand outstretched, fingers splayed, and wiggled back and forth ("only so-so"). Vocalic emblems include the trilled sound called a "raspberry" and the "tsk-tsk" or "tut-tut" sound used to express disapproval. Vocalic qualities that take the place of punctuation in print might also reasonably counted as emblems; certainly they should be considered part of language. A falling tone on the final syllable of an utterance signals "full stop," unless it is drawn out, in which it may signal uncertainty. An increase in volume signals "exclamation," and a rising tone signals "question mark." A change of pitch often signals a quotation, as does the use of "air quotes" (index and middle finger of each hand extended and moved downward in front of the speaker). Most of these examples can be quite ambiguous, used to express a range of meanings; even

---

[31] This automated error correction is one reason why it is so difficult to proofread one's own writing.
[32] Arundale (2010); see Chapter 9.

their status as "emblems" is subject to debate. However, they serve as part of language.

Like phonemes and complete words, these and other emblems are perceived and observed on an analog continuum, but they have readily recognized canonical forms (within a given speech community), and observers will often digitize the signal – either recognize a motion as a "head nod" or not (i.e. either assign it to the "head nod" emblem category or not).[33] Like phonemes and words, there may be ambiguous gestures (the shrug is barely a subtle dip of the shoulders, or it is performed quite slowly), in which case the perceiver may need to assess the context in order to determine whether or not it truly qualifies as the emblematic shrug and thus counts as an equivocating response. A morpheme or a complete word can be emphasized (or deemphasized) through vocalic qualities, altering its interpretation without affecting its recognition and categorization.

Similarly, a head nod (or any other emblem) can be emphasized, deemphasized, or otherwise qualified through alterations in its manner of production without affecting its recognition and categorization. The head can be nodded vigorously or subtly, rapidly or slowly, and still be recognized as a head nod. In this sense, to achieve code-like qualities such as precision and identifiability, both spoken words and emblematic gestures may require considerable cognitive effort on the part of the perceiver as well as the producer, and the meaning of both words and emblems can be emphasized, qualified, or subtly transformed by varying incidental qualities of the signal. The resulting subtle differences of meaning are best understood as analog, not digital.

Emblems are often produced in tandem with speech, to reinforce, supplement, or even contradict a spoken utterance ("He's probably the best person for the job," accompanied by an emphatic head nod, a slow head nod, or a shrug). Emblems frequently substitute for speech: a nod or shake of the head is accepted as an answer to a question, particularly if another person is speaking or a spoken reply is otherwise inconvenient or inappropriate. Both visual and audial emblems are also frequently used as back-channel communication to support, comment on, or disagree with what another speaker is saying (here again, the emphatic head nod, slow head nod, or shrug may be pressed into service).

Illustrators. Less code-like gestures also contribute to expressing meaning. Hands may indicate shape of an object being described, speed or direction of motion, relative location, or sequence of events. Metaphorical gestures may

---

[33] Burgoon et al. (2010). Students sometimes have trouble distinguishing *analog* from *ambiguous*. A shrug is analog if the intensity, speed, and height to which shoulders are raised affects how it is interpreted; it is ambiguous if in context it could be understood as "I don't know," "I don't care," or "I don't want to answer."

illustrate or reflect verbal metaphors: A common example is a sine wave motion, indicating "*up and down*" as a metaphorical expression of variations in emotional valence, interest level, quality, value, and so forth. A pinching gesture of index finger and thumb may help describe literally picking up something small or metaphorically "*nit-picking*" an argument. Expanded hands may indicate the size of an object, prototypically a fish; the motion is also often observed as a metaphorical indication that another person's story is "a *fish tale*" (i.e. an exaggeration). A chopping motion of one hand, fingers outstretched, metaphorically signals that it is time to bring a story or other performance to an end ("*cut*"); a finger drawn across the throat can serve the same metaphor – or metonymically characterize something as potentially lethal (literally or metaphorically). The motion of the entire body may be used to describe a motion or the size of an object – and, as with the previous examples, this can also be used metaphorically, as, for example, when an inflated chest and raised shoulders metaphorically mocks the subject of a conversation for being pompous or self-important. Metaphoricity, like intentionality, is often marked by ostensive qualities that signal the intention that an action be interpreted as intentionally metaphorical.[34]

Vocal qualities (vocalics) are also used to illustrate an idea being expressed – a story about a petulant child (or an adult who was acting "childishly") may be illustrated by quoting the subject of the story in a whining voice; the same whining voice may also serve as a metaphorical expression of discontent. A falling vocal tone may metaphorically express sadness, and a rising tone may express jubilation or excitement; greetings are often expressed in a rising, high-pitched tone to signal the speaker's excitement and pleasure in an unexpected encounter. A faked accent may metaphorically express an evaluation of someone else's performance or self-presentation, or illustrate the quality of a described social encounter. The possibilities are effectively infinite.

Utterances

Texts in printed English are divided into units of meaning through a hierarchy of typographical conventions. In English, topics are organized as paragraphs, ideally one to each specific topic. Discrete ideas (e.g. propositions) are presented as sentences, culminating in a period, question mark, or exclamation mark. Sentences are composed of discrete units of meaning, words, and phrases. Intermediate between words and sentences, units of thought are divided by commas (and other punctuation marks) to indicate how units of thought are organized in relation to what precedes and follows them.

---

[34] See Chapter 11.

In spoken language, a variety of signals can fulfill functions similar to punctuation. However, unlike written language in which there is a clear marker (the blank space) to separate one word from the next, in an animated conversation a series of words may be produced in one continuous flow. This flow of sound tends to be broken up into *phonemic clauses*[35] or *intonation units*,[36] usually marked by a falling pitch on the final phoneme, often preceded by a rising pitch on the penultimate phoneme. The end of an intonation unit may also be slightly louder, and dragged out, and intonation units are usually followed by a slight pause. Walter Chafe argues that each intonation unit comprises a complete thought, and that each thought emerges into consciousness as the preceding intonation is finishing. If the speaker has not yet completely formulated the next thought, a particle such as *um* or *uh* will appear as filler, a signal that more is coming and that the speaker is encountering cognitive difficulties.[37] Like other words in the lexicon, these particles are also often used metaphorically, to express the *idea* of cognitive difficulty, as, when one is preparing to decline an invitation, "*um*" may metaphorically indicate "I had to think about it before declining" (whether it is true or not). Hand gestures are also often used to indicate that more is coming (and to facilitate the production of the next intonation unit). Averted gaze, vocal pauses, head movements, hand gestures, and drawn-out words can all signal cognitive difficulty.

Depending on the nature of the conversation, speaking turns may be relatively short, expressing a single idea through a series of intonation units, or linking several ideas together, as in a story or explanation. Like figurative language use, brief stories and references to stories appear frequently in conversation and in other forms of discourse such as speeches.[38] It seems likely that conversation structure has evolved and developed in tandem with and as part of language itself, since it would be very difficult to use language in any complex way without some form of structuring.

Conversation Support

Conversation, the basic form of language use, ordinarily involves the entire body. Eyes, face, gestures, voice qualities, touch, even the posture and orientation of the body generate signals (*regulators*) that help initiate conversations, establish (and change) the purpose and tone of the conversation, include or exclude others, regulate speaking turns and topics, deal with interruptions, and eventually close the conversation. Body signals can extend, substitute for, or change the perceived intention and interpretation of the spoken language.

---

[35] Burgoon et al. (2010). [36] Chafe (1994). [37] Enfield (2017).
[38] Ritchie (2012, 2017). Stories and storytelling will be discussed in Chapter 13.

Ordinarily these conversation signals are produced automatically, with little conscious thought, but they can also be produced intentionally, even precisely – or ironically.

Supporting the Flow of Language. Speech is ordinarily accompanied by a wide range of motion. Gestures of the hands and arms help the speaker produce words and phrases,[39] and mark the rhythm of speech ("beat"). Similar gestures are also used to emphasize certain words or phrases. Signals, including eye contact, facial expressions, and gestures, sometimes but not always accompanied by vocalization, acknowledge the presence of others (greetings), initiate or avoid conversation, manage turn-taking, topic change, and the delicate process of bringing a conversation to a close. A similar variety of signals contributes to framing a conversation, the relationship, and specific utterances. Most of these signals are culture-specific or at least culturally modified, and learned as part of acculturation, beginning in early childhood.

Turn-Taking. Once initial greeting rituals have been completed, people take turns speaking, with speaking turns usually averaging about six seconds.[40] Although turn-taking is occasionally managed with verbal expressions like "Well, what about you?" or "What's your opinion about all this?," it is usually regulated by an array of gestures, facial expressions, and vocalic signals. Both turn-requesting and turn-yielding usually occur at the end of intonation units (phonemic clauses), marked by a change in loudness, falling pitch on the final syllable, and a pause. If the speaker wishes to keep speaking (deny turn-change), eye contact will be avoided, the pause will be short or filled with a sound (*um* or *uh*), and often accompanied by a hand or arm gesture.

If the speaker wishes to yield the floor, the pause will be longer, eye contact established, and often a pointing or extended open hand gesture used metaphorically to "*hand the topic over to*" another person. Listeners request a turn by gazing toward the speaker, leaning forward, nodding, raising an index finger (or entire hand), assuming a more erect posture, and an inhaled breath.[41] The most obvious way to avoid taking a speaking turn is simply to remain silent;[42] after about a minute, the speaker (or someone else) will usually resume speaking.[43] Listeners can also refuse a speaking turn by avoiding eye contact or maintaining a relaxed posture.[44] Either speaker or listener may also use the "stop" emblem, hand upraised, palm outward, to prevent another person from interrupting, to refuse a turn, or as a back-channel comment.

---

[39] McNeill (2000, 2005)   [40] Jaffe and Feldstein (1970).
[41] Wiemann (1973); Wiemann and Knapp (1975); Burgoon et al. (2010).
[42] An example of using lack of a signal as a signal.   [43] Enfield (2017).   [44] Knapp (1978).

Speaker Support. Listeners use *back-channel signals*, distributed throughout a listening turn,[45] to react to what a speaker is saying, encourage or support a speaker, or merely to indicate continued attention and interest. A listener may hurry a speaker along by nodding rapidly, encourage a speaker by smiling or nodding, display facial expressions appropriate to a story (a smile, frown, sad expression, or surprise). Wandering gaze, backward movement or leaning, or fidgeting may indicate waning interest and encourage a speaker to hurry a story along. Conversely, a forward lean and sustained gaze accompanied by nods, emotional facial expressions, and brief vocalizations indicate continued interest and encourage a speaker to continue and possibly to elaborate on a story.

If listeners do not display attention and involvement signals and cues, speakers usually find it disconcerting and may bring a story, and often the entire conversation, to a close. Deliberately suppressed back-channel signals may indicate that the listener doesn't follow what the speaker is trying to say[46] or that a listener is impatient or uncomfortable with what the speaker is saying – for example, if the speaker is telling an offensive joke or story. Cultural differences in conventions of back-channel communication often lead to misunderstandings.

Expressive Signals

The entire body, along with the face and vocal quality, expresses emotion and mood, social status, and other personal qualities, as well as personal affiliation and relationships.

Emotions. Distress, disgust, and interest are present at birth. Other emotional expressions are learned[47] at around the same time in most children. Most infants display their first social smile when they are between six and ten weeks old. By six or seven months old, most babies show anger, surprise, shame, fear, and joy. More complex emotions, such as contempt and guilt, usually emerge later.[48] These "basic" emotions incorporate physiological arousal, and often produce an autonomous response that can include facial expression, vocalization, gestures, and changes in posture, skin color, and so forth.[49]

Distress, aversion, interest, fear, and aggressive intent are all readily identifiable in other mammals, especially other primates, and in many cases the signals (facial expression, vocal quality, and bodily posture) are similar to those observed among humans. Playfulness is also observed among most

---

[45] Duncan (1974).   [46] Krauss, Fussell, and Chen (1996).   [47] See Chapter 5.
[48] Burgoon et al. (2010).   [49] Chapter 5.

mammals as well as in most human cultures; it is typically signaled with some version of the "play face," along with distinct vocalization and posture (similar to the signal for submissiveness). As discussed in Chapter 5, the degree to which common emotional expressions are innate or social learned is very much a matter of debate, but it is clear that emotional expressions characteristically involve an array of signals, including the voice, face, and body, all of which are strongly conditioned by cultural practices and social context.

Social Status and Power. The basic signals associated with status and power among humans and other animals are remarkably similar. Dominance (or aggressive intention) is signaled by exaggerated size and elevated position, often enhanced by raised hair and exaggeratedly erect posture, loud voice, prolonged gaze, motion toward the other, and aggressive gestures. Submission is signaled by reduced size and lowered position (including the deep bow or "kowtow"), lowered head and lowered or averted gaze, softer and sometimes higher-pitched voice, retreating movements, open and restrained gestures. Among humans, status and power are also signaled by dress and physical location (higher and closer to the center). Higher status is signaled (or claimed) by larger space (larger residence or office, greater separation from other persons) and by the quality of structures and furnishings.[50]

Sexual Interest/Availability. Among most sexual species of animals, signals indicating sexual interest and availability are unequivocal and emphatic. Females in estrus emit pheromones, exhibit color and shape changes in part or all of their bodies, and exhibit clear behavior changes. Males perform elaborate "dances" (like the American sage grouse), vocalize loudly, display flying, running, or fighting abilities, and otherwise advertise their fitness as a potential source of genes.

Humans are (usually) more subtle, probably because humans are embedded in large and complex social structures, and human expressive behavior, especially sexual behavior, is constrained by cultural rules and norms. Human females do undergo subtle changes in body shape and behavior during their fertile periods, but they often suppress or mask these biologically determined signals by means of cosmetics and garments. More overt (and intentional) signals of sexual interest and availability may include eye contact (either prolonged or brief), smiles and other facial expressions, touch, vocal inflection, and posture,[51] all of which, unlike changes in body shape and chemistry, *are* subject to volitional control, and consequently can be produced with varying degrees of ambiguity. Culture-specific signals include accessories (like fans, drink containers, cigarettes, and garments). Ordinarily, there is a gradual

---

[50] See Chapter 11.
[51] And, of course, the cue provided by the "*boner*" that has recently motivated plotlines in a certain variety of romantic comedies.

escalation of signaling that preserves deniability (in the interest of minimizing loss of face – which does not appear to be a consideration for other species).

Relationship and Affiliation. Social affiliation (friendship or intimacy, common group membership, etc.) can be signaled by proximity, orientation toward each other, frequency of eye contact, and touch. Similar or identical clothing, hair styles, bodily adornment are all used to signal affiliation. Sometimes this simply reflects converging tastes, but sometimes it is formally decided or at least deliberately adopted by people who wish to belong to a group or to advertise their relationship. Similarities in posture, facial expression, and behavior can signal affiliation. Similar accents and style of vocalization and gesture often signal affiliation and identity; when people spend more time together, their communicative behaviors tend to converge.

Digital or Analog?

Discussions of "nonverbal communication" often refer to signals as "codes," implying that they are *digital*, each type represented by a small and countable number of discrete options, each option expressing a unique, consistent, and particular meaning. At a first pass, this seems reasonable: She nodded or she shook her head; he smiled or he didn't, we kissed or we didn't, we shook hands or we didn't. For many purposes, this seems adequate, and in many interactions, we undoubtably do make just this sort of binary assessment. But each of these signals exists on an analog continuum. A smile can be faint, warm, radiant, and many gradations between. A kiss can be a mere brushing of lips against cheek (or even a slight touch of cheek on cheek), or it can be a prolonged, passionate encounter of lips and tongue that leave both parties breathless – with a deliciously ambiguous spectrum between these extremes. A handshake can be a quick palm-to-palm clasp, too brief even to be classified as limp or firm, or it can be limp and clammy or firm to the point that it is almost painful; it can be brief or prolonged, include a clasp just above or below the elbow with the other hand, and so forth. It can be preceded by a fist bump or followed by hooked thumbs. Like the smile and the kiss, the handshake lends itself to endless, and endlessly interpretable, variations.

Whether people experience and process these signals as digital (binary) or analog depends on the context, nature of the relationship, how the encounter is framed, and many other factors. One person may process the same signal as binary ("Well, I *did* kiss you goodbye!") and the other as analog ("It wasn't much of a kiss"). If anything, "nonverbal" signals are even more ambiguous than verbal. As researchers, we have to classify things in order to count and compare them, and factors such as the size of a sample may require us to use rather crude classifications (kiss or not kiss, handshake or not handshake, smile or smirk).[52] But both as researchers and as practitioners of communication, we are well-advised to remember that most everyday signals are ambiguous, sometimes deliberately so, sometimes carelessly so, often unavoidably so, and cannot confidently be understood or analyzed as simple digital codes. It is impossible to measure signals accurately or to assign them to unambiguous categories; quantification is by nature imprecise and essentially metaphorical.[53]

To function effectively, signals need to be produced in a way that will reliably attract the attention of an intended audience and will be readily recognized as a signal. However, there are some circumstances in which a signal is strategically intended to be perceived and recognized by a particular audience – and no one else. In such a "strategic signaling" situation, the perceptual characteristics of the signal may be "damped down" either by reduced amplitude (size, loudness, intensity) or by qualities that barely distinguish it from random behavior. Instead of a broad, emphatic wave of the hand, the originator may barely move the hand; eye contact may be brief but intense, a smile may be restricted to a brief twitch of the lips. People who know each other well may rely on actions that will appear meaningless or inconsequential to outsiders, or exchange signals only when no one else is watching or listening.

In sum, human communicative signals, like neural signals, combine analog with digital elements. The vocal, gestural, and written signals of language are produced on an analog continuum but sometimes intended by the speaker, and sometimes classified by the listener, as digital. However, often the analog qualities of a signal are intended or interpreted as expressing a meaning that is not readily digitized. Most of the nonlexicalized signals that may appear either independently or in combination with language are inherently analog, but they may also be digitized by the persons using them and interpreting them, or at least by researchers observing them. For these reasons I prefer to avoid terms like "*encode*" and "*decode*" for ordinary communication, reserving them for the work of spies and computer programmers.

Ad Hoc Signals

As noted at the beginning of the chapter, anything that humans can move, reshape, adjust, or alter in any way that is obtrusive (noticeable and distinguishable from simple random actions) can be turned into a signal. Like the

---

[52] Discourse analysis researchers who attempt to code the analog nature of conversation signals quickly find that their notation systems become burdensome to the point of incomprehensibility. This usually leads to the decision to sacrifice accuracy and detail for simplicity and practicality.
[53] Horgan (1998); Jones (1982).

pile of rocks used to mark a trail, these ad hoc signals often become conventionalized, but people can be quite inventive at devising signals from available objects or activities. An example was recently observed during a group backpacking trip in Yellowstone National Park, where the park service has installed pit toilets near each campsite. As a signal that the toilet was in use, the hikers agreed to leave a fallen branch across the trail to the toilet ("*door closed*") when it was in use, and parallel to the trail ("*door open*") when it was not.

As Sperber and Wilson[54] explain, to serve a communication function, an action or object must be ostensive: it must call attention to itself in a way that implies communicative intention. To communicate effectively, it must satisfy the assumption of maximal relevance, that it will precipitate a sufficient change to the mutual cognitive environment (one or more mutual cognitive contexts) to justify the effort of accessing the context in which it is relevant. This may be established by prior agreement, like the agreement to use a fallen branch to signal that the toilet is in use, but an object can activate a mutual cognitive context in many other ways – for example, by using a personally significant object or an unexpected action.

Summary

We humans use a wide range of signals to communicate with each other (and with our animal companions). Some of the signals we use are evolutionarily continuous with signals common among other social species. However, unlike most other animals, humans have volitional control over almost all aspects of our appearance and behavior. We can turn *any* perceptible action, sound, or artifact into a signal. To be effective, a signal needs to be distinct enough from random behavior to be perceived, recognized as a signal, and interpreted by the intended audience, but there are many circumstances in which it is desirable to use a minimally detectable signal, or even to produce a deliberately ambiguous signal. Most humans become quite adept in early childhood at making an action sufficiently obtrusive to be readily recognized as a signal. The ability to make a signal sufficiently subtle to be ambiguous, or recognized only by a particular other person, is a more sophisticated skill.

It has been customary to distinguish between signals that are and signals that are not part of language. However, observation of actual conversations shows that humans routinely incorporate a variety of so-called nonverbal signals into the flow of language, and that many of these signals play thoroughly lexical and syntactic roles in language use. It has been customary to conceptualize and

---

[54] Sperber and Wilson (1986).

Summary 145

discuss communicative signals as digitizable codes, but most signals are analog, not digital, in the way they are produced and interpreted, and quite frequently the analog components of a signal contribute significantly to the intended meaning.[55] Most signals, including well-defined words, are fundamentally ambiguous, capable of a range of interpretations according to accompanying signals and the communicative context. Terminology like *encoding* and *decoding* should be used sparingly if at all, and only when the referenced signals are sufficiently precise to justify the implicatures. Actual communication among humans is rarely truly code-like.

---

[55] There are often good methodological reasons for digitizing observed analog signals for purposes of analysis. That does not imply that those categories are meaningful to research participants.

7 Context

A central function of the brain and nervous system is to maintain a simulation model of the body in its physical and social environment, and a central function of perceptual systems is to provide information needed to keep that simulation model up to date and project it into potential futures. For humans the social environment is a crucial aspect of the environment, and communication is a core function of perception. In addition to building and maintaining relationships, communication obtains information about the physical and social environment to help maintain the brain's representations of the environment, especially the social environment.[1] Conversely, knowledge about the physical and social environment, represented in the simulation model, interacts with and shapes communication processes.

The brain's simulation model of the social environment includes the communication process(es) in which the person is currently engaged: what topics have been discussed, what ideas and feelings have been expressed and by whom, what is likely to happen next. All this is part of *context*, which also includes the social and physical setting and participants' general knowledge. Relevant aspects of the social setting include the identity of the participants, the nature of their relationships, values, beliefs, habits, and quirks. Context also includes metacommunicative information about others' emotional and cognitive states and processes.[2] Relevant aspects of the physical setting include the nature and location of the space, potential threats and resources.

At a surface level, the physical context may constrain the interaction – for example, if it is too noisy for comfortable speech. More important, what participants know, and reasonably believe other participants know, their "*common ground*," influences how thoughts are expressed, what can be assumed and what must be declared or otherwise established. Even the most basic and rudimentary functions of communication, grooming, play, and social hierarchy, require some mutual recognition of context, the physical and social

---

[1] A more detailed discussion will be provided in Chapter 8. [2] Heyes et al. (2020).

situation and past interactions. For more elaborate and sophisticated interactions, context plays an increasingly important role in understanding.

I will begin this chapter with a discussion of context and meaning, then discuss several aspects of context, beginning with cognitive context (ideas known by and salient to all participants) and the relevance of a signal to cognitive contexts as a factor in understanding communication. Then I will discuss the social context, the participants in a conversation, the setting, nature of the conversation, what has gone before, the nature of the relationships, and the purposes and nature of the conversation itself. I will discuss various means of framing a conversation or relationship and the contribution of politeness norms and behaviors to relevance and understanding.

Cognitive Context and Relevance

Successful communication relies on common ground between speaker and audience. This has often been expressed as "*shared*" contextual knowledge, but the concept of shared knowledge raises insurmountable epistemological difficulties.[3] Each participant in a conversation knows about the various aspects of the conversation only through what has been perceived and can be readily recalled. What has been perceived depends on attention, and what is represented in memory depends on several factors, including the individual's values, beliefs, and assumptions. Given the differences among individuals with respect to each of these factors, it is unlikely that any two persons will ever have exactly the same contextual knowledge – and there is no way to know whether they do.

Sperber and Wilson[4] analyze the basis for communication in terms of *cognitive contexts*, conceptual schemas and scripts and representations of the social and physical environment. The cognitive contexts that are both known and salient to an individual at any moment is that person's *cognitive environment*. In place of "common ground," Sperber and Wilson propose that communication is based on *mutual cognitive environment*, the cognitive contexts that all participants believe to be known and salient to themselves and other participants. This formulation recognizes that cognitive environment is fluid and constantly changing, but, like "common ground," "mutual cognitive environment" is unavoidably limited by solipsism, the impossibility of knowing precisely what is known and salient to others.

The concepts represent different assumptions, but both are useful. I will use *common ground* to refer to interlocutors' assumptions about the general cultural knowledge, beliefs, and expectations that are known to all participants.

---

[3] Clark (1996); Sperber and Wilson (1986). [4] Sperber and Wilson (1986).

I will use *mutual cognitive environment*, consistent with Sperber and Wilson, to refer to the specific knowledge and so forth, the cognitive contexts, that interlocutors believe to be both known and presently salient to all participants.

The idea of cognitive context also underlies Sperber and Wilson's concept of relevance, which in turn provides a reasonable basis for the slippery concept of *meaning*. Sperber and Wilson[5] argue that humans have a basic drive for relevance, both in processing perception generally and specifically in communication. *Relevance* can be understood generally as the efficiency with which interpreting a signal will affect the mental state of speaker and audience members, their mutual cognitive environment. Relevance is directly proportional to the effect a message has on one or more mutual cognitive contexts, and inversely proportional to the amount of effort required to achieve that effect. There is an element of circularity in this definition, since it includes the effort required to identify a relevant cognitive context as well as the effort required to decide how the message is relevant and update or reinforce the associated beliefs and knowledge.

The relevance/meaning of an utterance or interaction can include changes to multiple contexts, changes to representations of the physical and social environment, relationships, the other person's character, personality, and intentions, one's own social status, and so forth. Even one's own self-concept and sense of personal identity can be altered by an interaction, and this is part of the meaning. Social schemas and scripts may also be altered, as when a young adolescent learns how to flirt or learns which types of humor are acceptable at a funeral. Crucial contexts also include other participants' identities and emotional sensitivities in relation to cultural norms of politeness.[6] A thoroughly detailed analysis of *any* social interaction must be open to *all* dimensions of context.

Cognitive environment is similar to Damasio's concept of representation of the state of the body in the social and physical environment, although Sperber and Wilson restrict the concept to those aspects of the overall representation that are salient at any given time. The cognitive environment includes representation of the physical surroundings, the activities currently taking place, the persons who are present, and the nature of their participation in the present activities, each as a separate *cognitive context*. It also includes knowledge about the physical surroundings, activities, and relationships among those present, including associated social norms and expectations (more *cognitive contexts*). Knowledge about the history of each of these elements (the surroundings, the activity, the persons present and their relationships) may be more or less salient (as *cognitive contexts*) to different participants.

---

[5] Sperber and Wilson (1986/1995); Wilson and Sperber (2004).   [6] Leech (1983, 2005).

Expectations and hopes for future action within and future changes to these various elements (Damasio's concept of *forward projection*) may also be salient as cognitive contexts.

Mutual cognitive environment is updated throughout an interaction as participants' interpretations of others' reactions lead them to update their beliefs about others' cognitive states. Maintaining and updating the mutual cognitive environment is a requirement for satisfactory communication and an implicit task throughout an interaction, although it frequently happens that some participants take more responsibility for it than others.

Context and Interpretation

Sperber and Wilson argue that all signals, including language, are inherently ambiguous. Interpretation relies on the mutual assumption that speakers will use the most relevant signal available (maximum effect/minimum effort) and that, if the relevance to the most salient context is not apparent, listeners will seek a context in which the signal *is* relevant. Initially Sperber and Wilson argued that the search ceases when any relevant context is found,[7] but in later writings, they acknowledge that a signal can be relevant to more than one context,[8] and complete understanding often requires an extended search for relevance. Consider a possible interaction between two sisters. As Judy walks toward the door, Jill says, "Don't forget your umbrella." The remark is only relevant if Jill believes that it is going to rain, which changes Judy's belief about the weather. It is also potentially relevant to Judy's perception that Jill believes she, Judy, is careless and forgetful, so Judy replies, "Yes, Mother." Since Jill is her sister, not her mother, the reply is only relevant in the context of Judy's attitude toward their relationship, leading Jill to interpret the reply as an ironic put-down.[9]

Establishing Common Ground. As Clark notes, one of the benefits of common cultural membership is that it enables us to make reasonably valid assumptions about common ground. If two Oregonians encounter each other in some remote part of the world, they can each safely assume that the other has similar knowledge about political institutions, Oregon's typical mountains, forests, and deserts, the major universities and their athletic teams, and so on. Beyond these culture-based assumptions, we often assess the probability of common ground based on language, dialect, and pronunciation, dress, and personal adornment. If uncertain, we may use preparatory questions to ascertain the extent of common ground and mutual cognitive environment, or supply a brief summary of the context required to understand a joke, story,

---

[7] Sperber and Wilson (1986/1995).   [8] Wilson and Sperber (2004).   [9] See Chapter 12.

or comment. When common ground or mutual cognitive environment is uncertain, people commonly use prefatory (or post hoc explanatory) remarks to reinforce the salience of relevant contexts. This might consist of a reminder (prefaced by a face-saving phrase like "as you probably realize . . .") or an explanation ("I was referring to . . .").

In the following sections, I will discuss several types of context that are part of people's representation of the physical and social environment. I will return to a more detailed discussion of relevance at the end of the chapter..

Social Settings

Even the briefest and most casual conversation occurs in a social setting; indeed, every communication interaction *creates* a social setting. Asking a stranger for the time, or even making eye contact, creates a social setting, with certain implicit rules for the engagement. Social settings vary along several dimensions, including participants and roles as well as features such as formality, intimacy, duration, expectation of privacy, and so on. These dimensions vary from one culture to another, but are usually taken for granted within a given culture, and performed automatically and effortlessly.

Clark[10] lists several categories of social settings. *Personal settings* include conversations of various sorts, ranging from asking a stranger for the time through street corner gossip to a rambling conversation at a party or reception. *Nonpersonal settings* include monologues of various sorts, such as political speeches, stand-up comedy, and lectures. *Institutional settings* are somewhat similar to ordinary conversation, but their function, topics, and structure are established and limited by institutional rules. Examples include classroom discussions, news conferences, courtroom testimony, and debates. *Prescriptive settings* are a subset of institutional settings, in which words to be spoken are completely or largely fixed beforehand. Examples include wedding ceremonies, induction into an organization, and swearing in officials. In most of these settings, prescribed language is used to create a new "social reality," to change the social status, rights, and obligations of one or more participants. *Fictional settings* include plays and other performances, in which speakers represent ideas and responses of someone else. These may represent an author's idealized version of a casual conversation, but they usually differ in important respects from actual conversations. In *private settings*, people speak only to themselves – for example, rehearsing an idea, exclaiming about something surprising, and so on. These utterances may be *potentially* social, in the case of rehearsing language for an expected future conversation, but

---

[10] Clark (1996).

often they are social only in the metaphorical sense of an internalized dialog, a "virtual" social interaction in a nonsocial setting.[11]

Members of a culture share schemas and scripts for various types of social setting such as banquets, flirting, sporting events, and business meetings; these culturally shared schemas and scripts are part of *common ground*, but the schema for a particular social setting will ordinarily be salient, part of our *cognitive environment*, only when we are thinking about that setting. When engaged in a particular social interaction, we also have (as a cognitive context) a detailed knowledge of the present social interaction, along with an implicit understanding of how this particular interaction compares to the abstract script in our culture.

Participants. Clark also lists several categories of participants who may be involved in a conversation. The primary participants are the *speaker* and the *addressee(s)*. If a remark is addressed to only one member of a group, the persons not directly addressed are *side-participants*. Other people within hearing of the conversation may be *overhearers*, a category that includes *bystanders* (their presence is known) and *eavesdroppers* (their presence may not be known.) The presence of side-participants may require the speaker to specify who is addressed. The presence of known overhearers or the possibility of eavesdroppers may require the speaker to take precautions such as concealing actual meanings, avoiding sensitive topics, or expressing sensitive or controversial ideas with particular care.

Secondary Audiences. A category not discussed by Clark is *secondary audiences*,[12] other people who may not be physically present but who may learn of the conversation from a participant or other secondary source. This may be particularly relevant to public discourse, as in political speeches, news conferences, and so on, but it can also be relevant to interpersonal conversation. In a child's conversation with one parent, the other parent is potentially a secondary audience, and other relatives and family friends may also be secondary audiences. Talk by politicians and other public figures is almost always at least partly intended for secondary audiences; in the case of news conferences and interviews, the implicit secondary audiences are more important than the primary audience.

Lynne Cameron and I examined a public meeting that took place several years ago in Portland, Oregon, following the controversial death of an African American woman, Kendra James, who was shot and killed by police officers

---

[11] It might be reasonable to regard "social" as a fuzzy category, a matter of degrees rather than "yes or no." That is, when I think about how my mentor might respond to this passage and how I would reply to him, it can reasonably be argued that the conversation is neither fully private nor fully social. See Chapters 9 and 15 for a more detailed discussion.

[12] Ritchie and Cameron (2014).

during a routine traffic stop.[13] In an attempt to address concerns about police use of lethal force among members of the community, the mayor and chief of police held a public meeting that included a long presentation by police officers who had investigated the incident. Prior to the formal presentation, the mayor and police chief each gave an informal speech, and a community leader responded. The police chief, in particular, seemed to be phrasing his responses to questions and concerns from the audience with the expectation that, should the officer who shot the woman be brought to trial, any public statement he had made at the meeting might be entered as evidence. Thus, the prospective jury was an unacknowledged secondary audience. The mayor apparently chose her phrasing to avoid the risk of antagonizing voters from other parts of the city – another unacknowledged secondary audience.

These secondary audiences were apparently not salient to many members of the physically present (primary) audience, and the officials' cautious phrasing contributed to the perception, among members of the primary audience, that the community's concerns were neither acknowledged nor addressed. The community leaders who spoke also appeared to choose their phrasing to please *their* constituencies within the community, reinforcing the impression that the mayor and police chief were ignoring their concerns. In part because of the failure to acknowledge explicitly these secondary audiences, the meeting completely failed, leaving police-community relations even worse than before.

Another example occurred during the 2016 US Presidential campaign, when Hillary Clinton referred to the White Supremacists and others who supported Donald Trump as "deplorables." She was directly addressing an audience of urban liberals, but the remark was reported widely in more conservative rural communities, where it was not at all well-received. Clinton's failure to consider how her remark would be understood by these secondary audiences is one factor that cost her the election. In general, in a casual conversation, a remark critical of an absent third party, if it is subsequently reported to that person, can have serious relational consequences.

Face-to-Face vs. Mediated. Clark argues that casual, face-to-face conversation is the basic form of language use, and all other forms are derivative of conversation. Certainly face-to-face conversation affords the widest range of signals, particularly when people are close enough to touch each other and to observe each other's facial and vocalic expressions. In face-to-face conversation, we attend to subtle changes in voice quality (tone, loudness, talking speed, etc.), facial expression, and gesture. We may perceive subtle scents, which can influence us even if we aren't consciously aware of them. The more

---

[13] Ritchie and Cameron (2014).

a communication situation differs from this basic setting, the fewer of these signals and cues are available.

Another important feature of face-to-face communication is its extemporaneous nature: because utterances are heard and processed as they are produced, they can be repaired, but they cannot be deleted or revised. Speakers can monitor listener's responses and make repairs to correct apparent misunderstandings and clarify their intentions; they can also shape subsequent utterances in response to cues from listeners. Speakers can anticipate potential responses and consider alternative ways of expressing an idea, but this is likely to take more time than is available, and requires that the speaker receive permission to interrupt the ordinary flow of conversation. Participants' awareness of this is part of cognitive context, part of the (presumably mutual, but often differentially salient) cognitive environment.

Ordinarily there is no record of a face-to-face conversation.[14] In ordinary conversation, participants can recall the exact words that were spoken for no more than a couple of intonation units. As each utterance is processed, its general meaning is added to a mental representation of the conversation.[15] That general meaning is what both speaker and hearers recall, and it constitutes the discourse context. (If an utterance is remarkable in some way, it may be stored verbatim, as part of the discourse context, accessible to subsequent recall and reference.) The recalled representation of the gist of the conversation thus far, the discourse context, is available for subsequent reference, and it is continuously updated as new utterances are produced and processed.

Each of these participant roles is part of the overall schema for conversation, with implicit rules for each type of social setting. Specific knowledge about the participants in the present interaction, including the possible secondary audiences, is part of the "present interaction" cognitive context, presumed to be salient to all participants, continually updated by each participant, and accessible for inferences of relevance.

The Discourse Context

When someone complains about a remark having been "taken out of context," they are usually referring to the discourse context, the nature of the conversation, the gist of what has been said, and the immediate sequence of utterances that preceded and followed the remark. The discourse context is ordinarily the most salient to participants and the primary focus and source of relevance. Like the social setting and participants, both the nature of the conversation and the

---

[14] Technology, particularly the cell phone, seems to be changing this assumption (Chapter 14).
[15] Chapter 4.

gist of the sequence of preceding utterances[16] are part of participants' (and observers') cognitive context.

Nature and Purpose of the Talk. As discussed in Chapter 3, language and talk probably originated in signals exchanged for a very limited range of purposes or functions: grooming, alert, status negotiation, play, and sexual interaction. All these still figure prominently in language use, but the functions of conversation have expanded to a much larger range, as human cultures continue to invent more and more needs that communication can satisfy – and more and more types of signaling to fulfill these needs. Among the most common purposes, relationship maintenance is still an important part of almost every type of conversation. But this simple function has been elaborated, refined, and transformed, even as entirely new conversation functions and purposes have developed.

Other purposes for talk include economic (business negotiations and transactions of various sorts), instruction, inquiry, and decision-making. Each type of conversation follows known and shared scripts; these shared scripts are examples of mutual cognitive contexts. Each affects the mental state (cognitive environment) of the participants, and may affect their perceptions of the relationships and the physical environment (all part of the cognitive environment).

In addition to these are the institutionalized, ceremonial conversations by which language is used to solidify and alter social reality. Institutionalized ceremonies of this sort sustain the status of the sponsoring institutions (schools and the "institution" of marriage as well as the civil and religious authorities that authorize the ceremonies). Participants attain a new social status by virtue of the sponsoring institutions, and witnesses affirm the validity and reality of the institution and the new social status by their side-participation.

The relationship maintenance function has been elaborated to include sub-genres such as flirting, teasing, confiding, complimenting, scolding, joking, telling jokes, and storytelling. These types of interaction play a role in many of the uses of conversation, particularly but not exclusively in relationship maintenance. Several of them will be discussed in more detail in later chapters. All these are represented as "contexts" (schemas, concepts, scripts), accessible for inferences of relevance, and liable to be updated while processing signals and utterances.

What Has Been Said Before, by Whom, and in What Sequence. The most basic and most common meaning of "context" is what came immediately before, but utterances often refer to other utterances that came earlier in the

---

[16] In ordinary conversation, the actual words we hear are recalled for little more than a few seconds; after a few minutes not more than the general meaning of what was said will be recalled (Enfield, 2017; see Chapter 8 for a more detailed discussion).

same conversation or even in previous conversations.[17] Sometimes the connection is only implied, sometimes it is explicitly stated. It may be important who made the prior statement; in an argument or debate, this can be particularly important. In a debate or an instructional conversation, the sequence of prior utterances may be important as well. Given the limits of short-term memory, in an ordinary conversation the exact words will be forgotten within a few seconds, leaving only the gist and emotions.[18]

Conversation rarely proceeds according to one topic at a time. Even storytelling is often scattered over several speaking turns, interspersed with other comments that are marginally relevant if at all. The extended context of the present discourse can be quite important for making sense of a story, argument, or explanation. Many of these forms, including stories and explanations, can be produced by a single speaker (sometimes in one speaking turn, sometimes scattered over several), or they can be coproduced by several speakers. All this is part of participants' "cognitive environment," their representation of the social and discursive environment.

Relationship to Broader Discourse. Utterances can refer to other conversations in several ways. In scholarly, scientific, and religious discourse, the entire preceding body of discourse about the topic is potentially relevant, but may be only briefly or fleetingly mentioned. Each lecture, discussion, sermon, or publication is part of a conversation that may have started many centuries ago and may continue for many more decades or even centuries. In any discourse, ideas, images, and stories from the broader culture may be referenced or echoed. Often an utterance can be understood without reference to the cultural antecedents, but the cultural context provides richer opportunities for relevance.

Even casual conversations among friends and family members often refer to events and conversations that may have happened years ago. This knowledge about collective and individual past experiences is part of common ground and, potentially, part of the mutual cognitive environment, subject to alteration by relevant utterances in the present interaction. Within a conversation, participants are expected to produce appropriate back-channel responses, and to connect each utterance to what has gone immediately before, as well as the overall history of the conversation. This requires that participants maintain a representation of the conversation and project where it might lead.

Relationship

The nature of the relationship has a strong influence on how a conversation progresses and, conversely, can be altered as relationship-relevant signals are

---

[17] Chapter 9.   [18] Chafe (2012).

processed. Relationships can be defined along several dimensions, including purpose, status, affective valence, commitments and obligations, and prior history. Each of these dimensions implies roles and expectations, which in turn has implications for what Goffman[19] called *face*. Knowledge, beliefs, and expectations about these relational dimensions are crucial contexts that shape and are affected by communication. Participants' ideas about present relationships are usually affirmed, but can sometimes be radically changed by an utterance or even a single signal. For example, even a subtle indication of sexual interest can change *friendship* to *love affair* – other, equally subtle signals can have the opposite effect. An unmitigated face threat can change *trust* to *wariness*; an act of unexpected kindness or a face-supporting act can have the opposite effect.

Affective Valence. If the relationship is intimate, more informal language may be used, and participants will make more assumptions about common ground. If the relationship is hierarchical, the lower-ranking participants may exercise greater care in how they conduct themselves, the kind of language they use, what ideas they express, and so on. Family members, lovers, and very close friends may engage in teasing and other banter with each other that they would not use with casual acquaintances.[20] Even within a relationship type, rules and expectations may vary. For example, in traditional families, the parent–child relationship and even the relationship between spouses is commonly hierarchical, whereas members of more "open" families assume both greater equality and greater intimacy.[21]

As with other aspects of context, behavior in a conversation is influenced by how participants *perceive* the relationships – the *actual* nature of the relationship is not otherwise knowable. This distinction can be important if two participants have different perceptions of a relationship (e.g. one believes the relationship is one of sexual intimacy and the other does not, or one believes it is hierarchical and the other believes it is equality). Different perceptions often lead to misunderstanding and conflict.

Framing

Framing generally refers to using language (or any other signal) to influence how others understand a relationship, topic of discourse, or conversation.[22] An interpersonal example of conversation framing occurred several years ago when a former coworker with whom I had been on friendly terms called me on the telephone. After a few minutes of gossip, catching up on old friends and what we had both been doing since we both left the organization, he asked,

---

[19] Goffman (1963).   [20] Chapter 11.
[21] Fitzpatrick and Ritchie (1994); Ritchie and Fitzpatrick (1990).   [22] Chapter 4.

"Hey, why don't we do lunch sometime?" While I was looking over my calendar to identify a suitable date, he continued, "By the way, I've been meaning to ask: have you updated your life insurance recently?" Abruptly, my conversation frame, "What kind of conversation is this?," changed from "old friends catching up with each other" to "a sales call." Consequently, my event frame for (and interest in) the proposed lunch date underwent a rapid change. This abrupt change in understanding of what kind of conversation I was in changed how I interpreted not only his *subsequent* remarks but also everything that had gone before, and the nature of the relationship.[23] The *"four walls"* persuasion strategy hinges on a similar strategic reframing: A series of questions, framed as discussion of personal opinion or tastes, creates a sense of commitment to a product or a cause; the final question reframes the entire series as a request to make a purchase or donation consistent with the previous responses.

"What kind of conversation is this?" is one type of *frame*, and the process by which people invoke or activate a particular conversation frame is one type of *framing*.[24] My former coworker's initial friendly greeting framed the call as *social*, invoking one familiar script, but his question about life insurance abruptly reframed it as *sales*, invoking a very different script. Conversations can be framed in several ways, including aspects of the physical setting, use of formal or informal language, and many other cues. Like my phone call with the former coworker, conversations are often reframed as they go, sometimes repeatedly during the course of a long conversation.

We routinely engage in several types of conversation, often within the space of an hour or two. In addition to marketing calls and old friends catching up, we engage in gossip, content-free chatter about sports, celebrities, and other inconsequential topics, requesting and giving advice, giving and receiving orders, arguing, evaluating alternatives and making decisions, and so on. Each type of conversation has implicit and generally understood scripts (which may differ both between cultures and between persons). Sometimes the type of conversation is signaled explicitly ("Can I ask you a question?" "Could you explain how to use this?" "Did you see the game last night?"), but often the framing is more subtle, only implied by such cues as the kind of language used, gesture and facial expression, and so on.

We learn and use scripts for many kinds of conversations, including greetings. These tend to be automatic. We learn scripts for ordering at a restaurant, introducing people, getting acquainted, offering congratulations or condolences – and passing a stranger on a narrow sidewalk or trail. Most of us have several scripts for each social setting, and select from these accessible scripts

---

[23] Chapter 9; Arundale (2010).   [24] Tannen (1991); Tracy (1997).

"on the fly." We may not even realize we are following a script until another participant deviates from it or, like my former colleague-turned-insurance salesman, switches to a different script. Scripts are closely related to frames;[25] activating a frame usually activates one or more relevant and often well-rehearsed scripts. A conversational frame tells us what kind of conversation we're in and triggers a relevant script (and a relational frame tells what kind of relationship we're in – possibly helping shape the activated script). Once activated, a conversation script establishes or at least influences how the conversation will proceed, how utterances follow one another, how signals will be generated and exchanged, and so on..

Physical Surroundings

Various aspects of the physical surroundings influence the nature of the conversation, and may also furnish topical content. Most obvious is the effect of specialized spaces such as an art museum, church, shopping center, or wilderness trail. Furnishings provide clues to the appropriate nature of an interaction as well as providing topical content. Both the size and shape of open space and the arrangement of furnishings and other objects influence and constrain physical proximity and movement, as well as the number of people who may participate in a conversation and their disposition with respect to each other. (Often spaces are arranged or selected precisely for this purpose.)

The physical environment is itself available as a topic of conversation, in part because by default it is assumed to be perceptible to all, hence automatically part of the mutual cognitive environment. The weather or recently blooming flowers are ready and salient mutual cognitive contexts. In face-to-face conversations, all participants are ordinarily potentially aware of the nature of the space and the furnishings, although they may not all be equally aware of associated cultural assumptions and practices. Moreover, participants don't always notice relevant aspects of the physical surroundings unless they are made salient. In mediated conversations such as telephone or texting, the participants may occupy and be influenced by physical and social spaces that are not perceptible to other participants.

Culture

Culture can be understood as an enduring pattern of beliefs, behaviors, values, and expectations common to a large group of interacting people that guide or at least influence their interactions. Cultures are learned informally and are

---

[25] Tannen (1991).

usually accepted with little thought as "the way we do things." Large complex cultures usually include multiple "subcultures" and "cocultures," that share many of the features of the inclusive culture but are distinctive in various ways. Within the overarching "American" culture, for example, rural Midwestern farm culture and urban Mexican American culture both share many of the features of the overarching culture but also express easily identified features unique to them. Each of these is a *subculture* within the inclusive national culture, a *coculture* with respect to each other. Enduring organizations, occupations, even families and friendship groups also tend to develop distinctive cultures; most people belong to multiple and often overlapping cocultures (e.g. academic, family, urban, etc.), and readily adapt their behavior and expectations to the culture that is most salient at the time.

Broadly defined cultures (e.g. associated with a nationality or ethnicity) vary along several dimensions that are relevant to communication, including individualism versus collectivism, immediacy, power distance, context, immediacy, and masculine versus feminine orientation.[26] Individualist cultures tend to give priority to individual expression and needs, and emphasize personal relationships; collectivist cultures give priority to social harmony and the needs of the social group, and emphasize membership in a primary social group. *Power distance* refers to the importance of hierarchical versus egalitarian relationships. In higher context cultures, people are expected to understand meanings that are implicit in the context; in lower context cultures, meanings are more likely to be explicitly stated. *Immediacy* refers to the amount of interpersonal contact expected as part of communication; higher immediacy cultures generally expect a higher level of sensory stimulation than lower immediacy cultures. *Masculine-oriented* cultures emphasize more stereotypically gender behaviors (men suppress emotional expression; women behave more submissively). In *feminine-oriented cultures*, both males and females have more freedom of nonverbal expression, and there is greater equality between genders.

Within these broad generalizations, specific cultures usually include implicit rules about the use of communicative signals, including touch, language (e.g. vocabulary and pronunciation), loudness, vocal inflection, talking speed, eye contact, turn-taking, and so on. Academicians and even advanced students often find that the communication practices that serve them well in a school setting are less appropriate in a family setting or among close friends. Conversely, the communication styles associated with family and close friends may not be well-received in an academic or business setting – particularly if they involve use of profanity, sexual references, or ungrammatical sentence

---

[26] Burgoon et al. (2010).

structure. All these are part of our culturally conditioned scripts, assumed to be part of the mutual cognitive environment. Signals are interpreted according to these scripts, and, if they are not mutually accessible (as is often the case in intercultural situations), the differences may lead to serious misunderstanding.

Cultures and subcultures also include assumptions about what is "common knowledge" and can be taken for granted. Academic subcultures assume knowledge about theories, concepts, methods, and terminology – as well as about academic practices and the organization of academic institutions. Other occupational cultures such as business, religious, athletic, and recreational cultures have their own taken-for-granted bases of knowledge, methods, relationships, and specialized language. Within each of these broad cultures, subcultures have unique practices, knowledge, and assumptions. Most of us belong to many crosscutting groups, each with a unique "dialect" as well as a particular set of beliefs, attitudes, and knowledge. The knowledge, practices, and beliefs associated with the culture of a particular social group or organization constitute a kind of schema and, like other schemas, can be made more salient by encountering any part of it. When I encounter an academic colleague who is also an avid hiker or skier, any of a number of cues may raise the salience of one of these shared cultures – that is, may *frame* the ensuing conversation as "academic," "hiking," or "skiing." Acculturation or socialization includes learning these implicit norms, practices, and assumptions.

Politeness and Relevance

Politeness (face) theory can be traced to Goffman's insight that our social interactions take the form of a drama-like performance, in which we present a social *self* by playing a *role* based on cultural norms and social expectations.[27] Role performance, self-presentation, and social status are highly dependent on the support and cooperation of others with whom we interact. Any situation or event that impairs one's role performance diminishes one's *face*, the public perception of competent role performance.

Goffman introduced concepts of "face" and "facework" to express the processes through which people perceive and maintain their social status, standing in their community,[28] and role performance. Two basic concepts are "positive face" and "negative face." *Positive face* is the perceived state of being accepted and approved by other members of one's community. *Negative face* is the perceived state of having personal autonomy, the freedom to act according to one's own wishes and impulses. Any action or communication that implies that another person is not fully accepted and approved

---

[27] Goffman (1963, 1967).   [28] Goffman (1963, 1967).

(positive face) or is not free to act as they wish without constraint (negative face or perceived autonomy) is a *face-threatening act* and, as such, is subject to sanction and potential retaliation. Politeness norms and practices that support one's own and others' face and avoid or ameliorate face threats are taken so much for granted that they are scarcely noticed, though they are part of virtually every social interaction.

These factors – positive face and perceived autonomy, the effects of face-threatening acts, and cultural norms of politeness – are assumed, at least within a common culture, to be part of common ground and at least potentially part of the mutual cognitive environment in every interaction. The face needs of conversation participants and their responses to face threats and impoliteness are also part of the mutual cognitive environment. All these contribute to relevance and to the relevance-based interpretation of signals and utterances. Leech[29] supplemented Grice's[30] maxims of conversational cooperation with six politeness maxims – Tact, Generosity, Approbation, Modesty, Agreement, and Sympathy – and developed a general theory of politeness combining these maxims with Relevance Theory, itself a distillation of Grice's cooperative principle.[31]

Indirect communication was one of the motivations for Relevance Theory, and facework is often a motivation for indirect communication.[32] The search for a context in which a signal is relevant plays a role in every aspect of conversation, especially beginning and endings, in play, metaphor, and humor.

Summary: Context and Homeostasis

Humans are inherently social, and the growing complexity of human social organization has apparently played a driving role both in the initial evolution of language and in its subsequent elaboration and development. In ordinary conversation, we spend much of our time and attention discovering the extent of and maintaining our common ground[33] and mutual cognitive environment. This is necessary for maintaining and enriching interpersonal relationships as well as for coordinated action of any sort. Maintaining a mutual cognitive environment is a necessary part of maintaining an accurate collective representation of the social and physical environment, which is in turn essential for maintaining the group-level homeostasis. It is also essential for individuals as a basis for maintaining an accurate representation of body-in-environment, as a basis for forward projection and choosing among alternative actions in the present, hence for individual homeostasis.

---

[29] Leech (2005).   [30] Grice (1975).   [31] See Chapter 8 for a more detailed discussion.
[32] Chapters 8 and 9.   [33] Berger and Calabrese (1975).

Context is a multifaceted concept. It includes the immediate physical and social environment, the physical setting, the people who are present, and the nature and extent of their participation in the conversation. It also includes perceptions about the nature of the relationships among participants, and the nature and purpose of the conversation. More broadly, it includes perceptions about cultural knowledge – knowledge of extended physical environments, knowledge of relevant scripts and schemas, knowledge of personal history and shared cultural history. The use of language and other signals often frames the nature of an interaction, evokes or changes scripts. Conversely, scripts and schemas are learned and changed primarily through conversation; even perceptions about a relationship itself may be altered within a single conversation. Context is socially constructed, primarily through ordinary conversations.

In any conversation, the mutual cognitive environment will include what has gone before, and contexts directly relevant to the topic. However, a wide range of other contexts are potentially relevant, including the nature of the conversation and the relationship, social and cultural norms, and so on. The extended contexts may become salient at any time as part of the search for relevance, with implications for conversation structure that will be discussed in Chapter 9.

8 Relationships and Groups

Among the social primates, including humans, basic relationships are a function of the social structure of the primary group. A primary context for conversation, language use, and social interactions generally is the group in its various manifestations, ranging from small family, friendship, and work groups to the larger organizations of 150 to 200 people that constitute the primary group.[1] This chapter addresses the homeostasis-maintaining role of communication in relationships and groups, with particular attention to facework, social status, and social control.

Primate troops are organized around a dominance hierarchy; dominance and submission are communicated by vocal, gesture, and posture signals, reinforced by threat displays and occasional instances of actual violence. Mutual support coalitions of alliances, friendships, and kinship relations are created, maintained, and reinforced by grooming, social play, and sharing of food and other resources. Among other primates, parenting and family relationships are usually restricted to mothers, grandmothers, aunts, and sisters. Sexual relationships are more complicated. Among many species, access to sex partners is a function of the dominance hierarchy, limited to one or perhaps a few dominant males. Because of consistent high levels of stress, the lowest-ranking females are often effectively sterile. In some species the situation is more fluid, with mating opportunities contingent on elaborate signaling and display rituals. Signals of fertility, sexual availability, and sexual interest vary accordingly. Relations with members of other groups are often hostile, based on mutual aggression signaled by threat displays.

Basic Human Relationships

Basic communication relationships within human societies support a similar but larger and more nuanced set of relationship types. Hierarchical status (dominance and submission) is competitive, often involving some degree of

---

[1] Dunbar (1996).

aggression, usually regulated by cultural and group norms. The amount of cooperation and support varies among cultures and individual relationships. Peer relationships (friends, social groups, and teams) and family relationships are primarily cooperative and supportive, but often with some degree of competition and aggression. Relationships across social and cultural boundaries (in-group/out-group) can be competitive, aggressive, even hostile, or cooperative and supportive, often a combination of competitive and cooperative. All these relationships are created and maintained through communication, and they are the primary settings for conversation and language use. These relationship types have been expanded and elaborated over the centuries as cultures have grown increasingly complex and elaborate, but they are all subject to the same basic processes of homeostasis.

As society becomes more complex, both communication and its interaction with homeostasis become more complex. Conversation almost always has both a paratelic "grooming" and a telic, informative function, although the balance between them varies. In a business or professional relationship, telic communication may motivate most interactions, although social bonding through paratelic social communication is still important, and accounts for two-thirds of all language use.[2] In a romantic relationship or friendship, paratelic communication is more likely to dominate, though planning and decision-making requires some telic communication.

These basic relationships and social contexts have been elaborated in many ways as cultures developed and expanded their reach, facilitated by and interacting with language and technological development. Most relationships and groups are characterized by some combination of competition and conflict on the one hand, cooperation and support on the other hand. All cultures and groups have norms and practices (if only implicit) that regulate the balance of competition and conflict with cooperation and support in order to maintain group and individual homeostasis. As language and relationships have become more complex and conversation has developed as a means of recruiting and maintaining relationships, language use has developed the potential to increase as well as decrease stress. Accordingly, stress-reducing facework is vital to almost all social interactions, and it is built into the communication norms and practices of most cultures and relationships.

Homeostasis, Relationships, and Social Groups

Homeostasis includes the ability of conscious and deliberative minds to create new forms of life regulation.[3] Weapons, monuments, and central air

---

[2] Dunbar (1996).   [3] Damasio (2018).

conditioning are all examples of how culture affects homeostasis by regulating bodily and cognitive functions and by altering the environment. Other examples include the blossoming of complex relationships and social groups that satisfy various needs and desires – then generate new needs and desires.[4]

Many of individual humans' homeostasis needs are addressed by social interactions, including gaining and maintaining social status, building and maintaining relationships, avoiding or winning conflicts, social and environmental surveillance, access to sexual opportunities and food. Given the importance of groups (and other forms of social organization) for coping with ecological threats and opportunities, the group's homeostasis is itself important to individual group members: "No brain is an island."[5] A similar argument applies to relationship. To the extent that the Self's homeostasis depends on or is at least improved by interacting with a particular Other (a mate, friend, or ally), the Other's homeostasis becomes important to the Self. Threats to Other will be perceived as indirect threats to Self, and resources for Other as indirect resources for Self. Conversely, if interacting with an enemy or member of a hostile group *decreases* the homeostasis of Self, then threats to the enemy will be benefits and benefits to the enemy will be threats to Self.

Thus, extended relations of cooperation and conflict, love and hate develop from homeostasis-directed feelings. The biochemistry of relationship – endorphins that are released by casual conversation, sex, and friendly touch, and stress chemicals like cortisol that are released by even the presence of a dominant or aggressive Other – is itself part of homeostasis processes. Interacting with a friend or lover, shaking hands or exchanging smiles with a casual acquaintance or even a stranger, all release endorphins and add to homeostasis; interacting with an enemy, a sneer or insult or even the dreaded *possibility* of a sneer or insult, all release cortisol and adrenaline, increase stress and anxiety, and detract from homeostasis.

Relationships, like individuals, are characterized by homeostasis, a forward-projected balance of inputs and outputs, emotions, and responses. Individual representations of a relationship and its homeostatic balance are part of the representation of the social environment, and perceptions and actions related to a relationship are integral to maintaining personal homeostasis. Every member of a relationship or group has a cognitive representation of the relationship and group that shapes communication. Moscovici characterized the aggregate of all these interactions as *social representations*[6] because an individual's perception of how a group collectively understands itself and its environment can differ

---

[4] Consistent with Dennett (2017), some of the features of modern culture, including the needs and desires they generate, are harmful to both group and individual homeostasis, and others are neutral, neither beneficial nor harmful (see Chapter 3).
[5] Everett (2017, p. 121).   [6] Moscovici (1961; Farr and Moscovici, 1984).

from the individual's private assessment; this can even be true of a dyadic relationship. As individuals, we participate in maintaining the homeostasis of our relationships and the groups to which we belong, as part of and in parallel with our own homeostasis.[7]

Individual-level homeostasis extends to the level of relationships and groups, and eventually to entire cultures. To the extent that a group or relationship is of either practical or emotional importance to an individual, the stability, future-oriented welfare, and homeostasis of the group has a direct bearing on the homeostasis of the individual. An implication of this is that behavior that detracts from the homeostasis of the group or other members of the group will be indirectly detrimental to the individual. The detriment may also be direct, including banishment, termination of relationships, ridicule, or scolding. Individual communicative behavior will tend to be guided by the norms, values, and practices typical of the group (i.e. by the group *culture*). Another implication is that relational partners and primary group members will be motivated both to support each other and to assert control over each other's behavior, to maintain the homeostasis of relationships, groups, and the self. Many aspects of communication within relationships and groups are influenced by the need to maintain the collective homeostasis, including gossip, storytelling, play, and humor.

Communication is primarily about relationships, and communication is central to developing and maintaining relationships and social groups. It follows that behavior that undermines the basis for effective communication risks damage to the homeostasis of the group or relationship and, often, to the homeostasis of other group members. This would include communication offenses such as lying, gratuitous insults, and breaking promises, as well as other widely sanctioned offenses like theft, adultery, and physical assault. Norms of morality and ethics develop in every culture to sanction and repair the damage resulting from these and other communication and relational offenses.

Facework:[8] Politeness and Impoliteness

A primary form of social "*grooming*" is providing support for other peoples' positive and negative face by supporting and reinforcing their role enactment

---

[7] In a perverse way, that is true of negative as well as positive relationships: Enmities, like friendships, are part of the external social environment we strive to maintain in the dynamic stability of homeostasis that allows us to predict and plan for future situations and interactions. It is sometimes as important to predict and be predictable to our enemies as it is to predict and be predictable to our friends. Conversely, the ability to surprise (pleasantly) a friend and the ability to surprise (unpleasantly) an enemy are also important.

[8] See Chapter 7.

and by reassuring other persons in various ways that they and their performance, including their autonomous actions, are socially acceptable and approved. This is accomplished in many direct ways, including compliments and praise, agreeing with the other person, laughing at the other person's jokes and quips, expressing appreciation for clever comments, and so on. Joking and being playful can also support the other person's positive face.[9] These are all likely to activate the other person's internal reward systems, releasing endorphins and otherwise creating positive feelings that increase liking and attachment. Polite phrases like "please" and "thank you" support autonomy (negative face) by sustaining the polite fiction that the addressee is free to decide whether to comply with a request, whether or not it is actually the case.

A *face-threatening act* contradicts either positive face or autonomy. Anything that implies the other person is not an accepted and valued companion and member of the community is a threat to positive face – for example, failing to greet an acquaintance or refusing an invitation. Anything that implies the other person is subject to someone else's control and not an autonomous, self-directed agent is a threat to perceived autonomy. A prime example is giving the other person a direct order or stating an imperative such as "You *have* to do it."

In terms of Goffman's drama metaphor, *positive face* is the ability to perform one's social role smoothly and flawlessly. It can also be described as one's self-esteem and one's sense of being respected and esteemed by important others. Positive face can be threatened or devalued in many ways. Direct insults (bald on record) are the most obvious, in particular name-calling, including use of adjectives ("weak," "ugly") and epithets ("scoundrel," "liar," "thief"). Declining an invitation or failure to include someone in an invitation or event threatens the other person's positive face by implying their companionship is not valued. Delay in returning a letter or telephone call implies the other person is not important enough to deserve a prompt response. Failure to greet or at least acknowledge another person's presence implies the other person is not worthy of notice. Once we have theory of mind, the ability to represent or imagine how others think about us, and to project that representation forward into the future, we have the ability to imagine the worst, to invent stories about why we weren't invited, why a phone call wasn't returned, what it means for the relationship and for our own future homeostasis. *Facework* is all about how we avert or minimize threats both to own and to others' positive face and perceived autonomy, how we preserve the homeostasis of our relationships and, thereby our own homeostasis.

---

[9] Chapters 9 and 11.

Except in the context of open hostility, any face-threatening act (FTA) is discordant with and not relevant to the "civility" schema, and consequently invokes a search for some *other* context in which the act would be relevant. In the context of the relationship itself, the FTA will lower the hedonic value of the relationship. The goal of facework is to provide and raise the salience of an alternative context in which the FTA is relevant without impairing the hedonic value of the relationship – for example, by providing an alternative explanation that is not face-threatening.

Negative face refers to a sense (one might say an *illusion*) of personal autonomy. This is obviously relative to one's perceived position in the status hierarchy, especially the status hierarch of one's primary reference group. The higher one's status, the fewer people can impinge on one's autonomy. As with positive face, there are endless ways to threaten or diminish another person's perceived autonomy. Bald on-record autonomy threats involve a direct order ("Move!" or "Do it now!"), but implied imperatives and implied contradictions also threaten perceived autonomy. "There is no evidence supporting the claims of astrology" and, in the era of pandemics, "You should wear a face mask while in public" both seem to be understood as face threats by many people. Even citing an authoritative source to support a position in an argument can be perceived as a threat to autonomy, inasmuch as it constrains the arguments the other person is able to make. Resistance to autonomy threats is an expression of *reactance*, the universal tendency to respond to an order or even an implied order by doing the opposite.[10]

Friends can support one's perceived autonomy in several ways. In terms of Dunbar's basic argument, friends and allies should be willing and able to support each other in an intragroup conflict over hierarchical status, which directly affects autonomy as well as positive face. Selecting friends and associates who will support one's own performance is an important part of protecting own positive face. Many politeness rituals protect others' perceived autonomy. "Please" is short for "if you please" or "if it pleases you," which carries the pretense that you are not obligated to perform the "requested" action if it *doesn't* please you. Indirect commands like "if you have time . . ." or "you might consider . . ." have the same effect; they imply a choice even if in fact you don't really have a choice. Greeting rituals, gifts, and compliments all reinforce perceived autonomy.

Facework frequently involves a kind of exchange. When I honor another's perceived autonomy by saying "please," I compromise my own positive face by conceding that I am not inherently deserving of the favor I am requesting. When I honor another's positive face by apologizing for declining an

---

[10] In the United States especially, reactance against the threat to negative face posed by face mask rules posed a serious impediment to containing the COVID epidemic from the very beginning.

invitation, I compromise my own autonomy by acknowledging some level of obligation. When I honor another's perceived autonomy by apologizing for jostling or stepping in front of them, I compromise my own perceived autonomy by acknowledging that I do not have the right to move freely through space. When I honor another's positive face by apologizing for asking them to repeat something I did not understand, I compromise my own positive face by acknowledging that I may not be worth the trouble of providing a clarification, and that I was at fault for failing to hear correctly. Apologizing for a potentially face-threatening act and using polite formulae like "please" and "thank you" mitigate the face threat by accepting a reduction to the apologizer's face. Politeness formulae in general compensate the other person for a face-damaging act by sacrificing the speaker's face. (Conversely, replying to an insult or face threat with an equivalent or stronger insult or face threat helps restore a sense of equity.)

These concepts are related to homeostasis in obvious ways. Any face threat increases stress by undermining one's confidence in one's social status or supportive relationships. Conversely, efforts to avoid or ameliorate a face threat reinforces one's confidence in one's social standing and thereby reduce stress. The various polite formulae used to minimize threats to other people's face imply an increased valuation of the other person and are likely to be experienced as rewarding, much like a compliment, and as such constitutes a kind of grooming. Face-threatening acts can disrupt relationships and so threaten to disrupt the homeostasis of the social group. Consequently, politeness is as important to group- and social-level homeostasis as it is to the homeostasis of individuals.

Presenting oneself as socially skilled and able to support others' face according to culturally accepted politeness norms is part of positive face, so using these polite phrases is part of self-directed facework. However, autonomy (*negative* face) implies freedom from such social constraints. If one is genuinely autonomous, there is no need to consider other persons' face needs: "When you're a star, they let you do it. You can do anything."[11] For those who are not "stars," who are subject to the routine constraints of social interaction, there is an inherent contradiction between the demands of positive face and perceived autonomy.[12]

Impoliteness. Politeness theory has been criticized because it focuses unduly on the *individual* rather than on the interaction.[13] Culpeper and his

---

[11] Donald Trump, discussing his habit of sexually molesting women. *Access Hollywood* tapes. www.voanews.com/archive/transcript-donald-trumps-conversation-billy-bush-access-hollywood, accessed May 28, 2020.
[12] See Chapter 11 for a discussion of how face threats contribute to humor.
[13] For example, Arundale (2010).

colleagues have proposed an extension of politeness theory, *im*politeness theory.[14] According to Culpeper, behavior is considered "impolite" when it contradicts ordinary social expectations and norms. Impoliteness strategies generally involve deliberate use of face-threatening acts (FTAs): Bald on-record (overt impoliteness), implicatures, polarization (e.g. "we/they" with disparagement of the Other), exaggeration and outright lies, sarcasm/irony, and invidious contrasts. Impolite rhetorical strategies include attacks on others' positive or negative face, self-presentation as superior to others, and deliberate violation or discrediting of conventional social norms.

Deliberate use of face threats (*strategic impoliteness*) diminishes the target's face and undermines the target's homeostasis. Reducing an *enemy's* homeostasis increases one's own homeostasis, and reducing the homeostasis of a threatening or hostile out-group or out-group member increases the collective homeostasis of the in-group.[15] Face-threatening acts and the politeness formulae (facework) through which they are avoided or minimized play an important role in many aspects of communication, including relevance and conversation management.

Strategic impoliteness is closely aligned with what Mutz[16] calls "incivility," and has become a staple of contemporary political discourse,[17] recently identified with former president Donald Trump in particular. According to Mutz, incivility/impoliteness is often viewed as entertaining,[18] and does not detract from the speaker's credibility when it is viewed as "just entertainment."[19] Donald Trump's political and business rhetoric, for example, relies almost exclusively on strategic impoliteness, including insults, boasting, exaggeration, belittling, implicatures, lies, sarcasm, invidious contrasts – mostly bald on-record.

Theory of Mind and Moral Judgment. Theory of mind (ToM) entails the ability to represent how another person represents one's own mind and understands one's own motives and actions. This leads to the ability to perceive oneself as an acting and thinking object. Facework implies the ability to represent how others represent oneself. How do others view my social worth and status (positive face)? To what extent do others perceive me as an autonomous agent (negative face)?

ToM also entails the ability to represent how one's own actions affect others' face. Are my actions consistent with supporting others' sense of being socially acceptable and valued? Are my actions consistent with supporting others' freedom of action, and their sense of being respected as an autonomous agent? Do others perceive me as polite?

---

[14] Culpeper (1996, 2011; Culpeper, Bousfield, and Wichmann, 2003).   [15] See Chapter 2.
[16] Mutz (2007, 2016; Mutz and Reeves, 2005).   [17] Stohr (2017).
[18] It is also a staple of late-night comedy talk shows.   [19] Chapter 12.

The ability to perceive oneself as an object also implies the ability to evaluate one's own actions and explain them to others (metacognition and metacommunication). Are my actions consistent with my sense of social worth, my positive face? Are they consistent with my sense of personal autonomy, my negative face? Are they consistent with my feelings about other persons? Are they consistent with my beliefs, values, and morals? Do I present myself as socially skilled? Am I enacting my social role in this context in a competent way? In sum, how do I feel about my own actions?

Morality. A number of theories have been proposed to explain and justify morality and moral judgment. Greene[20] emphasizes a distinction between *deontological* moral judgments, which are based on a priori concepts of natural rights and duties, and *consequentialist* moral judgments, based on reasoning about the anticipated effects of alternative actions and selecting the action with the best anticipated balance of desirable and undesirable outcomes. Greene argues that humans have a "dual-mode" brain, and uses the metaphor of a point-and-shoot camera compared to a camera with manual settings for shutter speed, exposure, and focus. In the "automatic" mode, our decisions are based on "*pre-set*" emotions, reflexes, and intuitions; in the "manual" mode, we use a "general-purpose reasoning system" to evaluate alternative courses of action based on detailed information about the current situation plus general background knowledge.[21] Here I am going to take a different tack, based on how communicative actions in particular affect individual and group homeostasis.

Facework, Homeostasis, and Morality. The homeostasis of one's friends contributes to (and the homeostasis of one's enemies detracts from) one's own homeostasis. Group-level homeostasis is dependent on both the sum of individual group members' homeostasis and the quality of interactions among group members. *Positive face* and *perceived autonomy* both reflect and contribute to individual homeostasis. Face-supporting acts within a group support the homeostasis of individual members as well as of the group. Conversely, face-threatening acts toward outsiders who are considered hostile to the group and toward deviant in-group members also contribute to group-level homeostasis, thus indirectly to individual homeostasis. Impoliteness toward personal enemies contributes to individual and group-level homeostasis *if* and only if they are also hostile or detrimental to the group as a whole. Otherwise, impoliteness toward other members of the group, even if it contributes to individual homeostasis, will undermine the group homeostasis.

---

[20] Greene (2014).
[21] These modes are roughly the same as what Petty and Cacioppo (1981) call the "peripheral" and "central" route to persuasion.

Considerations of facework and homeostasis appear to be involved in many different topics commonly considered part of morality. *Lying* implicates both the positive face of the liar and the autonomy of the person lied to, since it interferes with the ability to make and execute fact-based decisions. Inartful lies detract from the target's positive face – for example, "If you think I'm going to believe that you must think me a total fool!" Deception is often a means to support another person's positive face. "White lies," such as deceptively praising another person's actions or appearance, are associated with social tact, as, for example, when a speaker asks "What do you think of my new hairdo?" On the other hand, since it forces the addressee to choose between lie and a face-threatening act, a direct question of this sort threatens the addressee's autonomy.

Sexual morality poses similar contradictions. Positive face implies "I recognize you as a moral and socially acceptable person," but autonomy also implies "I recognize you as a sexually autonomous person." But from a different perspective, the positive face of the other member of an established intimate relationship is threatened by infidelity, with the implication that the other person is inadequate in some way. If the cultural norms of the group emphasize abstinence or monogamy, these norms threaten individuals' sense of personal autonomy, but violating the norms undermines solidarity and so threatens the positive face of other group members and, collectively, of the group.

Similar considerations can be generalized to privacy. For other members of the group to claim the right to know about and sanction individual behavior violates individual members' autonomy. Conversely, concealing behavior that might affect the group may violate other members' sense of autonomy (by limiting their ability to act on the information) and positive face (because it risks impairing the group's reputation). Privacy marks a dialectical tension between desire and autonomy on the one hand and social order on the other hand (reputation, minimizing interpersonal conflict within the group).

Strategic Impoliteness and Morality: Trade-Offs. President Donald Trump famously used strategic impoliteness as his primary rhetorical strategy against his perceived enemies. It appears that this is part of the reason he has aroused such passionate support,[22] since many of his enemies are perceived by his supporters as outsiders, their own enemies. Thus, by detracting from the homeostasis of Democrats, Liberals, scientists, "politically correct" advocates, and other "enemies," Trump supports the homeostasis of Republicans, Conservatives, anti-vaxxers, white supremacists, and others among his core support.

---

[22] Mutz (2016).

Given the importance of group-level homeostasis both to the group and to its members, homeostasis-supporting acts can be considered *moral* in the sense that they contribute to the health and success of the group and thereby of all members of the group. Consistent with conventional ideas about ethics and morality, face-supporting acts (politeness) toward other members of the group and toward the group itself are also *moral* acts. However, face-threatening acts (impoliteness) toward out-group members perceived as hostile toward the in-group and its members might *also* be considered moral – from the perspective of an in-group (such as Trump supporters).

As president, Trump's oath of office was to the constitution and by implication to the nation as a social entity. From this perspective, face-threatening acts (impoliteness) toward any group members, any other citizens, support the homeostasis of the group (the nation as a whole) only if they are directed toward deviant members of the group, specifically toward members of the group whose actions have been detrimental to the homeostasis of the group as a whole (not merely toward certain individuals or subgroups). Otherwise, face-threatening acts detract from the homeostasis of the group as a whole (the nation), and from that broader perspective would be considered *immoral*. From this broader perspective, both politeness theory (conventional face theory) and impoliteness theory can contribute to a theory and critique of leadership.

I have argued that the actions of all group members toward other (in)-group members affect group-level homeostasis and by implication affect the homeostasis of other group members. If a leader is responsible for the welfare, homeostasis, and success of the entire group, then a crucial responsibility of leadership is to promote face-supporting acts and discourage face-threatening acts within the group, and direct face-threatening acts (i.e. strategic impoliteness) only toward hostile out-group members. If a group needs to cooperate with other groups, face-threatening acts toward out-groups and their members must *also* be minimized.

Social Control. Homeostasis of a relationship or group requires mutual support of each other's positive face and autonomy, primarily through politeness and other forms of facework. It also requires mutual control, to limit violations that threaten the homeostasis of other members, hence indirectly threaten the homeostasis of the group. This is accomplished in several ways, both direct and indirect. Direct control takes the form of bald on-record criticism and chastisement, which is itself face-threatening and will often precipitate conflict. Preemptive control often takes the form of simply reminding the (potential or suspected) offender of the norms or expectations. Storytelling is a common vehicle for expressing and reminding group members of group norms, and perceived violation of norms may be addressed through a metaphorical story that readily maps onto the literal story of the violation but minimizes face threat by allowing everyone to avoid explicit acknowledgment.[23] Humorous teasing and ironic put-downs are often used for social control by providing a partially face-saving context of "just joking around."[24]

Among the greatest threats to group homeostasis are aggression (usually directed toward struggles for dominance or sex partners) and sexuality. In addition to humor and irony, cultures and social groups often develop courtship rituals and rigid codes of sexual morality to control potentially disruptive sexual behavior, and higher-status members of a group will often defend lower-status members from any aggression, including aggressive humor.[25]

Power and Status

Among humans, like other social species, power and social status contribute significantly to reproductive fitness. Dominant individuals have greater access to sex partners and experience greater reproductive success. They also have greater access to food, shelter, and other resources, both necessities and luxuries. They are accorded more space and more freedom of movement and action, and they are less likely to be challenged or punished for perceived transgressions or norm violations. Lower-status individuals, particularly near the bottom of a group's status hierarchy, experience more stress and more stress-related health problems (including diseases and, among humans, heart attacks). In larger, more complex societies, power and status also extend to entire groups, and the status of one's primary reference group relative to other groups extends to individual status – as is evident in the deleterious effects of racial, ethnic, and religious stereotypes. In sum, power and status are crucial components of homeostasis; for humans, an important consideration in forward projection of the state of the body in its environment is social status, and the potential effect on social status is important in choosing among alternative courses of action.

Until recently, both social theory and evolution theory emphasized conflict and competition as basic determinants of social interaction. However, recent research has shifted the focus to include cooperation and collaboration, both within and across species. In human societies, both cooperation and competition are important, and groups such as families, work groups, and social groups are characterized by how they balance these contradictory norms.

For example, much of the early research on humor in conversation was conducted among adolescent males. Adolescence is notoriously a time of coming to terms with sexuality and conflict and establishing a place in the status hierarchy. Not surprisingly, research with this age group revealed an emphasis on tendentious (sexual and aggressive) humor. However, research

---

[23] Chapters 11 and 13; Norrick (1993, 1997).
[24] Chapter 12; Billig (2005); Fine and DeSoucey (2005).
[25] See, for example, Terrion and Ashforth (2002).

among mature adults tells a different story: Social norms tend to discourage aggressive humor targeted against lower-status or otherwise vulnerable group members, and bullying is likely to be punished.[26] By the time people reach retirement age, the preference has shifted strongly away from aggressive and tendentious humor toward more playful humor, including humor directed toward coping with the vicissitudes of the aging process.[27]

Signals of Power. Among both humans and other animals, size, strength, and aggressiveness are associated with power and dominance. In a confrontation, each participant will maximize apparent height; the effect is often amplified by hair rising up. Sustained eye contact and a loud, deep voice signal claims to dominance. Conversely, a lowered posture, downcast eyes, and soft, higher-pitched voice ("whining") signal submission. The association is bidirectional: Taller people are judged to be more powerful, and, conversely, people introduced with titles of authority or power are judged to be taller. Among humans in virtually all societies, a high position signals power: Corporate executives usually have their offices on higher floors of a building, and palaces and temples are built on high ground. All this is expressed in the conceptual metaphor POWER/AUTHORITY IS UP.[28]

Physical attractiveness is also a universal marker of social status. Markers of good health, such as facial symmetry and skin condition, are universally considered attractive, but otherwise cultural norms are quite variable.[29] Clothing and adornments are universal markers of social status; like physical attractiveness, the details vary among cultures, but, in general, the more expensive the costume, the higher the status. However, at extreme levels of wealth and power, status is also displayed by extreme simplicity, in effect advertising "I am so rich and powerful that I do not need to prove it by dressing up or wearing expensive jewelry."[30]

Bases of Power. In a classic study, French and Raven[31] identified five bases of social power: *coercive, reward, legitimate, expert,* and *referent. Coercive* power is based on the ability to punish through physical aggression or symbolic violence, such as an attack on the other person's face through overt insults or more subtle "microaggressions." *Reward* power is based on the ability to provide needed resources or symbolic rewards such as reinforcing the other person's face (e.g. praise). Coercive and reward power are inversely related: Withholding an expected reward is experienced as punishment, and failing to administer an expected punishment is experienced as a reward.[32] *Legitimate* power is based on selection through a legitimating process such as a

---

[26] See Chapter 12; Fine and DeSoucey (2005); Terrion and Ashforth (2002).
[27] Giapraki et al. (2020).   [28] Chapter 11.
[29] Chaiken (1979); Montepare (1995); Wilson (1968).   [30] Veblen (1973).
[31] French and Raven (1959).   [32] Bandura (1965, 1971).

democratic election or anointing by a religious authority. *Expert* power is based on recognized relevant skills or knowledge; *legitimate* power is often based on perceived or demonstrated expert power. *Referent* power is based on personality factors such as likeability and "charisma."

Among other primates, hierarchical power and social status are determined primarily through physical aggression or a credible threat of physical aggression, a prime example of coercive power. However, even within a group of chimpanzees, coercive power may be qualified or limited by the formation of coalitions, groups who can be counted on to come to each other's aid in the case of attack. Sometimes a coalition of second tier, "beta" males may succeed in overthrowing the "alpha" male. Forming and maintaining supportive coalitions is a primary purpose of grooming,[33] both the physical grooming among other primates and the symbolic (e.g. language) grooming among humans. This could be interpreted as an extension of reward or possibly of referent power, but it doesn't quite fit; perhaps a sixth category of power should be added, something like *social network power*.

Successfully asserting power increases positive face; an unsuccessful assertion of power decreases positive face. Yielding to an assertion of coercive power reduces both positive face and perceived autonomy; this is especially pronounced with coercive power. Yielding to reward or legitimate power can have a subtly negative effect on perceived autonomy, but the larger the difference in status or the size of the reward, the less the face threat. Because referent power is based on identifying with the higher-status individual, yielding to referent power may be experienced as an increase in positive face.

Dessalles[34] argues that language serves primarily to advertise the speaker's value as a potential friend, by displaying desirable qualities such as the ability to recognize and resolve contradiction. This suggests a combination of reward, expert, and referent power. The different bases of power frequently appear in synergistic combinations; for example, expertise is often the basis for selection by a hiring committee and the consequent granting of legitimate power, and legitimate authorities almost always have the power to punish and reward, including the symbolic punishments and rewards of disapproval or recognition.

Managing Social Distance. "*Grooming*" also contributes to the stability of hierarchical relations within the group: Lower-status individuals may groom higher-status group members by way of appeasement, but, conversely, the winner of a fight may groom the loser to reestablish group harmony. In human relationships, if the status is nearly equal (low social distance), both people are likely to engage in more dominance behaviors[35] as they jockey for position. In

---

[33] Dunbar (1996); see Chapter 3.   [34] Dessalles (2014); see Chapter 3.
[35] Burgoon et al. (2016).

an individualist culture like the United States, this can be especially problematic for a person, such as a young teacher or recently promoted manager (legitimate power), who is not perceived to have referent, expert, or coercive power. This kind of disparity can sometimes be ameliorated by emphasizing legitimate power and increasing referent power through dressing "*up*" with more expensive clothing and other trappings of social status, and by using dominance signals such as a lower and firmer voice and more direct eye contact.

When the difference in status and power is unambiguous, the higher-status person is often more relaxed and casual, but extreme differences in power and status may generate so much anxiety in lower-status individuals that they are effectively incapacitated. They may feel reluctant to ask for clarification or instructions, and they are unlikely to object to harsh or unfair treatment, and instead to harbor resentments that undermine group identity and solidarity.[36] This can be especially problematic in settings where discussion and asking questions are basic to the purpose of the interaction. Higher-status people can *reduce* social distance by minimizing dominance signals and substituting signals that mitigate the effects of status in various ways, including wearing more casual or less expensive clothing and arranging furniture in a sociopetal fashion (such as meeting at a small round table). Behavior that increases immediacy can also help to reduce social distance: smiling, voice modulation and animation, use of an open posture, and so on. Higher-status people often use self-directed humor to lower the social distance and put lower-status people more at ease.[37] However, this can also have the ironic effect of threatening the face of the lower-status people by forcing them to decide quickly how to respond (a threat to perceived autonomy) and the potential of losing positive face if their response is deemed inappropriate or excessive.[38]

Relationships of Equal Status

Peer relationships are essential to homeostasis. They are also fraught with risk of face threats from beginning to end. Initiating a friendship can be a delicate process because of the risk of rejection. Any attempt to initiate a relationship beyond a simple casual encounter constitutes a claim on the other person's time, and consequently a potential threat to perceived autonomy.

Because of the potential face threat, friendships usually develop in a sequence of stages, with friendly overtures presented in ways that preserve

---

[36] Burgoon et al. (2016).
[37] Lehmann-Willenbrock and Allen (2014); Plester and Sayers (2007); Terrion and Ashforth (2002); see also Chapter 12.
[38] Schnurr and Chan (2011).

deniability and reduce the risk of face loss to either person. Most peer relationships begin with casual encounters, with people who live or work in close proximity, or encounter each other in clubs, churches, social events, or other locales where casual conversation carries little face risk. Initial conversation usually includes exploring commonalities and establishing common ground. As a relationship continues, humor and other forms of playful communication contribute to bonding. Trust is built through storytelling (in the United States, women are more likely to share personal stories) and exchange of friendly humorous put-downs (more common among men).

In a modern, individualist society like the United States, sexual relationships are even more fraught with face threats. For this reason, courtship stages can be considerably more complex, especially in the early stages, involving display of ambiguous signals that are easily denied. These may include verbal teasing and use of metaphors and jokes as well as subtle variations in gaze and facial expressions, proxemics, and touch. The arranged marriages common to more traditional societies greatly reduce the face threats associated with courtship by delegating some of the face threat to the matchmaker – in exchange for a considerable sacrifice in autonomy.

Culture and Representation

Within any social context, a person will typically interact regularly and intensely with only a handful of others, and may interact less frequently with 100 or more people. These interpersonal relations are based on mutual knowledge acquired and maintained through routine interactions, elaborated and generalized by applying theory of mind. Each person sustains a representation of what others know and think (common ground), including how others represent one's own thoughts, what others expect, and how they are likely to react. All this contributes to the forward projection of how a particular conversation is likely to proceed and how the relationship itself is likely to develop, as well as how the interaction fits in with relevant cultural norms and expectations. The more prior contact people have, the more accurate their forward projection and the more efficient (and rewarding) their communication is likely to be. As people interact in various contexts, their mutual representations become increasingly complex and their ability to predict others' responses becomes increasingly accurate, all part of building and maintaining common ground,[39] the basis for mutual cognitive environment.[40]

During initial stages of acquaintanceship, conversation is often directed toward learning more about the other person[41] as a basis for assessing and

---

[39] Clark (1986).   [40] Sperber and Wilson (1986).
[41] Berger (1979); Berger and Calabrese (1975).

Culture and Representation   179

establishing common ground. Learning about the other person's group memberships, occupations, and hobbies as well as personal tastes and opinions helps expand and improve one's representation of the other and increase the accuracy of forward projections of the other's responses both to external events and to the conversation itself. As people encounter each other over time and relationships develop, they will often reveal increasingly intimate details about their personal tastes, past history, and so forth. This kind of personal information expands common ground and provides the basis for more efficient communication. How much people reveal to each other depends on factors such as their level of mutual trust and their perceptions about the nature of the relationship.[42]

Each person's representations of other persons include their expectations and how they are likely to react to unexpected behaviors. This includes normative expectations, what sorts of behavior (including communication) is expected and considered to be proper or improper, moral or immoral. Some of these expectations may be represented and understood as unique to the other person, but many of them will be associated with the culture of social groups and collectivities. For example, faculty members and students in a university have one set of expectations and norms; members of an extended family have a different set of expectations and norms. Representations of other persons may also include representations of how they think about social groups, organizations, and so forth, especially those to which both self and other belong.

In a hierarchical organization such as a corporation or military unit, each person's relationships will include both hierarchical and peer relationships, both cooperative and competitive relationships. Each type of relationship is shaped by general cultural norms and expectations, qualified by norms and expectations particular to the group and organization. Individuals differ in both their motivation and their ability to conform to group norms and expectations, and in their social skills.

Group norms and expectations may be set forth in formal documents and oral teachings, or they may be only implied. Religious organizations have doctrines, social clubs have charters and rules, business and military organizations have personnel manuals and codes of conduct. At least as important as these formal documents and teachings are the informal understandings and expectations implicit in everyday interactions and conversations. Each member of a group or organization has a representation of its collective expectations and norms; the aggregate of these personal representations and the behaviors and interactions they foster is one way to define the group's *culture*. Culture, like language,[43] is cognitively represented as a network of interconnected

---

[42] "Social penetration."   [43] See Landauer and Dumais (1997), and the discussion in Chapter 3.

concepts and perceptual simulations, and this network of connections is constantly changing in response to new experiences, new interactions with other members of the same culture, and sometimes by interactions with out-group members based on their beliefs about the culture. Cultural norms and expectations are developed, promulgated, and enforced through routine interactions,[44] including ordinary conversations, storytelling,[45] teasing, and humor.[46]

Relationship Dimensions

In a small community, a village or small town, relationships are likely to be stable and fixed, and people are likely to interact almost exclusively with people they know well.[47] In a larger city, many social interactions occur in relationships with strangers, or with other people who are encountered routinely in particular contexts. A city dweller may have friendly relationships with a barista, a few food servers and store clerks, an automobile mechanic, and so on. These relationships are usually limited to a particular context, but they are an important part of the social structure, of the texture of urban life as it is experienced on a daily basis,[48] and they contribute in subtle but important ways to maintaining and enforcing cultural norms of behavior.

Relationships vary according to several qualities or "*dimensions*," such as purely social versus task-oriented, hierarchical versus equal, competition versus cooperation, formal versus informal, personal attraction, emotional valence, and similarity. These dimensions are marked by a similar array of relational signals.[49] Some of these characteristics are likely to be stable across time and situations, but others are likely to vary according to the situation, especially social versus task orientation and formality versus informality.

Each participant in a relationship has a representation of the relationship based on cultural norms and expectations, past interactions, and personal hopes and needs. Representations of relationships and communication norms are subtly updated during every interaction, and may also be influenced and reshaped by other interactions and by new information from cultural sources. In a complex relationship, only the situationally relevant aspects of the relationship may be activated during a particular conversation – but as the topic and tone of the conversation changes, other aspects of the relationship and memories of particular past interactions may become more salient. All this is

---

[44] Berger and Luckmann (1966). Contrary to Berger and Luckman's initial argument, however, at least in modern societies social reality is highly fluid as a result of wide-spread and routine interactions with members of other cultures, as Peter Berger (1979) later recognized.
[45] Chapter 13.   [46] Chapter 12.   [47] Berger and Luckmann (1966).   [48] Jacobs (1961).
[49] Burgoon and Hale (1984); in addition to these, relational signals also include information about arousal and affect, which often influence the future course of the interaction.

part of the communication context, and influences how individuals interpret each other's signals.

Summary

The combination of expanded theory of mind and empathy with complex language has greatly expanded and elaborated the range of human relationships, well beyond the simple biological categories of dominance/submission, sexuality, infant rearing, and supportive alliance/friendship. Most human relationships, including interpersonal and group relationships, include some balance of hierarchical power with alliance and social support. The complexity of human relationships is greatly increased by the expansion of theory of mind and self-awareness, combined with a more sophisticated ability of individuals to represent and project forward in time their social status, their personal autonomy and positive face, their status as respected members of society, and of their primary reference groups. This introduced a new form of risk into social interactions, the risk of disrespect and loss of face.

Healthy and active social relationships, based on mutual trust and respect, are vital to homeostasis, to mental and physical health. All conversation and most other forms of communication are conducted according to implicit rules and practices that accommodate and minimize threats to all participants' positive face and perceived autonomy. These rules and practices of politeness and facework, both implicit and explicit, are always part of the communication context, essential to understanding conversation, play, metaphor, humor, and storytelling.

The expansion and elaboration of language interacted with theory of mind, what Baron-Cohen[50] calls "cognitive empathy." Amplified by the imitation, refinement, and elaboration characterized by Dennett[51] and others as "meme propagation," this led to accelerating expansion and elaboration of material as well as social and intellectual culture. Language has played a central role in this cultural expansion, and the telic use of language has expanded accordingly. These developments, the social-supportive role of language, telic use of language for intellectual and material production, and development of face threats and compensatory facework (politeness), must all be considered in any account of language use and conversation.

---

[50] Baron-Cohen (2020). [51] Dennett (2017).

9 Conversation

Clark posits conversation as the basic and original context of language use and argues that all language use is best understood as variations on the structure and practice of conversation.[1] Dunbar[2] claims that language evolved in response to the pressures of living in large, socially complex groups. Language and conversation serve as an extension of *grooming*, a way to maintain supportive friendship coalitions. This chapter begins with an evolution-based discussion of how conversation contributes to social organization and homeostasis. Then it discusses how conversation is organized. Finally it turns to the structure of conflict talk and argumentation, both as social interaction and internalized into individual reasoning and planning.

Conversation and Homeostasis

The homeostasis of an individual living in a complex social group with a marked status hierarchy is affected in several ways by interactions with other group members, both higher-status individuals who control access to resources and may pose a threat of violence and equal-status individuals who can offer support and share resources. Grooming affords the potential to cope with more powerful group members both through appeasement and by cultivating alliances and friendships with other group members who can offer support and protection. Grooming also strengthens bonds of cooperation, both within peer relations and in hierarchical structures. Among humans, this ordinarily involves figurative "*grooming*" (compliments, storytelling, entertainment, and politeness) as well as literal grooming through proximity and physical touch. Communication with other group members also affords the opportunity to maintain up-to-date information about the group in general and about its status and power hierarchy (gossip). The number and quality of an individual's social relationships is a direct aspect of homeostasis, important in its own right.

---

[1] Clark (1996).   [2] Dunbar (1996).

Roughly two-thirds of language use and signaling in conversation is social talk, paratelic interactions[3] associated with developing and maintaining interpersonal relationships.[4] However, Dessalles[5] argues that there has to be more to the origins of conversation than social bonding, which could be accomplished with a very simple syntax and a limited range of signals. He acknowledges the importance of language for exchanging information, but argues that informative communication can't be the primary function of language either, because information actually has a "negative value." People routinely *compete* for the opportunity to talk (i.e. to provide information). Dessalles points out that the invention of weapons increased the risk of murder, specifically killing the alpha male. Dessalles refers to this as "risk-free killing," but "lower-risk killing" is more accurate, since weapons can be used by the higher-ranking as well as by lower-ranking members of the group. Language increased the risk to the alpha male even more, by making it easier for lower-ranking males to form coalitions to demote or even kill an excessively domineering member of the group.[6] This dynamic adds rhetorical and interpersonal skills to physical strength as a source of social dominance.[7]

Dessalles argues that language serves primarily as a medium for advertising one's qualities as a potential friend, thereby attracting friends, which contributes to homeostasis. He claims that humans choose friends for their conversational competence, and conversation provides a medium for displaying competence in crucial rhetorical skills, including storytelling and argumentation; this explains why people compete for the right to talk and rush to be the first to relate a new tidbit of gossip or other information. An ideal friend should anticipate danger and help avoid being taken by surprise: Unexpectedness in a narrative signals alertness to unexpected events that may be a sign of danger. This explains the emphasis on narrative skills. It may also help explain the pleasure people derive from creating, identifying, and resolving incongruities, which includes activities like puzzles and riddles as well as humor[8] and irony. The ability to create amusing incongruities displays creativity and imagination and contributes to social status.[9] An ideal friend should be able to detect and resolve inconsistencies, thus, argumentative skills are valued.[10] Finally, by

---

[3] Actions undertaken for their own sake, rather than to achieve an extrinsic goal; by contrast, *telic* actions are primarily directed toward accomplishing an external (utilitarian) goal.
[4] Dunbar (1996); see also Chapter 3.   [5] Dessalles, Jean-Louis (2014).
[6] For example, on the Ides of March.
[7] See the discussion of French and Raven in Chapter 8. The tendency among other primates of the winner of a fight for social status to groom the loser suggests that social skill is an important attribute even prior to the development of weapons and language.
[8] Chapter 12.   [9] Koestler (1964).
[10] This is closely parallel to the explanation of humor proposed by Hurley, Dennett, and Adams (2011). They argue that the ability to resolve the incongruity that is basic to humor helps hone a

displaying emotion, we make ourselves vulnerable and predictable, thereby displaying trust and the quality of not being a danger to our friends.[11]

Dunbar's grooming-based account and Dessalles's "advertising" account help explain the inconsequentiality of much of our talk. Even conversations that have primarily telic purposes, such as business or political conversations, include a large component of "*grooming*," gossip, and chitchat, typically about 65 percent[12] of a typical conversation, which contribute to homeostasis at both the group and individual level[13] even when much of it (e.g. yesterday's football scores) is of no consequence. Dessalles's account also helps explain why conversations rarely have a single focus, but typically range over a variety of topics and frequently over a variety of moods, from serious to playful and back to serious. In sum, Dunbar and Dessalles frame conversation as an intermediary between individual and group homeostasis, serving a function at the social level similar to the function of neural and chemical signal systems for the individual human organism. Conversation serves to initiate, form, and maintain relationships as well as to reflect on them, understand them, and communicate about them. It provides a means for sustaining and coping with status hierarchies and for cooperation and cultural transmission of memes.

The ability to project representations forward evolved to anticipate and choose among alternative plans according to potential outcomes. Conversation coevolved with both language and neural systems for forward projection, integrating the ability to predict the course of a conversation, anticipate others' utterances, and prepare a response into conversation skills from the outset. The ability to anticipate others' actions, including language and other communicative signals and thus to respond quickly, "in real time," accomplishes several important objectives. It demonstrates mental agility, and it increases one's control over the direction of the conversation.

As this capacity for forward projection of conversation gets worked into the structure of conversation, it accomplishes a third objective, more entertaining conversations. The ability to formulate a clever response rapidly creates and then fulfills a desire for intellectual as well as emotional stimulation, what Cacioppo and Petty [14] theorized as a "need for cognition." Friendly conversation maximizes the opportunity to demonstrate mental agility and create entertaining conversation. In telic conversation (e.g. economic and political

---

person's incongruity recognition and resolving skill; the pleasure and laughter we experience is the brain's reward. See Chapter 12.

[11] We also *fake* emotional signals, which renders the story more complicated. See Chapter 5.

[12] Dunbar (1996).

[13] These aspects of conversation are inconsequential in terms of material production and direct economic benefit, but in terms of emotional and social homeostasis, they are anything but inconsequential.

[14] Cacioppo and Petty (1982).

negotiation), forward projection maximizes the ability to control the direction of the conversation and formulate responses rapidly.

The subversion of strength-based dominance by language use in conversation, both as an extension of grooming and as a means of displaying desirable social qualities, leads to another extension of grooming behavior, politeness.[15] Politeness practices serve to maintain social competence, reputation, and position in the social structure of the group ("face"), and thereby wards off threats to homeostasis. Politeness also helps maintain the face of others, which is equally important to homeostasis. Failure to support others' face weakens friendship bonds and can turn friends into enemies; skill in supporting others' face strengthens friendship bonds and can turn enemies into friends. Conversely, *impoliteness*, deliberately attacking the face of an out-group member, an enemy, or a violator of group norms, supports individual and in-group homeostasis[16] by strengthening group boundaries and norms and lowering the status of the target.

Conversation, from the first word to the last, incurs a series of face threats to all participants. The almost ritualistic quality of ordinary conversation ameliorates these face threats, which might otherwise bring what Enfield[17] calls "the *conversation machine*"[18] to a grinding (and mutually hostile) halt. Even greater face threats arise (and must be resolved) in wordplay, hyperbole, humor, and especially irony, each of which I will address in later chapters.

Telic Communication. As the abilities to recognize and resolve inconsistencies and forward-project representations develop, along with the ability to project the course of a conversation forward in order to formulate a response, skills and social practices of argumentation also develop. These skills are internalized as memes, and they are honed and developed into systems of logic, coevolving with the brain and spreading by way of ordinary imitation and social influence.[19] Forward projection helps to optimize the use of logic by extending lines of reasoning, anticipating, and countering others' arguments. Logic is a meme, a "practice worth learning,"[20] although most people are not very good at it.[21] Its adaptation may have coevolved with the brain even as different forms and standards of logic developed in diverse cultures.

---

[15] Chapter 8.
[16] People also apparently find deliberate impoliteness entertaining, as is evident in the popularity of talk radio and late-night comedy shows – and in Donald Trump's successful use of "strategic impoliteness" as his primary medium of political discourse.
[17] Enfield (2017).
[18] Enfield's metaphor emphasizes the spontaneous but reliable regularity of the process – but downplays its spontaneity and creativity.
[19] Dennett (2017); see Chapter 3.   [20] Dennett (2017).   [21] Kuhn (1991); Ritchie (2003c).

Highly organized signal systems, such as language and mathematics, have also come to play a central role in telic functions associated with material needs, getting, creating, and maintaining the resources for sustaining and enriching our material lives. Telic functions include informing, maintaining up-to-date representations of the body (and the relationship or group) in its physical, social environment both through surveillance and through formal and informal teaching. They also include argument, decision-making, and coordination. Several functions derived from the complex structure of society merge paratelic and telic communication, including achieving and maintaining social status and power. Perhaps as a reflection of its economic importance, much of research and theorizing about conversation has focused on these telic functions, with the unstated assumptions either that paratelic communication is secondary and unimportant or that it follows the same logic, rules, and structure as telic communication.

At some point in the evolution of language, forms of conversation branched out and different genres developed, including paratelic forms like humor, storytelling, flirting, and dramatic performance, along with telic forms like negotiation, planning and coordinating joint activities, and resolving disputes. All these follow a common structure based on the capabilities of human signaling and perception and the logic of social interaction, with modifications to this basic structure developing according to particular conversation contexts and modified by local cultures. Paratelic interactions like flirting, banter, storytelling, and gossip are adaptations of the basic structure, governed by culture-specific expectations. The same is true of telic interactions like informing, teaching, reasoning, and debate.

Structure of Conversation

All communication is inherently cooperative;[22] the need for cooperative interaction is especially evident in conversation because of the way facework, coherence, and time constraints interact with the nature of the underlying cognitive processes. In addition to our close friends and members of our primary groups, an even larger number of acquaintances, students, and strangers can, from time to time, present valid claims on our attention. On the one hand, time and attention are limited, and, on the other hand, conversation is important to personal homeostasis; consequently every stage of a conversation presents a potential face threat to all participants. Time is a scarce resource, and we (usually implicitly) budget our time according to our priorities.[23] Another person's willingness to allocate time to conversing with

[22] Grice (1975).   [23] Linder (1970).

oneself implies how much (or little) that person values our own company, and vice versa. Every interaction poses a series of potential face threats to both parties.

The structure of virtually all conversations is shaped in part by the need to anticipate and avoid or mitigate face threats and, conversely, by the possibilities of extended grooming through face-supporting acts. It is also shaped by physical and physiological constraints such as audial and visual acuity that limit the distance at which we can monitor others' voices, facial expressions, and gestures. All this interacts with the time constraints within a conversation and the relatively slow speed of cognitive processes to produce a complex set of communication practices and behaviors so familiar that we hardly notice them.

Fine Structure of Conversation – Moment by Moment. Every utterance involves three roles or actions: A thought (or response to a previous utterance) is generated, it is formulated into signals, including language, and it is performed or vocalized. Each of these is reflected in listeners' actions: The listener perceives and attends to the signals, interprets them into utterances, and understands their meaning.[24] This usually occurs so automatically that it is scarcely noticed, but if the thought to be expressed is complex or the situation is ambiguous, it may require considerable deliberation in a process akin to negotiation among the meanings to be expressed, the utterances available to express them in the current context, and the speaker's array of available signals. A similar process of deliberation may be required for listeners as they strive to ascertain the speaker's intended meanings.

Arundale[25] observes that most current theoretical models conceptualize communication as one individual "*encoding*" meanings into perceptible units; other individuals recover these meanings by drawing inferences in a "script or schema-driven alternation." In the absence of reciprocal causality, conventional explanations of these communicative behaviors reduce to the simple sum of the independent behaviors. "The individuals are engaged in 'joint' activities . . ., but only in the sense of the summative *transfer of power between two meshed gears*."[26] In contrast, Arundale claims that accounting for interactional organization requires "the distinct conceptual commitments of 'interactional achievement' models of communication that take the dyad rather than the individual as the minimum unit of analysis, and that conceptualize communication as a non-summative phenomenon involving mutual affordance and constraint over a sequence of at least three speaking turns."[27]

Arundale proposes the Conjoint Co-constituting Model of Communication, in which understandings of a present utterance are constrained by one or more

---

[24] Clark (1996). [25] Arundale (2010). [26] Arundale (2010, p. 2079).
[27] Arundale (2010, p. 2079).

preceding utterances and subject to revision by future utterance(s). One speaker produces an utterance (*first position*), which both affords and constrains the possible interpretations. Until another speaker produces a response (*second position*), the first speaker's projection of how the first-position utterance will be interpreted is only provisional. Another speaker's *second-position* utterance provides evidence of how the first-position utterance was interpreted. As the first speaker interprets this evidence, it may confirm the provisional projection or, if it is inconsistent, force modification of the projected interpretation. Any subsequent utterance (*third position*) will need to account for the confirmed or modified interpretation.

Throughout any conversation on a given topic, there is an interlocking sequence of these triads. Each utterance subsequent to the initial one and prior to the final one is a first-, second-, and third-position utterance in a progression of triads, with interpretations afforded and constrained by prior utterances and retrospectively revised to account for subsequent utterances. If a subsequent "third position" utterance forces modification of a previous utterance, it may force a chain of modifications of preceding utterances. To say that interpretations are jointly constructed implies that the projected interpretations are always provisional and fluid, subject to modification to account for evidence provided by subsequent utterances, even several speaking turns in the future. This includes evidence about the nature and purpose of the conversation[28] as well as about the intention of particular utterances.

Arundale uses an example of a routine office conversation, in which Marty requests a wall calendar from Loes. Marty begins the exchange by asking, "Do you have a calendar?" Loes initially interprets his question as an inquiry about her own possessions, relevant to a "schedules and dates" schema as an indirect request to consult her calendar. In the belief that she is cooperating with his implied request, she reaches for her own desk calendar, a second-position response that furnishes evidence of how she interpreted the intended relevance of his question. Marty perceives her misconstrual of his inquiry and corrects her interpretation by a more specific request (third position): "Do you have one that hangs on the wall?" This activates an entirely different schema (cognitive context) and forces her to reevaluate her initial interpretation of his first-position utterance as relevant to the now-salient context of her role as a supplies coordinator. She revises her original second-position response accordingly to fit his revised first-position request, "Oh, you want one." As Arundale observes, each utterance in a series is at once in a first, second, and third position with respect to earlier and subsequent utterances. I will return to the topic of repair sequences later in the chapter.

---

[28] The "conversation frame," discussed later in this chapter.

In an example from Chapter 7 – when my former colleague suggested "Why don't we do lunch sometime?" – this first-position utterance was relevant to what I perceived to be the mutual cognitive context of "catching up with an old friend," so I responded, "Let me look at my calendar," a second-position utterance that provisionally confirmed what I understood to be the intention of his first-position utterance. When he asked about my life insurance (third position), that precipitated a search for relevance, completed only when I activated previously nonsalient contexts of "sales call" and "exploiting friendships for financial gain." This disconfirmed my understanding of the first-position utterance, and at the same time precipitated a reinterpretation of the entire preceding conversation. It also altered the basis for future utterances by reframing the entire interaction (and the relationship).

Humorous banter often incorporates reframing and incongruities that force activation of different cognitive contexts (schemas) and reinterpretation of the relevance of previous utterances.[29] Emotional and relational messages are subject to modification in much the same way. If anything, emotional and relational messages are even more fluid. When a message has to do with feelings or relationships, the experience that is being communicated is often reinterpreted and modified.

Arundale specifies three principles that generally govern the sequence of utterances within and across triads:

According to the *adjacent placement principle*, speaker and hearers alike assume (unless the speaker indicates otherwise) that the current utterance is designed with previous utterances in mind and with the expectation that it provides grounds for subsequent utterances, including the immediately subsequent utterance.

According to the *sequential interpretation principle*, hearers expect and are expected to interpret the current utterance using knowledge and expectations developed from prior utterances,[30] ascribe their interpretation as the producer's meaning and hold the producer accountable for it, revise interpretations of prior utterances as necessitated by apparent inconsistencies, and form expectations and projected interpretations of future utterances on the basis of their interpretation of the present utterance. These first two principles are complementary to the assumption of maximal relevance[31] posited by Sperber and Wilson: The expectation of sequential placement and interpretability implies that each utterance will efficiently alter the mutual cognitive environment in a cumulative way.

---

[29] See Chapter 12. This is a staple of, for example, Marx Brothers and Abbot and Costello routines.
[30] The discourse context (Chapter 7).   [31] Sperber and Wilson (1986).

According to the *recipient design principle*, speakers frame each utterance based on interpretations of and expectations from previous utterances and expectations for hearers' uptake of the current utterance. Speakers attribute to hearers both knowledge of the interpretation of ongoing utterances and the necessary resources for interpreting the utterances (based on assumptions about the mutual cognitive environment), and presume that hearers will ascribe their interpretation of the utterance to the speaker and hold the speaker accountable for it. Speakers are "specifically accountable for designing their utterances for the particular recipients they target."[32] The knowledge and capabilities of the recipient are part of the mutual cognitive environment, updated as a conversation progresses. This consideration implies an expectation, consistent with Relevance Theory, that both speaker and listeners will access the most salient features of their mutual cognitive environment as needed to narrow the range of plausible meanings and resolve perceived ambiguities.

The triadic structure of communication identified by Arundale clearly depends on theory of mind and the ability to project the present situation forward to anticipate future situations. Specifically, what is the other person likely to say next, and how will the other person react to one's own possible utterances? The ability to project how the other person will finish a present utterance and how the other person might respond to what oneself says next is critically dependent on the accuracy of one's own representation of the other person's perceptions, thoughts, beliefs, and so on. This in turn depends on accurate representation of the mutual cognitive environment, what is known and salient to all participants. Neither Sperber and Wilson nor Arundale specifically address facework, but it is apparent that the other's face concerns and the other's awareness of one's own face concerns are part of the mutual cognitive environment, and are ordinarily taken into account in forward projections of a conversation.

Arundale argues that models of language use based on encoding/decoding models cannot explain the nonsummative effects of even ordinary communicative interactions because they address only the effect of one person's utterance on another, ignore reciprocal conditionality as well as the sequential organization of talk. They cannot account for even a commonplace interaction like the Marty and Loes example. This is in large part due to the assumptions that language units have discrete, fixed, and code-like meanings independent of any context of use and that each utterance is relevant to one and only one cognitive context. "The Conjoint Co-constituting Model of Communication represents a radical shift in framing from conventional models because

---

[32] Raymond (2003, p. 950), as quoted by Arundale (2010).

meaning and action are explained as social, and specifically as interactional, rather than simply as cognitive in nature."[33] I would extend this formulation by emphasizing the nontelic nature of conversation as a means of relationship maintenance. I would also suggest that the co-constituting nature of conversation often extends, at least in close relationships, across multiple interactions. Speakers often assume prior interactions as well as prior utterances within the present interaction as background knowledge and expect hearers to account for this extended background.

Conversation Scripts

Beginnings. Sometimes conversations begin just because two people happen to meet; at other times, one person decides to begin a conversation. Either way, to initiate a conversation presents a claim on the other person's time and attention, an assertion of one's own positive face ("I am worth your time and attention") and a possible threat to the other's autonomy, because of the implied obligation to participate in the conversation. For this reason, greetings are often ambiguous with respect to whether a conversation is expected. "Hello" and the more informal "Hi" or "Hey" demand only a similar greeting in reciprocation, but they leave open the possibility of an extended conversation.

More extended greetings such as "How are you doing?" are more complex. They imply a concern for the other's welfare (support for the other's positive face) but also imply an obligation to respond (a threat to the other's autonomy). In most circumstances, these implicit questions are treated as formulaic greetings, and the expected response is a neutrally positive word or phrase ("Fine") followed by a reciprocal inquiry ("What about you?") However, under unusual circumstances like the 2020–2022 pandemic or known health problems, the formulaic question may be intended as a literal question and receive a literal account of the respondent's state of health. Conversely, it may also elicit a playful response, such as "Couldn't be better" or *"Fine as frog's hair."*[34]

Either person can signal readiness for a conversation in several ways, including the tonal quality of the greeting, a marked orientation toward the other person, and so on. The next step might be extended eye contact, usually accompanied by a question or a particle such as "say, ..." Any one of these escalations presents the other person with a face-maintenance dilemma, in that refusing the engagement entails an overt face threat to the person initiating the conversation. A rejection is ordinarily prefaced by an apology, and either

---

[33] Arundale (2010, p. 2085). Note that Clark (1996) developed a fully specified theory of communication as a co-constitutive interaction.
[34] Ritchie and Dyhouse (2008).

prefaced or followed by an account – for example, "I'm so sorry, I don't have time to talk now because I'm late for an appointment" – and often by a promise of restitution: "Can I call you tonight?" Similarly, a request for a conversation is often prefaced by an apology and an offered excuse – for example, "Excuse me, do you have a moment?"

Beginnings usually include implicit negotiation about the nature and extent of the interaction. Sometimes it is explicit: "I only have a minute" establishes an expected duration (short, but not necessarily literally one minute) and "I'd like to ask you about ..." establishes a central topic. Often it is implicit: The maddening propensity of people to block stairways and entrances while they chat is probably as much as anything due to the fear that, if they move to one side, out of other people's way, they are committing to a prolonged conversation.[35] By stopping in the middle of traffic, both participants signal that the conversation will be short and assert both their own and the other's positive face by implying that they both have many things on their agenda,[36] while minimizing the threat to negative face by minimizing the expectation for prolonged engagement. (On the other hand, it is a face threat to other pedestrians, whose freedom of motion is constrained, with the implication that their convenience is of less importance than that of the two interlocutors.)

Terminations. Ending a conversation can pose as many face threats as beginning one. Signaling an intention to end a conversation implies a limit to the other person's value as a companion, and ordinarily requires mitigating action, including accounts ("I'm running late") and reassurances ("It was great talking to you; let's have lunch soon"). Extralinguistic signals ordinarily include some blend of orientation toward departure with signals of reluctance to leave. Because of the absence of visual signals, ending telephone conversations can be infamously difficult, sometimes requiring many speaking turns to accomplish.

Topic Changes and Framing. The less telic (purpose-driven) and more paratelic the conversation, the more likely it is that it will range over many topics. Topic changes can pose their own face threats: Is the other person finished with the current topic? Does a topic change signal boredom? Additionally, a topic change can pose problems for common ground: Unless the background information is already salient, coherence may require prefatory remarks that raise the salience and establish common ground for the new topic.

If a topic change also changes the nature of the interaction, for example, from paratelic to telic, "socializing" to "business," or vice versa, reframing

---

[35] It may also signal an exclusive focus on the interaction – a strong support for the other's positive face.
[36] The face threat to others, to passersby whose movements are blocked or restricted, is usually unintentional.

signals may be required. These include stock phrases like "on a more serious note," "If you don't mind, I'd like to talk business," or phrases that reframe the conversation in the opposite direction, "on a more personal note" or the general-purpose "by the way." Extralinguistic signals often serve similar functions – for example, laughter or changes in gesture, bodily posture, facial expression, or vocal tone.

Power and Status. Almost every interaction involves social status and power in some way, but the Hobbesian claim that all interaction is a power struggle is not supported by actual observation. To the contrary, the more paratelic the interaction, the more likely it is that it will include signals that *deemphasize* status differentials. Even conversations that are primarily telic are often characterized by equalizing signals such as self-deprecating humor if the status differences are perceived to be detrimental or irrelevant to the primary purpose of the interaction.[37]

Under some circumstances, it seems likely that large and well-established status differences might reduce the face threat involved in conversation management, and thereby simplify openings, topic changes, and closings. If one person is of much higher status – for example, a supervisor or professor talking with an employee or student or a celebrity talking with a fan – the higher status implies the right to open and close the conversation, change or reframe topics, and so on. The greater the status difference, the less face threat might be involved in asserting control over the conversation (but the greater the face threat from an insult or slight). When a higher-status person uses face-preserving signals in such a context, it has the effect of enhancing the face of the lower-status person, a "*grooming*" effect. This can also enhance the status, and the face, of the higher-status person by demonstrating a high level of both concern for others and self-confidence (in effect, "My status is so secure that it is not impaired by using self-effacing phrases like 'please' and 'if you don't mind.'")

Turn-Taking. In ordinary conversations, people take speaking turns that are of varying length (not predetermined), and the transition between speakers is usually tidy, with minimal overlap or delay between speakers. This seems obvious primarily because it is so familiar, but in practice it requires a highly tuned process of attention and cooperation.[38] Enfield[39] uses the metaphor "conversation *machine*" to emphasize the automatic and almost mechanical reliability of turn-taking in ordinary conversation.[40]

---

[37] Schnrr and Chan (2011); Terrion and Ashforth (2002). [38] Clark (1996).
[39] Enfield (2017).
[40] Unfortunately, Enfield's "conversation *machine*" metaphor also downplays the attention, imagination, and effort that is often required to keep the "*machine*" running smoothly.

There is a fundamental contradiction within conversation between the slow speed at which the brain processes language and our expectations about coherence and fluency; the way we resolve this contradiction tells us a lot about how the brain processes language as it engages with the interactive nature of conversation. On the one hand, we know that it takes about a half second to process and understand a typical word and slightly longer, about 600 milliseconds, to access, formulate, and utter a word – for example, in a task requiring subjects to recognize and name familiar objects such as a horse in a series of pictures.[41] On the other hand, across a variety of languages, the time that elapses between the completion of an utterance by one speaker and the beginning of an utterance by another speaker averages about 200 milliseconds, with overlaps occurring in all languages. There is some variation between cultures: For example, Japanese has a very short lag, only averaging about 7 milliseconds, and at the other extreme, Danish has a relatively long lag, averaging about 470 milliseconds.[42] Overlapping speech is observed in all cultures, although the overlap rarely exceeds about 400 milliseconds. Near the other end of the spectrum, lags longer than a full second are also rare: In every language, a delay of more than one second is uncomfortable. When lags occur, they often evoke corrective measures from the initial speaker.

In sum, people routinely start speaking a full second (or more) before they have finished processing the final phrase of the previous utterance. Moreover, if they need time to finish processing the previous utterance and begin formulating a response, they typically signal the delay with a word like "uh" or "um."[43] It is apparent that listeners begin formulating a response at least a full second before the end of the previous speaking turn. This apparent contradiction raises the question, how do people do that?

Enfield describes several cues that indicate the end of a speaking turn. Sometimes the end of a turn is apparent from grammatical indications – for example, phrasing that implies a question. Other important cues include a drawn-out final syllable and a drop in pitch or loudness. Gestures and a shift in gaze (for example, sustained eye contact with a person who is expected to speak next) are also often used to indicate the end of a speaking turn.

To test the effectiveness of vocalic characteristics in signaling the end of a speaking turn, DeRuiter et al.[44] played segments of white noise and segments of spoken language to subjects and asked them to press a button as soon as possible after the moment when they thought the speaker's turn would end.

---

[41] Enfield (2017).   [42] Enfield (2017).
[43] Enfield (2017). These particles, "uh" and "um," like everything else people volitionally control, are also used as signals with relevance to other cognitive contexts beyond the turn-taking scripts, in particular for facework, as I will discuss later in this chapter.
[44] DeRuiter, Mitterer, and Enfield (2006).

The researchers found that subjects needed about 1.5 seconds to indicate when white noise ends, but only .2 second to identify the end of a recorded speaking turn. A flattened pitch did not affect response time, but when the researchers muffled the words to make them unintelligible, response time increased to about a half second. These results indicate that lexical content, grammatical features, and prosody all provide predictive cues to the end of a speaking turn .

Listeners attend closely to prosodic features, gesture, gaze, and the grammatical structure of what is being said as well as content in order to predict when a speaking turn is ended and accomplish a smooth speaking turn transition. However, there must be more to it than that. The features described by Enfield do not account for turn transitions that begin with an overlap. It appears that the end of a turn is often ambiguous, and when beginning a turn under ambiguous circumstances, people usually attend to cues that assist in a smooth transition. These cues are strictly vocal in telephone and other voice-only mediated conversation, but include gaze and other signals in face-to-face communication or mediated conversation with a high-quality visual channel. More basically, the prosodic cues discussed by Enfield, as well as other indicators such as gaze and gesture, occur at or very near the end of a speaking turn, usually on the final word or phrase. Given that it takes a full second or longer to process an utterance and formulate a response, it is apparent that something else is contributing to smooth turn-taking.

The implication is that listeners anticipate, well in advance, not only when the speaker will finish but also what the speaker is going to say.[45] The brain maintains a "forward projection" simulation model of the current situation and how it is expected to develop over the next few seconds. This includes a model of what the speaker is probably going to say, how the speaker will finish the current speaking turn, and how the ideas being expressed fit in with the listener's prior representation of the world, the listener's knowledge, beliefs, attitudes, and so on. Do the ideas the speaker is expressing and is expected to finish with agree with, contradict, qualify, or extend the listener's prior representation? What kind of response will be called for?

Depending on the conversation, this simulation model may include a model of several paths the speaker might take, and how the conversation will proceed from there. Comprehension in real time also requires that listeners continually connect the ideas expressed by the speaker with the mutual cognitive environment, the contexts (schemas) most relevant to the topic and previous utterances, salient features of the listener's own prior knowledge, attitudes, and feelings. Unless these ideas are entirely new to the hearer, the simulation model will include the hearer's own potential responses to what the speaker

---

[45] See also Bergen (2012).

is expected to say. Will the hearer disagree, agree, or extend what has just been said? Will the hearer ask for clarification or examples, or provide new examples? Will the hearer tell a story that supports or contradicts what has just been said? Will there be an opportunity for a bit of wordplay or a humorous quip? Much of this forward projection is only partially conscious[46] (and it is interspersed with other thoughts, often unrelated to the present social situation).

Social and cultural norms, participants' personalities and interpersonal relationships, and the social implications of the speaker's utterance and the hearer's ongoing potential response will all be part of the Mutual Cognitive Environment: For example, how might the ideas expressed by the speaker, and alternative possible responses to these ideas, affect the hearer's relationship with the speaker? How might they affect the progress of the conversation? Depending on the nature of the conversation, these background factors may not be at all salient.

As the speaker continues, the topic-related contexts and other activated and salient contexts will be updated according to the relevance of the speaker's utterances and other signals; the projection of how the current speaking turn may play out and the formulation of one or more potential responses will also be continually updated. This forward projection enables the hearer, once it is evident that the current speaking turn is drawing to a close, to commence the partially formulated response almost immediately, sometimes even before the speaker has entirely finished (producing a brief overlap).

This forward projection and anticipation is a feature of virtually all conversations, including gossip, flirting, storytelling, and so on. It incorporates a crucial part of the process through which we comprehend language (by relating what is said to what we already know and believe) into the process through which we produce language and use it to engage in social interaction. It also represents the intersection of cognitive processes of producing and comprehending speech with social processes of maintaining relationships and conducting communicative interaction – all under the influence (and regulation) of cultural norms and practices.

Delays. If a listener delays the beginning of a speaking turn any longer than a second, the speaker will either issue a prompt or assume the listener has nothing to say at this point and resume speaking. The variation within what Enfield calls the "one-second window" of turn-taking is itself quite complex. A pause longer than one second may indicate that both parties are "*at a loss* for words," but it is often deliberately produced as a signal of discomfort or a desire to disengage from the conversation.

---

[46] Baumeister and Masicampo (2010).

When a response is required (as to a question, request, or invitation), a delay beyond a half second or so will be taken as either a cue that the respondent is having difficulty formulating a response, or as an intentional (and meaningful) signal. A question, especially if it was not anticipated, may require extra time for accessing relevant knowledge or beliefs. Even a request or invitation may require extra processing time (e.g. Do I have other obligations that prevent me from agreeing to the request or accepting the invitation?). Politeness norms play an important role here. If the response is negative ("dispreferred"), additional processing time may be required to devise a way of "*softening the blow*," reducing the face threat to the person who issued the question, request, or invitation. To signal an intention to respond, or just to buy time to formulate a response, a listener may stake a claim to a speaking turn while delaying its beginning by use of an initial "um" or "uh."[47]

Even in the most casual conversations, people tend to act in a way that preserves both their own and others' face, their sense of being socially accepted and esteemed, and their sense of autonomy. "Yes," even in response to an apparently neutral question, is usually preferred to "no." This is particularly true if the preceding utterance is a request or invitation. Requesting a favor represents an imposition on the listener, hence threatens the listener's autonomy, but it also implies a belief that the listener might be willing to comply (based on the listener's expected valuation of the relationship) and thus exposes the speaker to a loss of positive face. Extending an invitation similarly exposes the speaker to a loss of positive face, while affirming the positive face of the invited person.

When the listener is motivated to save face for the person making a request or issuing an invitation, some time may be required to think of a way to phrase a refusal that will reduce the face threat. Time may also be required to consider whether compliance is possible (e.g. "Do other obligations prevent compliance?") An extended delay before replying is a cue that the respondent had to think about the request, or may signal a reluctance to refuse the request or invitation. Conversely, too quick a response is a cue that little thought was required: A quick refusal increases the damage to the requestor's positive face, but a quick acceptance increases the support for the requestor's positive face. Like most cues, the delay due to cognitive difficulties can be and routinely is turned into a signal. Even when addressees have no intention to comply with the invitation or request, they may delay a refusal long enough to reduce the face threat to the initial speaker. Conversely, a delayed acceptance may be used to express a lack of enthusiasm. Since this is general knowledge, a delay (whether or not accompanied by "uh" or "um") may be interpreted as a signal

---

[47] Enfield (2017).

relevant to *other* cognitive contexts, leading to inferences about the respondent's degree of interest in the request or invitation or even about the respondent's commitment to the relationship.

People deal with all this in several ways. Speakers may phrase a request or invitation in a way that makes a refusal easier, provides a built-in excuse, and thus reduces both the threat to the listener's autonomy and the potential damage to the speaker's positive face. For example, "I know you're busy right now, but ..." or "I realize this is a last-minute invitation, but ...." Similarly, the respondent may begin a refusal with an apology, or offer an account instead of an explicit refusal – for example, "I'm sorry, but I promised to attend a meeting tomorrow at that time."

Even "yes or no" questions are subject to the positive response preference. Stivers[48] found that three-fourth of "yes/no" questions are answered affirmatively. Enfield explains that this is likely to be the result of a tendency to phrase questions in a way that reduces the probability of a negative response. When a negative response is more likely than a positive response, the question may be phrased in such a way that a negative response seems more cooperative, hence preferred. This may often result from an extra-long delay (over 600 milliseconds) in response, which leads the person who posed the question to rephrase it in a way that is easier to answer.

Preferred responses are usually produced quickly, within a half second at most, and are rarely preceded by nonword fillers. (The major exception would be if significant cognitive effort is required – for example, mentally reviewing scheduled activities or obligations – in which case the respondent may use a turn extender like "Let me see ..."). Dispreferred responses, on the other hand, begin with an intake of breath or a particle such as "tut" or "um." Either preferred or dispreferred responses may begin with a half second or so of silence, prolonged silence is more likely to precede a dispreferred response. Aside from the utterance of a particle, an actual response occurs after 500 milliseconds in half of all dispreferred responses but only in 20 percent of all preferred responses.[49]

Formulating a Response. Most people experience a constant flow of thoughts, some random, some more or less loosely connected to the current social interaction. These are characterized by the interaction of semantic and syntactic resources, perceptual simulations, introspection, interoception, and evaluation (primarily emotional).[50] Thoughts pertinent to the current conversation (cognitive contexts) include thoughts about the topic and related concepts, about the participants and relationships, cultural norms and expectations, and the progress of the conversation itself. Thoughts in the

---

[48] Stivers (2010).   [49] Kendrick and Torreira (2015).   [50] Chafe (2012); Chapter 4.

"stream of consciousness" include partial representations of relevance to some of the more salient cognitive contexts, particularly those related to the topic but also some related to relationships and social norms.

The brain maintains and continuously updates a representation of the social situation, relationships, and the conversation. This includes a representation of what has gone before and a forward projection of how the interaction is likely to proceed. In particular, the forward representation includes expectations of what the present speaker will say, when their turn will be completed, and various alternatives for a response. Potential responses are influenced by and may be drawn from thoughts in the "stream of consciousness," often supplemented with language, representations, and emotions emerging from preconscious thought. This constantly updated representation and forward projection enables listeners to anticipate the end of a speaking turn and commence a reply almost immediately.

Since thoughts involve perceptual and evaluative as well as lexical and syntactic features, formulating an utterance begins with categorization, as a basis for selecting words that express the category. Both word choice and syntax are selected to fit the evaluative and perceptual features. Because the fit is rarely precise, the same thought may be expressed in quite different ways on different occasions – including during a metacommunicative exchange that may ensue if the utterance doesn't sound right to the speaker or is challenged by a listener.[51]

Chafe argues that thoughts are expressed in *intonation units*, often five to seven words, marked by brief pauses and a falling intonation on the final syllable.[52] These intonation units emerge, like actors from behind a stage curtain, as the next thought is being formulated. Under some circumstances, a speaker will hesitate long enough to formulate a complete utterance, but ordinarily the speaker plans the general direction of the speaking turn while it is in progress, and perceives the exact words, phrases, and gestures as they are being produced – along with the listeners, or slightly in advance of them.

Because responses must be formulated "on the fly" and constantly updated, relevance and potential relevance can be considered with respect to only a small part of the Mutual Cognitive Environment. The result may be that the wrong idea is extracted from the jumble of thoughts, or a temporary failure of semantic memory leads to the wrong word or a mangled or mispronounced word. Speakers monitor their own utterances along with listeners and may notice the inaccuracy or error as they speak or shortly after speaking. They may also notice unattended secondary meanings or previously unnoticed relevance to secondary cognitive contexts, including unintended face threats

---

[51] Chafe (2012).   [52] Chafe (1994, 2012).

or violations of cultural norms. If the "mistake" is detected by the speaker, it may result in a start-over or self-initiated repair; if it is detected by a listener, the listener may initiate a repair. Either way, an account may be expected and offered along with the repair, to minimize the damage to speakers' and listeners' face.

Repairs. Because of the rapid pace of turn-taking, speakers often begin a speaking turn with only a general idea of what they will say, and formulate utterances on the fly, one intonation unit at a time.[53] One result of this is the need for frequent repairs, about once every minute and a half. Repairs may be needed for any of a number of reasons: a word is mispronounced or the wrong word used, or a phrase has unforeseen negative and potentially face-threatening implications. Sometimes the speaker misjudges the "common ground," and refers to information a listener doesn't have or that is not currently salient. Sometimes the utterance is well-formed but does not satisfy the speaker's intention. Sometimes a hearer derives implicatures (either about the topic or implied face threats) that were not intended by the speaker. Although utterances are sometimes constructed in advance, most frequently we hear our own utterances as we speak, and often fail to understand some of the implications of what we have said until we monitor listeners' reactions, which may signal the need for a repair (or the opportunity to accept undeserved credit for an inadvertent but clever pun).

Repairs may be initiated by speaker or listener. When a problem is recognized, the person who recognizes the problem must quickly decide whether it is sufficiently important to call attention to it (and disrupt the flow of talk) by correcting or requesting a correction. Most adults are proficient at mentally correcting perceived errors (and assessing whether an implied face threat was intentional or not), and we often silently make the repair or disregard the face threat.[54] However, the frequency of repair sequences shows that people often prefer not to let such problems go uncorrected, but to point out and solve the problem.[55] I haven't found any research on why some problems are allowed to go uncorrected,[56] but it is likely a function of the importance of the conversation and the seriousness of the error, weighed against the disruption of the speaker's performance, and the face threat it poses.

Recursion

A powerful feature of both language and conversation structure is the ability to embed language sequences within each other, either in full (as a quotation or

---

[53] Chafe (1994).   [54] Schegloff, Jefferson, and Sacks (1977).   [55] Enfield (2017).
[56] As my colleague Jeff Robinson (personal communication, October 2020) pointed out to me, this would be very difficult to research.

paraphrase) or referentially. Repairs often occasion metadiscourse about the error to be corrected. In particular, if the meaning of a "first-part utterance"[57] is ambiguous or has been challenged, it may lead to a metadiscussion about the language used, its relevance to the topic, or even the nature of the present conversation.

Clark[58] discusses two additional examples of recursion, *levels* and *layers*. *Levels* refers to the three actions involved in an utterance (discussed earlier in this chapter): meaning something, formulating utterances to express the meaning, and vocalizing the sounds. In ordinary conversation, these actions are performed by the same person, in the role of speaker. However, in other, nonbasic settings such as a political press conference, the three actions may be decoupled and assigned to different persons. In these contexts, the person who produces a string of signals, often an utterance of some length, is not necessarily the person who formulated the utterance itself, or the thought behind it. In the trope "the White House issued a statement ...," the press secretary is usually the *vocalizer* (Level 1), who actually utters or writes a string of words (and answers or evades questions about it). The President (or a committee of advisors) formulated the thoughts (Level 3). The words themselves may have been formulated (Level 2) by any of these actors – President, committee, or press secretary – or by someone else entirely. In more complicated examples, Shakespeare (Level 2) wrote words to express thoughts he imagines Macbeth might have had (Level 3), and an actor utters these words (Level 1) to an audience.[59] An interesting wrinkle is a political speech, in which the actual words spoken by the politician (Level 1) may have been formulated by a speech writer (Level 2) to represent the politician's thoughts (Level 3). The political example highlights an important feature of the process: There is likely to be extensive negotiation among all three roles,[60] especially the President and the speech writer, to ensure that the President's thoughts are expressed with suitable accuracy and relevance; the press secretary who must present the ideas may also advocate for wording that will be easier to explain or justify.

Layers refer to the "story" that is represented. The highest layer, Layer 1, is the present conversation. If one person quotes or paraphrases another person, that is Layer 2. The concept of layers helps analyze and explain a "story within a story," for example. In *Midsummer Night's Dream*, Bottom and his crew perform a play (Layer 2) *within* Shakespeare's play (Layer 1). If I describe a

---

[57] Arundale (2010).   [58] Clark (1996).
[59] If the actor is skilled, the members of the audience hear them as if they were originated and spoken by Macbeth.
[60] This occurs even when one person occupies all three roles. Orators may struggle over how best to word their ideas, then alter the phrasing while giving the speech. As I write this footnote, I am engaged in copy-editing the manuscript – and changing some of it to express my ideas (I hope) more accurately.

recent performance of *Midsummer Night's Dream* to a friend, my conversation with my friend is Layer 1; the performance is Layer 2; the play, *Midsummer Night's Dream*, is Layer 3; Nick Bottom's play is Layer 4. As Clark observes, the characters in each layer can know about the actions and utterances of those in each *lower* layer, but cannot (in principle) know about higher layers: Pyramus and Thisbe know nothing of Bottom and his recent amorous misadventures,[61] and none of them know anything about the performance of Shakespeare's play. Neither Shakespeare nor the actors who presented the play know anything about my use of it as an example here. Layers and Levels often occur together. In *Midsummer Night's Dream*, in the play within a play (Layer 3), actors (Level 1) playing Bottom and his crew (Level 2) utter words Shakespeare wrote (Level 3) to represent thoughts attributed to the characters, Pyramus and Thisbe (Level 4).

Layering is important in logical argumentation. Rhetors routinely represent (or sometimes misrepresent) the ideas of an opponent to explain why they are wrong. Sometimes this can go three or four layers deep: In Chapter 5, I represented (Layer 1) Barrett's (Layers 2 and 3) representation and criticism of Ekman's theories of emotion expression (Layer 4), then summarized LeDoux's qualifying remarks about Barrett's claims (Layers 2 and 3). Understanding theoretical arguments requires close attention to layering; miss a layer, and it is easy to attribute ideas to an author that the author is specifically criticizing and rejecting.[62]

Settings and Genres

The elaboration and branching of conversation produce an array of conversation types, too many to discuss here. The basic structure of conversation discussed in this chapter is adapted, often in an ad hoc way, for each setting. *Telic* conversations such as business and political meetings and negotiations are *about* something, primarily engaged to achieve a purpose that may be private or shared. In a formal meeting, turn-taking, the sequence of topics, and ending the conversation are often specified in advance and almost always controlled by an appointed or elected leader. Ritual gatherings like weddings and funerals are even more tightly constrained, by both custom and explicit

---

[61] Authors love to play against this constraint. A favorite passage in Tolkien's *Lord of the Rings*, unfortunately absent from the movie version, occurs in Book 3 when Frodo and Sam discuss how people in the future will react to the story of their trials and adventures.

[62] This is apparently a difficult skill to master: Even advanced students in my communication theory classes often miss the words and phrases that signal a change in layer, such as "According to ...," "however ...," and, more straightforward, "I disagree." My own writings have also been misquoted more than once by an author who represented my work as endorsing a view that I have explicitly criticized.

rules. An example of an *informal* telic conversation is the "Reconciliation Talks" between Jo Berry, whose father was killed by a bomb planted by the IRA and Pat Magee, who planted the bomb, that have been extensively analyzed by Lynne Cameron.[63] In these talks, the topics ranged from the bombing itself to Magee's motives for planting the bomb and Berry's emotional responses, then to the possibility for reconciliation between the warring sides in the conflict. An example of a more formal telic conversation is a meeting about police-community relations researched by Lynne Cameron and myself.[64] The police-community meeting was initially organized and controlled by trained facilitators, but it was characterized by a struggle over control of the topic sequence, the framing of the meeting, and the emotional tone. Instructional communication is usually controlled by the person giving instruction, but it may be driven by the learner's questions.

Although they are sometimes initiated for a particular purpose (such as issuing an invitation or requesting a favor), ordinary sociable conversations are usually not *about* anything in particular. Turn-taking and topics are spontaneous and informal, and the tone of the conversation may change several times. Dinner party conversations usually fall in between the extremes of control: the host may control the conversation's beginning and ending and exercise a flexible degree of influence (and, less frequently, actual control) over topics and turn-taking.

Language play and humor occur in almost every setting; they are usually bracketed by establishing a *play frame* by means of facial expression, intonation, and other signals. Signaling a play frame indicates that what follows is not to be taken seriously, and relaxes most of the rules of ordinary conversation, including the expectations of truth, relevance, and coherence. *Flirting* is a subgenre within playful communication, and may include joking, teasing (mock-aggression), and double-entendres that suggest a potential sexual interpretation.[65]

Conflict Talk. Disagreement can arise in any of these settings. It may be framed as logical *argumentation* in which positions are stated and supported or challenged by evidence. In informal conversations, the interaction is frequently framed as *conflict talk*, with its own almost ritualized script. Conflict talk is characterized by a sequence of at least three speaking turns, an initial assertion followed by a contradiction and a reinstatement.[66] A simplified example from Norrick and Spitz illustrates one general pattern: "You're skinny—no, I'm not

---

[63] For example, Cameron (2007). [64] Ritchie and Cameron (2014).
[65] Language play and humor are discussed in greater detail in Chapters 10 and 12.
[66] For example, Hutchby (1996); Muntigl and Turnbull (1998); Schiffrin (1985); Norrick and Spitz, (2010).

—yes, you are."[67] Once the conflict script has begun, the normal preference for agreement is reversed. Because *disagreement* is the unmarked (expected) response, even the most innocent comment, including citing supporting evidence, may be taken as contentious, and the structure of the conversation becomes oppositional rather than collaborative. However, as one of my students has pointed out, the "yes — no — yes" sequence can and often is interrupted by a challenge to the other person's underlying assumptions, which shifts the topic and sometimes the nature of the conflict.

Conflict sequences can end in only a few ways. In *submission*, one party concedes; in *compromise*, the parties agree to some middle position. In a *standoff*, both parties maintain their initial position, leading to either an abrupt topic change or *withdrawal*, in which one party ceases to respond and the interaction terminates. Humor can help in several ways, including facilitating a topic switch or allowing one party to concede with less loss of face. Humor can also defuse tension, reduce face threats, and facilitate resolving the conflict.[68] Because the conflict talk script is so familiar, it is often the focus of playful humor – for example, when people argue jokingly over a topic of little consequence, exchanging humorous put-downs. Conflict talk is often parodied or simulated within a play frame as a form of humor[69] – and flirting.[70]

Argumentation and Logic. Yet another function of conversation is to deliberate about individual and collective actions by projecting the current representation forward as a story about how the situation would be affected by each of the alternative actions. In group deliberations, two participants often have divergent or contradictory opinions, in which case the deliberation may develop features of conflict talk. Maintaining the mutual representation or "social reality" involves pooling information from the experiences (perceptions) of various group members; this information must also be evaluated and interpreted according to the knowledge and beliefs already common to the group. In some cases, the interpretation may not be obvious, and two or more participants may present contradictory interpretations (or may report experiences and perceptions with contradictory implications). This situation may also develop features of conflict talk.

Both individually and as groups, people face the need to make decisions frequently. We make dozens of trivial decisions every day, but we also make consequential decisions about relationships, food, shelter, and other resources, about safety, and work. We deliberate about these decisions in various ways, sometimes through an extension and adaptation of conflict talk. Even in informal conversations, when conflict arises, people offer evidence that

---

[67] Norrick and Spitz (2010, p. 90).   [68] Norrick and Spitz (2010).
[69] See Chapter 12 for examples and discussion.
[70] Norrick and Spitz (2010) provide an example of flirtatious conflict talk in a phone conversation.

supports their claims and contradicts opposing or alternative position(s). This often takes the form of one or more stories, or references to a mutually known story. Sometimes a generic story ("things that typically happen") is introduced as evidence; sometimes a metaphorical story is recalled or invented to support a claim. Claims are often supported by citing facts and supposed facts, which may be backed by media accounts, recognized authorities, formal education, hearsay, or personal observation. Stories and facts introduced as evidence may themselves be disputed through extensions of the basic conflict talk. Thinking often takes the form of silent argumentation, in which contrasting decisions or courses of action are imagined, each supported by recalled data and examples.

Argumentation, both to maintain mutual representations, the "social reality" of a group, and to decide on a course of action, follows patterns and rules that have been formulated in many ways, based on prevailing assumptions about the nature of reality (ontology) and of knowledge (epistemology). Deliberation is often guided by rules (usually implicit but made explicit in formal or institutional settings) about what constitutes evidence and how it is to be evaluated, and about how arguments are constructed and conclusions justified. In Medieval European thought, *knowledge* was based on reasoning from "first principles," using systems of logic dating to Aristotle; inductive reasoning from observable evidence could lead only to *opinion*, and characterized the "low sciences," alchemy, geology, astrology, and medicine.[71]

As empirical science gained power and status, the status of these two approaches to deliberation was gradually reversed.[72] According to contemporary empirical epistemology, knowledge is based on inductive reasoning from observational evidence and tested through deductive reasoning about the results of controlled experiments.[73] Although most people are not very good at this kind of formal theory-based reasoning,[74] conclusions based on observational evidence are generally valued above conclusions based on "mere opinion." Outside of academic settings and quasi-academic settings like law and some medical practices, deliberation often follows the *form* of reasoning from evidence, providing evidence to support a preferred conclusion or to contradict a dispreferred conclusion, but without the *substance* of reasoning from evidence. Evidence is commonly selected, interpreted, and evaluated according to prior beliefs and opinions.[75] As a result of "motivated reasoning," even when deliberation takes the form of reasoning from evidence, it often has

---

[71] Ritchie (2003d).
[72] The recent upwelling of anti-science sentiment – for example, in anti-vaccination and climate change denial – marks a resurgence of an even earlier version of Medieval European thought, in which knowledge was based on reasoning from revealed truth.
[73] Kuhn (1991).   [74] Ritchie (2003c).
[75] Ziva (1990). This happens even in scientific and scholarly reasoning, which is why criticism and replication are so important.

the substance of selecting and interpreting evidence to support prior commitments or emotion-based preferences.

Summary

The basic structure of conversation developed in tandem with language and with the increasingly complex structure of social relationships that language supports. Both language and conversation coevolved with the physiological structures (including the brain) necessary for complex signaling and social interactions. As language and conversation became increasingly complex and sophisticated, cultural norms and practices developed and, in turn, influenced the further development of language and language use in conversation. Conversation forms have branched out and elaborated into a variety of genres, ranging from informal socializing to highly structured institutional discourse such as religious rites, legal proceedings, parliamentary debate, and so on. In turn, many of these forms are internalized as the silent dialogues of individual thought, in which we silently debate and deliberate about alternative courses of action, rehearse for anticipated conversations, recall and replay remembered conversations, and fantasize about possible conversations.

As social structure expanded and became more complex, initially in response to agriculture and the growth of towns, division of labor and the development of socioeconomic and political class structure, relationships and group memberships also became more complex. In a modern urban culture, an individual may belong to many groups, each with a distinct common (shared) representation of the group and its members within the social and physical environment. Individuals impart information from one group in conversations in other group settings, evaluating, distorting, and synthesizing information in a complex process that constitutes public *discourse*.[76]

Language play, humor, stories, and metaphor are part of both the social conversations and the private, internal stream-of-consciousness conversations. These forms of language use are the topic of the next four chapters. The final two chapters will address the effect of communication media on interpersonal communication and relationships, and how these processes generate and shape public discourse.

---

[76] Chapter 15.

10   Play[1]

As I write this chapter (during the 2020 pandemic), I am sitting on a bluff watching powerboats plying back and forth on the Willamette River, each towing a person on one of an amazing array of floating platforms. Play is a major industry, a mainstay of the world economy, and a primary locus of social interaction and interpersonal bonding for children and adults alike. Many forms of play, those that require personal proximity or contact, are greatly missed in this season of contagion, and the urge to engage in social play is a strong inducement to flout the recommended pandemic distancing and isolation protocols. Humans (like laboratory rats and other animals) will risk – and sacrifice – a lot for the opportunity to play.

Oddly, play, intentionally pointless activity undertaken for no reason other than the pleasure it gives, has not received nearly the attention it deserves from social science. The attention it has received tends toward trivialization (play is something children and juveniles of other species do), commercialization, or humorless utilitarianism. The occasional admission that *some* adults do, *sometimes*, play in an utterly frivolous way is usually mitigated by shifting the focus at once to "child's play,"[2] or by convoluted explanations of how humor and playful language are thinly disguised aggression in the pursuit of power and social status.[3] In this chapter, I begin with a discussion of the nature and evolutionary development of play. I discuss language play as an element in conversation and humor, and end with a discussion of the contribution of play to homeostasis.

The Nature of Play

Theorists often ignore lighthearted or whimsical play and equate adult "play" exclusively with competitive games of skill or chance.[4] Genuinely frivolous and incongruous behaviors (such as deliberately distorting the sound of

---

[1] Sections of this chapter are based on and adapted from Ritchie (2005, 2009, 2011); Ritchie and Dyhouse (2008); Ritchie and Negrea-Busuioc (2014); Ritchie and Schell (2009).
[2] Bateson (2005).   [3] For example, Billig (2005); Zillmann and Cantor (1976).
[4] Huizinga (1955); Malaby (2006, 2007).

familiar words or phrases) make no obvious contribution to reproductive fitness, social standing, or economic success, and so they are not deemed worthy of serious attention.[5] And yet, this kind of frivolous behavior is a common occurrence in everyday life, especially in casual conversation. It appears not only at dinner parties[6] but also in university department meetings, science conferences,[7] and corporate boardrooms.[8] Frivolously playful use of language and other signals is an ubiquitous part of humor and metaphor.[9]

Although people sometimes claim that competition adds to the pleasure of a game, or at the extreme that competition is *necessary* for enjoyment,[10] Kohn[11] has shown that adults as well as children generally enjoy games more when competition is deemphasized or removed altogether. In a series of studies with young children, Lepper[12] demonstrated that offering a reward for playing with a game or toy greatly reduces children's subsequent interest in it. If one must be rewarded to do it, it may not feel like *play*.[13] Although play has many social and psychological benefits, these are incidental to its essence: Play is activity undertaken for its own sake, for the pleasure it gives.

Humans and other social animals regularly engage in both social and object play, including play with sounds and motion. Social play includes various forms of touch, including mock combat as well as chasing, jumping, and so on. Object play includes manipulating various objects (sticks and stones, leaves, smaller animals). This is often an expression of curiosity and may include combinations of objects. Social and object play are often combined, as in tug-of-war, collaborative manipulation of larger objects, throwing objects, and so forth.

Play often involves reframing – for example, reframing aggression as play or reframing an object as a doll – and it almost always involves an element of incongruity. For example, in play the stronger and ordinarily dominant participant often submits to mock-attacks from a weaker and ordinarily subordinate participant (Figure 10.1). A stone or stick may be cuddled as if it was an infant. This element of incongruity extends through humor, metaphor, and other tropes, and into storytelling and religion, where incongruity and paradox are elevated to the status of divinity.

Hurley, Dennett, and Adams argue that the enjoyment of humor is the brain's reward for recognizing and resolving incongruity,[14] a feature of all forms of play. Often incongruity is not just recognized, but actively created and left unresolved: Many religions are founded on "mysteries," incongruities

---

[5] Sutton-Smith (1995); Sherzer (2002). [6] For example, Tannen (1984).
[7] Ritchie and Schell (2002). [8] Coates (2007).
[9] Ritchie and Dyhouse (2008); Coates (2007). [10] For example, Gruner (1997).
[11] Kohn (1986). [12] Lepper, Greene, and Nisbett, (1973).
[13] Professional athletes, artists, and scientists *do* enjoy and get pleasure from their "work," just as I enjoy and get pleasure from teaching – and from writing this book.
[14] Hurley, Dennett, and Adams (2011).

Figure 10.1 Lioness with her sister's cubs

that are intended not to be resolved.[15] Playful incongruity is trivial, hence manageable and safe, fostering a reassuring sense of control for an indirect contribution to homeostasis.

Juvenile Play

Play is observed among juveniles of many species, including birds and fish as well as mammals.[16] Commonly observed play includes stylized jumping and running, stalking and pouncing on inanimate objects, carrying an inanimate object like a "baby doll," and roughhousing. Consistent with utilitarian claims, some of these behaviors imitate adult activities, and may serve a rehearsal function. When juveniles of "prey" species such as horses and deer jump and run about, they *may* be rehearsing actions to elude predators, and when juveniles of predator species stalk and pounce, they may be rehearsing for actual hunting – or they may be simply enjoying the feeling of their muscles at work. Rough and tumble play may develop skills needed for future sexual and

---

[15] Religious rituals provide believers a partial resolution of the incongruity.
[16] Bateson (2005).

social hierarchical competitions, while establishing a position in the emergent social hierarchy among other juveniles – but it is also a form of physical contact, endorphin-releasing grooming.

For human children, competitive team games are said to help the child develop and practice skills useful for success in the modern capitalist economy,[17] or for success in actual war. Famously, if apocryphally, "The battle of Waterloo was won on the playing fields of Eton."[18] For humans, language and communication play is particularly important, beginning with social-interactive games such as "peek-a-boo," the babbling of prelinguistic infants, and word and sound games between caregiver and child. All these contribute to acquiring social and communicative skills, as well as cognitive skills such as object constancy and perspective-taking.[19] However, the potential utility can't be the *motivation* for play activities for juveniles, who know nothing of "reproductive fitness" or "preparation for adult roles," and, as Lepper's research shows, emphasizing the usefulness of an activity often takes most of the fun out of it.[20]

Simpler forms of play might be an innate reflex, similar to the sucking reflex of a newborn infant; the human infant's endless babbling of meaningless syllables[21] seems to have a reflexive quality. However, an innate reflex can't explain the child's love of skip-rope rhymes, silly puns, and nonsensical wordplay.[22] Nor can it explain why more sophisticated forms of nonsense verse, puns, wordplay, and so on, continue to engage adults. For children and adults alike, these activities are *pleasurable* – they stimulate the release of endorphins and activate "pleasure circuits" in the brain for a kind of self-administered temporary "high," at the extreme leading to the state of self-transcendence Csikszentmihalyi[23] referred to as "*flow.*"

For laboratory animals, the chance to engage in play, solitary or social, has been found to be as effective as food in conditioning experiments.[24] Animals (including humans) will engage in play activities whenever the demands of more urgent needs (fear, hunger, exhaustion, anxiety) allow it. It is often claimed that play is observed among adult animals only in domesticated species, but as Figure 10.1 illustrates, adults of many species do play in the wild, just like domesticated animals.

---

[17] Cook (2000).
[18] Attributed, probably falsely, to Wellington. The chess clubs of Eton are more likely, since chess is associated with foresight and strategy.
[19] Cook (2000).
[20] The label "educational" may help sell a toy to parents or gift purchasers, but it is likely to decrease the appeal to the child who receives the gift.
[21] Lee (1986).   [22] (Carter, 2004; Cook, 2000).   [23] Csikszentmihalyi (1980).
[24] Fagen (1995).

Adult Play

Once the play-endorphin habit is acquired in childhood, if the more urgent survival needs are taken care of,[25] play is likely to persist into adulthood. Adult animals of many domesticated species, and many adult animals in zoos (where they are regularly fed and protected from predators), routinely play with toys provided by their human attendants. Adult play is also observed in the wild – for example, among wild dogs, big cats (Figure 10.1), several species of primates, cetaceans, and octopuses.[26]

Cook[27] lists four categories of play: *agon*, or competition; *alea*, games of chance; *mimicry*; and *ilinx*, the feeling of vertigo or giddiness that accompanies such activities as riding a swing or merry-go-round. Cook also refers to the feeling of "*flow*"[28] that can arise while engaging well-honed skills, including communication skills. Most of the social science discussion of play, including communication play, has focused on *agon*, competition, and *alea*, games of chance; and these two categories embrace many of the forms of both adult and children's play that come immediately to mind, including organized sports, card games, board games, and gambling. All these activities have the potential for building and asserting social power and dominance, and at least some of them may also hone skills that are useful in telic activities: chess and games that combine chance with skill hone planning and strategic thinking skills that generalize to utilitarian activities.

It is more difficult to devise a convincing utilitarian (telic) explanation for water-skiing, snowboarding, punning, writing haiku or sonnets, solving puzzles, snorkeling, surfing, hiking, rock-climbing, or needle-point. Some of these activities engage *ilinx*, feelings of vertigo or at least elation (and release pleasurable amounts of adrenaline); others may engage the feeling of *flow*. Some but not all allow for display of physical skill (needle-point, rock-climbing, and water-skiing) or cognitive skill (writing poems or solving puzzles), but enjoyment of these activities does not seem to require a high level of skill or an appreciative audience. All these activities involve both incongruity and aesthetics.

Adults also have adult versions of playing *house, cops and robbers*, and other "childish" role-playing, which might fit into *mimicry*. Adults "*dress up*" in antique uniforms and reenact historical battles, complete with more or less realistic weapons, or dress up in medieval, futuristic, or simply absurd costumes and enact scenes from the age of chivalry, *Star Trek*,[29] and *The Rocky*

---

[25] Maslow (1943). However, children have been observed playing even amid the ruins of war-torn cities.
[26] Montgomery (2015).   [27] Cook (2000).   [28] Csikszentmihalyi (1980).
[29] Wise (1979).

Horror Picture Show.[30] Mimicry seems a poor fit for these games, or for elaborate fantasy-world, role play games like *Dungeons and Dragons*. They all engage and exercise the active imagination, the brain's ability to represent (and enact) detailed narrative representations of alternative realities. This in turn strengthens and exercises our ability to construct elaborate simulations of possible future or alternative realities.

It is frequently claimed that when children play house or doctor, they are rehearsing for possible roles, or more likely trying out possible roles. When they play war or cowboys, that seems a little less likely. When adults engage in role play, whether historical (Civil War reenactments) or fantasy (*Star Trek* or *Dungeons and Dragons*), they are creating and entering an alternative reality (and the elaborate costumes usually involve aesthetic appreciation). At least some of children's role play games have a similar quality; most children certainly know they are not going to be a cowboy or outlaw, or a fairy princess or pirate captain. Adult play is more sophisticated than that of children, but *play* describes what both adults and children are doing, and it seems to be important to both mental health and social functioning, along with deep and often unalloyed pleasure.

None of these activities is competitive,[31] and they are enjoyed at all levels of skill. The relationship between playfulness and competition is more complex than is commonly recognized, and the human proclivity for competition and games of chance is balanced by a frequently-expressed preference for cooperation and for noncompetitive forms of play.[32] Even overtly aggressive forms of language play such as mockery and teasing often enhance rather than undermine affection and group solidarity within a family, among friends,[33] and within a work group.[34] In addition to the intellectual pleasure of wordplay, playful teasing demonstrates common ground, shows that relationships need not be constrained by conventional politeness norms, and displays mutual trust and solidarity.

Most people who are in good health find the use of well-toned muscles, senses, and cognitive skills intrinsically enjoyable, in part due to chemicals released by muscle tissues. Playing socially adds at least two dimensions to the pleasure. One is the increment to *positive face* that comes from even a minimally successful performance (and the increment to *negative face* that comes from overcoming obstacles). The other is the release of endorphins associated with social grooming.

By telling jokes or making puns and clever quips, we give pleasure to one another, and thus cement amicable relationships. Sharing a pleasurable activity

---

[30] Sharman (1975). [31] For example, Huizinga (1955); Malaby (2006, 2007).
[32] Kohn (1986). [33] Norrick (1993).
[34] Lampert and Ervin-Tripp (2006); Plester and Sayers (2007).

releases endorphins that become associated with the companionship and strengthens social bonds. Wordplay and verbal teasing displays language and social skills that reinforce social status while entertaining everyone present; by building on group history, they also demonstrate and reinforce the sense of group identity and membership.[35] Various forms of joking provide a "safe" and acceptable way to make mild criticisms and thus reinforce group behavioral norms[36] without serious damage to the emotional bonds. These are intrinsically enjoyable, but they also have social and psychological benefits – which are dependent on the intrinsic pleasure of the play, the combination of incongruity and aesthetic display/appreciation.

Play is a feature of cognition, communication, and social life for humans as well as many other animal species. These activities are rewarding because endorphins and other reward systems evolved to motivate homeostasis-building physical and cognitive activities;[37] some aspects of play, such as curiosity and pattern recognition, may also be directly fitness enhancing, but other aspects may reduce fitness. Forms of play are "*memes*"[38]; they spread and "*evolve*" because they are intrinsically rewarding, independent of both benefits (such as reduced stress and social bonding) and risks (such as injury while rock-climbing or loss of face from an unsuccessful attempt at humor).

It is likely that play contributed to cognitive evolution and the development of language and language-related skills. Playing with objects will eventually lead to serendipitous discoveries: Striking two pieces of flint together makes interesting sounds, and may eventually produce a sharp flake that becomes a useful tool. Playing with a piece of tough grass may produce a useful knot. Playing with sounds may produce enjoyable harmonies or regularities that develop into music or expand a rudimentary vocabulary. Playing with metaphors may lead to new insights and expanded vocabulary. Creativity and inventiveness are powered by curiosity combined with play.[39] Humans are not the only species to use objects as toys for intrinsic pleasure, but we excel at devising elaborate toys,[40] and we alone invent elaborate ways to play with signals – especially language.

In the next sections, I will briefly introduce playful use of metaphor, humor, and other tropes; in the next two chapters, I will give a more thorough account of metaphor and humor, followed by a chapter on storytelling, which often employs all these forms of play and is at least partly motivated by playful creation of coherent alternative realities.

---

[35] Fine and DeSoucey (2005). [36] Norrick (1993). See Chapter 12. [37] Chapters 2 and 3.
[38] Dennett (2017). [39] For example, Koestler (1964).
[40] Like many other animal species, human children are adept at creating toys out of mundane objects – a scrap of wood, an empty box, even food items.

Language Play

Whether or not it was instrumental in the early development of music and language, play is presently implicated in much of language use. Adults as well as children play with sounds, distorting real words and inventing new words. Conversations are frequently loaded with exaggeration (over- and understatement, exaggerated accents, etc.), alliteration, metaphor, irony, and humor. Storytelling often combines many of these and other tropes – as does reasoning and argumentation. Music, dance, and other arts are intrinsically playful; although they can be bent to telic purposes (such as advertising and political organizing), in their purest form they are developed and enjoyed for their own sake. Mathematics has a strong element of play in it, demonstrated by the popularity of mathematical puzzles.

In language play, both adults and children exploit and distort every feature of language, including phonology, lexis, and grammar,[41] and many features of conversation structure, including turn-taking and back-channel support.[42] Poetry and the poetic effects achieved by good prose play with phonology (in rhyme, alliteration, and rhythm), with lexis and grammar in double entendres, metaphors, metonyms, and irony. Each of these elements is also used in the nonsense rhymes, skip-rope rhymes, and jokes common on playgrounds as well as in the playful talk of adults. Children derive great pleasure from reciting "tongue twisters" and riddles, as adults do through "verbal dueling," quips, and other forms of verbal wit.

Many forms of language play subvert the expected relationship between language and reality.[43] Puns, rhyme, and rhythm require that words be chosen first for their forms and sounds, which are usually independent of meaning, and second for their *meaning*; at the extreme (i.e. *Jabberwocky*[44]), meaning plays no role at all. In nonsense rhymes like Lear's "The Owl and the Pussycat,"[45] an entire story is developed according to the requirement of the rhyme and meter, rather than any attempt at *meaning*. Lear builds on the *local* sound and meaning of words and phrases, with disregard for the ordinary requirements of coherence and sense-making. "The fiction thus created ... thus seems to incorporate a wild and random element, to be controlled by language itself rather than by reality or the will of the writer."[46]

Many genres of wordplay and humor follow a similar subversive logic, inducing a shift from a conventional and expected frame to an unexpected and often counter-normative frame, subverting both ordinary language norms and

---

[41] Cook (2000); Johnson-Laird (1993).
[42] Norrick and Spitz (2010) provide several examples of playful use of the conflict script.
[43] Cook (2000); Ritchie (2011).   [44] Carroll (1871).   [45] Lear (1871).
[46] Cook (2000, p. 49).

accepted social norms and expectations.[47] At the pleasurable extreme of nonsense, the meaning of this sort of wordplay is *that it has no meaning*; it is offered and enjoyed as the distilled essence of language. However, overtly nonsensical jokes and quips often reveal or imply a "truth" contrary to taken-for-granted ideals, and enlist listeners in the illicit pleasure of contradicting accepted social reality.[48] Adopting formal "rules" such as rhyme, alliteration schemes, or meter for composing a narrative or poem[49] inverts the usual relationship of language to reality and creates a new realm of possibilities and imagination. As with active role play games, the best nonsense verse creates an impossible alternative world and invites the listener or reader to inhabit it for a while.

Cook's observation that play subverts ordinary reality helps elucidate the oft-observed relationship between play and creativity, both in language and in puzzles and object play generally. Lakoff and Johnson argue that complex concepts are built by combining simple conceptual metaphors, based on experienced correlations among sensory experiences.[50] This is a playful process, and a similar process of testing and building new concepts by combining simpler concepts is part of the creative process in many fields (including social science).

Expressive language, including wordplay and humor as well as metaphors, activates many emotional and introspective simulations, which may contribute more to interpreting utterances than the primary lexical meanings. Words, phrases, and other signals chosen to activate one set of simulations may activate different and unanticipated simulations and semantic connections in some hearers and readers, leading to interpretations neither intended nor desired by the originator. Figurative language such as metaphor is particularly apt to activate secondary associations and novel connections with other concepts.[51]

Cook suggests that the possibilities of language become more constrained by meaning as it is more fully mastered, and associates this with a sense of adulthood as a time when "the magic of childhood" is lost.[52] Conversely, the enjoyment of imaginative wordplay suggests that the relaxation of meaning constraints in favor of formal constraints can help adults to recapture this "lost innocence," at least for a while. The most successful children's books and movies often feature language play that is sufficiently clever that adults enjoy reading the book or viewing the video again and again, as often as the child insists. In recent decades, a sizable market in "children's literature" has been picture books purchased by adults as gifts for other adults.

Cook's diagnosis of adulthood seems excessively dreary. A more positive framing is that, with intellectual maturity, adults gain the ability to control and indulge the magic so the world becomes a less terrifying place, but without necessarily losing its numinous qualities. The popularity of adult role-playing

---

[47] Ritchie (2005). [48] Ritchie (2005). [49] Chapter 12. [50] Lakoff and Johnson (1999).
[51] Ritchie (2006, 2008). [52] Cook (2000); Ritchie (2011).

activities, costume parties, and so forth, supports this more generous characterization of adulthood. Recent research applying discourse analysis to conversations in families, friendship groups, and workplace conversations shows that imaginative language play is not peripheral but often central to building and maintaining relationships.

Many forms of play rely on pattern completion. Complex musical and poetic rhythms, rhymes, riddles, jokes all provide a pattern that is either left to the hearer to complete or completed for the reader. More complex patterns provide greater contextual effects[53] and greater satisfaction.[54] A large part of the pleasure of solving a riddle or working out how the final line of a haiku ties together several themes is derived from the pleasure of exercising one's own skill. Hurley, Dennett, and Adams[55] argue that the pleasure of humor is the brain's way of rewarding itself for resolving the incongruity posed by a joke; this also applies to puns, quips, and nonsense verse.

The kinds of play Cook describes, in which ordinary reality is deliberately subverted and new realities created through application of incidental rules (rhyme and rhythm in "The Owl and the Pussycat," sound in alliteration and puns), appear in other arts, such as dance and architecture. Shakespeare uses wordplay in his histories and tragedies as well as his comedies. A similar kind of subversive element occurs in forms of "intellectual play" beyond language, including mathematics, theoretical science,[56] and other forms of *"high play."*[57] Andy Clark[58] proposes a strategy of reconstructing the world in a form our brains can compute; simultaneous play with objects and ideas, engaged for its intrinsic pleasure, provides a means for accomplishing this, and is integral to creative thinking. It is easy to imagine an early hominid playing with two stones, clinking them together until a sharp-edged flake falls from one. This may have happened thousands of times before one of the players cut herself on the flake, and realized its utilitarian potential. In more recent examples, Shannon was known for riding a unicycle about Bell Labs (where he was employed while working out the details of Information Theory[59]), and the process through which Crick and Watson discovered the structure of DNA was marked by strong elements of play[60] with objects, images, and ideas.

Play in Conversation

Conversation appears to have developed initially as a means for social bonding. Dessalles argues that conversation provides a venue for

---

[53] Sperber and Wilson (1986). [54] Ritchie (2005, 2006).
[55] Hurley, Dennett, and Adams (2011). See Chapter 12. [56] Byers (2007); Ritchie (2009b).
[57] Bro (1971). [58] Clark (1997). [59] Shannon (1948; Shannon and Weaver, 1949).
[60] Watson (1968; see also Ritchie, 2009b).

demonstrating one's attributes as a potential friend.[61] Everts shows how playful conversational humor contributes to maintaining family solidarity,[62] and several studies have demonstrated a similar role in work groups.[63]

Everyday conversations often include frequent bursts of spontaneous verbal play.[64] Coates argues that most humor in ordinary adult conversation occurs in a play frame that can be spontaneously activated by any participant through a variety of signals, including laughter, an abrupt alteration of vocal tone or facial expression, or simply an utterance that makes sense *only* as play (e.g. "deadpan humor"). The play frame marks everything that is said as nonserious, and normal rules of turn-taking and coherence are suspended. Conversational play is inherently both collaborative and subversive, with everyone taking part, if only through laughter or back-channel comments that further the play. A play frame is often established and characterized by features such as laughter, simultaneous speech, fanciful metaphors, and collaborative elaboration of fanciful metaphorical stories to create an amusing (and often ironic) alternative reality.

Coates provides an excellent example from a recorded conversation among three women friends during a shared meal in Surrey, England. One participant, Sue, mentions that she brought a rabbit home from school for the weekend. Later in the conversation, she tells about a couple she knows in which the wife forbids the husband even to have a guitar in the house, much less play it, which leads to a discussion of relationship norms and obedience. After Liz comments "He doesn't have much of a life . . .," Sue signals a switch to play frame with laughter and compares the husband to the rabbit, leading to collaborative construction of a metaphorical imaginary story about the husband as rabbit. An excerpt will give the flavor of the exchange[65]:

SUE: He doesn't really [laughing] | he's like the rabbit
LIZ: | he is really, isn't he? | she should
SUE: Yeah [giggle] I think | I should bring him - | I think I should
ANNA: | introduce them
LIZ: Get him [giggling] | I wonder why she doesn't | get him a RUN in
SUE: Bring him home for | weekends [laughs]
ANNA: Introduce them | then you'll be able to
LIZ: The GARden [giggling]

The friends continue in this vein for several more speaking turns, often speaking simultaneously and repeating phrases. They develop an elaborate

---

[61] Dessalles (2014).   [62] Everts (2003).
[63] For example, Fine and DeSoucey (2005); Lehmann-Willenbrock and Allen (2014); Terrion and Ashforth (2002).
[64] Coates (2007); Tannen (1984); Ritchie (2010, 2011c; Ritchie and Dyhouse, 2008).
[65] Adapted from Coates (2007, p. 34); original notation simplified. See Chapter 12 for a more extended discussion.

fantasy in which Sue brings the husband/rabbit home and introduces him to her school rabbit, where the wife provides a run for him in the garden and feeds him a few lettuce leaves. As Coates points out, the metaphor of husband as *"rabbit"* plays on the stereotypical timidity of rabbits, emphasizing the women's scorn or dismay at the apparent power imbalance in the relationship they are discussing. The elaborate playful fantasy culminates with Liz's remark that "It's strange, isn't it, the life some people lead?," which marks a shift out of the play frame back into a serious frame. It appears that the playfully humorous metaphorical story provided a means for thinly veiled criticism of the couple's relationship (and an implied contrast with the "ideal relationship"), but, at the same time, it has the quality of collaboration typical of a jazz performance, which Coates metaphorically expresses as CONVERSATIONAL PLAY IS JAZZ PERFORMANCE.

Fine and DeSoucey[66] provide a quite different example from their study of a meteorology office in Chicago. Two female employees, Joan and Heather, keep little aquariums with small fish on their desks. Several of the male employees in the office tease the two women with threats to "do something" to the fish, inventing fanciful scenarios, such as performing a scientific experiment on the fish; the women respond by threatening retaliation ("I'll get out my bat"). In one sequence, two of the men threatened to send the fish into space on a rocket ship, bury them, and staple a banner onto a fish's tail. On another occasion, while working the night shift, two of the men wired a bunch of batteries together to look like a bomb and placed it on Heather's fish tank with a "ransom note." The women "victims" collaborate in the play by pretending to take the threats seriously and threatening physical retaliation.

In the *"rabbit"* sequence discussed by Coates, the scenario is collaboratively developed over the course of part of just one conversation. The fish-tank example discussed by Fine and DeSoucey is part of what they call a "joking culture," in which many different elaborate scenarios are developed around a single theme of threatening harm to the fish. In Coates's example, the playful scenario serves as a vehicle for social commentary about power imbalance in an acquaintance's marriage. In the fish-tank example, the primary purposes seem to be lightening the monotony of the workplace and providing a focus for lighthearted social interaction.

People also play with the form of conversation. An example from my own research comes from a conversation about police-community relationships among a group of friends, all with "new left" political leanings.[67] This

---

[66] Fine and DeSoucey (2005). See Chapter 12 for a more extended discussion.
[67] Ritchie (2010); the conversation was organized and transcribed as part of an assignment for an advanced Communication class. Ritchie and Zhu (2015) discuss this and the next example as Grammatical Metaphors; see Chapter 11.

sequence occurred after several minutes of conversation, and had no apparent relationship to anything that had previously been said.

TYLER: Are you a cop? Are you a cop?
CELESTE: No.
TYLER: Are you a cop?
CELESTE: No.
TYLER: That's three times, okay. We're cool.

"Are you a cop?" is presented as a bona fide request for information in the overt form of a hostile interrogation. This apparently satirizes the belief, common among drug users and political radicals, that evidence from an undercover police officer is inadmissible in a criminal trial if the officer has denied being a police officer three times. Given their prior relationship, it is evident that Tyler knew Celeste was not an undercover police officer – and given the innocuous nature of the conversation, it wouldn't have mattered if a police officer were present. The sequence of questions takes the form of a hostile test of identity, but it is only playful teasing, creating a fantasy reality in which the participants are doing something more exciting, dangerous, and politically important than helping complete a class assignment for one member of the group.

In an example reported by Norrick and Spitz,[68] two men play with the form of "conflict talk" blended with "science talk." The conversation involved a middle-aged woman, FR; her son, DV, in his early twenties; and another male, MK, also in his midforties. FR is planning a meal for a coming event and discussing the possible menu with the other two. She suggests they might make a quiche. Her son DV objects to having quiche because "real men don't eat it." This is apparently intended as a satirical reference to the pop-culture book, *Real Men Don't Eat Quiche*,[69] DV then presented a riddle:

DV: How many real men does it take to change a light bulb?
FR: Tell me.
DV: None, real men aren't afraid of the dark.

MK asked, "What's the light bulb got to do with the dark?" DV initially responded, "Well, if you have a light bulb on, it's NOT." MK challenged this claim, and DV launched into a mock-science explanation of light bulbs: "They suck in darkness, they're darkness suckers. They suck the darkness out of the air." This was followed a sequence of nearly thirty speaking turns, in which MK fed straight lines to DV, enabling DV to elaborate his account of light bulbs as darkness suckers, claiming to have learned it in physics class.

---

[68] Norrick and Spitz (2010, pp. 97–100). See Chapter 12 for a more extended discussion.
[69] Feirstein, (1982).

A similar example comes in a famous scene from the Abbott and Costello movie *In the Navy*,[70] in which Costello plays with the conversational form of mathematical proof to demonstrate that 7 x 13 = 28.

As Norrick and Spitz argue, these long exchanges are "akin to banter, that is to say talk oriented toward humor for the purpose of play, but it is organized into the structure of conflict talk with a clear preference for disagreement."[71] However, they also illustrate a genre of humorous discourse sometimes referred to as "*stringing a line*," based on a common thematic metaphor, FOOLING SOMEONE IS FISHING. The game is to invent a fantastic story and embellish it – whether the listener is fooled or not is less important than how well the story hangs together, how elaborate it gets, and how long participants can keep it going.

The opening gambit, "real men don't eat it" (quiche), a satirical reference to the book by that name, was a stock humor line for several years after the book came out. DV may have used it intentionally to set up the long elaborate "*line*," but the "*darkness suckers*" sequence may have been spontaneously produced. Even if it was spontaneous, it is also possible that DV and his friends at college had previously explored the comic possibilities of that inversion of physics, and he repeated and extended the joke here.

All these examples involve construction of a coherent play world with its own logic and rules. In the *rabbit* example, the interactants construct a metaphorical story; in the *fish* example, they construct a series of pretend plots that imply stories without fully developing them. The *light bulb* and *math* examples play with the *explanation* form of conversation, which is blended with *conflict* talk in *light bulb*.

Play and Homeostasis

Previous chapters discussed how pleasure may have evolved as a reward for activities – resolving the incongruencies of humor and solving puzzles, finding food, engaging in sexual activity, and so on. Social play, like conversation, activates simultaneous (shared) rewards, increasing social bonds. Both social and solitary play, which can lead to new insights or inventions, activate rewards that help motivate future play. Play also contributes to homeostasis by reducing anxiety and stress and cultivating a sense of personal well-being.

Play, including play with incongruencies, contributes to imagination and creates space for trying out new combinations, exploring new possibilities.[72] It can also free the mind to consider events from different perspectives and to reframe experiences and situations. Playing with alternative realities enhances

---

[70] Lubin, A. (Director, 1941) *In the Navy*. Universal Pictures.
[71] Norrick and Spitz (2010, p. 100).   [72] Koestler (1964).

the forward projection and incongruity-recognition functions of the brain. Fantasy and fantasy-related activities such as role play can help externalize the imagination and contribute to the brain's forward-projected modeling of possible futures, both to anticipate and prepare for future contingencies and to explore alternative courses of action.

In language play, both the use of nonsense and invention of metaphors help to expand language and create new possibilities for expressing new or difficult ideas. Play with language and with conversation structure helps to elaborate existing literary and art forms – and often to create new ones. As Dessalles[73] points out, the display of language and cognitive skills through language play displays desirable qualities for recruiting friends – and for flirting and recruiting sexual partners.

Play and the Origins of Language Use

Play and grooming both originated well before Homo sapiens. Grooming was originally primarily a matter of touch, but sounds and other proto-signal systems such as motion and gesture may have become part of grooming early on. Many species engage in rhythmic motion, and several engage in a kind of vocal chorus, almost like singing. Arbib suggests that singing and chanting along with dance-like rhythmic motion may have developed into a group bonding ritual that contributed to the early development of language.[74] With the development of theory of mind, early hominids may have gained the ability to see not only themselves and their fellows as objects, independent of themselves, but also to the group and, eventually, the chanting, swaying, gesturing, and grooming as objects with an independent existence. As these come to be associated with certain sounds, a rudimentary vocabulary might develop. Here, the recognition and enjoyment of incongruity would contribute by facilitating the incongruous action of treating social interaction as an object independent of the interacting persons.

Bruner argues that the mastery of fire permitted primitive hominids to extend the waking day.[75] The group would gather around the fire for protection against predators, for warmth in cool weather, for light, and especially for companionship. The singing plus a developing proto-language would facilitate the development of storytelling. Storytelling provides a way to represent the group, its history and present conditions of homeostasis, to the group members. Recounting stories of the past, including stories of heroes and gods, provides a means of forward projection and planning.[76]

---

[73] Dessalles (2014).   [74] Arbib (2012); see also McNeill (2012).   [75] Bruner (2002).
[76] See Chapter 13.

Mirth is an element of play, and as language develops, the incongruity of play provides a means and motivation for development and refinement of humor. Storytelling may have included elements of incongruity and incongruity-resolution from the outset, both in a heroic and in a comic (humorous) vein. Metaphor and other tropes (exaggeration, irony, etc.) may also be an outgrowth of play, as similarities among objects, actions, words, and ideas are developed and exploited for aesthetic, religious, and comic purposes.

In play, the incongruency is usually not really resolved, except by termination of the play frame and dissolution of the play world. In humor, the incongruency is resolved by reframing some part of the situation to force a change in assumptions – but the fundamental incongruency often remains (Tyler and Celeste both know that he knows that she is not a cop, and that their conversation would be of no interest to the police even if she were a cop.) In metaphor, the incongruency is resolved by experiencing *some aspect of* the topic as *some aspect of* the vehicle in a way that adds relevance to the topic. In irony the incongruency is resolved by reversing the explicit meaning of the ironic statement to derive an implied meaning. A well-constructed narrative sets up an incongruency and resolves it through a plot element such as the intrepid action of the protagonist or the intervention of a god or helpful stranger.

Summary

Play is widespread among mammals, and at least some other classes (e.g. cephalopods) and universal among humans. Play contributes to the development of motor and social skills among juveniles of many species, but among both juveniles and adults, it is indulged primarily for its own sake, for the pleasure it gives. Play contributes to homeostasis in several ways. Language play provides a means of grooming[77] and displaying cleverness,[78] so contributes to social interaction and structure. All forms of play release endorphins and reduce stress. Play, including language and object play, contributes to imagination and creativity. These functions are vital for discovery and invention, and increase the power and range of forward projections as a basis for planning and problem-solving. Play is also a central component in humor, metaphor, storytelling, and language development. These themes will be developed in more detail in the next few chapters.

---

[77] Dunbar (1996).   [78] Dessalles (2014).

11   Metaphor

Language enables individuals to collaborate with each other in developing more accurate and extensive representations as well as in developing complex social relationships. However, the expressive and communicative power of language is constrained by two factors. First, because people learn language through unique streams of experience; they also use and understand language in subtly different ways: Language is not a code, but a system of using signals to construct roughly similar representations. Conversation helps to update and maintain these mutual representations. The second constraint: Our bodies are able to act and our senses able to perceive with complex nuances that vastly outnumber the potential of any practical language to represent accurately.

We overcome these constraints in several ways. By extending and refining syntax, we combine signals to extend and qualify their expressive ability. We extend conversation by incorporating stories, quotations, allusions, and so on. We explain our experiences and ideas, then sometimes we explain our explanations. We extend vocabulary by combining words, coining new words, and reusing old words in new ways. A particularly powerful way to extend the range and subtlety of language is through indirect communication, which extends the expressive power of language indefinitely, but at the cost of even greater increase in ambiguity.

In this chapter, I will discuss two closely related forms of indirect communication, *metaphor* and *metonym*. I will discuss two approaches to metaphor, semantic association and conceptual metaphors. I will criticize a tendency to treat metaphors as code-like and propose a refinement to conceptual metaphor theory that avoids this error. Then I will discuss grammatical metaphors, multimodal metaphors, metaphorical stories, and playful metaphors. Finally I will discuss theories regarding the interpretation of metaphors, and the contribution of metaphors to social structure and homeostasis. In Chapter 12, I will discuss humor, irony, and other forms of indirect communication that contribute to humor.

Lexical Metaphor and Metonymy

Metonymy refers to the use of a word or phrase to denote a related concept: In general, a metonym can be use of a part for the whole ("*Lend me a hand*," when the speaker actually wants the help of the entire person), closely associated concepts ("*boots on the ground*" refers to the soldiers wearing the boots), place for institution and/or process ("The *White House* issued a statement"), and so on. *Metaphor* generally refers to using one word or phrase to express something about a totally unrelated concept, although this formulation understates the complexity of the concept. Metaphor and metonym are closely related, and it is not always easy to tell where one ends and the other begins. A person who asks a colleague to "*lend me a hand*" may want help proofreading a manuscript, in which case the utterance is both a metonym and a metaphor (the requested hand may be used to wield the proverbial red pencil, or to enter corrections on a computer keyboard, but the colleague's *mind* and *attention* are actually wanted).

Until recently, theorizing about metaphor was conducted in terms of "noun is *noun*" metaphors invented by a linguist or philosopher to support a particular point. Common examples include "Achilles is *a lion*" and "My lawyer is *a shark*;" familiar literary metaphors such as "Juliet is *the sun*," usually taken out of context, also appear frequently in these discussions. However, metaphors in actual discourse rarely take the form "noun is *noun*." In one sample, Cameron[1] found that 63 percent of all metaphors are verbs and verb phrases; nouns account for only 22 percent. A passage from a campaign speech by President Obama provides at least fourteen metaphors, only three of which are nouns.

The *document* they *produced* was eventually signed but ultimately *unfinished*. It was *stained* by this nation's *original sin* of slavery, a question that *divided* the colonies and *brought* the convention to a *stalemate* until the founders chose to allow the slave trade to *continue* for at least twenty more years, and to *leave* any final resolution to future generations. . . . This is *where we are* right now. It's a racial *stalemate* we've been *stuck in* for years.[2]

Often the topic is not even stated, but must be inferred from the context, as when Obama said that the US Constitution "was *stained* by this nation's *original sin* of slavery," leaving it to listeners or readers to work out that "*stain*" is a metaphor for something like *dishonorable* or *immoral*. "*Stain*" is a common metaphor in many cultures; related metaphors include "*defile*," "*corrupt*," and "*dirty*." Metaphors can be identified on a range of familiarity from "*dead*" or "*sleeping*" metaphors, metaphors so familiar that most people don't even recognize them as metaphors, through a range of commonplace metaphors like "*stain*" to fresh and newly coined metaphors that are readily recognized as metaphorical. An example of a thoroughly "*dead*" metaphor is "*salary*," from the Latin for *salt*, which was once paid as wages to Roman

---

[1] Cameron (2003).
[2] Then Senator Barack Obama, *A More Perfect Union*. Philadelphia, PA. March. 18, 2008.

soldiers. "*Sleeping*" metaphors, that most people would recognize as metaphorical only when it's pointed out to them, include familiar and idiomatic phrases like "*rising*" prices, "*inflation*," "*warm* feelings," and so on.

An example of a newly coined metaphor was "*glass ceiling*," initially coined by Gay Bryant,[3] a former magazine editor quoted by Nora Frenkel[4] in a 1984 article about Bryant's frustration after being repeatedly passed over for promotion. "Women have *reached* a certain *point*—I call it the *glass ceiling*. They're in the *top* of *middle* management and they're *stopping* and *getting stuck*."[5] Since that initial use, "*glass ceiling*" has appeared in writing, speeches, as a visual metaphor, and as the name of a unit of US government, the Federal Glass Ceiling Commission (1991–1995). It has become so commonplace and lexicalized that it is often generalized to refer to *any* situation in which a process or development is interrupted by some external factor. This progression, from fresh and original phrases readily recognized as metaphors through commonplace but still recognized metaphors to thoroughly *lexicalized* metaphors that are used and understood as literal language, is partly how language expands and changes.

Semantic Association and Simulation

Children acquire their first few words through association; they hear words like "mama," "daddy," and "puppy" when these entities are present. However, this is soon supplemented, then largely replaced, by learning from the language context. Children typically acquire ten to twelve new words every day from early childhood until well into adolescence, and most of these words are at least initially understood through their relationships with the contexts in which the words are encountered, including other words as well as perceived objects, actions, and social interactions.[6] Landauer and Dumais claim that word "meanings," how we understand them in natural discourse, are subtly changing throughout life as we encounter them with related words in new contexts.

Psychologists have known for decades that words will activate connections to words that are related,[7] either by belonging to the same *schema*[8] or by having been recently encountered together; *which* related words are activated and the strength of activations are strongly influenced by context. For metaphor comprehension, an implication of this idea is that a vehicle word or phrase, such as "*stain*" or "*glass ceiling*," will activate related and

---

[3] Bryant (1984).   [4] Frenkel (1984).
[5] Every italicized phrase in this passage is metaphorical; the literal meaning of each phrase is completely incongruous with the context.
[6] Landauer and Dumais (1997).   [7] Tabossi (1989); Hoey (2005).
[8] A set of interrelated ideas about a topic. See Chapters 4, 6, and 7.

context-relevant words, phrases, and ideas. These, along with the background knowledge and perceptual simulations that are at least briefly activated,[9] will contribute to understanding the metaphor and the context in which it is encountered.[10]

The neural connections among words and phrases are part of language comprehension, including metaphor comprehension. Background knowledge and perceptual simulations associated with the connected words and phrases may be weakly activated as well as those associated with the word or phrase itself. In "*stained* by the *original sin* of slavery," "*stain*" may activate both perceptual simulations and schemas associated with blood and other bodily fluids, along with emotion-related words and simulations related to shame, guilt, and humiliation. Obama's use of the metaphor is likely to have increased the salience of these simulations and concepts in relation to both *slavery* and *the Constitution* as well as to the connection of slavery to the constitution.

Conceptual Metaphors

Traditional theories held that metaphors are simply literary embellishments in which a more interesting and striking word or phrase (the *vehicle*) is substituted for a less interesting word or phrase (the *topic*), and qualities or characteristics associated with the vehicle are attributed to ("*transferred to*") the topic. In these theories, metaphors are strictly features of how language is used. However, Lakoff and Johnson[11] challenged this view, arguing that metaphors are *conceptual* and *cognitive*. Each metaphor observed in language use expresses an underlying relationship in which a more abstract concept is experienced as and understood in terms of a more explicit and common concept. They argued that ordinary phrases (previously classified as lexicalized metaphors) demonstrate the underlying conceptual structure through which we understand the world and our experience.

"*Rising*" prices and "*low*" opinion" express underlying conceptual metaphors MORE IS UP and GOOD IS UP. "Price *inflation*" and "*inflationary bubble*" express MONEY IS A SUBSTANCE/AMOUNT IS SIZE. "*Warm* feelings" and "*icy* glare" express EMOTION IS TEMPERATURE. "*Stain*," "*defile*," "*dirty*," and "*corrupt*" all express MORAL IS CLEAN; IMMORAL IS DIRTY, and a related conceptual metaphor MORAL IS PURE; IMMORAL IS IMPURE.[12]

---

[9] Bergen (2012); Gibbs (2008).
[10] Kintsch (2008) has successfully used this idea to develop a computer program that derives interpretations of simple, direct metaphors that are similar to the interpretations provided by humans.
[11] Lakoff and Johnson (1980, 1999).
[12] Lynne Cameron argues that interrelated metaphors of this sort do not necessarily always reflect underlying conceptual metaphors; she coined the term "*thematic metaphors*" to describe groups

"*Glass ceiling*" blends at least three conceptual metaphors, SEEING IS KNOWING, POWER IS UP, and A CAREER IS MOTION THROUGH SPACE (or more generally, A CAREER IS A JOURNEY). Bryant was "*moving up*[13] *in*[14]" the organization when she encountered a "*barrier*" to "*climbing higher*" in the organization. She could "*see*" the positions of "*higher*" power and authority, but she could not "*reach*" them.

Thus, "*glass ceiling*" and the underlying conceptual metaphors also imply another kind of metaphor, a *metaphorical story*. In brief, "*glass ceiling*" implies a vehicle story in which a person is trying to climb a ladder that appears to lead from one floor of a building to another. The protagonist encounters a barrier, and realizes that the way is actually blocked by a transparent pane of glass: She can't see the glass barrier until she bumps into it, but she can see through the glass to the upper story. She can see all of the upper story's luxurious furniture and appointments, but she cannot pass the barrier, cannot reach the destination. This maps onto a topic story about a female executive (Gay Bryant) who has been successively promoted to positions of ever greater authority until abruptly the promotions stop short of the executive ranks ("*upper* management"). She is fully aware of the power and privileges of executive ranks (she can "*see*" them), but she cannot achieve ("*reach*") them because of unacknowledged but insurmountable gender discrimination (an "*invisible (glass) barrier*").

Metaphors often imply metaphorical stories,[15] and these stories potentially make a substantial contribution to understanding the metaphors that evoke or activate them, whether or not the audience actually processes the metaphor. The process of identifying and resolving the incongruity, and the fact that the incongruity is usually not fully resolved, lends interest and expressive power to a good metaphor. The process of familiarization whereby a metaphor becomes lexicalized gradually reduces the incongruity, until it takes a creative use of the metaphor to call attention to the incongruity and thereby "*bring it back to life*." Hillary Clinton's use of "*glass ceiling*" in her 2008 concession speech effectively "*breathed new life into*" the by then familiar metaphor.[16]

Common abstract concepts like affection, argument, and marriage are expressed in many cultures through multiple conceptual metaphors, each based on different sets of physical and social experience, according to different aspect of the topic concept. Argument, for example, may be experienced as LOCATION ("*take* a *position*"), WAR ("*attack* a *position*"), or JOURNEY ("*reach* a

---

of metaphors in which the vehicles are all drawn from a common conceptual source, but that do not necessarily reflect underlying conceptual relationships.

[13] This conceptual metaphor, STATUS IS UP, is also commonly expressed in "career *ladder*."
[14] Note that "*in*" also expresses AN ORGANIZATION IS A CONTAINER.   [15] Ritchie (2018).
[16] Ritchie (2017).

228   Metaphor

conclusion"). ARGUMENT IS WAR, which Lakoff and Johnson discuss at length, can also be understood as a metonym, since arguments and war are both parts of a broader concept of CONFLICT. Similarly when Obama, in his *More Perfect Union* speech, says that he chose to "*continue the long march* of those who came before . . .," he is speaking both metonymically (the Civil Rights movement has been marked by many literal marches, notably the march on Selma portrayed in the movie by the same name) and metaphorically (POLITICAL CHANGE IS A JOURNEY).

Conversely, the same metaphor vehicle can express many concepts. A career, lecture, or marriage can be A JOURNEY. Any of these can reach a "*fork in the road*," "*rough patch*," "*turning point*," or "*dead-end*." As Cameron points out in several of her writings, the same metaphor is often developed and used in several passages, applied to different topics, which can increase the coherence of a text. The JOURNEY metaphor appears throughout Obama's speech: "This is *where we are* right now," "we can *move beyond*...," and "*continue on the path* of a more perfect union."

From Code to Conceptual Metaphor – and Back?

If "code" is understood literally, as a one-to-one mapping of meaning onto signal, language is clearly not a code.[17] Both because of how it is learned (through connections with experience, perception, and other language) and because of the creative, careless, and generally "*loose*"[18] way it is used, language is inherently ambiguous, operating as much by implicatures and inferences as by "meanings" or definitions. Language changes subtly with new experiences, encounters, and connections; consequently (unlike a code) it is unique for each person and different for any one person from time to time; usages and "meanings" are usually similar, but probably never identical, and there is no way to know exactly what another person intends or understands.

It follows that metaphors are not coded, but people still speak and write in terms of the "meaning" of a metaphor, as if they did have clear, coded meanings. Conceptual Metaphor Theory (CMT) provides an alternative perspective – but an overly literal and often overly precise interpretation/specification of the theory has sometimes implied a code model. An example discussed at length by Lakoff and Johnson, ARGUMENT IS WAR, can be construed as metonymic, inasmuch as both arguments and war are examples of a common concept, *CONFLICT*. However, much of the discussion of CMT treats each application of the same vehicle to a different topic as a separate and unique Conceptual Metaphor (CM), and many theorists treat the "*mappings*"

---

[17] Chapters 1–3 and 6.   [18] Sperber and Wilson (1986).

between topic and vehicle as fixed either in a culture or in an individual mind. These are qualities of a code.

I have previously argued against the first of these two assumptions by suggesting that CM vehicles are mostly *generic*;[19] for example, ARGUMENT IS WAR, MARRIAGE IS WAR, BUSINESS IS WAR are all expressions of the same generic metaphor,[20] WAR. Other common generic metaphors that accommodate a wide variety of topics include JOURNEY, UP, OBJECT/SUBSTANCE, and CONTAINER. Each of these can be applied to many different topics and express something distinct about the way the topic is experienced. For example, in X IS A SUBSTANCE ("that idea *lacks weight*"), the topic (an idea in this example, but an investment, effort, or contribution can also be "*substantial*") is experienced as a *substance* with attributes that somehow evoke the properties of an actual substance.

This explanation still leaves a code-like residual. It dispenses with the idea that, for example, HAPPY IS UP fixes something about *happiness* in a code-like relation to something about *verticality*, but it can be and often is interpreted as establishing a "*mapping*," a metaphor that implies a set of determinate relationships.[21] A frequently discussed example is ANGER IS LIQUID IN A CONTAINER UNDER PRESSURE. This CM is apparently motivated by expressions like "*boiling mad*" and cartoon characters with steam coming out their ears. Both LIQUID and PRESSURE imply specified qualities that can be mapped onto particular qualities of the topic, ANGER.

For example, in their analysis of the emotion metaphors in Tim O'Brien's stories about the Vietnam War,[22] Esmaeili et al.[23] apply the LIQUID IN A CONTAINER UNDER PRESSURE METAPHOR to passages from one story in a way that deviates markedly from the way O'Brien expresses the emotions in the broader context of the book. The story begins with a wound to his buttocks: An new and inexperienced medic (Jorgensen) freezes up, fails to detect and treat O'Brien's shock, and fumbles the treatment of his wound, which becomes badly and almost fatally infected. O'Brien is evacuated from the battlefield, hospitalized, released but reassigned to the relative safety of a headquarters company. Because of the incompletely healed wound, he had to sleep on his stomach. Describing his sleepless discomfort, he writes, "I'd lie there all

---

[19] An extension of a concept initially introduced by Tourangeau and Rips (1991). Generic metaphors receive a more detailed discussion later in this chapter.
[20] This idea is similar to what Lakoff and Johnson, Kövecses, and others call *image schemas*.
[21] I have often used the "*mapping*" metaphor in my own writing; only recently have I realized how it works to sustain the *code* metaphor.
[22] O'Brien (1990). Esmaeili et al. characterize the book as a memoir, but O'Brien presents it as a collection of stories, based on his Vietnam War experiences, that are not necessarily literally true.
[23] Esmaeili, Akhavan, and Amjad (2015).

fidgety and tight, then after a while I'd feel a swell of anger come on."[24] Esmaeili et al. acknowledge that "[T]here is no implication of heat here," but they go on to ascribe heat to the author anyway: "since anger is usually conceived of as heat, it is plausible to infer that the narrator has conceptualized anger as a fluid in a container, i.e. his own body, which is coming up with the increase of the heat, in line with two other entailments: WHEN THE INTENSITY OF ANGER INCREASES, THE FLUID RISES."[25] Very little of this is in the original text: No fluid, no heat, no container, and Esmaeili et al. ignore the context.

O'Brien was lying in an uncomfortable position on his stomach. He was literally "fidgety" (small movements of muscles, probably in legs and arms) and "tight" (the same muscles, along with others in his abdomen and other parts of his body, tensed as if for action.) He experienced a gradual onset of a blend of feelings and an intensifying physiological response he retrospectively describes as "a swell," which could represent his physical discomfort or a physiological reaction to the emotion; as muscles tense, they also literally swell. There is no mention of heat, container, or liquid.[26] If the swell was in his stomach, it would be sideways, not upward. Perhaps the swell was *"contained in"* his body, but he expresses it as an active *feature of* his body. It may refer to the tensed stomach muscles, or it may simply express a general feeling of intensity; there is no basis for concluding that it refers to any *contents* of his body. Esmaeili, Akhavan, and Amjad's conceptual metaphors provide a plausible way to analyze and classify the metaphors as independent linguistic units, but they do not fit the context, and there is no reason to think that they played any role in O'Brien's cognitive or emotional processes.

The more general context is a story about a failed revenge plot. O'Brien's old company is brought in from the field for rest. Over beers and shared stories, it becomes evident that he is no longer one of them, while Jorgensen, who has gained experience and competence, is now an accepted member of the group. O'Brien encounters Jorgensen, who apologizes, but O'Brien can't bring himself to accept the apology and let go of his obsession with revenge, his need to make Jorgensen feel some of what he himself had felt.

For weeks it had been a vow—I'll get him, I'll get him—it was down inside me like a rock. Granted, I didn't hate him anymore, and I'd lost some of the outrage and passion, but the need for revenge kept eating at me.[27]

In their analysis of the first sentence, Esmaeili et al. draw on Lakoff and Kövecses's[28] discussion of the social model of retributive justice as a

---

[24] O'Brien (1990, p. 192).   [25] Esmaeili, Akhavan, and Amjad (2015, p. 140).
[26] *"Swell"* could be a reference to an ocean swell, but nothing in the passage suggests anything like that.
[27] O'Brien (1990, p. 200).   [28] Lakoff and Kövecses (1987).

responsibility to punish wrongdoers. They argue that this is metaphorically expressed as ANGER IS A BURDEN, which joins with THE BODY IS A CONTAINER: The "*rock*" is a "*burden*" "*down inside*" the container of his body. For the second sentence, they note that "*lost*" implies EXISTENCE IS PRESENCE (an equally plausible interpretation might be OUTRAGE AND PASSION ARE POSSESSIONS). They argue that "*kept eating at me*" implies that anger has "an *insatiable appetite*" (p. 141); implicitly ANGER IS A HUNGRY ANIMAL. The authors summarize, claiming that "The negative valence of this emotion has given rise to negative conceptualizations," which they identify as BURNING, BURDEN, and GLUTTONOUS.[29]

In this passage, O'Brien is retrospectively depicting his obsession with anger and revenge, which was almost painful. Did he experience his anger as a BURDEN? Or as something "*hard*" and "*cold*"? Did he experience his anger as an OPPONENT or HUNGRY ANIMAL? Esmaeili et al. go way beyond O'Brien's representation of his experience, and it illustrates how the implicit code-like assumptions of CMT as elaborated by Lakoff and Kövecses can lead a textual analysis far afield from the actual experience expressed in a text.

A more straightforward approach would begin with the text, in this case with O'Brien and his attempt to understand and express a strong emotional experience and his complex feelings about those emotions. The overall context of this passage is important: The story, which was written twenty years after the war, continues with an account of an elaborate practical joke in which O'Brien and an accomplice, Azar, sought revenge by simulating an enemy sneak attack while the medic is on night guard duty, alone in a foxhole on the perimeter of the base. They hope to reduce Jorgensen to a state of quivering terror, but Jorgensen is not taken in, and O'Brien is the one who ends up humiliated in front of Azar. The story ends with a reconciliation between O'Brien and Jorgensen.

The point of the story is O'Brien's ambivalence about the plot and his regret when the joke went too far, his humiliation when the medic was not taken in, and his subsequent reconciliation with Jorgensen. The revenge story, O'Brien's account of his feelings of guilt and regret, and his reconciliation with the medic force a reinterpretation of the hospital passage itself,[30] which serves to set the stage for the self-reflective moral reckoning and the reconciliation in the final scenes.

The overall context of the story is crucial to interpreting the metaphorical description of O'Brien's anger. The narrator feels victimized (by the medic, not by his anger); the desire for retaliation *may be* part of a social/cultural

---

[29] Esmaeili, Akhavan, and Amjad (2015, p. 141).   [30] See Chapter 9.

model of retributive justice, but it is described as an innate physiological response, and as an obsession. Nothing in the passage suggests a social or cultural model or norm. He experiences a combination of emotional responses, both cognitive and physiological (i.e. literally actions/states of his body). Does he feel his anger as a "burden"? Or simply as a hard, cold object? Granted that "*kept eating*" suggests "an insatiable appetite" (ANGER IS AN ANIMAL), but it equally suggests ANGER IS A CORROSIVE ACID, and that is arguably more consistent with the overall context.[31] Rather than BURDEN and GLUTTONOUS, it is at least as plausible to summarize his characterization of anger as HARD, COLD, CORROSIVE or AGGRESSIVE, and PERSISTENT. Nor is it apparent that the narrator necessarily experiences his anger as *negative*; people in the throes of reactance often seem to cherish and sustain their own anger. "*Lost some of . . .*" supports reading his experience of anger as a possession that he could not let go of until after the failed attempt at revenge.

Homeostasis applies not merely to the self but also to the primary reference group, a set of bonds that looms particularly large during wartime, when soldiers develop intense and complex interpersonal bonds: This story is about the complexity of one of those relationships. It is also about morality and human weakness, about our universal failure to live up to our own ideals. Humans (probably uniquely among animals) reflect on and try to understand our own responses in relation not merely to our own homeostasis but also in relation to our social environment, our primary group in particular. When we reflect on (or agonize over) threats to homeostasis, connections to other experiences activate or create metaphors. We employ and sometimes expand these, add them to our representation. People are not always aware of this process, but it seems to be the central theme of O'Brien's story.

I will illustrate this approach with Gay Bryant's "*glass ceiling*": "Women *reach* a certain *stage* in their career *where* they encounter a sort of *glass ceiling . . .*"[32] A conventional CMT analysis would go something like this: TO KNOW IS TO SEE, TRANSPARENT/VISIBLE IS KNOWN, POWER IS UP, A CAREER IS A JOURNEY/MOTION, and GENDER DISCRIMINATION IS A PHYSICAL OBSTACLE. I initially used this approach myself,[33] as a basis for showing how it implies (and is often used as) a metaphorical story.

How would the analysis develop if we start with Bryant's own experience, and her attempt to explain her experience to the interviewer? As she reflected on her experience, Bryant's thoughts may have gone somewhat like this:

---

[31] Even with the ANIMAL interpretation, the focus of the passage is on *persistence* and *aggression* rather than *nutrition* or *appetite*: ANGER IS A VICIOUS DOG, or perhaps ANGER IS A WILD ANIMAL.
[32] Bryant (1984).   [33] Ritchie (2017).

- She was able to perceive everything about ("*see clearly*") the executive suite.
- She had all the qualifications, the right strengths. (She compares her qualifications to those of top executives.)
- She was repeatedly denied promotion (couldn't "*get there*").
- She was *stopped* by *unacknowledged* sexist bias (an "*invisible barrier*").
- It was a "*glass ceiling*" (a structural metaphor that combines the two concepts, awareness ("*visible*") and obstruction ("*barrier*")).

It is misleading to take the lexical expression of conceptual metaphors, conventionally represented in SMALL CAPS, as literal descriptions, as preexisting units of thought.[34] It is more useful to regard them as suggesting plausible ways to describe a process of understanding and representing experience. In the case of "*glass ceiling*," Bryant (like O'Brien) was striving to understand a complex experience and express it, and her feelings about it, to others, especially to others in similar situations. As she reflected on her experience and her feelings about it, various aspects of her representation would become salient and activate connections to other experiences, and to metaphors. Many of these drew on the conventional conceptual metaphors that are widely known and readily available in Bryant's highly literate publishing industry culture. The CMT analysis is a useful post hoc explanation of this mental process, but it does not necessarily describe what actually happened as Bryant worked her way through her feelings and crystalized them in a very expressive metaphor.

For a reader, understanding Bryant's metaphor follows a similar path. When she describes her frustration, the reader empathizes; Bryant's metaphors resonate with that empathy so that the reader experiences simulations vicariously (but in terms of the reader's own experience). People may not *necessarily* think in terms of conceptual metaphors, but conceptual metaphors are there, a powerful rhetorical and conceptual resource ready to use. Thought takes the form of a combination of feelings, simulations, and language – and abstract neural representations of these. There is abundant evidence that these are organized in concepts or schemas or frames, interconnected sets of words, memories, simulations, and so forth. These concepts or schemas are probably interconnected (loosely) with each other in various ways, including ways of connecting more abstract with less abstract concepts as described by CMT. It is likely that conceptual thought employs these conceptual metaphors. But it is also likely that the experience, and the examination and consolidation of experience in thought, precedes as often as it follows from activation of a conceptual metaphor.

---

[34] Cameron (2007); Cameron, Maslen, and Low (2010).

Conceptual metaphors are useful tools for representing the relationship between thoughts and language. But we need to be careful not to reify them or treat them as a code-like specification of intentions and interpretations. Analysis should always start with the text, as close as we can get to the author's (originator's) social interactions and thought processes, and only then draw on conceptual metaphor analysis to illuminate *possible* connections.

Grammatical Metaphor

Lakoff and Johnson explain that conceptual metaphors lead us to experience a more abstract concept as a less abstract concept, but Halliday[35] explains the relationship as *transcategorization*, in which a concept from one conceptual category is expressed – and experienced – as a concept from a different category. Halliday and his colleagues show that transformation of a word or phrase from one grammatical category to another can also be usefully analyzed as a form of metaphor, which he calls *grammatical metaphor* (GM). Mao[36] provides a useful example: "these ideas have been subject to widespread criticism." Here, the action designated by the verb *to criticize* is transcategorized into a noun that designates an entity, criticism, an object or substance that is capable of being "*spread widely*." In this example, the grammatical metaphor produces an implied *objectification* metaphor, in which an abstract concept is presented as an object or substance.[37] In Obama's campaign speech, "*stained by* ... slavery" transcategorizes the noun *stain* to a verb, with *slavery* as the active causal agent. By extension this establishes *slavery* as an active agent in present-day political and cultural struggles. Grammatical metaphor can be usefully applied to relations between any parts of speech; nouns can be transcategorized into verbs or adjectives, adjectives into nouns or verbs, and so on. Analysis of these grammatical transformations in a text can often contribute significantly to understanding the author's underlying assumptions.[38]

Grammatical transcategorization also applies when one speech act is re-presented as another.[39] A rhetorical question may transform an imperative ("Ask permission!") and present it as an interrogative ("Don't you think you should ask first?") In an extended example from Norrick and Spitz,[40] a statement of personal taste is re-presented as a satirical comment. In a discussion of what to serve for a planned meal, DV's mother proposes quiche and DV objects that he does not like quiche, because "real men don't eat it."[41]

---

[35] Halliday (1985).
[36] Mao (2010). I will designate grammatical metaphors by underlining them.
[37] Ritchie and Zhu (2015). "Criticism" can also be understood as a metonym for "critics," who are dispersed in space and time.
[38] Halliday (1985); Ritchie and Zhu (2015).   [39] Mao (2010).
[40] Norrick and Spitz (2010). I will discuss this example in more detail in Chapter 12.
[41] This refers to the pop-culture book, *Real Men Don't Eat Quiche* (Feirstein, 1982).

Here, an intended criticism of the concept of "real men" is transcategorized and presented as a reason for disliking quiche. Irony generally takes the form of grammatical metaphor, since it transcategorizes an *intended* speech act into a (different) *apparent* speech act.[42]

Transcategorization is common in English usage, and often the only way to be certain whether a particular example fits the theory is to check the etymology of both the observed form and the supposed root form.[43] The issue at stake is whether the transcategorization makes any difference to the understanding of a passage[44] – and if it does, it isn't necessarily important which form is historically original. In the Obama speech discussed earlier, "*divided*" appears first in "*divided* the colonies" as a past tense of a verb, referring to disputes about slavery during the Constitutional Convention. In the following paragraph, it appears again as a noun, "racial *divisions*." Analyzing this transformation as a grammatical metaphor is useful because, reified as *things*, "*divisions*" can exist as independent agents that enter into causal relations. Similarly, in the now current phrase "climate change," "change" is transcategorized[45] from a verb to a noun, implying an agentive entity with causal powers.

Multimodal Metaphor

Until recently, discussion of metaphor focused entirely on language. However, once the idea of conceptual metaphors gains traction, it becomes apparent that any signal that represents a concept can be used metaphorically to induce the perceiver to experience it metaphorically. Visual metaphors are commonplace, appearing in the arts, in editorial and entertainment cartoons, and in the use of gestures. Location of palaces, government buildings, and religious buildings on physically high ground expresses POWER IS UP and SACRED IS UP. Pictures of icebergs express the idea of unknown ("*hidden*" or "*unseen*") dangers, and are often used to express a political or financial problem as a "*physical hazard*" capable of "*sinking*" a "*vessel*," often represented in political cartoons as "*the ship of state*." Flames or smoke coming out of a cartoon character's ears express EMOTION IS TEMPERATURE; ANGER IS HEAT. An emotionally volatile

---

[42] See Chapter 12.   [43] Ritchie and Zhu (2015).
[44] Ritchie (2017); Ritchie and Zhu (2015).
[45] Transcategorize is itself a grammatical metaphor. The noun *category* is re-presented as a verb categorize, transforming the abstract noun into an action that changes the essential nature of other language units; adding *trans* produces the capability of changing other language units across linguistic boundaries, so that the transcategorized unit becomes a completely different sort of concept, moving from one category to an entirely different category. *Category*, a member of the category *noun*, becomes categorize, then transcategorize, both in the category *verb*.

relationship is often expressed by moving a hand in a sine wave ("*ups* and *downs*"), and a thriving or failing relationship as an upward or downward curve (HAPPY or SUCCESS IS UP/SAD or FAILURE IS DOWN).

Sounds are also used metaphorically, in conversation as well as in music – for example, a "*falling*" tone for *sadness* or *tragedy*, a "*rising*" tone for *joy*[46] (UP IS HAPPY). Many instruments can be used to imitate the sound of a galloping horse or moving train, metonymically or metaphorically expressing motion or motion-related concepts like *rescue* or *escape*. Because of its long use as the theme for the TV program *The Lone Ranger*, a passage from *The William Tell Overture* became a common sonic metaphor for *rescue*, often metaphorical "*rescue*" from a socially embarrassing situation rather than literal *rescue* from a physically dangerous situation.[47] Thus, the music passage activated a metaphorical story (next section) in which the Lone Ranger riding to the rescue of an imperiled person or group expressed a bystander "*riding to the rescue*" of an emotionally "*imperiled*" person. Instruments can also imitate the sound of a vocal sigh, weeping, laughter, and so on, often metaphorically expressing an emotional response. The human voice is frequently used to imitate sounds of animals, machinery, wind, and so on, which can also metaphorically express other concepts: a "*purr*" for contentment, a "*growl*" for annoyance or anger, a fake cry of pain to express sympathy for a speaker's troubles.

Multimodal metaphors often portray language metaphors, and, in turn, multimodal metaphors and metonyms often provide the base for language metaphors. "Was my face ever *red*" describes embarrassment, whether the speaker blushed or not. A finger pointed toward a person's temple may metonymically express the idea of intelligence, but if it is perpendicular to the skull and shaped like a pistol, it may express "*shoot myself*" as a metaphorical admission of having made a blunder.

Metaphorical Stories and Story Metaphors

Storytelling is a crucial feature of both thought and conversation, since stories are central to the forward projection of situations, actions, and conversations, and comparing alternative stories is crucial to decision-making.[48] Stories are often metaphorical, and many metaphors are based on, and potentially evoke, stories.[49] The most familiar forms of metaphorical stories are the allegories, fables, and parables that have been told and retold over many centuries. In allegory, a central metaphor is elaborated, sometimes over hundreds of pages, often supported by metaphorical names for people and places, metaphorical

---

[46] Curtis and Bharucha (2010). [47] Often ironic. [48] Chapter 13.
[49] "*Glass ceiling*," discussed in the preceding, is an example.

descriptors, and so on. For example, in *Pilgrim's Progress*, the topic is implied but not explicitly mentioned; the central metaphorical mapping (A SPIRITUAL CONDITION IS A PHYSICAL PLACE) is supported by metaphorical names such as "Sinner," "Everyman," "Idleness," and "Christian," and metaphorical place names like "Slough of Despond."

A shorter and briefer literary form is the fable, stories like "The fox and the grapes," "The boy who cried 'wolf!,'" and "The emperor's new clothes." These are so familiar that the title alone is often used as an aphorism, with the power to evoke the story and guide its application to a relevant aspect of the current situation. Shorter yet is the parable, used by many religious teachers: A familiar example is "the prodigal son." In both fables and parables, the intended interpretation (the "moral of the story") is sometimes but not always explicitly stated in a coda. In others, like Jesus's parable of the wise man who built his house upon solid rock, the relationship to the topic is incorporated into the story.

Parables often take a form closer to metonym than to metaphor. The prodigal son in the well-known vehicle story rebels against his father, goes off to lead a sinful life, falls on hard times and repents, and is forgiven. This both expresses and provides an example of the general topic story of sin, repentance, and forgiveness. Similarly, the good Samaritan in another parable displays kindness and charity, providing an example of a topic story displaying the advocated moral qualities as well as mapping onto general stories.

Real-life events are also frequently used as metaphorical stories. Waterloo, the scene of Napoleon's final and total defeat, has been frequently used as a metaphor for *any* major reversal, financial, political, or personal – for example, "*Where will you meet your Waterloo?*" from the popular song "Waterloo"[50] that maps a major life reversal onto the story of Napoleon's disastrous defeat. A more contemporary story from American football expresses an attempt to recover from a partial setback: "Maybe it's time to *fall back and punt*." Politicians are frequently accused of "*kicking the can down the road*," based on a playful activity of rural youths.

Aphorisms (usually metaphorical) distill a bit of commonsense wisdom in a way that requires activation of at least a vehicle story and usually require mapping it onto a topic story. A "*bull in a china shop*" is merely something or someone in the wrong place until a story about a bull clumsily destroying the entire contents of the shop is mapped onto an already salient story about some behavior, usually metaphorically "*clumsy*" behavior that "*destroys*" social harmony, interpersonal trust, or some other valued social state of being. "*Let sleeping dogs lie*" merely seems like advice to be kind to exhausted pets until a

---

[50] Wilkin and Loudermilk (1959).

vehicle story about someone awakening a sleeping dog and getting bitten is contrasted with a vehicle story about the same person tiptoeing around the dog and not getting bitten, and both vehicle stories are mapped onto the topic, some potentially troublesome social situation.

Glucksberg and McGlone[51] provide an interesting example, "Cambodia is Vietnam's *Vietnam*," from media commentaries on Vietnam's 1978 invasion of Cambodia. This metaphor maps the story of the long and costly US engagement in Vietnam onto the story of Vietnam's subsequent (but not nearly so costly) intervention in Cambodia. A similar example is the aphorism *"boys will be boys."* Here, the first *"boys"* often refers to adult men, and the second *"boys"* refers metonymically to childish behavior of adolescent males, with the implication that the topic persons are behaving in a puerile manner. Both examples also exemplify the combination of metaphor with irony.

Playful Metaphors. Metaphors are prototypically used to express serious ideas, as in Obama's phrase *"stained by the original sin of* slavery," and, from later in the same speech, *"carries the blood of slaves and slave-owners"* and *"incendiary* language." However, they are also used playfully, as when a group of scientists discussing how to communicate science to the public extended and developed the metaphor *"ivory tower."*[52] The scientists' play with *"ivory tower"* also illustrates how metaphors can be developed into humor and stories. Even when the tone is serious, speakers and writers often "play" with language, including idiomatic metaphors. An example comes in a discussion of police-community interaction when one member of a group of African Americans criticizes adolescent lawbreakers, transforming *"we're all in the same boat"* into a story about a troublesome adolescent *"knocking a hole in the boat"* to *"get me some water"* and concludes with a metaphorical coda, "everybody *goes down."*[53]

People often create playful quasi-metaphors with little or no serious meaning, *"empty* metaphors" according to Ritchie and Dyhouse[54], who provide the following example of an exchange of greetings (from a rural town in southern Indiana):

> "Howdy, John, how doin'?"
> *"Fine as frog's hair*, Skeeter. You?"
> *"Fit as a fiddle."*

Both phrases take the form of metaphors, but the images they activate are playfully incongruous, and the only *"content"* is to affirm and reinforce their

---

[51] Glucksberg and McGlone (1999).   [52] Ritchie and Schell (2009).   [53] Ritchie (2010a).
[54] Ritchie and Dyhouse (2008).

social solidarity and provide evidence of their pleasant mood by engaging in lighthearted wordplay.[55] An exchange of this sort contributes to homeostasis in at least two ways: it reaffirms the emotional bonds, and it releases endorphins through the pleasure of the language play. Many playful metaphors can support a reasonable interpretation. A "*gully washer*" is a heavy rainstorm with the potential to erode loose soil into gullies, but its use is probably more a result of its amusing sound and sense of exaggeration, and is not intended to predict impending soil erosion. "*Raining buckets*," like "*gully washer*," has a quality as much hyperbolic metonym as metaphor, but "*raining cats and dogs*," like "*fine as frog's hair*," can be interpreted only in terms of the playful evocation of perceptual simulations. Similarly, "*a snowball's chance in Hell*" combines playful exaggeration with interesting rhythm (a *snow*ball's *chance* in *Hell*) and incongruous simulations.

Cleverly playful metaphors are often used in advertising, journalism, and other professional communication where it is important to attract and hold the attention of an audience, and to motivate a deeper level of processing. Carter gives the examples of an Irish petrol company called "*Emerald Oil*" and a hair salon named "*A Cut Above*"[56] (up is good; "*cut*" can refer to "*cutting*" a deck of cards as well as cutting hair). In the United States, there are many taverns with names like "*The Dew Drop Inn*" and (for singles bars) "*The Meet Market*" ("*meat*" is a commonplace crude reference for casual sex). Kövecses also cites playfully metaphorical sports headlines, including "Clemson *cooks* Rice" (TO DEFEAT IS TO COOK) and "Cowboys *corral* Buffaloes"[57] (TO CORRAL IS TO CONTAIN). In addition to play on word sounds, team names, and activities, all these potentially activate amusing perceptual and story simulations that reward deeper processing. Glucksberg provides a nice example of wordplay in a financial page headline: "Main Street bulls take bears by the horns."[58]

In serious discourse, metaphors are most often selected for their ability to activate simulations and semantic associations that express something complex and interesting about the topic. But these playful metaphors, like "*fine as frog's hair*," seem to have been created and used primarily for the amusement and pleasure of the simulations they activate, and secondarily to reward more extensive processing. The pleasure of using and processing playful metaphors serves a vital social-bonding function that contributes to both individual and group homeostasis while enriching the language resources of the speech community.

---

[55] Both metaphors are cultural commonplaces: "*Fit as a fiddle*" is or at least once was widespread in the United States, and I recently heard a service station attendant in eastern Oregon reply to a polite "How are you?" with "*Fine as frog's hair*."
[56] Carter (2004).   [57] Kövecses (2005).   [58] Glucksberg (2001).

Language play, storytelling, and humor are intrinsically enjoyable, and they reduce stress and contribute to a sense of well-being. The shared pleasure supports social bonding and contributes to social solidarity by emphasizing common group membership and cultural knowledge. This is no doubt one reason why skillful use of language is a valued trait that enhances social status and contributes to personal and group homeostasis.[59]

Understanding Metaphors

As discussed in previous chapters, thinking involves a combination of perceptual simulations and semantic connections. Concepts, both material concepts like *bird* or *swim* and abstract concepts like *love* or *metaphor*, are composed of densely interconnected simulations and words. Simulations automatically activate associated words, and words activate associated simulations as well as thematically related words. Concepts are also interconnected, both by related words and by related simulations, including simulations of objects, actions, emotions, and so forth. *Duck*, *fish*, and *water* are all connected with *swim*, and may or may not be activated depending on the context.

Words and phrases, including metaphors, at least briefly activate simulations[60] and associated words. A metaphor will usually activate simulations and words associated with the vehicle. The activation is stronger if the metaphor is new or imaginative; the more familiar it is, the weaker the simulation.[61] When language is processed at a deeper level, simulations are likely to play a more central role;[62] the depth of processing is itself partly a function of ability to process (freedom from distraction, background knowledge, language abilities) and motivation to process (interest and relevance).[63]

Like all language and signal systems, metaphors are ordinarily ambiguous. A given metaphor can often be understood in terms of more than one underlying conceptual metaphor, and even within a single conceptual metaphor, the vehicle-topic relationship may be explored in quite different ways by different people or by the same person in different situations. Speakers sometimes use "*tuning devices*"[64] such as "metaphorically speaking" or "in a sense" to help reduce the ambiguity and guide listeners to a particular interpretation, but the success of these is not assured.

Steen[65] argues that people will process a metaphor more deeply if it is perceived as *deliberate* – that is, used intentionally as a metaphor – and if the structure of the vehicle phrase suggests the need to shift attention from the topic to the vehicle. Evidence of deliberate metaphor use includes novelty,

---

[59] Dessalles (2014).   [60] Bergen (2012).   [61] Littlemore (2019).   [62] Barsalou (2008).
[63] Petty and Cacioppo (1981).   [64] Cameron and Deignan (2003).   [65] Steen (2015).

repeated metaphorical phrases based on the same conceptual metaphor, and surrounding language, including tuning devices.

Aspects of a metaphor that may induce cognitive elaboration and perceptual simulations include novelty and creativity, the use of unusual or particularly dynamic language, specifically calling attention to the metaphor, and extended development of the metaphor. If a metaphor is either presented as or implies a story, that may also motivate a listener to extend and complete the story. Conversely, if a metaphor is upsetting or contradicts deeply held beliefs, a reader or hearer may ignore it or reject it entirely.

Contextual Influences on Individual Interpretations. Discussions of conceptual metaphors[66] often imply a universal mapping of topic onto vehicle, but metaphors are often understood in a variety of ways, even by members of the same language community. For just one example, I have asked several English-speaking audiences to spell and explain the metaphor "t - - the line." Consistently the audience is equally divided between "*toe* the line" and "*tow* the line" – with a variety of explanations *within* each group. "*Toe* the line" may imply the imaginary line that soldiers "toe" when lining up in a military formation, or the starting line runners "toe" before a footrace. "*Tow* the line" has been interpreted as a tugboat, the rope in a game of tug-of-war, and an advertising banner behind an airplane. Each interpretation draws on different knowledge, experience, and associations. Each interpretation generally implies "conform to social expectations," but the particular implications differ. The explanations of "*toe*" all imply passive compliance, and the explanations of "*tow*" imply active compliance.

From Obama's speech, both "racial *wounds*" and "a racial *stalemate* we've been *stuck in* for years" may activate a wide range of simulations, depending on context and background experience. "*Stuck in*" might imply sticky mud, a narrow passageway, or rush-hour traffic. "*Original sin*" refers to a religious doctrine that varies widely among Christian denominations, and is not well understood by all Christians, much less non-Christians. If the concept of "*original sin*" as a guilt that is acquired at birth is more salient, the "*stain*" will have much greater immediacy and imply a shared guilt for the evils caused by slavery. For listeners unfamiliar with this doctrine, the "*stain*" of slavery may apply only to the time before the Civil War and the Emancipation Proclamation, and have no relevance to the present.

Convolution and the Cognitive-Affective Model. Thagard defines analogies as "systematic comparisons in which a source situation provides information about a target situation."[67] He argues that understanding analogies is difficult because two complex ideas can be compared in many ways, but

---

[66] For example, Lakoff and Johnson (1980; 1999). [67] Thagard (2011, p.132).

constraints of similarity, structure, and purpose can make this process easier. Thagard proposes a *convolution* account of how concepts are combined, and applied it to emotional experience[68] and creativity[69] as well as to analogy and allegory.

Thagard claims that readers or hearers develop simulations by which we can understand and predict the behavior of complex systems. Creativity involves combining mental representations, patterns of neural activity that represent previously unconnected concepts in working memory.[70] "The generation of new representations involves binding together previously unconnected representations in ways that also generate new emotional bindings,"[71] which is what Thagard means by *convolution*, "an operation that binds together wave functions or vectors" or patterns of neural activation. Thagard and Stewart demonstrate that patterns of neural activity, including appraisal and affective evaluation, can be bound together, in such a way that the constituent concepts remain separable and distinct. Through this process, aspects of *slavery* and *original sin*, including their conceptual meanings and our emotional (appraisal plus affect) responses, can be bound together into a new concept, *slavery-as-sin*.

Analogy Versus Conceptual Metaphor: Comparing To or Experiencing As. Gentner and Bowdle assert that metaphor is an extension of analogy in which attributes of the vehicle and its sub-concepts provide a basis for drawing conclusions about the topic.[72] Lakoff and Johnson claim that metaphor is distinct from analogy, and induces us to experience the topic *as* the vehicle.[73] Thagard's explanation of convolution is compatible with the conceptual metaphor view:[74] The topic is *combined with* the vehicle and creates an entirely new and distinct concept.

Barsalou[75] suggests that lexical processing is engaged for low-effort shallow processing, Petty and Cacioppo's[76] "peripheral route," but perceptual simulations are engaged for deeper, more elaborate processing, Petty and Cacioppo's "central route," which leads to more cognitive change and retention.[77] The central route, greater processing, is engaged only when the individual has sufficient motivation (interest and relevance) and ability (mental capacity, language skills, and background knowledge).

Thus, "*stained by* the *original sin* of slavery" would be more likely to engage multimodal perceptual simulations only if the person has a sufficient knowledge of both the history of slavery and the doctrine of *original sin*, as well as sufficient interest to justify the processing effort. Ideas and emotions associated with these concepts would be activated and blended into a highly

---

[68] Thagard and Aubie (2008). [69] Thagard and Stewart (2011).
[70] Thagard and Stewart (2011). [71] Thagard and Stewart, 2011, p. 2).
[72] Gentner and Bowdle (2001). [73] Lakoff and Johnson (1980). [74] Thagard (2011).
[75] Barsalou (2007). [76] Petty and Cacioppo (1981). [77] Petty and Cacioppo (1981).

charged composite emotion, possibly leading to a new set of cognitions about the US Constitution and its authors. For those lacking motivation and/or knowledge, only the most salient ideas associated with *sin* (it's wrong, and people don't approve of it) might be briefly activated and associated with the most salient ideas associated with *slavery* as a truism "forcing people to work for nothing is wrong," leading to little or no cognitive change.

Metaphor, Social Structure, and Personal Identity[78]

Extensive evidence suggests that social "*structure*" (SOCIETY IS A BUILDING) is experienced in primarily in metaphorical terms; our social experience shapes and is shaped by the metaphors we use to discuss both social structure and personal identity. Examples discussed earlier in this chapter include expressions of personal intimacy and social inclusion ("*warm*," "*close*") or exclusion ("*cold*," "*remote*") and "*glass ceiling*" (A CAREER IS A JOURNEY; POWER IS UP).

EMOTION IS TEMPERATURE: Williams and Bargh[79] asked subjects to hold a cup of hot or cold beverage and then assess personality traits for a randomly chosen person. Holding the hot beverage container was associated with ratings significantly more friendly than holding the cold beverage container. Zhong and Leonardelli[80] used a series of manipulations to induce feelings of social inclusion or exclusion. Participants led either to feel excluded or recall a time when they felt excluded estimated the temperature of the room to be significantly colder, and when offered a drink after the test, they were more likely to request a warm drink rather than a cold drink.

POWER IS UP is observed in architecture (the executive suite of most organizations occupies the top floor), city planning (palaces and temples have been located in high places throughout history), and social customs such as bowing and kneeling. So strong is the association that even the visual location of a word or phrase (e.g. on a page or computer screen) activates inferences based on the metaphor. In a series of experiments, Schubert, Waldzus, and Seibt[81] presented pairs of words – such as teacher and student, boss and employee – either at the top of a computer screen or at the bottom and asked subjects to identify the group with the most power and the group with the least power. Responses were both faster and more accurate if the higher-status group was presented higher on the screen and the lower-status group lower.

Metaphors related to VERTICAL POSITION and PHYSICAL/TEMPORAL PROXIMITY also influence self-perception. Given the opportunity to select a position

---

[78] I am indebted to my student Elise Stinnett for several of the insights and resources cited in this section.
[79] Williams and Bargh (2008).   [80] Zhong and Leonardelli (2008).
[81] Schubert, Waldzus, and Seibt (2005).

that is higher or lower in space, people who exhibit depressive symptoms or perceive themselves as low in power are more likely to select a lower location, and people who perceive themselves as powerful are more likely to select a higher location.[82] Wilson and Ross[83] report that subjects are more critical of their behavior in the "*remote*" past (i.e. more "*distant*" from them) than of their more recent ("*closer*") behavior, even when current evaluations show no actual improvement.

POWER IS UP also influences romantic and sexual preferences. When a group of college-age subjects were asked to rank potential dating partners, female participants ranked males as more desirable when their images were presented in higher locations. Conversely, male participants ranked females as more desirable when their images were presented in lower locations.[84] Commonplace metaphors also express love as an "*object*" that can be "*exchanged*, "*lost*," "*given*," or "*stolen*."[85] Relationships are often expressed as spatial relationships: "*circle* of friends," "*distant* cousin."

Synthesis: Context-Limited Simulation Theory (CLST)

Cameron[86] argues that it is impossible to determine whether a conceptual metaphor is activated on any particular occasion, and recommends discussing metaphors only in terms of *thematic* metaphors. While I agree that it is impossible to know what people are actually thinking, I am convinced by the evidence that abstract concepts are at least shaped by conceptual metaphors, and that many metaphorical expressions are based on these conceptual metaphors. However, the evidence does not support the claim that conceptual metaphors take an invariant, code-like form such as LOVE IS A JOURNEY, or the claim that they are always activated when a metaphor is encountered.

The accumulated evidence supports a more general claim, that repeated experiences such as movement through space, upward and downward motion, changes in temperature, and so forth, lead to the development of *generic* conceptual metaphors such as UP/HIGH, DOWN/LOW, WARM/COLD, JOURNEY, PHYSICAL CONFLICT (WAR), DIRT, and so on. These generic conceptual metaphors are available as abstract multimodal simulators with which to understand and express abstract concepts. MORE IS UP, POWERFUL IS UP, HEALTHY IS UP all draw on the same underlying experience-based conceptual field, vertical direction and motion. Since most abstract concepts are complex, we routinely "mix metaphors" and draw on *several* conceptual fields to express any complex experience. LOVE IS A JOURNEY as well as A CONSTRUCTION PROJECT, A DANCE, A GAME, and even WAR. However, metaphors often receive only a very

---

[82] Landau et al. (2010).   [83] Wilson and Ross (2001).   [84] Meier and Dionne (2009).
[85] Sato et al. (2015).   [86] Cameron (2007).

cursory, shallow lexical processing, and the associated perceptual simulations are often only weakly activated.

The context and perceived relevance and interest influence how a speaker draws on these conceptual fields to formulate an utterance, and how hearers understand it. These processes are usually more or less automatic, but they are sometimes deliberate, in that speakers and hearers actively consider alternative metaphors and metaphorical interpretations (consistent with Steen). This is the essence of Context-Limited Simulation Theory (CLST).[87]

Summary

Language has extended human cognition in many ways. Initially language increased and enhanced social structure, both peer relationships (bonding) and hierarchical relationships (dominance and submission). It also provides means for objectifying emotional and mental experience and for abstracting and representing relevant features of the social and physical environment. The expansion of vocabulary and increasing complexity of syntax expanded the range and complexity of experiences (real and imagined) that could be represented and communicated. Metaphor expanded both vocabulary and grammar even further, facilitating the expression of subtle nuances of experience while increasing the ambiguity of signals. Conversely metaphors, both lexical and grammatical, exercise a pervasive influence on both experience and the expression of experience – including social structure as well as personal identity and sense of self.

---

[87] Ritchie (2006, 2017).

12   Humor and Irony

Humor is an extension of play and, like play, performs many purposes in social interaction. This chapter begins by reviewing some of the primary theories of humor, then discusses the social functions of humor, including humor as a coping mechanism, and humor cultures. Irony, as a particular form of humor, gets a separate treatment. The chapter closes with a discussion of the contributions of humor to social organization and homeostasis.

Until recently, most research and theorizing about humor has focused on verbal humor, particularly canned jokes, often drawn from published joke books. Early research on humor in conversation focused on "joking sessions" in which participants tell a series of jokes, chaining off each other's performances.[1] However, retelling canned jokes typically accounts for only 11 percent of daily humor encounters, and they are completely absent from many social encounters. More typical forms of humor include interaction humor, irony, quips, put-downs, and playful interaction, which account for 72 percent of daily humor encounters. Humorous use of other signals (facial expressions, posture, gestures, etc.) is a separate category, important but less frequently studied.

Humor, and theories about humor, might be divided into two classes, "*bitter*" and "*sweet*." Both play a role in social regulation as well as in social bonding. "*Bitter*" humor functions to exclude, to emphasize status differences, to dominate, to wound, and to punish. Until recently, most mainstream theories of humor emphasized these functions, and focused on examples of humor (primarily off-color jokes and aggressive put-downs of the sort enjoyed by adolescent males) that serve these functions. "*Sweet*" humor functions primarily to entertain, to include, deemphasize status differences, strengthen social bonds, and alleviate stress. "*Bitter*" humor encourages the audience to laugh *at* some person or group identified as the butt of the joke.[2] "*Bitter*" humor can contribute to group homeostasis through aggression against a disliked outgroup and can also contribute to individual homeostasis (but possibly detract

---

[1] Coates (2007).   [2] Gruner (1997).

from group homeostasis) through aggression against a rival within the group. "*Bitter*" humor, including put-downs, often serves to reinforce group norms and rules by chastising violators.[3] "*Sweet*" humor encourages the audience to laugh *with* and contributes to both group and individual homeostasis by strengthening bonds, reducing stress, and ameliorating conflict.

Humor in ordinary adult conversation is characterized by wordplay, including puns and quips, amusing anecdotes from real life, retelling humorous incidents or anecdotes from mass media, role play, and enacting absurd scenarios. Aggressive humor appears primarily as humorous and humorously ironic put-downs, often self-directed and, within harmonious groups, is usually enjoyed by the target.

Theories of Humor

Humor as Sublimated Aggression. Most traditional theories of humor emphasize aggression or incongruity.[4] Gruner[5] argues that *all* humor is based on aggression, an implicit or explicit attack by the joke teller against an individual, either as a specific person (e.g. "*put-down*" humor) or as a representative of an out-group. The aggression approach is commonly supported by examples of sexist, ethnic, and other stereotype-mocking jokes, usually targeted at lower-status and relatively powerless groups.

For example, "light bulb" jokes ask how many members of some group (e.g. blonds, lawyers, disfavored ethnic groups, etc.) it takes to screw in a light bulb; the punch line (e.g. "five, one to hold the bulb and four to turn the chair") demonstrates the alleged stupidity of the target group and its members,[6] a metaphorical attack on all members of that group. Most racial, ethnic, and gender-based jokes disparage the targets, and exclude the target group while emphasizing the group solidarity of the joke teller and audience.[7]

The effects of disparagement humor are complex and ambiguous. Zillmann and Cantor show that a favorable view of the target group reduces and an unfavorable view increases appreciation of prejudice-based disparagement humor.[8] Telling a prejudicial joke increases the subsequent expression of prejudice against the target group by the teller – but only if the joke is appreciated by the audience. Acceptance of one prejudicial joke appears to have a releasing effect on other previously prejudiced group members – that is, it establishes a group norm of acceptability – but it does not increase the expressed prejudice of those who were not already prejudiced.[9]

---

[3] Billig (2005). [4] Martin (2007). [5] Gruner (1997). [6] Attardo (2001).
[7] Attardo (2001); Norrick (2003). [8] Zillmann and Cantor (1976).
[9] Ford, Richardson, and Petit (2015).

Aggression and disparagement evidently play a role in many examples of humor, but the evidence does not support the claim that genuine aggression or disparagement are part of all or even most humor. It takes considerable interpretive creativity to apply aggression theory to absurdist jokes such as those of the "elephant joke" genre[10] – for example, "How does an elephant hide in a strawberry patch? It paints its toenails red." Gruner claims that these jokes somehow constitute an "aggression" against the hearer – but the closest a typical hearer comes to a reaction consistent with the aggression explanation is an exaggerated groan. Aggression theory is not always easy to apply even to canned jokes, for example:

A kangaroo walked into a tavern and ordered a beer. The bartender served him and said, "Ten dollars, please." The kangaroo paid the money and sipped on his beer. The bartender kept glancing at the kangaroo out of the corner of his eye, then finally walked back over and commented,

"You know, we don't get many kangaroos in here."

The kangaroo replied, "Well, at these prices it's no wonder."

Who or what is the target of aggression here? Neither kangaroos nor bartenders fit the victim role. This might be considered as aggression against inflation as an *institutional process*, taken as an "ideological target."[11] But it is hard to interpret an action directed at an ideological target as *aggression* except in a metaphorical sense.

Another objection to the claims of aggression theory is based on the widespread use of put-down humor among friends and family members, where it is accepted and actively enjoyed by everyone, especially the target.[12] If the humor in these exchanges is experienced as genuinely aggressive, it will be protested – and usually, if a teasing remark "*goes too far*," so that it seems actually aggressive, it *is* protested, withdrawn, or negated. In a work group, other group members will often come to the defense of a lower-status member who is perceived to have been the target of an aggressive joke.[13] The most frequent exceptions to this occur when the target is perceived as an "outsider" – for example, a woman in a job perceived as stereotypically masculine – or the aggressive joke is a response to the target's violation of group norms.

Within a family, work group, or friendship group, use of mock-aggressive teasing is usually governed by explicit norms and occurs within a "play frame" that can be established either contextually or by paralinguistic signals such as vocal tone or facial expression.[14] Contrary to the tenets of aggression theories,

---

[10] Martin (2007). [11] Attardo (2001); Everts (2003); Terrion and Ashforth (2002).
[12] Everts (2003); Terrion and Ashforth (2002). [13] Terrion and Ashforth (2002).
[14] Chapter 10.

mock-aggressive humor is often directed toward higher-status rather than lower-status group members, and avoids truly sensitive issues and topics.[15] Similarly, among the college students in Gibbs's research on humorous use of irony, aggressive humor that might risk disrupting relationships was carefully avoided.[16]

Incongruity and Frame-Shifting. Another approach emphasizes the "surprise" element in humor and a sudden flood of incongruity created by the punch line.[17] The kangaroo joke sets up an *initial* incongruity, which the listener accepts through suspension of disbelief (a common feature of the "play frame"). The punch line states a familiar truth that is not incongruous; the incongruity exists only because it forces a frame shift.[18] The bartender's statement and implied question sustains the frame of the initial incongruity (kangaroos do not actually walk into bars to order drinks.) The punch line obtrusively ignores this context-setting major incongruity and shifts to a minor incongruity in an "ordinary consumer economics" frame, leaving the major incongruity unresolved. The elephant in a strawberry patch joke (like most elephant jokes) works exactly the same way, by activating an initially incongruous frame that is *not* resolved. Contrary to incongruity resolution theory, the humor seems to come from the incongruity itself, and the fact that the punch line resolves a secondary incongruity but leaves the most salient incongruity unresolved. It appears that the punch line legitimates or naturalizes the incongruity for the hearer's enjoyment.

Gamson[19] reports the following bit of teasing between two male firefighters following the completion of a focus group:

KEN: I didn't *pull any punches*.
JOE: You didn't *throw any*, either.

The teasing put-down relies on a common metaphor based on boxing (in a practice sparring match, the superior boxer will often "*pull*" his punches to soften the blow and avoid injuring an outmatched sparring partner.) Joe's quip appears aggressive toward Ken, and it serves as a mild rebuke for Ken's minor violation of the "don't brag" social rule. However, like Norrick's examples,[20] it was apparently intended and understood in good humor, within an established friendly relationship. Rather than assert superiority, the put-down reestablishes equality. Ken's boxing metaphor is arguably incongruous with a friendly discussion, and Joe's response ironically reverses the incongruity, but neither incongruity nor aggression fits the example very well. Raskin,

---

[15] Everts (2003); Terrion and Ashforth (2002); Schnurr and Chan (2011). [16] Gibbs (2000).
[17] (Raskin, 1985; Perlmutter, 2002). [18] Coulson (2001). [19] Gamson (1992).
[20] Norrick (1993). See Chapter 10.

Attardo, and other incongruity theorists acknowledge these difficulties,[21] but their attempts to resolve them are not convincing.[22] As with aggression, it may be useful to distinguish between a deep level of incongruity (walking into a pub and ordering a beer is profoundly incongruous with what we know about kangaroos) and a purely linguistic incongruity, as between the commonplace metaphor, "*pull your punches*" and the less common extension, "*throw a punch.*"

Another example of a frame shift comes in a joke about hunting:

Two hunters are out in the woods when one of them collapses. He doesn't seem to be breathing, and his eyes are glazed. The other guy whips out his phone and calls the emergency services. He gasps, "My friend is dead! What can I do?"

The operator says, "Calm down. I can help. First, let's make sure he's dead."

There is a silence, then a shot is heard. Back on the phone, the hunter says, "OK, now what?"

The 911 operator introduces an ambiguity that is not noticed until the punch line. Idiomatically, "*make sure* he's dead" in such a context is understood as "check to see if he is really dead," and activates a frame that includes checking for heartbeat and breathing. The punch line activates a very different frame associated with crime fiction or gangster movies (if he isn't dead, kill him), which creates an *unresolved* incongruity with the initial frame that is only partially resolved. Here also, rather than resolve the incongruity, the punch line raises its salience and apparently naturalizes it (as if killing a friend to "make sure he's dead" is perfectly ordinary). In all three examples, perceptual simulations, including simulations of the characters' emotional responses, may add to enjoyment of the incongruency.

A Cognitive/Evolutionary Account of Humor. Hurley, Dennett, and Adams[23] argue that humor has evolved to reward the brain for identifying and correcting false assumptions. Evolution has rewarded development of two contradictory skills. One is the ability to anticipate future events rapidly and shift attention from one context to another. This rapid development of expectations frequently leads us to have erroneous assumptions and expectations, which undermine the integrity and usefulness of our representations and forward projections. The second, compensatory skill is to detect and correct erroneous assumptions and projections – which can require significant cognitive effort and attention. The pleasure associated with mirth is a reward for discovering and resolving contradictions, which encourages future engagement in the task. It is not the incongruity as much as the sudden and

---

[21] Attardo (2001); Raskin and Attardo (1994).   [22] Brône and Feyaerts, 2004).
[23] Hurley, Dennett, and Adams (2011).

unexpected identification and correction of false and contradictory assumptions that produces the pleasant mirth.[24]

As a joke or comic scene unfolds, we set up a frame representing the comic character's beliefs, assumptions, inferences, and intentions, and another frame representing what we know about the actual situation. Mirth is produced when these frames are merged or blended, and we identify the contradictory assumptions and correct the false assumptions. This enjoyment is enhanced by combining with other positive emotions, including feelings of superiority to the comic character, sexual arousal, appreciation for cleverness or skill, and enjoyment of wordplay and aesthetic elements such as images or the sounds of language. In conversational humor, the conversational situation and topic establish and maintain a mutual cognitive environment of salient contexts; a quip or jest introduces an incongruent context that activates contradictory assumptions. Mirth is produced when the contradictions are resolved.

Relevance. Sperber and Wilson claimed that the search for a relevant context proceeds only until a sufficiently relevant interpretation is discovered, then ceases. A joke setup activates a familiar context, and the buildup strengthens its activation. When the punch line introduces elements that are not relevant to the initial context, it activates a new search for relevance and a new interpretation based on a different context, often one that was initially either less salient or rejected entirely. This produces a "flood of relevance" that accounts for the humorous effect.[25] If the ambiguity is resolved in a particularly *clever* way, so the resolution unexpectedly "*fits*," the joke is enjoyed much more than if the resolution requires a "*stretch*," in which case a loud groan is more likely than laughter.

Giora has extended relevance theory in a discourse-based theory of humor.[26] According to Graded Salience Theory, any well-formed utterance or text is relevant to an established topic, a context that is salient in the mutual cognitive environment. It also conforms to a "graded informativeness condition," in that each proposition is as informative or more informative than what went before. Finally, deviations from relevance or informativeness are acknowledged or marked. Humor or irony conform to relevance but violate the informativeness expectation because the immediately salient meaning is either insufficiently or excessively informative.

According to Giora's account, the most salient meaning of a phrase such as "make sure he's dead" is accessed first, but the punch line forces reconsideration of other schemas that were initially activated but contextually

---

[24] This explanation fits nicely with Dessalles's (2014) account of the social advertising function of conversation.
[25] Sperber and Wilson (1986). [26] Giora (2003); Norrick (2003).

suppressed.[27] Giora predicts that the original interpretation is actively suppressed: "Whereas understanding irony and metaphor involves retention of salient, though contextually incompatible meanings ..., joke interpretation does not."[28] However, at least in these examples, the frame shift resolves one incongruity only by introducing another, potentially more shocking, incongruity, which remains unresolved.

Relevance Theory and Graded Salience Theory implicitly assume that listeners activate only one context at a time. At first reading, this seems accurate with respect to the hunter joke, in which a *hunting trip* script is activated, then blended with a *health crisis* script. The 911 operator's utterance activates a *calling for help* script that blends easily into the *hunting trip/health crisis* script, but the punch line activates an entirely different script that forces reinterpretation of "make sure he's dead." However, for the reinterpretation to be relevant, all three of the previously activated scripts must be revised.

The kangaroo example poses more difficulties. The setup blends an *animal joke* script with a *bar joke* script, and it is incongruous from the outset. The *kangaroo* provides a context in which the bartender's hesitant question is relevant, although perhaps insufficiently informative – but insufficiently *inquisitive* is a more accurate characterization. The punch line is relevant to the previous information about the price of the beer, but requires activation of an *economics* schema, and leaves the incongruity of *kangaroo* unresolved, with no apparent relevance to anything.

In the hunting joke, the punch line resolves an apparent incongruity by activating a less-salient interpretation of "make sure he's dead," revealing that it was "insufficiently informative" because it was ambiguous. In the kangaroo joke, the salience of a major incongruity (a kangaroo orders a beer) is reduced, and the salience of another, relatively minor, incongruity (the high price of the beer) is elevated. *Informativeness* doesn't quite seem the right concept. And both jokes leave the *most* salient incongruity unresolved.

Both examples suggest that multiple cognitive contexts are activated at once. This claim is even more important for conversational humor. The exchange between Ken and Joe ("You didn't throw any, either") requires the simultaneous activation of the familiar BOXING metaphor, a *focus group/conversation* schema, and a *friendship/friendly put-down* schema. The quip changed the mutual cognitive environment of Ken and Joe with respect to, hence was relevant to, all these schemas.

In general, the more dimensions of ambiguity are resolved by the punch line, the better the joke. A punch line that activates more than one relevant context produces an unexpected boost in relevance and increase in cognitive

---

[27] Giora (2003).   [28] Giora (2003, p. 175).

effects. A really *good* joke or quip expresses a deeper, often partially suppressed social truth, leading to changes in social and cultural contexts as well as cognitive and emotional contexts. For example, the kangaroo joke expresses a suppressed feeling of outrage people feel when faced with an unexpectedly large restaurant or bar tab.[29]

None of these accounts deals adequately with humor that uses frame shifts to highlight and resolve an incongruity based on a false assumption while leaving a contextual incongruity unresolved (the kangaroo and elephant joke) or introducing another incongruity (the hunter making sure his friend is dead). This would seem to support the possibility that playful incongruity is enjoyed for its own sake[30] (when it is genuinely harmless), and that the creation of (clever) incongruities, as well as the resolution of incongruities, is rewarded by the endorphins associated with merriment.

Playful Humor. It is apparent from the popularity of nonsense verse and fantasy role play[31] that adults as well as children enjoy incongruity for its own sake. Most of the humor encountered in ordinary discourse is playful (*"sweet"*) at least in some sense. Humor often plays with the form, sound, and meanings of words and phrases, and sometimes plays with our expectations of a social context or topical frame. Humor frequently involves creation (and celebration) of incongruities, and almost always plays with and distorts our sense of reality.

Several examples of language play discussed in Chapter 10 illustrate the enjoyment of incongruity. The *"rabbit"* metaphor developed by a group of women gossiping about a friend's marital relationship and the long riff on light bulbs as *"darkness suckers"*[32] both introduce and develop incongruities with no attempt to resolve them. The "Are you a cop?" tease[33] develops a fantasy identity for the target, the group, and the conversation, again with no attempt to resolve it.

The same group of young radicals who produced the "Are you a cop?" tease produced another example. The group had been asked to discuss excessive use of force by police officers. Tyler, the same participant who asked "Are you a cop?" three times, compared police officers to a breakfast food server who messes up an order:[34] "If a waitress approached you with saying, oh I'm really sorry, you said 'over medium,' but I got you over easy. Cops just fucking *pepper sprayed your baby*, even more so, right?" A few lines later, he returned to this metaphor, initiating the following exchange:

---

[29] Ritchie (2005). [30] Chapter 10.
[31] For example, Carroll (1871); Lear (1871); see Chapter 10. [32] Norrick and Spitz (2010).
[33] Ritchie (2010); Chapter 10.
[34] Ritchie (2010). I will return to this example later in the chapter, as an example of a group's humor culture.

TYLER: If you're a waitress and you're not getting good tips and you think people hate you, then you should *quit pissing in their soup.*
MICHAEL: Of course, the fallacy of that assumption ... the waitress is doing something blatantly crazy unethical.
CELESTE: Some places you get tipped more for that.
MICHAEL: Like, I love that sauce. {Laughter}
TYLER: You guys have the best soup. {Laughter}
CELESTE: We do.

The participants clearly enjoyed collaboratively developing this crude incongruity. Instead of resolving the incongruity, they made it even more absurd, just as DV enjoyed elaborating the fantasy physics of light bulbs as *"darkness suckers."*[35]

All this suggests that people derive pleasure and mirth from developing and entering a fantasy world that is incongruent with ordinary reality. Often, as in the kangaroo and hunter examples, the punch line serves to resolve a minor incongruity while naturalizing and legitimating a major incongruity, a fictional world in which kangaroos drink beer, left-leaning college students are dangerous subversives, waitresses urinate in the soup, and customers enjoy it. Perhaps the pleasure of entertaining these incongruities is associated with the brain's vitally important forward-projection faculties, the ability to invent, elaborate, and project oneself into fanciful, future, and even impossible worlds.

Social Functions of Humor and Play

Humor plays a complex and important role in social interactions.[36] Family, friendship, and work groups develop unique styles and traditions of joking and teasing, which help define the group and build commitment to the group. Humor also helps reinforce group norms, soften criticisms, and negotiate status. Humor provides a way to criticize a violation to group norms in a less confrontational way that preserves "deniability" and alleviates face threats by allowing the target to accept and laugh along with the humor. Early research often emphasized the disruptive and distractive role of humor, but more recent research has taken a more nuanced approach. Humor often helps to strengthen social bonds within the group, and can facilitate discussion of sensitive topics.

In the example from Gamson, the playful give-and-take between two firefighters expresses the teasing that is basic to their friendship and restores equality between them by deflating Ken's claim. Good friends can tease each other back and forth precisely because they trust each other's intentions and

---
[35] Norrick and Spitz (2010); Chapter 10.
[36] Everts (2003); Fine and De Soucey (2005); Holmes and Marra (2002); Plester and Sayers (2007).

interpretations.[37] By reaffirming their equality and displaying mutual trust, this type of teasing confirms and strengthens their friendship.

Humor plays an important role also in organizations and groups. Lehman-Willenbrock and Allen show that work groups are more productive if their culture is characterized by humor patterns, in which a humorous remark is followed by one or more other humorous remarks. Humor patterns contribute to positive socio-emotional communication, positive procedural structure, and new solutions.[38]

Humor Cultures. Fine and DeSoucey[39] studied a group of mushroom collectors and a workplace group in a weather-forecasting office, and found that both groups developed and maintained a distinct humor culture. According to their research, joking is embedded (in the group's processes, history, and relationships), interactive, and referential – to the group's common history. Joking helps to sustain interpersonal bonds and helps establish and enforce group norms. Humor cultures are usually historical in that joking and teasing build on past events known to all members of the group but not to outsiders. Outsiders are often mystified by the humor of a family or friendship group, which is often difficult to explain.

The group of left-leaning students who produced the "Are you a cop?" and "Pissing in the soup" riffs are a good example. Throughout the conversation they developed a series of extravagant and demeaning metaphors for police officers, and developed a number of deadpan humor sequences that played on their fictional identity as "dangerous radicals." Tyler took the lead in much of this fantasy play, but every member of the group contributed.

An extended example of a humor culture comes from an ethnographic study of mid-level Canadian police managers attending a six-week training session.[40] Both joke-telling and put-downs occurred frequently throughout the session, and group norms quickly developed. Many of the put-downs were self-directed; PS, from Newfoundland, introduced himself as "a goofy Newfie." PD, a Francophone, introduced himself with "I'm trying to learn English, so if you'll help me out . . .," and HE (a Scotsman) followed up with "Like my friend over there, I'm trying to learn English, too." The initial focus of the put-down humor was almost entirely the speaker's self or the shared occupation of police work. By the second week, put-downs expanded to external groups, for example, during a discussion of values:

RESOURCE PERSON:	What do they teach in military schools?
HE:	[in his thick Scottish accent]: How to kill people.
RESOURCE PERSON:	No, I meant in military primary schools.
HE:	How to kill wee people.

---

[37] Fine and De Soucey (2005).   [38] Lehman-Willenbrock and Allen (2014).
[39] Fine and De Soucey (2005). See Chapter 10 for a more detailed discussion.
[40] Terrion and Ashforth (2002).

This exchange illustrates a common feature of spontaneous humor. The initial claim that military schools teach "how to kill people" states a truth that is ordinarily papered over; the incongruity lies in the bald, frank way HE states it. The second quip extends this logic by blending it with the implications of the phrase "primary schools" into an apparent truth that contrasts and creates a shocking incongruity with our ordinary sentimentality.

As the group's status structure emerged, put-downs began to be directed at other members of the group – but almost always toward *higher* status members, and usually following a line the target had already invited, for example, Newfoundlander jokes directed at PS, the self-styled "goofy Newfie." In general, put-down jokes were enjoyed by everyone, including the target, as long as they followed implicit rules. Less popular members were less likely to be targeted, put-downs were not directed at someone who was not present, the target was expected to be able and willing to share the laughter, and the put-down should not offend the target, except violators of group norms, who were considered fair game.

The put-down jokes had the effect of leveling status differences, reinforcing group solidarity, and signaling acceptance of the put-down target. If any of these rules were violated, the offender would be punished in some way, often by temporary ostracism and absence of laughter, and the target would be protected. Put-downs were not accepted from outsiders (e.g. the resource person), and humor that highlighted differences (such as sexist humor, since there was only one woman in the group) and undermined group solidarity was not appreciated.

Schnurr and Chan provide an example of both self-deprecating humor and teasing across levels of power and authority in an IT company. Donald, the CEO, and Ann, a project manager, are interviewing Michael, a job applicant.

DONALD: Things are looking like this year will probably be our best year ever, um, but it does come on the back of, you know, fairly tight fairly lean times we're just now ... there's four main shareholders, um, so it's, you know, it's however deep our pockets are and ... you can see the quality of my suit//[laughs]\
MICHAEL: /[laughs]\\
ANN: He's got shoes on, so he must be having//a good day\
DONALD: /[laughs]\\ oh yes ...[41]

Schnurr and Chan focus on the face threats implicit in this exchange: In particular, Donald threatens his own positive face by implicitly making fun of his own suit, and implying that the company he heads is not doing all that well, and Ann reinforces the face threat and extends it with the implication that

---

[41] Schnurr and Chan (2011).

Donald often appears shoeless. All this threatens Michael's face in at least two ways, first by implying that he is applying for work in a failing company, but more deeply by forcing him to decide, quickly, how to respond.

Forcing Michael to decide how to respond was probably one motivation for the joking, a test of Michael's social skills and his ability to "think on his feet." But the exchange also displays an easygoing social environment, a joking culture in which a mid-level employee, Ann, is comfortable joking with the CEO, and the CEO, Donald, has a degree of self-confidence that he is comfortable engaging in a humorous series of threats to his own face. The exchange exhibits several layers of incongruity. Joking about one's own clothing is incongruous, launching a humorous attack against the positive face of one's employer is incongruous, and exhibiting a joking exchange that *appears* to be overtly hostile during a job interview is incongruous. In addition to *testing* the applicant's social skills, this also displays information about the social climate that may help Michael decide how comfortable he would be in this environment.

For Donald and Ann, the teasing serves to strengthen as well as display their interpersonal bonds, supporting both individual and team homeostasis. As a test of Michael's interpersonal skills and level of comfort with this kind of informal teasing, it also plays a defensive role, by helping to assure that new hires will contribute to and strengthen, rather than undermine, the joking culture of the organization.[42] Thus, the teasing contributes to group homeostasis in several ways, and accomplishes several personal and organizational objectives at once.

Humor as a Coping Mechanism

Humor and irony are frequently used (and recommended) as a way to cope with unpleasant and even tragic situations. Sometimes this takes the form of simple distraction, for example, watching a silly comedy, a movie, or TV show. But often it takes the form of joking and irony about the situation itself. Demjén[43] provides an excellent example in her detailed analysis of a long-running joke on a British cancer survivor's forum. This thread was explicitly set up "For those with a warped sense of humour" as a way to "cope by being irreverent and silly and able to laugh at all the bad stuff."[44]

---

[42] This is consistent with Dessalles's (2014) claim that display of one's desirable social characteristics is a major function of conversation.
[43] Demjén (2016, 2018).
[44] Demjén (2016, p. 18). The "warped" thread carried an explicit warning for potential readers who might be put off or distressed by the raw humor about a difficult and potentially life-threatening illness.

Cancer and cancer treatment pose inherent incongruities. In cancer, the normal processes of cell division and growth get out of control. Common treatments include exposing the cancer (and the surrounding tissues) to not-quite-lethal doses of poisonous substances or radiation – another incongruity. Because the cancer cells are growing faster, they are more susceptible to these treatments; however, both treatments have extremely unpleasant side effects. Cancers of the bowel also involve symptoms, diagnostic procedures, and treatments that violate norms of privacy and modesty and activate disgust reactions. Discussing any of this openly violates taboos of ordinary polite conversation, yet cancer patients must somehow deal with all these incongruities. The raw humor on the "warped" thread provides a way for the participants to address and acknowledge the incongruities, to normalize the taboo topics and thereby (partially) resolve the incongruities by reframing them in various ways and laughing at them.

Reframing was accomplished in several ways, including assigning names to the tumor, such as Mr. Crab, Mr. Cancer, Mr. C. One participant named her tumor *Hefty*, after her doctor remarked that she "had had 'a hefty tumour.'" The personification also included ascribing mental states, personality traits, and intentions to the tumor. The mischievous and "evil Mr. Crab" plays "funny little jokes" like preventing the patient from eating at regular mealtime, then demanding food in the middle of the night. Musical taste is ascribed to another participant's cancer, who is expected to run "screaming NO!NO!NO! holding his fingers in his ears" at the songs she listens to – a lighthearted tease combined with a humorous way of deflecting attention from the serious nature of the tumor.

The anxiety of waiting to see whether a treatment was successful and the tumor is gone or just *"hiding"* is metaphorically reframed as *"playing hide-and-seek."* The originator of the thread, "HoneyBee," developed the *"hide-and-seek"* metaphor in a different direction, launching a running joke that was taken up and developed by her and other participants over a span of nearly a year. Discussing the prospect of an uncomfortable and embarrassing rectal exam due at her next appointment with her doctor, she mused about placing some object in her rectum for him to find. Another participant suggested a *Rolo*,[45] and the suggestion was quickly taken up, with jokes about how to hide it, how the doctor will respond, *"Hunt the Rolo"* as a euphemism for a rectal exam, and many jokes playing on the advertising slogan "... give him your last *Rolo*." Naturally, the name became tainted, so that a new member of the thread was warned to "be wary of accepting Rolos ...."

---

[45] A brand of suggestively shaped chocolates packaged in long, thin cylindrical tubes.

Humor, either self-directed or directed toward the situation, is an effective way of coping with face-threatening and socially taboo situations and topics, including diseases of socially taboo body parts (bowel cancer) and being more or less naked in front of fully clothed medical staff during diagnosis or treatment. Humor and playfulness in general releases endorphins that help mitigate pain and discomfort. Shared with other patients or with medical staff, humor can increase interpersonal bonds, thereby reducing the face threat by reframing the encounter as personal rather than public. Generally, the humor must stay within proper bounds, to avoid reframing the encounter as *intimate*. The joking about "*hunt the Rolo*" on the cancer thread often veered close to this boundary – but the joking about HoneyBee's fantasy romantic relationship with her physician was kept within the play frame, and presumably was *not* shared with the doctor.

Irony

Irony is common in conversation – Tannen found examples of irony in 7 percent and Gibbs found examples of irony in 8 percent of conversation turns[46] – but it is not easy to define, and it is frequently unrecognized or misunderstood. Irony is sometimes defined as saying one thing but meaning the opposite, or speaking in a way that highlights a contrast between an ideal state of affairs and the actual state of affairs. Like humor and play, irony focuses attention on incongruency – but without resolving it. In a study of ironic speech among college-age friends, Gibbs identified five common types of irony: jocularity, sarcasm, rhetorical questions, hyperbole (overstatements), and understatements. Gibbs quotes a conversation in which two students, Kayla and Sarah, tease two others, Cherie and David, for studying Latin. The extended interaction ends with the following:

CHERIE: Why you guys dissin' on Latin?
DAVID: (mocking tone) What, wo-ah, you're dissin' my Latin.
KAYLA: Actually, Latin helps because, doesn't it, it helps with etymology; it helps with words, breaking words down.
DAVID: Totally ... yeah, yeah, she got it ... yeah.
CHERIE: Structure, parts of speech, yeah.
DAVID: I'm a changed person since the last couple of weeks of Latin.

Irony presents an ideal or expected representation of a situation and implicitly contrasts it with the actual situation.[47] From this perspective, Kayla and Sarah's response to the news that their friends are studying Latin might be

---

[46] Tannen (1984); Gibbs (2000). [47] Ritchie (2005).

better characterized as surprise than criticism, but Kayla's later contribution to justifying this counter-normative behavior mitigates the potential criticism.

Each of the ironic statements in this interchange constitutes a face threat (itself an incongruity when it appears among friends), and Cherie's question, "Why you guys dissin' on Latin?," though spoken in an ironic tone, appears to be defensive. David echoes Cherie's defensiveness in a mocking tone, "What, wo-ah, you're dissin' my Latin," that both supports and implicitly criticizes Cherie's apparent sensitivity. Kayla responds by breaking the play frame and mitigating the ironic criticism with a serious concession about the usefulness of Latin. After accepting and extending her offered justification, David reinstates the play frame with an ironic overstatement, "I'm a changed person since the last couple of weeks of Latin." A crucial aspect of this exchange is the collaboration of all members of the group in downplaying and mitigating the potential face threat and developing the interaction as playful humor, which strengthens the homeostasis of the group.

Gibbs and Izett provide an example of an exchange in which irony is used to mitigate the potential face threat of calling attention to a possible or potential breach of interpersonal ethics. Melissa and a friend are talking in the kitchen of the apartment Melissa shares with Jeanette. Jeanette, from her own bedroom, hears her name being mentioned:

JEANETTE: (yelling from her room) Are you talking about me again?
MELISSA: I have no life, Jeanette. All I do is talk about you. All the time.
JEANNETTE: (laughing) Get a life![48]

Jeannette's initial question activates the cultural frame of "gossip," in which talking about a friend in her absence is rude, but the question itself is presented in an open way that invites interpretation as irony. Melissa's response accepts the "gossip" frame along with the "ironic protest" frame, and extends it with an ironic self-accusation that can also be interpreted as implying that Jeannette egotistically assumes that she is so important or interesting that Melissa can talk about nothing else. Jeannette's final response accepts Melissa's ambiguous ironic frame and substitutes it for the initial "gossip" frame, thereby defusing the literal implications of both utterances, and reinforcing the frame of friendly ironic banter. The substance of the irony is an entirely fictional fantasy, cooperatively constructed by the two roommates. The irony criticizes the implied situation (gossip) from the perspective of another (amiable jocularity),[49] but the irony is used to emphasize that the criticized state of affairs is fictitious and to affirm the actual situation as one of trust and friendship, strengthening solidarity.

---

[48] Gibbs and Izett (2005, p. 136), previously discussed in Ritchie (2005). [49] Giora (2003).

Gibbs and Izett (2005) suggest that irony divides the audience between "*wolves*," who recognize the irony and "sheep," who do not recognize it, and between "confederates," who agree with the irony and "victims," who do not agree with it, or would not if they understood it. Both examples illustrate the relationship work involved in sustaining all members of the group as "wolf/confederates," characteristic of "*sweet*" humor and consistent with supporting and building homeostasis.

Both examples illustrate how ironic and humorous banter sustains the homeostasis of friendship groups, by addressing and defusing potentially divisive tensions. Studying Latin (a language commonly associated with serious and esoteric scholarship) and gossiping about one's friends are both counter-normative, hence potentially divisive. The ironic tone allows participants in these exchanges to acknowledge and discount the violation of expectations, convert them to shared humor, and reaffirm their social bonds.

Irony is often used in political humor. A recent example is an opinion column by Alexandra Petri, ironically titled "Relax and do not panic. Donald Trump is in charge."[50] The column was written in response to the revelation that President Trump didn't tell the American people that he knew from almost the outset that the coronavirus was airborne, extremely deadly, and much worse than even a "strenuous flu," and that his reason was that "he did not want anyone to panic. He wanted people to keep calm."

The column is written with deadpan humor – for example, Petri refers to a passage in which Trump "likened himself to Winston Churchill, who apparently was constantly scrambling up to the rooftops of London to speak with what Trump described as 'calmness.'" She follows up with a summary of Churchill's "calmness":

Churchill addressed the people and filled them with confidence during the Blitz (or as he called it, the Nothing), no doubt saying such ringing, reassuring things as, "There is no need to fight anyone on the land, on the beaches, or the landing grounds, because everything is under control and the Nazis will just vanish, like a miracle," and, "We DON'T have before us an ordeal of the most grievous kind," and, "Now this IS the end. It is the end of the end. We're way past the end of the beginning. It's over, lads!"[51]

Unlike the previous examples, this is an example of "*bitter*" humor, an ironic contrast between Churchill's famous speech rallying the British public to the fight against Nazi Germany (the ideal situation) and a version of the speech that would be consistent with Trump's explanation (the actual situation). It

---

[50] Petri (2020).
[51] This is also an example of a *story metaphor* (Ritchie, 2017), which I will discuss in more detail in Chapter 12.

relies on readers (wolf confederates) having at least enough historical knowledge about Churchill and WWII to recognize the reversals and ironies.[52]

With Gibbs and Izett's classification scheme, readers who were shocked by the revelations in Woodward's taped interviews are "wolf/confederates" in Petri's ironic fantasies. Trump and presumably his supporters by extension are the "victims." This leaves a question about the "sheep" category. Do Trump's supporters recognize the irony? Does Trump himself recognize it? There is some evidence that he might, in his bitterly ironic comment to Woodward, late in the sequence of interviews, that "you'll probably screw me."

With respect to Trump's supporters, the evidence from past research on the persuasive effects of irony is not encouraging. In a classic study of the ironic humor in the 1970s sitcom *All in the Family*, Vidmar and Rokeach found that viewers with preexisting racist views did not understand that the show was making fun of Archie Bunker's bigoted statements. To the contrary, previously bigoted viewers were more likely to applaud Archie for "telling it like it is."[53] In a more recent study, LaMarre, Landreville, and Beam studied viewer reactions to Stephen Colbert's deadpan ironic humor and found the same results:[54] Liberal viewers understood Colbert's overt positive comments about Trump as ironic and believe that Colbert is liberal, but Conservative viewers understood them as sincere and believe that Colbert is conservative. These results are all consistent with the theory of "motivated reasoning":[55] People are more likely to pay attention to and to believe messages consistent with their prior views, to ignore or discount messages inconsistent with their views, and to distort or reinterpret messages to fit their prior values and beliefs.

Humorous messages activate a play frame within which audiences take them less seriously. Humor increases audience's liking for the source, leads to more in-depth processing of the message and less counterarguing, so it would be expected to increase persuasiveness. But it also increases discounting, treating the message as irrelevant to the issue, which neutralizes the persuasive effects (although a "sleeper effect" is sometimes found, in which persuasion effects show up after a week or so).[56]

Summary

Humor is an extension of play. Both are commonly undertaken for their own sake, for the intrinsic pleasure they provide, and both require establishment

---

[52] This example also illustrates the common risk in using irony, that naïve members of the audience will miss the irony and take the ironic statements as literally true, concluding that Churchill actually did speak these lines.
[53] Vidmar and Rokeach (1974).   [54] LaMarre, Landreville, and Beam (2009).
[55] Kunda (1990).   [56] Nabi, Moyer-Gusé, and Byrne (2007).

and acceptance of a play frame that separates them from ordinary conversation. Both humor and play create alternative worlds, often marked by deliberate incongruities. Humor goes further and reveals incongruities in the actual world, and at least partially resolves these incongruities in a clever and surprising way. However, contrary to previous theories based on incongruity resolution, both jokes and conversational humor often leave incongruities unresolved – and this appears to contribute to people's enjoyment.

Like play, the shared enjoyment of *"sweet"* humor, including the mock-aggression of irony and playful put-downs, enhances and strengthens social bonds, a direct contribution to individual and group homeostasis. *"Bitter"* (genuinely aggressive) humor and irony directed at an out-group can also contribute to the bonding among in-group members, while emphasizing their separation from the out-group and its members, also contributing to the homeostasis of the in-group (at the expense of the out-group).

Both humor and play, by creating and developing alternative realities, can contribute to projecting the state of the body in its environment in the form of alternative states and alternative futures, sometimes expanding the range of possibilities for action in the world – a key component of creativity.[57] Irony is particularly effective representing a desirable situation and contrasting it with the actual state of affairs. The incongruity characteristic of most humor often carries ironic overtones: The focal irony in both the Kangaroo and Hunter examples discussed in this chapter is resolved through an ironic frame shift.

---

[57] Koestler (1964).

13   Stories

A primary function of the brain is to represent the current state of the self in its physical and social environment, projected forward as alternative futures representing alternative courses of action. Both these forward projections and the memories they draw on take the form of stories.[1] Storytelling permeates language use in almost every context; it was very likely part of language use from the beginning, and may have contributed to the evolution of language.[2]

In this chapter, I begin by defining story and describing some of the characteristics and functions of storytelling. I discuss collaborative storytelling in conversations, then discuss stories that establish and support identity. I close with a discussion of the contribution of storytelling to social structure and homeostasis.

Defining *Story*

Story and *narrative* have been defined in a number of ways by different scholars. Some scholars differentiate between the two concepts[3] but others do not.[4] Some scholars define narrative or story quite broadly, as a sequence of two or more events.[5] Schank and Berman define narrative in similar terms as a "structured telling," which will ordinarily include "themes, goals, plans, expectations, expectation failures (or obstacles), and perhaps, explanations or solutions."[6] Bruner argues that "for there to be a story, something unforeseen must happen,"[7] there must be an incongruity to be resolved. Labov recognizes a minimal narrative as any sequence of independent clauses, but a "fully developed narrative begins with an abstract, an orientation with information on persons, places, times and behavior involved; the complicating action; an

---

[1] Schank and Abelson (1995); Schank and Berman (2002). The construction of stories continues in deep (REM) sleep, even when the processing of sensory input is largely shut down (which may account for the chaotic nature of dreams).
[2] Bruner (2002). See Chapters 3 and 9.   [3] For example, Snaevarr (2010).
[4] Bruner (2002); Schank and Berman (2002).   [5] For example, Abbott (2008); Labov (2013).
[6] Schank and Berman (2002, p. 287).   [7] Bruner (2002, p. 15).

evaluation section, which identifies the point of the narrative; the resolution; and a coda …."[8]

Many of the stories I have observed in my own data, drawn from unstructured casual conversations, fall somewhere on the continuum between a simple story and a fully developed narrative; parts of Labov's structure are often omitted or merely implied. Stories that are expected to be familiar to other participants in a conversation are abbreviated and sometimes merely indexed with a name or a brief clause. An example of a sparsely narrated story appeared in a conversation among a group of African American men about relations between the community and the local police force.

> Tony Stevens was ex-Marine, Vietnam era. He had a guy came in. Robbed a gas station. Tony grabbed the guy and held him down. The police came in. In spite of what everybody in the surrounding area was telling them, the police jumped on Tony, and choked him to death. Why? The perpetrator was white and Tony was black. And this was a detective that did it. This was when Potter was chief of police. There are certain *patterns* that happen.[9]

Although it is sparsely narrated, this example represents the complete structure, including a *setting* (the gas station), *persons* who *attempt to accomplish something* (the robber and Tony), *opposition* (Tony opposed the robber; the police opposed Tony), or conflict leading to *a reversal* (the police jumped on Tony instead of on the robber), followed by a *resolution* (Tony was killed) followed by a *coda* that explains the story, including the resolution. The coda implies but does not state the story's relevance to group identity and to the topic of the conversation.

When relevant cultural and historical context is known and salient, a name ("Emmett Till," "Adam and Eve"), location ("Garden of Eden," "Appomattox Courthouse"[10]), or theme ("forbidden fruit," "first kiss," "police shooting") may serve as a *story index*[11] with the potential to activate relevant parts of the associated story. As "first kiss" and "police shooting" illustrate, the same phrase may activate quite different stories for different people, depending on their background experience, knowledge, and presuppositions.[12] In the same conversation in which the Tony Stevens story appeared, another participant remarked, "Well, it has happened here too. Kendra who got shot over there on … on the bridge by a police officer." The city where this took place has a relatively small and cohesive African American community; the name *Kendra* by itself was sufficient to activate the entire story of Kendra James, who was shot and killed during a routine traffic stop.

Complex narratives often weave together many constituent stories. Brief as it is, the Tony Stevens story incorporates two stories and indexes several other

---

[8] Labov (2013, p. 5).   [9] Ritchie (2010).
[10] The place where General Robert E. Lee surrendered to General Ulysses S. Grant, effectively ending the US Civil War.
[11] Schank and Berman (2002).   [12] Ritchie and Cameron (2014).

stories. "Ex-Marine, Vietnam era" indexes the Stevens's military service and the Vietnam War. "Robbed a gas station" furnishes the background and motivation for Stevens's actions. "What everybody in the surrounding area was telling them" implies an alternative story in which the police recognized Stevens as a hero and thanked him. The contrast with that alternative story that should have but did not happen sets up the bitter irony of the actual story. It also provides evidence to support the coda, "patterns that happen." The second part of the coda, "this was a detective that did it," implies a story (also bitterly ironic) about the training and experience assumed to precede promotion to police detective and the behavior ordinarily expected of a high-ranking police officer. In the context of the conversation, the Tony Stevens story is embedded within a complex story about the troubled relationship between the police department and the African American community, the topic of the conversation.

Labov and Waletsky[13] assert that events must be narrated in chronological sequence to count as a narrative, but flashbacks are often used to supply information needed to understand an event, and flash-forwards to alert the audience to an irony in a character's actions. An example comes at the beginning of a TED talk by NASA scientist Jim Hansen about climate change. He begins with a question how the distant past affects the recent past: "What do I know that would cause me, a reticent, Midwestern scientist, to get myself arrested in front of the White House protesting?" Rather than directly answer the rhetorical question, he flashes back to a story about his youth that explains how he came to be involved in climate change research. "I was lucky to grow up at a time when it was not difficult for the child of a tenant farmer to *make his way* to the state university. And I was really lucky to go to the University of Iowa where I could study *under* Professor James Van Allen who built instruments for the first U.S. satellites." He then went on to relate a story about his research on the "*greenhouse* effect," with several other flashback stories and one flash-forward hypothetical story, set in an alternative future in which he failed to act on this knowledge and his grandchildren criticize him: "Opa understood what was happening, but he didn't *make it clear*." By shifting back and forth in time, rather than telling the events in sequence, Hansen invited his audience to participate in making the causal and motivating inferences for themselves, consistent with well-established persuasion principles.

Master-Plots, Setting, and Character Types

Abbott argues that humans organize our understanding of time primarily around narrative.[14] He also argues that our understanding of actual life events is organized around *master-plots* such as betrayal, revenge, rags-to-riches, a

---

[13] Labov and Waletsky (1967). [14] Abbott (2008).

quest, and so on; many of these are universal, but each culture has its own variations.[15] Schank and Abelson argue that memory is constituted primarily by stories, which are gradually refined through mental recall, rehearsal, and retelling, and gradually reshaped to fit one or more familiar master-plots. The master-plots of each culture are represented by folktales, biography, and literature, in romantic or heroic form (*Cinderella, The Odyssey*, and Jim Hansen's progress from farm-boy to world-famous scientist), in tragic form (*Othello, Macbeth*), and in comic form (*Don Quixote, Huckleberry Finn*). Hogan[16] narrows the field even further: Based on analysis of narrative themes in a variety of literary works, Hogan found that the most common themes are relationships, particularly love and conflict; this finding is consistent with Dunbar's[17] research on the predominance of social themes in ordinary conversations.

Master-plots usually involve stereotypical character types, commonly associated with familiar characters like Iago, Judas, Lear, Oedipus, Cinderella, Willy Loman. Tragic characters like Othello are usually complex and multi-dimensional – "*round*" characters, which Abbot contrasts with the "*flat*," uncomplicated characters of satire and comedy.[18] Abbott's distinction seems too simple: Are Don Quixote, Arthur Dent in the *Hitchhiker's Guide* series,[19] or even Bottom in *Midsummer Night's Dream*, truly "*flat*"? In any event, familiar types are encountered in many genres – the flirt, the scoundrel, the hypocrite, the well-meaning fool – and they also appear regularly in conversational storytelling. As stories are recalled and retold repeatedly, they tend to be modified toward the most relevant master-plot. Sometimes this happens deliberately; more often it happens as part of the memory reconstruction process. Often audience expectations and responses contribute to reshaping stories (and memories).

Setting. Events in a story occur in a time and place, which may be precisely stated (Jim Hansen anchors his story in a tenant farm, at the University of Iowa, and in a time that can be calculated from his current age) or only generally inferred. (The Tony Stevens story is loosely anchored in time and space by the reference to his Vietnam service and the location of a gas station.) Time and place, along with other narrated details, create what Abbott calls a "story world."[20] This may be actual (recent or distant past), future, or fictional/fantasy. Stories also frequently activate *possible worlds* in which things might be different. Elements of the Tony Stevens story imply an alternative possible world in which police officers do not automatically assume that the dark-skinned person is the culprit and the light-skinned person the victim; the Garden of Eden story implies a possible world in which Eve would have

---

[15] Master-plots can reasonably be classified as a type of meme, and they develop in much the same way.
[16] Hogan (2003; see also Mar and Oatley, 2008).   [17] Dunbar (1996).   [18] Abbott (2008).
[19] Adams (1979).   [20] See also Gerrig, (1993).

resisted the serpent and continued to live in blissful innocence with Adam. Often, as in these two examples, the implicit or explicit contrast with an alternative world is the point of the story.[21]

Stories contain and take place within their story world as well as within the world of the narrator. A story is characterized by the time in which the events occur as well as the time it required to tell (or read) the story. There may be long gaps within the story ("a few years later ...") as well as in the telling, because of interruptions of one sort or another. In some complex stories (*Tales of 1001 Nights*, *Lord Jim*), the story is narrated within a (fictional) story world, what Clark calls *layering*.[22] Even true stories may be several layers deep, as when an interview is described in a news account, complete with interviewee's account of a previous conversation. Skillful narrators often play with time, setting, and layering; this can encourage audiences to "enter into the story world," and thereby render the story more immediate and more convincing.[23]

Stories are frequently used in persuasive communication.[24] Stories that encourage people to enter the story world increase involvement in the story and message-processing. Identification with the main character reduces counterarguing and increases message acceptance.

Types of Story. Researchers and scholars have classified stories in a number of ways, according to features such as whether they report events that actually happened (*experiential* stories) or were invented (*fictional* stories), whether they are reported as having happened to the narrator (*first-person*) or someone else (*third-person*). Experiential stories include bragging, embarrassing stories, humorous retelling of an actual incident, and retelling of dreams or fantasies.[25] The *myth* or *mythic story* is often but not always told as having actually happened. *Generic* stories[26] or *pseudo-narratives*[27] recount events that typically happen to the narrator, or that anyone might experience, and are often signaled by conditionals such as *would*[28] or by phrases like "Every time I ..." or "Sometimes ...." These story types are not always clearly distinguished, and they are sometimes blended.

Storytelling in Conversations

Until recently, research on storytelling relied on structured contexts like interviews,[29] reflecting pragmatic interest in diagnostic and therapeutic stories as well as the ready availability of interview data. However, storytelling is a

---

[21] Lewis (1943) developed just such an alternative world in the second book of a theological/science fiction trilogy.
[22] Clark (1996); see Chapter 9 for detailed discussion.   [23] Green (2004).
[24] Moyer-Gusé (2008).   [25] Norrick (2010).   [26] Norrick (2010).   [27] Labov (2013).
[28] Labov (2013).   [29] Norrick (2007).

central feature of conversation, and conversational storytelling exhibits several features that distinguish it from storytelling in interviews and other highly structured social contexts. Compared to interviews, conversational storytelling is less formal and more spontaneous and interactive, marked by frequent digressions and disfluencies, interruptions, uncompleted thoughts, and extraneous comments. Conversational stories are also often dispersed over several speaking turns, and are frequently co-narrated.[30]

Norrick reports that storytellers clearly mark the opening and closing of a story, and summarize the action or point of the story. He further claims that storytellers respect norms of "storytelling rights" and "tellability" and are punished for violating these norms, as well as other group norms having to do with topic, disgust, and so forth. In my own data, these "rules" are frequently violated without comment, which may reflect the casual socializing context.[31] The relative freedom with respect to "rules" such as "storytelling rights" and "tellability" may also reflect the population from which I have gathered most of the data, men and women in late twenties and early thirties, most of them attending college and working but not yet in established careers. Members of this demographic group may be less concerned about irrelevant, disgusting, or immoral content as well as less likely to compete for the floor than is observed among adolescent subjects. Most researchers also include "newsworthiness" as a feature of "tellability," but in my data conversation, participants seem to enjoy stories that are well-known to most or all participants. This is particularly true of shared stories about a family, social group, or relationship,[32] or stories about shocking or titillating occurrences. Similarly, members of tight-knit groups often retell stories that illustrate "what typically happens," whether positive or negative.[33]

Audience participation is important both in eliciting and in telling stories.[34] Stories sometimes occur in thematic chains, in which a story follows up a theme or topic introduced by a previous speaker, but in my own data, the contextual relevance is not always obvious. Labov claims that extended narratives of fifteen minutes or more are common in natural conversations,[35] but in my own data, stories longer than two or three minutes are rare.

An example of generic "things that typically happen" stories came in a conversation about police-community relations among a group of middle-class professionals. Referring to recent incidents in which police officers have shot

---

[30] Ritchie (2010, 2011a, 2011b, 2011c).
[31] I typically assign students to organize and record a conversation about a topic of general interest such as homelessness or police-community relations, and encourage them to organize it as a social event, so as to obtain samples of ordinary casual conversation. Standard IRB procedures with respect to consent, anonymity, and so forth, are carefully followed.
[32] Everts (2003); Norrick (1997).   [33] Ritchie (2010, 2011b).
[34] Norrick (2007); Labov (2013).   [35] Labov (2013).

270   Stories

and killed unarmed civilians, one participant characterized a typical alibi with the following story:

whenever I hear a an officer say ... it seems like the *magic words* ... like the *get out of jail free card* ... is ... "I felt ... that ... my life was in .. that I was being threatened or ..." like these *magical phrase* that police officers it's like ... they're trained that's the word like if anything bad ever *goes down* say ... "I felt you know I felt that my life was in jeopardy."[36]

The phrase "*magic words*" is familiar from fairy tales and fantasy novels. In this context, it encouraged listeners to experience the story as a fairy tale or fantasy story and the police officer's use of the stock phrase "my life was in jeopardy" as a ploy in a fairy tale. "*Get out of jail free card*" evokes the popular game *Monopoly*, specifically a subplot within the larger narrative of the game. In the "*jail*" subplot, a player is suspended from participation ("*in jail*") and either "*pays a fine*" or uses the card to "*get out of jail*" without paying. The phrase has become an idiomatic metaphor for any situation in which some irrelevant principle or status is claimed to excuse a violation of norms in a nonsensical way. Both the topic and the vehicle story have all the features of a narrative – a protagonist (the police officer, the player) with an objective (escape blame for a shooting, continue with the game), a context, a setback, and a resolution. The role of this story in the conversation is to express the speaker's cynicism about the officers' motives in these incidents, and by implication to express support for members of the minority community who claim that police officers frequently abuse their power and use excessive force.

Metaphors often imply stories ("*good Samaritan*," "*glass ceiling*"), and people frequently expand them into metaphorical stories, either as part of a playful tease or to make a point. An example of both appeared in an informal focus group conversation among scientists about the role of scientists in communicating science to the public.[37] The participants were coworkers, with a well-established joking culture. In response to a comment about the continual need to secure research funding, one participant, Jack,[38] remarked, "Ya. There really is *no more ivory tower*." This remark implies a story about an idyllic "*ivory tower*," isolated and protected from the world below, and maps it onto a world of scientists happily conducting research without worrying about funding or funding agencies. A few speaking turns later, another participant referred back to this metaphor, developed it and explicitly connected it to their

---

[36] Ritchie (2011b).
[37] This was part of a day-long meeting sponsored by the Department of Energy; for details, see Ritchie and Schell (2009); Ritchie (2011).
[38] Here and in other examples from informal conversations in which speakers are not public figures, names have been changed to preserve anonymity.

current situation, leading to a put-down, followed by a collaborative story development:

LARRY: Jack said something, one way of ... of *capturing* part of that, ah, *change of role* is, ah, *no more ivory tower*. It's probably, we're, we're *not there* now ... it's probably *not too far in the future*.
JIM: I've never really *seen the ivory tower*. (Laughter)
LARRY: You haven't. They never did *let you in*, did they?
JACK: Is that *what you dream about, in the night,* Jim? *Ivory tower* you just go to sleep, and the first thing you get is the *seven million dollar grant* from ... to do whatever you want from the *MacArthur Foundation*? And you *go up into the ivory tower*. What the, *open pit, unstable wall*.
JAN: Ya, the *unstable*.
LARRY: Ya, *instead of the ivory tower, we're in an unstable foundation*.

As the tease ("They never did *let you in*") is developed into a story about Jim's dream, it exhibits all the elements of narrative – person, scene, objective, setback, resolution by a foundation. But then the coda develops a pun on "*foundation*" that ironically reverses the mood of the story, and returns it to the cynical tone suggested by Larry's opening comment.

In this passage, the teasing reinforces the group's sense of a shared situation, enhancing their solidarity. The entire sequence can be understood as a collective representation and forward projection of their situation. Within the context of the overall conversation, it also functions as motivation – this is why they need to expend the effort to communicate their science, and its importance, to nonscientists, so they can build support for the funding needed to continue their research.

A quite different example of developing a common metaphor into a metaphorical story comes from Ritchie and Cameron's analysis of a public meeting about a 2003 incident in which police officers shot and killed an unarmed African American woman,[39] Kendra James. One of the community leaders elaborated the commonplace "*blind* justice" into a contrasting pair of metaphorical stories. He complained that the District Attorney had refused to seek an indictment of the police officer who fired the fatal shot and contrasted it with the District Attorney's aggressive pursuit of an indictment in other criminal cases, finishing with the following:

Somebody said that "justice is *blind*," but we as Portland citizens, we need to know, or I need to know, that our elected and sworn officials are not *taking advantage of her* or us just because she's blind.

Here the customary metaphorical interpretation of "*blind*" as implying a disregard for irrelevant individual characteristics is ironically contrasted with

---

[39] Ritchie and Cameron (2015; Ritchie, 2011).

272 Stories

a literal interpretation of *blind*, implying a story about officials who "*take advantage of*" the visually impaired Justice, allowing malefactors to get away with crimes that she is unable to see. This is also an example of a *contested identity story*, in which the same story is told from different perspectives, reflecting the core identities of different social groups. I will return to this topic in a later section of this chapter.

Two examples of collaborative construction of metaphorical stories come from a conversation about police-community relations[40] among four "new left" activists, all with a bawdy and subversive sense of humor, as demonstrated in the "Are you a cop?" example discussed in Chapter 12. Throughout this conversation, the participants emphasized the role of police officers as "public servants." On one occasion, Tyler elaborated on the "*servant*" metaphor, leading to the following exchange:

TYLER: Cops are more like a *servant*, like a *waiter or waitress*, right? So if they *fuck up*, they say, oh, I'm really sorry. You want to talk to my boss or manager?
DEKE: If you're a cop and you *screw up* at work, like you *pepper spray a baby*, or you shot someone who didn't deserve ... it is just weird. *Stakes are a lot higher* than they are in our jobs.
TYLER: I'm sure. If a waitress approached you with saying, oh I'm really sorry, you said "over medium," but I got you "over easy." Cops just fucking *pepper sprayed your baby*, even more so, right? {Laughter} ... They *feel a sense of* "*it's a tough job*," but fuck, you know, we all have *tough* jobs. You should be held accountable *at all levels*.

Here a commonplace vehicle story about a food server in a short-order café who gets an order wrong is developed as a metaphor for a topic story of a police officer's malfeasance, dramatized with a baby as the victim. It is likely that a baby has occasionally been the victim of police use of pepper spray, but Tyler did not refer to any actual incident. "*Pepper spray a baby*" here is a blend of hyperbole with metonym, representing all forms of police violence. The two stories are tied together by "we all have *tough* jobs" and the discriminating metaphor "*at all levels*," acknowledging the difference in status and responsibility between food servers and police officers. After several speaking turns in which the implications of the *pepper spray* story were developed, Tyler pushed the envelope even further, leading to the collaboratively developed "pissing in their soup" fantasy story discussed in Chapter 12.

Coates[41] uses a metaphor of "*jazz performance*" to characterize the combination of imaginative creativity and collaboration exemplified by this example.

---

[40] Ritchie (2011). This and several of the other examples in this book that were drawn from conversations about police–community relations were recorded and transcribed by students in an advanced theory class as part of their final assignment.
[41] Coates (2007).

Michael responded to Tyler's exaggerated metaphor in a totally serious vein, but Celeste's deadpan incongruous response established a play frame, which Michael immediately accepted and the rest of the group collaboratively developed, much as members of a jazz combo might respond to and elaborate on a playful theme introduced by one of them.

Another example of a collaborative story came in a conversation about homelessness, among six college-age adults, four males and two females. As is common in conversations among members of this age group, profanities and scatological humor appeared throughout the conversation. Some of the comments and stories were hostile to homeless people, and some were quite sympathetic. About thirty minutes into the conversation, J began a story that he had heard from an acquaintance:

J: On the east coast I think, Boston or somewhere, my friend was telling me about this.

It was all over the news ... like ... homeless people were taking shits in people's cars,

inside their cars ... because they didn't ... have a place to go the bathroom ... they, they would like get arrested or ... whatever because they, yah know.

P: That's the number one public nuisance in Amsterdam.
J: So they started shittin' in people's cars ... like inside their cars they'd get in, take a shit, get out, and you come back to your car.
(general laughter)
And there's shit.

R: That's brilliant! That's subversive ... people who own cars wait!
(general laughter)

P: Get a bike!
R: Shit! I drove. (laughter)
B: You can't shit inside somebody's bike.

This story has the characteristics of "a good story," a picaresque narrative where a loveable scalawag momentarily overturns the social order. It has the hallmarks of what Brunvand calls an "urban legend,"[42] a story that is told and repeated as if it really happened – often even appearing in news stories – that can't be traced to an original source or an actual event. It appears the group enjoyed participating in the development both because of the incongruity and for the comeuppance of middle-class automobile owners ("Get a bike!"). It

---

[42] Brunvand (1981).

also highlights an interesting incongruity in language between the frequent and casual use of "shit" (and other expletives), that J used the euphemistic "to go the bathroom" where "shit" would be literally applicable. This apparent ambivalence is also apparent in the repeated transition back and forth between a literal use of "shit" to an exclamatory use.

Although one of the frequently cited criteria for story "tellability" is newsworthiness, families and other groups frequently enjoy retelling a familiar story, either because it reflects group identity or norms or because it is intrinsically amusing. These stories are often collaboratively narrated, as in the following example from a discussion among another group of college-age friends, gathered for a conversation about police-community relations. One participant, Ellie, had just related a story about the failure of the police to investigate a classmate accused of collecting child pornography from the internet, "not that he enjoys it, but he has it just to have it." This led to a collaborative retelling of a story that had just appeared in the news.

ALEX: Yeah, that reminds me of, like, that case they had a little while ago about the kids . . .
BETH: Oh, the sex thing?
ALEX: Yeah, the setting up . . .
BETH: That was in Pennsylvania, sending naked pictures of themselves. Not even naked pictures, scantily clad pictures of themselves.
ALEX: Yeah, teenage girls sending . . .
BETH: [Interrupting.] Several teenagers.
ALEX: Naked or partially naked pictures of themselves . . .
BETH: None of them are full nudity.
ALEX: To . . . um, I'm not sure, to their friends, uh, both male and female. And . . .
BETH: And some of them were never sent.
ALEX: And, so, they got caught on child pornography.
BETH: Yeah.
ALEX: For both the girls who took the pictures and the guys who received them.
FRED: Not all the girls got charged . . .
BETH: I heard a couple people got caught, even though they actually never; it was just picture of themselves, and they didn't have any other pictures, just pictures of themselves. And at least one picture was only of a girl in a bikini. Nothing scantier than that.
ALEX: And yeah, the fact, that, you know, that gets brought up in this debate and that . . .
BETH: And then something like THAT.
ALEX: Doesn't get . . .
ELLI: Where it was actual real life eww kiddie porn . . .

Although the topic introduced for this conversation was "public safety and police–community relations," the participants focused on the inability of police and other authorities to control the behavior of young people, and on the frequent violation of community norms regarding drugs and sexual behavior.

The participants' expressions of disgust about "kiddie porn" demonstrates that it violates their own moral standards – but they considered *talking about it* to be acceptable and entertaining. Clearly they were all aware of the story, so it had no "news value," but they contributed tidbits of information as if they were news. Their collaborative retelling suggests *"transportation into the story world,"*[43] a dynamic and sustained simulation of the story world that increases involvement and interest.[44]

In a conversation about police–community relations among a group of American Muslims, two participants, Sarah and Samira, collaborated in developing a future scenario based on the internment of Japanese American citizens during World War II:

SARAH: Well, you were talking about, like, the Japanese and how they were detained like after World War II, and what happ—well, not after World War II, what happened after the Pearl Harbor bombing, and then, even like, during that time, like, all Ger—almost all German Americans were *put in* detainment, even though, like, after the fact, like, only 10 percent of the German Americans that were detained were even *part of* the Nazi party, and then they found out that *none* of the Japanese Americans were *part of* espionage. And two-thirds of them were like American. American, they had like already [had been here for generations].

SAMIRA: Right, but they were in camps. They put them [in camps].

SARAH: [But they] put them in camps.

SAMIRA: Yes, they did.

SARAH: And then, it's *past*, and now they *feel* safe in their commu—like, you know what I mean, that's past. So I think, *Insha'Allah*, maybe, as *awareness grows*, this will pass too.

SAMIRA: 'Cause I was just waitin' for the time when they was gonna *try* and *round up* all African Americans and put 'em in a camp, which would've been a *mess* ... [laughter]

SARAH: And my—my own mother said to me, like.

SAMIRA: You know?

SARAH: Don'—did you know that they're going to try to do the same kind of thing to Muslims? Like, aren't you scared? Aren't you, aren't you scared that being Muslim now that, umm, if ... if, you know, they have some new thing in the war, that they're going to *round up* all, all *Muslims*? In the United States, and put you in some camp? And I was like ...

AISHA: Did you ... did you hear that recently?

SARAH: No, my *mother* said this to me.[45]

Like the "kiddie porn" story, this story was co-constructed from information that was generally known – but possibly not to everyone. As in several of the other examples, it appears that a primary motive was to "get it on record,"

---

[43] Gerrig (1993). [44] Green (2004). [45] Ritchie (2017).

establish the information as part of common ground. It appears that Sarah and Samira have thought about and discussed this scenario before; it may have begun circulating widely among American Muslims in the post 9/11 panic. Aisha's question "Did you hear that recently?" could indicate either that it was news to her or, conversely, that she thought it was "old news." By expressing group-relevant concerns, the story reaffirms group membership and identification through a sense of shared vulnerability.[46]

Identity Stories

The "Muslim internment camp" story reflects a co-constructed present representation of the group in its cultural and political context, projected forward as a plausible scenario. Both individuals and groups create and tell stories that reflect personal identity, group identity, and individual relationship to their reference groups. These stories are sometimes contested, usually when members of a family or other group disagree either about the nature of the group or about the meaning of commonly experienced events, or even about the events themselves.

New York Times columnist Ross Douthat, in a column written shortly after the election of Donald Trump, raised the issue of a *national* narrative. Until relatively recently, political and cultural discourse in the United States has been dominated by a *settler* narrative in which European pioneers conquered, tamed, and settled a basically "*empty*" wilderness, sparsely populated by "*savages*," who sometimes assisted but often violently opposed the intrepid settlers, which necessitated the removal of the savages to reservations.[47] This narrative was blended with an intellectual narrative that celebrated the efforts of the "*founding fathers*" to create an enlightened political system based on "*checks and balances*" and "the rule of law." It was also blended with a narrative of the Civil War as a conflict between advocates of prioritizing national unity and valiant "*Lost Cause*" advocates of giving priority to "states' rights."

Almost from the beginning, this narrative has been challenged by counter-narratives that focused on the evils of slavery and the genocidal treatment of native Americans. These counter-narratives have gained increasing strength throughout the past century, until the "culture wars" struggle between the traditional story and the counter-narratives culminated in Donald Trump's

---

[46] The conversation took place and the analysis was completed before the campaign rhetoric of Donald Trump greatly increased the plausibility of the scenario.

[47] Douthat (2017); Ritchie (2019).

openly anti-immigrant and racist presidential campaign. Douthat argues that restoring any semblance of national unity requires that, somehow, a new national story must be created that blends the positive elements of the traditional narrative with the truth-telling impulse of the counter-narratives. The new narrative must recognize the contributions of traditional heroes like Washington, Jefferson, and Andrew Jackson while honestly criticizing their moral failings – owning slaves, massacring Native Americans, and so on. It must, at the same time, recognize, valorize, and celebrate the contributions of previously unacknowledged or weakly acknowledged heroes and groups.

These stories reflect different perspectives on our national identity, including, for example, what it means to be "patriotic." What many Americans understand to be the national story is also woven into their own personal story and their personal identity. This drives the cultural and political polarization decried by Douthat and many other observers.

To the extent that individuals identify with any particular group or classification (Protestant, African American, Republican, union member), the status and welfare of that group will be central to their own homeostasis. The narratives of these groups, the stories they recall and tell, shape their collective forward projection of the state of the group in its social and political environment. They also influence each individual's personal story, as it projects forward into the future, with its sense of constraints and possibilities. Both group and individual narratives include narratives about "enemies," individuals, and other groups with conflicting interests, and how they oppose and block the group. Douthat argues that understanding these narratives and their interactions and contradictions, and resolving the contradictions, is essential if a new, unifying national narrative is to have any chance. I will return to this theme in Chapter 15.

Summary

Humans are a storytelling species. We understand and explain things with stories, and we reason in terms of stories. Stories are told frequently in conversation and alluded to even more frequently. We enjoy telling stories and listening to stories, and the shared enjoyment of stories is a strong factor in developing and maintaining interpersonal bonds as well as personal identities.

Early researchers in storytelling emphasized the informative aspects of stories (e.g. Labov), but the mounting evidence that people enjoy telling and retelling stories that are known to most or even all members of a group challenges this view. Norrick emphasizes how these "retold stories" establish and maintain group norms (his examples mostly come from family groups) and socializing new members into the group.[48] However, many of the stories in my own data appear to be retold for their entertainment value. This is consistent with Dessalles's[49] claim that conversation serves to advertise one's values as a potential friend, hence to recruit new relationships and solidify existing ones. The shared enjoyment of storytelling enhances bonding among group members, and if the story has playful or otherwise satisfying elements to it, it may not matter if it has been told and retold many times.

People often enjoy collaboratively creating and enacting fictional, ironic, and even impossible stories (like the *"pissing in your soup"* example); this celebrates group identity and reinforces group solidarity and bonding. Collaborative story creation also enhances creativity and sharpens individual and collaborative skills for forward projection and for *"thinking outside the box."*[50]

The central role of stories in ordinary conversation may reflect their contribution to cognition, as means of projecting and assessing the possible outcomes of alternative courses of action. This extends to collaborative storytelling that contributes to groups' collaborative reasoning and planning. The constant flow of thought that is characteristic of individual thought and the frequent storytelling in conversation hone our story-inventing skills and respond to our basic enjoyment of stories.

[48] Norrick (1997). [49] Dessalles (2014). [50] Koestler (1964).

14   Media Technology, Social Reality, and Discourse

In this chapter, I will discuss how conversation interacts with communication media and the growth of larger and more complex social organization to develop into public discourse. I will start with a brief overview of media technology and its effect on cognition and social organization, focusing on language and conversation, visual images, writing, print, electronic media, and the internet. I will discuss how expanded social organization and the media technology that facilitated it created audiences separated from speakers, and led to the fragmenting of society into publics, organized around discrete stories about shared histories and possible futures. I will use the recent social and political polarization in the United States as an example to explore how different media have disrupted and reshaped public discourse.

Communication Technology

To understand the effects of a technology or practice, it is useful to start with its affordances and constraints. How can people interact with it? What does it allow people to do or to do more easily? How does it extend human capabilities? What kinds of relationships and interactions will it support? What practices or relationships does it interfere with or displace? What does it require people to give up or sacrifice to use it? How does it change time and energy budgets? How will it affect the spread of ideas and practices (memes)?

Language and Conversation. The development of language and conversation extended and amplified the relationship-building power of grooming, permitting a tripling of primary group size,[1] and the recruitment and development of more complex social relationships.[2] Language extended the surveillance function of individual perception, allowing people to learn about objects, activities, and events indirectly through conversation. The relationship-building and surveillance-extending functions of language fostered joint attention to objects and events, solidifying and extending

---

[1] Dunbar (1996).   [2] Dessalles (2014).

common ground. Language precipitated, facilitated, and coevolved with the development of neural systems that support conceptual thought and concept-based social interaction. It precipitated and facilitated the development of culture as a medium for improving individual and group homeostasis and reproductive fitness that has become increasingly independent of biological evolution.

Social Reality. Within a primary group, conversations cluster among small overlapping subgroups. The history and current state of the primary group as well as the more stable subgroups (e.g. families and teams) is dynamically developed and represented in the stories that are told and retold in the various conversations, the conversation practices, metaphors, humor, and colloquialisms. These constitute the "social reality" of the group, the assumptions and expectations that are taken for granted, form the backdrop for everyday social interactions, and are reproduced in everyday social interactions.[3] Within the primary group and its subgroups, there may be different opinions, but conversation and discussion about topics that are relevant to everyone are usually coherent and inclusive. Deviant views and assumptions, if they threaten group cohesion and group homeostasis, are discouraged through humor, mockery, and other means, backed up by the implicit threat of social isolation.

Each subgroup will have some conversations in which they exchange, compare, and debate information about the history and the current status of their own group and of the entire primary group, with at least some projection into and stories about potential futures. Each member of the group has some potential input, if only indirectly, into the primary group's stories. Inevitably, some members have much more input than others, due both to their social status and their communication skills. The aggregate of all these conversations constitutes the *discourse* of the group. As new media develop and social organization expands and becomes increasingly complex, the result has been fragmentation of discourse and development of discrete "publics."[4] In this section, I give a brief overview of media technologies and their effects on cognition and social interaction; in later sections, I explore the consequent organization of public discourse.

How Media Affect Cognition. Cognition, the representation of experience as part of the representation of the body in its environment, includes awareness (external perceptions, interoception, and introspective awareness of thought), memory, and imagination (representation of future, alternative, and impossible experiences). Each new medium has expanded the range of possibilities for social interaction while changing the nature of social interaction, and that in turn has indirectly changed the nature of cognition. Language greatly

---

[3] Berger and Luckmann (1966). [4] Price (1992).

expanded the possibility of collaboration and *extended* cognition[5] as people pool their knowledge, exchange and compare perceptions and analyses to solve problems that would be beyond the capabilities of a solitary person working alone.

Beginning with language, new media enhance the ability to abstract, generalize, imagine, and facilitate communicating about experience. Some new media extend memory and make recalled experiences more objective, more public, and more permanent; some extend the reach of communication in space and time and allow people to represent experiences and intentions and express thoughts to people in remote locations[1] and future times. Speech and music emphasize sound; visual art and print emphasize and objectify vision; video and television emphasize both. Sculpture and dance emphasize tactile and sensual features of experience as well as visual and temporal; cuisine emphasizes taste and smell as well as visual and tactile senses. Print reduces the importance of spatial distance and time. Electronic media render spatial distance almost irrelevant and greatly alter the experience of time. Print standardizes as well as objectifies memory and enhances the importance of vision. Electronic media project individual "presence" across thousands of miles.

Visual Images

Just as language objectifies abstract concepts, including perceptual features of experience, visual images objectify visual experience, establishes it as independent of the individual perceiver and as a potential focus of joint attention and an anchor to memory. As visual images are developed in sophistication and complexity, they allow for inspecting and understanding the relationships of parts to each other and to a whole, and for giving form to imaginary objects and combinations.

Both two-dimensional images and three-dimensional models allow contemporary scientists, engineers, and architects, among others, to display their ideas in physical form where they can be seen, touched, and manipulated. Because of the limitations of short-term memory, it is difficult to think about the relations among more than a few parts of a complex object or process, or about how an array of abstract concepts might interact. Constructing a model, image, or diagram makes it possible to think about and to recall the nature of many sets of parts and their relationships, to inspect them and compare them again and again. The model or diagram becomes an extension of memory and reasoning.[6] Because two or more people can see the same image at the same

---

[5] Clark (1997); Hutchins (1994).   [6] Clark (1997).

time, it facilitates discussion, debate, and collaborative reasoning.[7] However, visual representations can also reify concepts, treating abstractions as objective reality.[8]

Written Language

Like imitation, writing creates language as a set of objects independent of both individuals and social interactions. It creates a permanent, correctible, but objective record of what was said. This greatly extends and supplements memory, and, as Plato argued, weakens individual memory. Over time it supplants speech, allowing the direct representation of complex ideas in a permanent form, subject to inspection and comparison by both the writer and potential audiences. Because a written record is literally an object, it reduces the possibility of disputing the events it portrays.[9] Written messages and records can be transported across great distances, which extended the possibilities for political, economic, religious, and cultural influence and control. Writing also created a new form of relationship: Long-distance friendships and even love affairs can be and are conducted by written letters (and now by email and text messaging).

Writing suppresses the sound of language, although people commonly experience weak simulations of the sounds of words as they read, write, and think. Writing almost totally divorces language from other signal systems such as facial expression, gesture, and vocalic intonation. The communicative functions of these "auxiliary" signal systems are replaced by punctuation and other devices (such as underscoring and metaphor). Writing both enabled and required new and more formal grammatical structures.[10] Alphabetical languages also break the intonation units of spoken language into discrete words.[11] Pictographic languages like Chinese and Japanese organize the stream of language in a different way, by concept, with greater unity of form and meaning. Like alphabetic languages, Chinese and similar languages also use punctuation, underscoring, and so forth, to accomplish the communicative

---

[7] For example, Crick and Watson created a model of the molecular components of DNA that they could manipulate and play with and used the model to explore possible physical relationships among protein molecules as they worked out the structure of DNA (Watson, 1968; for extended discussion, see Ritchie, 2009b).

[8] Relevant to this book, Shannon's (1948, 1949) elegant representation of electronic signal transmission in his well-known source – message – receiver diagram has contributed to the sustained popularity of the code metaphor for researchers interested in human communication and language. For a detailed discussion, see Ritchie (1991).

[9] Recent disputes and controversies over "fake news" admittedly weaken my confidence in this statement.

[10] Halliday (1998).   [11] Ong (2002).

functions of vocalics, face, and gesture. Writing is probably responsible for the widespread view that "nonverbal" signals are independent of language.

Spoken language tends toward objectifying the abstract features of thought, as if the thought is somehow independent of the thinker. It also allows two or more people to collaborate in formulating an idea, which then becomes both the collective property of all participants and independent of any of them. Written language amplifies this effect in several ways. The written expression of an idea exists in a permanent physical form that is clearly separate from any author. The text can be edited, revised, and modified by the original author, by another person, or by two or more people working together. Two independent ideas can be written, placed side by side, and compared, phrase by phrase and word by word. Writing makes it possible to conduct personal and commercial relationships and assert political power at a distance. It also makes it possible to engage in disputes and collaborations at a distance, and refine, revise, and reshape an idea or an argument from multiple perspectives, creating the possibility for entirely new forms of knowledge[12] and discourse. Electronic media both amplify and accelerate these effects.

Writing also makes it easy for authors to look at what they have written, think critically about it, argue about it, and revise their ideas as many times as they wish. These capabilities extend thinking and logic, objectify it, and create a new form of reasoning. Authors can internalize their critics, their collaborators, and their mentors, as Plato famously internalized Socrates in his dialogs, then externalized the dialog in what reads like a transcription of the conversations.[13] By separating object from subject, ideas and experiences from their expression, writing changed the nature of thinking, logic, and discourse. It also changed the nature of storytelling, and facilitated the development of entirely new art forms and new kinds of social relationship, spanning both space and time. By separating the origination of a message from its processing, writing created an anonymous *audience*, an effect that was greatly amplified by print.

Print

Writing changed both the form and the use of language, substituting abstract visual symbols for the (also abstract) sounds of spoken language. Alphabetic writing in particular digitizes language, in that every word is represented by a finite set of letters, each letter encoding a particular sound or set of sounds, and many of the most basic grammatical concepts are represented by punctuation

---

[12] Halliday (1998).
[13] I have internalized the critical voices of several mentors – Steve Chaffee, Mary Ann Fitzpatrick, Ray Gibbs, and Lynne Cameron in particular – and I engage in silent argument with one or more of them every time I write.

symbols. Since there was previously no canonical spelling for many words, the digitization was only perfected with the invention of print, the dictionary, and standardized spelling and usage. Moveable type also emphasizes the digital, code-like nature of language and emphasizes writing and language as repeatable, reduceable, interchangeable, and mechanical.[14]

The availability of inexpensive books in large numbers encouraged the spread of literacy and, with it, the spread of a concept of language that was based as much or more on written as on spoken language. It also greatly accelerated the development and dissemination of memes, both useful and pernicious. The invention of fiction as a popular form made the imaginative projections of other persons readily accessible to a large and growing share of the population, creating entirely new forms of cultural expression, leading to the fragmentation of intellectual and artistic experience, and separation of audiences into "popular" versus "high" cultures. This included new kinds of interpersonal relationships and communities of interest, based on knowledge and ideas gleaned from reading the same books.[15] Previously, for most people, knowledge and cultural norms were almost entirely acquired orally, by listening, which limited the size of an audience to a hundred or so, depending on the acoustic quality of the space. In the age of print, knowledge was large acquired visually, by reading, and reinforced or qualified through oral means (lectures and conversation).

Print also led to development of a new *parasocial* form of relationship, in which an individual develops a sense of intimacy with a total stranger, who might be the author of a book or tract or a totally fictional person. A skillful author can develop fictional characters with such depth and complexity that their readers experience them as real people and develop complex (obviously one-way) relationships with them. Goethe's novel, *The Sorrows of Young Werther*,[16] spawned what may have been the first in a long and continuing series of suicide epidemics based on the *suicide* meme, fueled by parasocial identification with a romantically depressive popular culture figure.

The Audience

One-to-many communication can be traced to the development of public speaking, (oratory) and formal drama, central features of public life in classical Greece and Rome. They were mostly one-way, although members of the audience could respond by shouted comments. Just as writing expanded conversation to include written exchanges over great distances, print expanded and greatly changed the nature of audiences. The audiences for written oratory

---

[14] Eisenstein (1980).   [15] Eisenstein (1980).   [16] Goethe (1774).

(e.g. the op-ed column) and written performance (e.g. the novel) are largely anonymous, solitary, individual, and scattered through space and time. Both reading and writing are solitary acts, separated in time and space from the social relationships they draw on.

Electronic Media

Beginning with the invention of the telegraph, then the telephone, instantaneous communication became possible across large distances. Although they share the features of effectively instant communication and making distance irrelevant, the media otherwise have sufficiently different features that they affect communication in quite different ways.

Radio and Television. Radio extends the effect of print from visual to oral. It creates a small audience that may be a single person or a small group, in a one-way "conversation." Even when the content of radio is oratory or performance, the nature of the medium, in which the voice comes through a small speaker, often located in a small space (a living room, bedroom, or automobile), lends it a sense of intimacy, as if this person "is talking to *me*." Television adds the visual element of conversation and performance back in, but the effect is still intimate and personal, with the face and shoulders of a speaker often filling the entire screen. The effect is nicely illustrated by the western genre. Western movies, especially during the 1950s and 1960s (the era of the wide screen), focused on action in a large, open, dramatic landscape. In contrast, radio westerns focused on dialog and sound effects; television westerns focused on relationships and developed the personalities of their characters, week by week, sometimes over several years.[17] With many of the features of gossip, radio and television greatly expanded and developed the new parasocial form of relationship in which listeners and viewers feel that they have a personal relationship with the characters portrayed in their favorite programs.

Audio recording and movies created a mass market for professional performers, musicians, and actors, and radio and television rapidly expanded the market for professional music and storytelling, at the expense of amateurs. The radio and the phonograph changed the experience of music from friends and family *playing* music together to friends or family *listening* to music – together or, often, as solitary individuals.[18] These media effectively inserted their content into ordinary conversation, which has come to be increasingly focused on televised sports, drama, the personalities and intimate lives of performance

---

[17] *Gunsmoke* is a good example. Even *Bonanza*, set on a large Nevada cattle ranch, resembled a television soap opera more than a classic cinematic western movie.

[18] Televised sports had a similar effect on athletics.

"idols," and both radio and televised talk shows. They also provided a means for political and cultural leaders to address mass audiences in a way that seems intimate and personal, with the speaker only a few feet away, apparently making direct eye contact with the viewer.

Computer/Internet. The internet began as an extension of intellectual discourse, allowing scientists and scholars to collaborate more efficiently. Works in progress can be transmitted for review, commentary, revision, and so forth, almost instantaneously. It was quickly adapted for personal conversations as well. At first, it was an extension of written correspondence, with instant delivery and with the possibility of a kind of hybrid of writing with conversation, combining the possibility with almost instant response with the ability to review and edit messages before sending and the lack of visual or vocalic signals.[19] As the medium matured and bandwidth was added, it became possible to transmit photographs and other images. Then inexpensive digital cameras were developed, permitting transmission of video as well as still images to supplement live vocal interactions. With a sufficient bandwidth, it is now possible to engage in a conversation complete with the full range of visual and vocalic signals, although with a slight delay that makes turn-taking awkward. Moreover, many people can connect at once, permitting remote classes, meetings, and even lectures, a capability widely exploited during the COVID-19 pandemic.

The Cellphone. The cellphone is at base an extension of the telephone, crossed with the internet, and supplemented with digital video recorders and with enough "apps" to create it as an entirely new and rapidly evolving medium. Because the cellphone is completely portable, it allows people to be available for conversations literally all the time, "24/7." In many relationships, the *possibility* of being available all the time creates an *expectation* of being available all the time. As a result, failure to answer a call may be viewed as a transgression, a face threat requiring an account and perhaps a repair. Another effect of 24/7 availability is that people in intimate relationships may share both intimate and trivial details of their lives, reinforcing the basic content-free "grooming" function.

App-based extensions of the cellphone include visual: With a good connection, the other person's facial expressions and some gestures are visible. Brief text messages – a return to the telegraphic writing style, but with instant delivery – are easy and convenient. It is easy to snap and instantly transmit a photo of a lovely landscape, a pet or grandchild doing something cute, the meal one is about to eat – or a "selfie" that shows what a great time one is

---

[19] Unfortunately, people often neglect to take advantage of this capability.

having. Other apps allow friends to play games remotely – word games, logic games, card games, and so on.

All this changes the nature of relationships, liberates imagination, and introduces the possibility of entirely new kinds of relationships. Courtship communication has expanded to include "sexting," sending erotic still or video images, as well as the more innocent exchange of trivial details of one's life ("I just saw a couple walking the *cutest* dog.") Text messaging is an ideal medium for exchanging a string of puns or other wordplay, short poems, and an infinite variety of emojis expressing love, annoyance, boredom, and so on. One result of this instant, on-demand communication seems to be radically shortened utterances as well as more frequent but shorter and arguably more trivial conversations.

The versatility of the cellphone has led to a proliferation of media apps, each with particular affordances and constraints, each with unique effects on communication, both interpersonal and public. Writing in the autumn and winter of 2020–2021, it is impossible not to comment at least briefly on the effect of media apps like Twitter and Facebook, which have accelerated and broadened the origination and transmission of memes. President Trump developed Twitter, with its telegraph-like length constraints, into a powerful gossip-like tool for assembling and directing a political movement. In the remainder of this chapter, I will discuss some of the implications of these developments for public discourse.

Elaborating and Fragmenting Social Reality

As Homo sapiens evolved in response to language, genetic evolution became less important and cultural adaptation more important, allowing humans to adapt to and thrive in a range of ecological niches and cope successfully with extreme environments and rapidly changing conditions. This resulted in rapid proliferation of diverse cultures. Reflecting the varieties of cultural practices and the local spread of linguistic and cultural memes, relationships and conversations became more varied and more complex, and languages developed in ways that supported the communication needs of each culture. As society became more extensive and more complex, and skills became more refined, requiring longer training and apprenticeship, division of labor and specialization expanded and became more fixed. "Interests" and sociopolitical classes developed, based at first on specialization, then on wealth and political influence.

Facts, obtained directly through perception and interpretation and indirectly through communication with others, extend, qualify, and amplify the common representations. When new perceptions seem to contradict elements of current individual or common representations, interpretation requires evaluation, critique, judgment, and synthesis, and may require revision of individual and socially constructed representations. This process of evaluation, critique, and judgment (argument or debate) is often part of conversation, and tends to be internalized into individual thought in the form of *reasoning*. As cultures become more complex and different groups develop unique shared representations, the direct and indirect basis of these representations becomes subject to dispute and debate. Narratives and other interpretive frames are developed and become part of the cultural "common ground" of cultures and groups, but these can also develop into different versions based on different background assumptions, then become subject to dispute and debate.

Larger and more complex societies are composed of many primary but overlapping groups of various sizes. The discourse of the society is constituted by the interaction of all the discourses of constituent smaller groups and organizations. The conversations themselves represent and are influenced by the discourses of various subgroups ("interest groups" or "publics") and of society as a whole. Individual members of larger, complex societies are unlikely to have direct input into public discourse, which is shaped by conversations among a small subset of powerful, higher-status people. However, even the discourse of elites is not entirely impervious to the everyday, insignificant conversations of ordinary people.

Modern societies are large and complex, organized in intersecting aggregates that include nations and their subsidiary states, cities, and communities, religious communities, occupational and professional identities, and so on. In a complex social structure of vocational specialization and sociopolitical classes, individuals look to peers and members of relevant social groups for the emotional and social support of friendships and alliances. In a modern industrial or postindustrial society, individuals also develop complex webs of relationships that involve membership in multiple groups, each of which maintains its own homeostasis. An individual may belong to workplace groups, religious and avocational groups, political parties, informal neighborhood friendships, and so on. Each of these groups and relationships has a distinct common representation of the group itself and members' identities with respect to the group, all within a distinct common representation of the social and physical environment and the group's identity and status within that environment. Each group is also a source of independent perception and interpretation, extended cognition that produces more or less unique "information" about the environment and about other groups. Individuals commonly inhabit multiple *social realities*, [20] each associated with a different community,

---

[20] Berger and Luckmann (1966).

and may occupy a distinct individual identity with respect to each of these communities.

Groups are defined in part by their boundaries, who belongs to the group (insiders) and who does not (outsiders). Group identities and memberships are also defined by their use of language, implicit rules of play, humor, and teasing, the stories they tell, and the way they tell them. Every group has an origins story, and most groups have stories that express group members' sense of personal and collective identity, "who we are and what we do."[21] The central stories are told and retold, to affirm group identity and membership and to help socialize new members into the group.[22] In a complex society (like the contemporary United States), many groups experience and recall parallel critical events, but because they experienced these events in quite different ways, they shape them into unique and sometimes contradictory narratives. These differences in experience and perspective inevitably lead to contestation, as the shared stories that unify a particular group around a common narrative may exacerbate conflict with other groups.

Public Discourse

A *conversation* can be understood as a communication-based interaction among two or more individuals within a relationship or group. A conversation ordinarily takes place in a single session, although people will sometimes continue a conversation after an interruption (usually brief), and occasionally over an extended series of interaction events. *Discourse* is sometimes used as a synonym for conversation, but it is also used as a more inclusive term that includes discussion, debate, lectures, and written communication. It is useful to distinguish between casual conversation and the extended, multimedia discussion that constitutes *"public discourse."*

Public discourse can be understood as communication among an identifiable set of people (which may embrace a large group or an entire society) about a topic or issue or a set of related topics, and will typically include many different conversations (as well as speeches, writing, etc.). An academic discipline, for example, is defined by discourses about its topics of study; each discourse is typically composed of written books and articles, lectures, and conversations that extend over many years. Public discourses usually include conversations organized around multiple perspectives and diverse arguments, often based on different assumptions, competing interpretations of evidence, and, at the extreme, different claims about what is and is not "fact." When

---

[21] Fine and DeSoucey (2005); Ritchie (2011b).
[22] Fine and DeSoucey (2005); Norrick (1997).

disagreements reach a certain point, public discourses will sometimes split into separate discourses, with limited communication among them.[23]

Up to a certain size and social complexity, dyadic and small group conversations sustain a coherent shared representation of the group in its environment. This may be extended by discussions in larger groups, formal or informal gatherings of a few dozen people, characterized by extended speeches that contribute to projecting the shared representation forward in time. Problems facing the group and the society may be identified and analyzed in the context of shared representations of the society's history, possible solutions, and expected outcomes. Interlocking membership in which individuals belong to several groups and participate in conversations in different groups and informal gatherings contribute to the society's ability to maintain a coherent representation shared among many groups and develop coherent shared projections of potential futures.

As a society grows in size and complexity, the conversations and gatherings, and the publics they constitute, may become less homogeneous, with fewer common memberships to sustain shared representations. Both small group conversations and informal gatherings will gradually organize into discrete clusters of interlocking groups. Inevitably the representations shared by the entire society will become more abstract, and more detailed representations will begin to fragment as subgroups develop their own distinct versions based on common interests and experiences. The larger, heterogenous public will fragment into smaller, more nearly homogeneous publics, each organized around its own stories and its own version of the overarching story of the society. In the United States, for example, each ethnic and occupational group has its own identifying stories, often embedded in a particular version of the national story – and, frequently, at least partially in opposition to it.

Groups and societies all have conventions of language, play, and humor, as well as identity-defining stories. These are disseminated, and collective homeostasis maintained, through conversations in interconnected networks of smaller groups, through religious and educational discourse, and through public discourse. At one end of a public–private scale are essays, books, and speeches, delivered to large groups in person or by means of electronic and print media. At the other end of the scale are conversations, typically two or three people but occasionally as many as a dozen or more. Internet and cellular technologies blend these extremes in interesting ways, supporting both genuinely dyadic conversations and mass messages (e.g. "tweets" and the like) that

---

[23] For example, for much of the past century the field of Communication has been split into Critical Theory and Empirical discourses that address only a few of the same questions, based on quite different assumptions, and are at best only partially comprehensible to each other.

take the form of personal communication even though they may be sent to and read or heard by millions of people.

The printing press provided a means to objectify knowledge (history, scientific research, philosophy) as well as imagination (poetry, fiction, religion, and speculative philosophy) in a more or less permanent form, independent of any author and subject to interpretation, critique, elaboration, and debate. It also provided a means to objectify and disseminate news (knowledge and opinion about contemporary events, implicitly based on interpretation of these events in relation to someone's understanding of the underlying background story). Print and other mass media expanded the audience for all these genres. Even when the various writers disagree about interpretations and even about the underlying facts themselves, print makes it easy to compare, contrast, and critique competing accounts.[24] Audiences may be fragmented and believe conflicting or contradictory accounts of historical and current events, but at least they have access to the competing accounts, which allows for a sort of quasi-unity.

In the United States, the rise of network television in the 1950s through 1970s and into the 1980s created an environment in which a handful of news sources provided a coherent and mostly uniform account of current events and interpretations.[25] The entertainment wing of these networks and the magazine and book publishers affiliated with them provided a narrative account of both history and contemporary life that was informed by and coherent with the news and history. As summarized by conservative columnist Ross Douthat, the result was development of a widely shared narrative of American history and the "American way of life." It was a narrative of courageous and intrepid settlers taming a wilderness and creating a powerful and benign democracy. A sub-narrative about the American Civil War celebrated the heroism of Confederate as well as Union soldiers,[26] reframing the Confederate soldiers' treason as "gallantry" and a "Lost Cause." This central narrative was based on and informed by the interpretation of observed events by journalists, historians, novelists, and so on, all within the context of the preexisting stories to which their writings contributed. As Douthat observes, this version of "the American story" was never totally unchallenged, but competing and contradictory stories were either restricted to small specialized audiences or coopted and neutralized by the dominant mainstream media. Even the recording of events portrayed by histories and cultural/national narratives has always been an interpretive act, based on the reporter's understanding of the underlying story.

---

[24] Eisenstein (1980).   [25] Beniger (1983).   [26] Douthat (2017).

The introduction of cable and satellite TV broadcasts beginning in the 1980s facilitated a proliferation of independent entertainment and news programming that led to fragmentation of the mass audience. An early and benign effect of the rise of independent programming was to enable the much wider dissemination of information, events, and interpretations that challenge and contradict the previously dominant narrative. The "heroic settler" narrative was confronted with and challenged by a narrative of subjugation and "ethnic cleansing" of the existing inhabitants and the "Lost Cause" narrative by a narrative of slave-era brutality and Jim Crow lynching and racial terrorism. However, these same factors also contribute to the dissemination of disinformation, rumors, and lies.

The fragmentation of the audience was accelerated and amplified by the rise of internet and cellular transmission technology and the introduction of social media services like Facebook and Twitter. These services, along with search engines like Google, use algorithms designed to deliver content that will attract attention to ads ("generate clicks") that have the side effect of building isolated audiences susceptible to misleading and false information. The cellphone makes it easier for events to be recorded by observers who interpret them within different and contradictory story frames, producing apparent facts that supplement, extend, and often contradict the "dominant" narrative, and to disseminate these alternative accounts. During recent years it has become apparent that these media also facilitate the invention of totally fictitious events as the basis for equally fictitious "facts" and a narrative that takes on the qualities of fantasy.

Narratives

An acceptable (and convincing) narrative is organized around one or more central figures or heroes with a common set of motivating purposes. Narrative emphasizes the actions and experiences of central figures or groups, the protagonists in the constitutive stories. Their actions, ordeals, and victories represent the group and are vicariously experienced by all members of the group as their own actions, ordeals, and victories.

In a smaller, coherent society, all members may identify with the central figure, the hero (e.g. a family's founding matriarch or a corporation's founding entrepreneur), and accept the hero's point of view as their own. Events that threaten or bolster the hero's homeostasis also threaten or bolster the homeostasis of the group and, by extension, the homeostasis of every member of the group. Retelling the story reinforces individual as well as group homeostasis. Individual members of the group understand their own identity in the context of the group's master narratives (there are often many smaller narratives within the overall narrative) and manage their own homeostasis in terms of the group homeostasis, as exemplified by and personified in the hero's homeostasis. Hearing and reading about the hero's doings and sayings, group members overcome doubts and vicissitudes and maintain their own homeostasis as part of the community. Thus the homeostasis of the community is maintained through sermons and lectures and conversations in which these doings and sayings are told and retold, discussed, explained, and relived.

In larger, more complex societies, many and diverse publics develop around different and often competing or conflicting interests and perspectives associated with ethnic identities, religious communities, labor unions, managerial workers and property owners, and so on. These publics/communities have more frequent conversations based on similar news and entertainment media.[27] They develop narratives about their own communities that include narratives about the society as a whole; these narratives may simply extend the overall narrative of the society, but they often compete with or contradict it.

Frame Conflicts. In many cases, topics and issues at the center of a discourse can be framed in multiple ways. The US settler narrative that has traditionally been framed in terms of the "intrepid pioneer taming the wilderness" can also be framed as "stealing indigenous peoples' land through ethnic cleansing." Missionaries who accompanied the early settlers who were framed as "bringing truth to uncivilized savages" can also be framed as "destroying coherent and complex cultures." In the eighteenth and nineteenth centuries, colonialism and slavery were justified by framing Europeans as a superior race and Africans and Asians as inferior races. Although it has been successfully challenged within mainstream US culture, this framing continues today, for example, in White Nationalism.

Example: Public Discourse about the US Civil War

To take an example pertinent to Douthat's argument, the US Civil War was initially framed as a struggle over slavery itself, confounded with and motivated by the dependence of the Southern cotton economy and the aristocratic culture supported by slave labor. During the Reconstruction and subsequent "Jim Crow" eras, the Civil War was reframed by emphasizing the political dispute about the distribution of power between the central government and "states' rights" (the "Lost Cause") and obscuring the role of slavery. Confederate soldiers, particularly those who had served as officers in the US army, were initially framed as treasonous oath-breakers, but their treason was pardoned, and they were reframed as heroic warriors in the "Lost Cause" struggle against modernity and a domineering central government. During

---

[27] Price (1992).

the late nineteenth and early twentieth centuries, this reframing was reinforced, for political reasons, by naming US military installations, highways, and other monuments after Confederate generals and erecting statues in their honor.[28] This reframing was carried forward in the late nineteenth and first half of the twentieth centuries when the brutal suppression of African Americans was also framed in terms of "states' rights" and "defending the Southern way of life." "Race riots" were reframed to distract attention from the culture of lynching and the murderous riots in which White mobs destroyed African American communities and to redirect attention to the riots that grew out of Civil Rights era protests against police brutality and vote suppression.

In the initial "Founding Fathers" narrative, the stories experienced by the slaves and by the indigenous people displaced by settlers were often omitted or suppressed.[29] Most of the individual experiences of these events were recounted, if at all, in the conversations of small communities, and, when told to a broader audience, rarely heeded. Their omission from the discourse was legitimated by portrayals of non-Whites in general as less than fully human in both "scientific" discussions and popular culture caricatures. All this was part of the traditional narrative that Douthat[30] contrasts with the liberal counter-narrative.

The Civil Rights movement of mid-twentieth century, abetted by introduction of new communication technologies, brought these previously suppressed events and stories into the light where they could more readily be read, heard, and experienced. The supposedly "scientific" accounts of racial differences were resoundingly discredited, both by critical scrutiny of the evidence it was based on and by new genetic and anthropological research, and the cultural caricatures based on the same prejudices and misconceptions were repudiated. This infusion of new information and new stories based on previously disregarded events and interpretations helped to precipitate cultural changes that have amplified the contradictions between these frames and contributed to increasing political turbulence.

Conflicting Narratives: "That's Not Who We Are." At a fundamental level, history is often thought of as a simple recounting of events. But it is impossible to recount *all* the separate events that constitute any composite event, and "simple" recounting without selection and interpretation is impossible. The "settler culture" and "Lost Cause" narratives were based on a particular interpretation of a small subset of all the events that shaped the United States, a subset that was selected and interpreted by heirs of the European intellectual traditions who dominated US political and intellectual

---

[28] For example, US Highway 99, which extends from the Canadian to the Mexican border, was named the Jefferson Davis Highway.
[29] For example, see Blow (2021). [30] Douthat (2017); Ritchie (2019).

culture well into the second half of the twentieth century. Inevitably this selection and interpretation was guided by the assumptions and narratives of their culture, the dominant culture of the time.

The Battle of Gettysburg, because it was a crucial turning point in the US Civil War, the "crisis of the house divided,"[31] provides a pertinent example for more detailed analysis. Over 104,000 Union soldiers and 71,000–75,000 Confederate soldiers fought (charged, retreated, dug trenches, bayonetted each other and shot muskets and cannon at each other) over three hot days in July of 1863. Casualties are estimated at 46,000–51,000. It is impossible to know even how many people were engaged in the battle, exactly how many were wounded or how many died; each casualty, each wound, and each death is an event within a turbulent and chaotic series of events. Most events are not recorded. The events that are recorded represent what someone remembered long enough and considered important or interesting enough to write in a journal or diary or relate to a reporter who might include it in a news story.

Converting events into history begins with the many decisions about which events are recorded and which are not. This selection process is itself shaped by individuals' representations, their stories about their selves and their groups within the social and physical environment – in this case the combat unit, army, battlefield, and war. The selection of events worth recording begins with making sense of particular incidents within the story, all part of the process of homeostasis, within a representation of personal identity that is changed by these very incidents even as they are interpreted.

A soldier writes a letter home, selecting events to narrate in the letter that will help to sustain the homeostasis of his relationships with the addressee, and with the friends and neighbors to whom the addressee may show or read the letter. Later, journalists and historians and novelists interview the soldiers and other witnesses and pick through these interviews and the letters and diaries they are allowed to read. They select the events that fit a story that is forming as they go, shaped by the stories they hear, by their own prior understanding, and by the "national story" they began with. All this, selecting, interpreting, and molding events into "the" story of a battle, is part of the writers' process of homeostasis. It all contributes to an ongoing discourse about the war, one of the many discourses that emerge through all these conversations and speeches and written news and historical accounts. There is nothing pernicious about this process: Filtering, selecting, and interpreting is necessary if a story is to be told at all, and it will inevitably reflect the biases and perspectives of individual writers.

---

[31] Douthat (2017); Ritchie (2019).

This same process extends through constructing a narrative of the war, the events both prior and subsequent to the war, so that *Gettysburg* is one narrative, one set of narratives within a larger set of narratives of *the Civil War*, within a larger set of narratives of *the United States of America*. There were 180,000 soldiers at Gettysburg, plus the civilian residents of the town and the slaves and liberated slaves who accompanied each army, each with a different set of experiences, different events interpreted according to different beliefs and assumptions. Out of these thousands of personal stories, a number of narratives emerged,[32] each supported by a particular subset of the events of those three days and each interpreted according to a different preexisting narrative.

Some stories are deliberately suppressed. Blow[33] gives the example of the Tulsa Massacre of 1921, when White citizens, with the aid of the National Guard, destroyed the prosperous African American community of Greenwood known as "Black Wall Street" and murdered 300 people. All evidence of the massacre was deliberately obliterated, victims buried in unmarked graves, news accounts excised, police records destroyed.

Another nation-defining race issue, scarcely even recognized at the time when the US Constitution was being drafted, was the displacement, subjugation, and genocidal slaughter of indigenous peoples. Like the battle of Gettysburg, this involved uncountable events, some trivial (like cooking a meal over a campfire), some (like the slaughter of Native American women and children depicted in the woodcut[34] that accompanied Douthat's column[35]) epoch-making and soul-shattering. Each of these, trivial and consequential alike, was experienced by different people from different perspectives. Most were quickly forgotten; many were remembered, retold, recorded, and interpreted according to the beliefs, prior experience, and understanding of the individuals who wrote the diaries and letters and the individuals who assembled them into histories. Like the Tulsa Massacre, many of the relevant stories were deliberately suppressed.

Both slavery and the subjugation of the indigenous peoples involved the experience of victims (slaves, former slaves, and natives) as well as victimizers

---

[32] Confederate and Union soldiers experienced the battle and every encounter within those three days from their own unique perspective. But officers and foot soldiers, infantrymen and artillerymen, and the residents of the town, sheltering however they could at the edge of the battle, all experienced these events from unique perspectives, recalled and interpreted them in different conversations according to different perspectives into fragments of stories about the battle. Most of these were lost in time; a few were collected and blended into "the" historical accounts that are told, revised and retold, in history books, fiction, movies, and classrooms.

[33] Blow (2021).

[34] "Enlightened Christian warfare in the nineteenth century. Massacre of Indian women and children in Idaho by White scouts and their red allies. Engraving, 1868." Getty Images.

[35] Douthat (2017).

(slaveholders, KKK mobs, armies, and militias) and bystander/witnesses, who usually accepted the perspective of the victimizers. The events associated with slavery and the war fought to preserve slavery, and with settlement of the frontier and the slaughter or removal of its previous inhabitants, were selected, interpreted, and recorded according to that same set of perspectives. At the same time, these events were also selected and interpreted according to their own perspectives, by the slaves and natives who survived, then recorded in oral histories and in written accounts by the victims and by sympathetic bystander-observers. A few of these alternative narratives, voiced by Abolitionist leaders like Frederick Douglas and Sojourner Truth and, later, by novelists like Richard Wright and James Baldwin, hovered at the edge of the national discourse, never quite integrated into the national narrative. Many more of the alternative narratives remained hidden, suppressed, or neglected by the historians and novelists and speechmakers until their recent gradual rediscovery and insertion into the national discourse.[36] Their long omission from the public discourse enabled the unified narrative that Douthat both regrets and criticizes.

History in the form of a foundational narrative begins with which events are recorded and interpreted and which events are ignored, relegated to "Black History Month," or suppressed altogether. The recording and interpretation are influenced by a perspective that includes the taken-for-granted interests and values, shaped to maintain the historians'/story-tellers' homeostasis and the homeostasis of their reference groups. When media capacity is limited and access to media restricted, the stories of subordinate groups may not be told at all, and are unlikely to enter public discourse, even when they are told and retold in the informal oral histories.

The new media technologies that began to appear with inexpensive audio and video recording equipment and accelerated with the development of personal computers and the internet provide a means for these counter-narratives to be recorded and collected, and eventually to be disseminated more broadly. The emergence and dissemination of these previously suppressed events and narratives into the popular culture of movies and music and best-seller novels contributed to the fragmenting of the US national story decried by Douthat.[37] Like individual memories, collective stories are always reshaped through telling and retelling, to fit concerns and values that are salient in the time and place. The "other" stories and alternative frames may be disregarded or suppressed, but they are always latent, with the potential to surface and disrupt previously stable narratives.

---

[36] For example, see Smith (2021).   [37] Douthat (2017).

In a uniform and restrictive media environment, both storytellers and audiences select events according to prior understandings and values (selective perception[38]). Consistent with homeostasis maintenance, they interpret these events to support their prior beliefs and values (motivated reasoning[39]). Over time people sometimes integrate new information into their knowledge and adjust beliefs and values to accommodate newly discovered facts. This is most likely to happen when enough new evidence enters the discourse that is too compelling to ignore, so that the cognitive dissonance produced by the contradictions can be resolved only by a radical change in the discourse.

The introduction of cable channels and internet facilitated selective perception and motivated reasoning. However, the same factors enabled previously ignored or suppressed stories to be told. The live TV coverage of the Vietnam War and of the brutal suppression of civil rights demonstrations in the United States contributed to the passage of civil rights legislation, which eventually led to the emergence and empowerment of journalists and media storytellers like Ava DuVernay, whose *Selma*[40] presents the story of the events of a crucial civil rights demonstration from the previously suppressed viewpoint of the demonstrators. Social media enable descendants of slaves and other victims to find each other, to find sympathizers in greater numbers, and to organize more efficiently to protest vote suppression, racialized violence, and discrimination. Social media also enables White Nationalists and conspiracy theorists to find each other, recruit more sympathizers, and organize counter-protests. Because they facilitate instantaneous communication with a large audience with minimal gatekeeping, these new media have also facilitated origination and dissemination of inaccurate and often deliberately distorted accounts of both actual events and events that never happened.

The upshot of all this is the splintering of public discourse into distinct and radically separate discourses, conducted in multiple conversations among like-minded people. The narratives Douthat identifies are part of these public discourses, taken for granted as the basis for the private conversations as well as the speeches, essays, sermons, and news stories that draw on and feed into the private conversations.

Lies and Fake News

Misinformation resulting from inaccurate observation and "disinformation," outright lies based on distorted representation of actual events and fabrication of events that never happened, have always been part of public discourse, and print media is susceptible to both. But print allows more opportunity for

---

[38] Vidmar and Rokeach (1974). [39] Kunda (1990). [40] DuVernay (2014).

context and nuance, can be quoted and refuted in detail, and invites review and reflection. The electronic media that appeared late in the twentieth century discourage context, nuance, and reflection, and afford a much more fertile ground for both inadvertent *mis*information and deliberate *dis*information.

Thanks to cellphone technology, events can be reported immediately, before they are fully understood. Images can be recorded and transmitted, which can provide an objective record of events or reinforce a partial and inaccurate account of events. Disinformation is even more insidious. With modern technology it is possible to create convincing images and reports of events that never happened and disseminate them faster than they can be detected and debunked.

Both misinformation and disinformation have been amplified and accelerated by at least two other features of recently developed technology. One is exemplified by Twitter, which reverts to the telegraphic style of language by means of a length limit but, unlike telegrams, messages on Twitter can be sent instantaneously via cellphone from virtually anywhere in the world, and delivered instantaneously to an unlimited number of readers. Even the current limit of 280 characters is insufficient to present evidence, reasoning, or context: Twitter specializes in starkly presented opinions, judgments, and outright fabrications stated as facts. Another significant feature is the development of algorithms that encourage readers' engagement and hold their attention by identifying their interests and prejudices and directing them toward increasingly radical content that will keep them engaged.[41]

The new media technologies of instant transmission of images and short, telegraphic messages, and the attention-directing algorithms that control these technologies, tend to increase the separation of discourses. People are directed toward messages that fit and support what they already believe, and engage in conversations with others who hold similar views and read much the same messages. Conversely, the same algorithms restrict opportunities for conversation with others who hold different views and read different messages. Even for topics that are not particularly controversial, these trends are likely to produce a fragmentation into separate discourses. This fragmentation into separate discourses is particularly pronounced for topics such as race/slavery and gender/sexual morality, because of the strong emotions these topics evoke. The subtle and complex synthesis of separate narratives into a new and inclusive national narrative requires that these fragmented discourses somehow be rejoined into a single, coherent discourse, somehow in spite of the forces keeping them apart.

---

[41] At the time of writing this chapter, both technologies are too new to have been extensively researched or understood.

Summary

In our complex modern society, most people have many primary reference groups. The homeostasis of each of these groups is a factor in personal homeostasis, perception, thinking, and communication. The homeostasis needs of these various groups are sometimes in competition or conflict, sometimes mutually reinforcing. But even within one's own personal homeostasis, as well as that of various reference groups, there is a constant trade-off between the need for accuracy of representations, including the predictive forward-representation, and the need for consistency and coherence. Personal consistency and sociocultural coherence reinforce selective perception and motivated reasoning, but these processes work against accuracy of representations.

Confounding things even further is the tendency most humans have toward empathy, at least empathy for those who are present and visible. We indirectly experience others' hopes and disappointments, their pain and suffering, and their elation when they achieve some minor success. Both modern media and the integration of communities and institutions render the victims of racism and poverty more visible, more present, and our vicarious experience of their suffering poses yet another challenge to personal homeostasis and, when they are part of a primary reference group, to the group homeostasis. When the victims are not part of a primary reference group but are part of an outsider group, an "Other" perceived as threatening to our group, empathy and vicarious experience of their suffering poses an even more severe challenge to group and consequently to individual homeostasis, a challenge that may require rejecting and denying the empathy, which in turn may require denying the humanity of the victims. A primary condition for empathy is the willingness and ability to recognize and to enter into the experiential world of the Other,[42] but in a situation of perceived threat to homeostasis, that may seem all but impossible. All these factors influence our perceptual processes, our selection of events as worth noticing and reporting, and our interpretation of these events as we integrate them into our projections of self and group in our social and physical environment.

---

[42] Ritchie and Cameron (2014).

15 Recap
Homeostasis and Communication

The fundamental guiding premises of this book are evolution, embodiment, homeostasis, and representation. The purpose of this book is to derive an account of communication that is thoroughly consistent with communication as a function of a biologically evolved brain, which is an integral part of a biologically evolved body, based on current research in neuroscience and cognitive science.

Homeostasis is a basic principle of life. To be alive is to be in a constant state of change, with a constant inflow of nutrients of energy and outflow of waste products. *Homeostasis* is a state in which the inflows and outflows are maintained within a stable range that is consistent with the overall pattern of relationships among parts. A living system is never either completely in balance or completely out of balance.[1]

A single cell acts as a unit of homeostasis, maintaining its own balance of inputs and outputs and responding to perturbations from the environment (fluctuations in the ambient temperature and presences of nutrients and poisons, including waste products of other cells). This is the basic level of homeostasis. When cells band together in multicellular organisms, the organism is a second level of homeostasis, maintaining the balance of inputs and outputs and responding to perturbations from the environment *by means of* the homeostasis-maintaining activities of the constituent cells. As each cell is dependent on the organism as a whole, information about the homeostasis of the organism as a whole is one input to each cell's homeostasis-maintaining processes.

Random variations in the reproduction of organisms (due to errors in transmission of genetic information) sometimes result in offspring that are more efficient at obtaining and using available resources in the present environment, – that is, more *reproductively fit*. Random alterations that lead to greater competitive ability are more likely to be reproduced in future generations. By accelerating evolution and adaptation to changes in the

---
[1] Damasio (2018); Maturana and Varela (1980).

environment, sexual reproduction and the ability to *cooperate*, with other organisms[2] both add to reproductive fitness. These three factors, sexual reproduction, competition, and cooperation, define basic parameters of *social organization*.

With the advent of sexual reproduction and social organization, individuals become dependent for resources and protection from predators on the social group, so that information about the group becomes input to the homeostasis of the individual. Thus, the sexual dyad and social group (herd, flock, troop, tribe) constitute a third level of survival and homeostasis. Social groups and relationships are characterized by different degrees of complexity, so the homeostasis of the group varies in importance as a factor in individual homeostasis.

Signaling is essential for cooperation and social organization. Social structure includes kinship networks and status hierarchies, which require some system of signaling both to establish and maintain the hierarchy and to minimize actual physical conflict. As social structures increase in size and complexity, signals also increase in complexity. The homeostasis of the group as a whole and of higher-status members of a complex group are improved if they can sustain their status and assert dominance through signals rather than physical aggression. The homeostasis of lower-status members of the group is also improved if they can use various signals (especially grooming) to appease higher-status individuals and to cultivate and maintain relationships with others who might support them in a conflict.

Cognition

Signaling within organisms takes several forms, including chemical and neural systems. Neural systems connect cells and tissues both directly and indirectly, via the brain. Chemical signals are emitted by many different cells throughout the body and affect the processes of other cells both directly and indirectly, by affecting the functions of neurons. A primary function of the brain, as part of the central neural system, is to coordinate the activity of the various organs and tissues throughout the body in the interest of the organism's overall homeostasis. The brain also maintains a representation of the state of the body in its environment, projected forward (in time) to anticipate changes in the environment, as they might affect the body.

As animals developed in complexity, brains evolved the ability to project forward in time a representation of alternative future states of the organism in its environment as a way to maintain homeostasis through present actions. The

---

[2] If the organisms are of different species, this is called *symbiosis*. Both cooperation and symbiosis are vitally important to human homeostasis.

ability to predict behavior of other organisms (especially predators and prey) improved the ability of brain to maintain and respond to forward projection. Memory of past states and events, abstracted and continuously fitted to the present, improved prediction and forward projection. Humans are able to project, maintain, and compare multiple alternative forward projections, based on different assumptions, as a basis for evaluating alternative responses. The forward projected representation includes more or less detailed predictions about what will be perceived. Actual sensory input is aggregated, filtered, and interpreted according to these predictions and, in turn, contribute to updating the representation. To a large extent, we see what we expect to see.

The representations, both memory and future, include a dimension of time and causality, the basic elements of narrative. Stories are a fundamental element of both memory and cognition.[3] Human mental life includes a constant series of thoughts, mostly stories, which appear to play a role in maintaining awareness of the environment and readiness for action.

External Signals. For both sexual reproduction and coordination, social species require the ability to generate, display, recognize, and respond appropriately to signals. A *signal* can be any perceptible change in the physical environment that is produced for the purpose (or intention) of altering the state or behavior of another entity. Between organisms a signal can be a perceptible action or substance (such as a pheromone), a visible change in characteristics such as shape, color, or action, or an audible sound. To be detected, a signal must be readily differentiated from the background, the ordinary situation. Usually signals correspond to detectors that have evolved to detect a particular chemical substance, sound, or visible action, but humans are very good at creating signals from whatever is available and under volitional control.

Extending Homeostasis. As the social structure of their groups increased in size and complexity and became increasingly important to individuals' homeostasis, social interactions became an increasingly important part of the environment. This led to evolution of increased ability to monitor other group members' behavior and relationships, make complex inferences based on these observations, and represent and forward project condition of the self in the social as well as physical environment. Grooming (including play and cooperation as well as touch) and signals of aggressive intention, dominance, and submissiveness developed to help manage relationships.

The brain evolved abilities to monitor and keep track of complex social relationships, both by direct visual observation and by monitoring others' signals. At some point, this developed to include a representation of the social group itself and its collective homeostasis. The brain also evolved the ability to

---

[3] Schank and Abelson (1995); Schank and Berman (2002).

represent how others experience the world, including the social world (theory of mind), as a means of improving predictions of others' behavior (aggression, response to possible aggression, trust). This facilitates both cooperation and deception.

Language, Personhood, and Conversation

Some combination of visual and vocal signals, along with the developing theory of mind and the development of more complex interpersonal relationships, provided the impetus for expanding the repertoire of signals into a protolanguage. Language greatly increased the power of grooming and the ability to create and maintain increasingly complex relationships based on mutual trust and predictability. It also increased the complexity of play and grooming, leading eventually to discovery of toolmaking and to the emergence of a sense of personal identity, an independent *self*, within the context of relationships, subgroups, and the primary group.

There is evidence that other animals, including other primates, are able to learn and use several hundred "words" and string together two or even three signals. Sometimes these strings combine vocalization with gesture, but it is not yet certain how much "meaning" they express. Some other animals, including some primates, show evidence of rudimentary theory of mind, the ability to represent what another animal sees and believes, and of the ability to use signals deceptively. None of this approaches the sophisticated complexity of human language, but it is a plausible beginning.

At least two levels of theory of mind seems necessary for genuine language use. The lowest level is the ability to represent how another entity might perceive and respond to an utterance. There is evidence of this ability, first-order theory of mind, among some other animals, including several other species of primates and some birds. The second-order of theory of mind is the ability to represent how the other person represents one's own thoughts and intentions. For language use, this implies the ability to represent another person's prediction of how oneself will understand and respond to a signal.

Third-order theory of mind confers the ability to represent how others represent one's own thought processes. By extension, third-order theory of mind allows one to experience one's own mind as an object in its own right. Representing how others represent oneself and one's thought processes facilitates developing a sense of *self* within a relationship, or as a member of a group or tribe. This implies the ability to recognize and explicitly represent one's own social status, and how various social interactions might affect others' views of oneself – that is, to represent one's own "face." The ability to forward project how a communicative act might affect one's own face, one's social standing, or the face of a friend or other member of the group, greatly expands the potential of language use in conversation for grooming – or for symbolic aggression. It also contributes to the structure of conversation, and constitutes a large part of the meanings people infer from both language and other forms of signaling.

Language, along with other forms of signaling such as touch and vocalics, contributes to social bonding in many ways, including supporting others' face through compliments and so on. It also contributes to social control, both directly (through instruction, admonition, and criticism) and indirectly, through gossip, humor and mockery, metaphor, storytelling, and innuendo. Language developed for conversation, probably social at first, but the more complex society it supported required regulation, coordination, some form of collective decision-making. Decision-making requires forward projection, which requires memory and some way to decide among alternatives. For the individual, projecting futures and experiencing the emotions they excite drive decision-making; collective, shared emotion is important for group decision-making. Leaders and persuaders learned ways to guide and direct the collective emotion, and so to influence both the projected futures and the decisions.

Languages have developed in a wide variety of forms, using a range of signals. Most languages use vocal signals, supported by gesture and facial expression. In response, the human vocal tract and hearing capabilities have coevolved to support the use, detection, and interpretation of complex combinations of sounds with remarkable speed and acuity. Written languages have developed independently in many different cultures, using various combinations of symbols and images. All these have in common some combination of more or less abstract symbols that, singly or in combinations, represent ideas, concepts, or emotions. They also have in common some way of combining symbols into utterances and texts, such that it is possible to express an effectively infinite range of thoughts, ideas, and experiences. In face-to-face communication, language-based utterances are usually produced in combination with other signals (intonation, facial expression, etc.) that can be produced and understood independently but also extend and qualify the utterance and, at the extreme, function as part of the language.

Both syntax and vocabulary tend to follow recognizable rules within a speech community, to the point that members of that speech community will recognize (and sometimes reject) deviant syntactic constructions, pronunciation, or usage. However, both syntax and vocabulary (including pronunciation and "meaning") constantly change within speech communities and consequently vary among speech communities within the same broader language community, sometimes developing into distinct dialects and, eventually, into entirely separate languages (as Latin separated into French, Italian, Spanish, etc.) Words themselves often originate in metaphors or other transformations such as hyperbole or irony, which become lexicalized to the point that the conceptual insight of the original trope is forgotten or lost entirely.

Conversation. Language is usually produced as a sequence of signals, intonation units, and utterances, which express ideas or units of thought. These may be assembled into a compliment or insult, a declaration, a story, an explanation, and so on. Conversation, the basic form of language use,[4] is composed of sequences of utterances, usually three or more, often ranging over several topics.

Conversation structure is influenced by many factors, including efficient use of time and energy. Turn-taking and the typical "one speaker at a time" structure is a result of limits on attention and ability to discriminate sounds while speaking. The relatively short typical gap between speaking turns is influenced by considerations of efficiency and the speed of language processing relative to language production, but it would be impossible without our brain's ability to project forward and predict what another speaker is going to say and when they will finish saying it. Opening and closing, turn-taking signals, and back-channel cues are all influenced by the need to preserve one's own and the other's face, both for grooming and maintaining positive relationships in the interest of maintaining personal homeostasis and for maintaining the homeostasis of the relationship and the group. Although the most basic features of conversation (e.g. turn-taking) are common to all cultures and language communities,[5] these are realized in different ways, typical both of broad cultures and of the microcultures of groups and relationships.

Discourse

As relationships and coalitions become more important and come to be perceived as independent features of "social reality," social homeostasis becomes important to individual homeostasis. Language probably initially developed as a contributor to individual homeostasis, in that it improved the ability to develop and maintain relationships and coordinate with other members of a group or tribe for balancing one's own homeostasis needs. It led to the ability to exchange information (gossip) about other tribe members and about the social structure. The ability to exchange social information through gossip and the ability to plan and coordinate collaborative action provides the basis for intentional action on social structure – that is, to planning, organizing, and politics. Discourse began to develop as gossip about other members of the tribe, extended to discussion of the group-level homeostasis (e.g. where to forage, or find shelter, how to organize a settlement, and how to avoid or resolve conflicts). Extending

---

[4] Clark (1996).   [5] Enfield (2017).

theory of mind to deceased tribe members and to forces of nature, including significant animals, led to development of religion, which became important to maintaining the tribe's homeostasis and a topic of common concern contributed to the development of discourse.

As communication technology developed in ways that enlarged the social world for significant portions of society, primary reference groups came to be represented not only as the social environment for individual homeostasis but also in relation to other groups. Expanded and extended communication also expanded the social reality, so that increasingly large aggregations of people in an increasingly complex organizational structure became relevant to the homeostasis of individuals and their primary reference groups. A further extension of theory of mind is the ability to represent one's group or tribe as an independent entity with definable characteristics and interests, as it is perceived (represented) by other members of the group and by outsiders. This also entails the ability to represent "society" and even "humanity" as independent entities, and to represent both one's own group and oneself as a member of a group in relation both to other groups and to "society" or "humanity" generally. Thus we have groups, societies, and nations, as well as races, belief communities, and even political parties as distinct units, with composite characteristics and interests, all with a complex relationship to our own homeostasis and that of the groups with which we identify.

This complex social and cultural structure is at least potentially part of each individual's social reality, and relevant both to individual homeostasis and the homeostasis of primary reference groups. The relevance of an out-group to homeostasis may take the form of threat or competition, of potential cooperation, or of a potential target for aggression. Forward projection in the form of stories about these out-groups and their relationship to primary reference groups will become a part of both public discourse and private conversations. When diverse groups within a nation (or any large organization) identify themselves in opposition to each other, as in the contemporary United States, the public discourse is likely to separate into isolated, mutually incompatible discourses, each organized around and motivated by the drive to maintain its own homeostasis in the face of what is perceived as threatening. Whether individuals and their primary reference groups will continue to develop to the point of recognizing the importance of humanity to their individual and group homeostasis, so that the out-groups come to be recognized as collaborators rather than competitors and threats, remains to be seen.

Emotions and Values

Initially homeostasis referred just to the individual organism's dynamic balance of energy, nutrients, and wastes, then expanded to include information about external resources and threats. As hominids became increasingly social, the interaction of individual with group-level and whole-tribe homeostasis led to the development of emotion as a blend of arousal and evaluation. Emotion provides an analog summary of the social environment as it impinges on the individual's homeostasis, and the arousal component of emotion prepares the body for whatever action might be indicated. Emotional expression is also a resource in negotiating social relationships, at least in part because of its presumed predictive and explanatory value. As sources of pleasure, satisfaction, and distress, emotions are themselves a major factor in individual and group homeostasis. Group chorusing and dance-like synchronous movement is typical of some other primate species, and occurs in many traditional human societies. Group emotional solidarity and collective homeostasis may have been maintained and increased through chorusing and dance, and this probably contributed to development of language.

As communication technology leads to confronting and incorporating an ever-expanding array of "Other" groups, societies, and nations into the social reality of individuals and their reference groups, the forward projection of the state of one's own body and group in the social environment becomes increasingly complicated. Out-groups can be represented as threats to own homeostasis, as support for one's own homeostasis, or as a complex combination of threat and support. One way of understanding *values* is as an analog summary of these threats to and support for the homeostasis of oneself and one's reference groups, a group-level function similar to the function of emotion at the individual level.

Summary

To develop an objective account of human communication, research and theorizing must begin with the recognition that human bodies, including our brains, have evolved through random changes to the genome, conditioned by our interactions with an unpredictable and constantly changing physical and social environment. Humanity is an intensely social species, and this is reflected in the dialectic of competition and cooperation, aggression and sociability. Our brains and the minds they express are remarkably powerful, but they are also flawed, in ways that reflect the haphazard "good enough" process of evolution, the quasi-independent development and spread of memes, and the interaction of often contrary impulses.

A primary function driving the evolution of the brain was to coordinate the various organs and tissues and regulate the intake and output of the body to maintain homeostasis. This entailed developing the ability to represent the state of the body (and social person) in its physical (and social) environment and project it forward in time as a basis for guiding homeostasis-maintenance action in the present. As human society became increasingly complex and social relationships (both supportive peer relationships and hierarchical relationships) became more important to individual homeostasis, language developed. Initially language apparently served both grooming functions to maintain interpersonal relationships and surveillance functions to expand individuals' ability to surveil and hence accurately represent the social structure. As the surveillance and informative functions of language were readily expanded to include ecological surveillance and coordination of both social and ecological activity, language became more powerful, society became even more complex, and the homeostasis of reference groups became increasingly important to individual homeostasis.

Development of writing and other communication technologies expanded the reach and complexity of social organization further, leading to more complex layers of dependence on groups and organizations for homeostasis as well as to more complex competition within and between groups and larger units of social structure. Conversation expanded and reified as public discourse, incorporating both small group conversations and one-to-many communication through hierarchical religious organizations, written texts, and eventually electronic media. Although individual-level homeostasis has arguably become more complicated and in many cases disconnected from group- and societal-level homeostasis, the fundamental biological processes of homeostasis are still operative, influencing discourse by way of individual emotional responses to perceived threats and opportunities and individual representation of group-level values and representations.

The signals human communication depends on, including language, are inherently ambiguous, both because we use them in complex combinations to express such a range of thoughts and feelings and because they are imbedded in a potentially infinite set of contexts that are usually inadequately specified in our perceived mutual cognitive environment. Both creating and understanding a set of signals as a "message" entails a process of interpretation that includes inference and sometimes attribution and often includes requests for clarifying signals, repair (through additional signals), or both. The extent of this ambiguity varies from the relative precision that can be accomplished by use of a short and strongly emphasized signal (e.g. a loudly spoken "No!" or "I want my hamburger *without* mustard!"[6]) to the almost complete ambiguity that results from the use of contradictory signals or obscure allusions.

What is important about this account includes the granular level at which thought takes place, the complex array of signals through which thought is expressed and communicated, the role of representation and prediction,

---

[6] These examples illustrate how signals are used to qualify other signals, sometimes reduce the ambiguity, but also sometimes increasing it.

including partial activation of perceptual, motor, and emotional systems, and the inherent ambiguity of most communication. We don't know exactly how the brain accomplishes it, but we do know that the process implicates, to different degrees at different times, global knowledge about the world and the other participants in a conversation as well as local and immediate knowledge about what was just said and what will probably be said in the immediate future. It also implicates the individual's own hopes, purposes, and likely future utterances and actions. The complexity of the cognitive environment on all sides of a conversation partially accounts for the ambiguity and unpredictability of even the most routine, mundane exchange.

At the broader level of discourse, these individual cognitive and communication processes interact with the affordances of various communication media and with social structure. These interactions produce cultural representations that in turn form part of the backdrop of individual discourse, enter into, and help shape the mutual cognitive environment assumed in ordinary conversation.

In sum, research and theorizing about human communication must start with what actually happens in the observable world when one person creates or enacts a signal with the intention that another person perceive, interpret, and respond to it, and how this is accomplished by evolved biological brains-in-bodies.

Post-Script, Methodological Implications: Polysemy and Objectivity

Signals, including language, are often ambiguous, with interpretation and response dependent on the social context. Cognition, even by trained philosophers and scientists, is often flawed by selective perception and motivated reasoning. Even our physical perceptions are strongly influenced by what we expect to see, and often distorted by the processing "short-cuts" our brains must use, short-cuts that produce common perceptual illusions. Does this mean that objective knowledge is impossible?

If by *objectivity* we mean precise, detailed, and accurate representation of the physical and social environment, including causal relationships that allow precise predictions, then it is clearly impossible. However, I would argue that a weaker version, which might be labeled *objectivity**, is not only possible but also necessary to both individual and collective homeostasis. We know that our perception is subject to distortion and bias. As social scientists, we know that our research instruments (self-report surveys and even the most well-designed experiments) depend on how human subjects perceive and report what they perceive, using language subject to a range of subjective interpretation. We also know that as researchers, we are susceptible to flaws in our own reasoning, and the language we use to describe and interpret our observations is susceptible to misinterpretation and misunderstanding. However, it is not only the best we have. Setting aside mystical revelation and fact-free *a priori* reasoning (with our bias-prone and hormone-saturated brains), *it's all we have*.

On the positive side, even prior to the rise of modern science, humans developed social and cognitive techniques for improving and validating our knowledge of the world. We look at obscure or ambiguous objects (including the metaphorical "*objects*" of abstract thought) from different perspectives; we look at them again at a different time, we compare what we see to what others see, and we compare it all to our memories of what we have seen on other occasions. As we become aware of the biases and flaws in our perceptual and reasoning faculties, we allow for these as well as we can. The "scientific method" of inductive reasoning, tested by deductive reasoning and systematic observation and refined through replication and criticism, extends and institutionalizes this intuitive epistemology. It does not and cannot guarantee absolute, error-proof certainty about anything. It can and does improve our understanding of our physical and social environment, our ability to represent and simulate our environment in various ways and to project these representations forward as a basis for making predictions about future events that usually turn out to be reasonably accurate.

Objectivity* is not guaranteed to be free of personal bias or simple random error, but it is all we have. My own work, as reflected in this book, is based on reasoning from the best evidence I have been able to find, subject to the rule that every claim, every interpretation, must be consistent with the best available evidence. That principle, the principle of objectivity*, acknowledges that the best available evidence is subject to potential error and misinterpretation in observation, and occasionally even to misrepresentation (sometimes but not always deliberate). As better evidence becomes available, some of the claims and representations in this book will be substantiated; many of them will be contradicted or qualified. Absolute objectivity implies a "truth" that will never change. Objectivity* implies humility about our own limitations and an asymptotic relationship to knowledge, in which our understanding continues to approach, but can never hope to reach, "truth."

References

Abbott, H. P. (2008). *The Cambridge introduction to narrative* (2nd ed.). Cambridge: Cambridge University Press.

Adelman, P. K., and Zajonc, R. B. (1989). Facial efference and the experience of emotion. *Annual Review of Psychology, 40,* 249–280.

Apter, Michael J. (1991). A structural phenomenology of play. In Kerr, John A. and Apter, Michael J., eds., *Adult play: A reversal theory approach.* Amsterdam, The Netherlands: Swets & Zeitlinger, pp. 13–30.

Arbib, M. A. (2012). *How the brain got language.* Oxford: Oxford University Press.

(2013). *Language, music, and the brain: A mysterious relationship.* Cambridge, MA: MIT Press.

Arundale, R. B. (2010). Constituting face in conversation: Face, facework, and interactional achievement. *Journal of Pragmatics, 42,* 2078–2105.

Attardo, S. (2001). *Humorous texts: A semantic and pragmatic analysis.* New York: Mouton de Gruyter.

Bandura, A. (1965). Influence of models' reinforcement contingencies on the acquisition of imitative responses. *Journal of Personality and Social Psychology, 1,* 589–595.

(1971). *Social learning theory.* New York: General Learning Press.

Baron-Cohen, S. (2020a). Our restless minds. *New Scientist,* Dec. 5–11, pp. 34–39.

(2020b). *The pattern seekers: A new theory of human invention.* London: Allen Lane.

Barrett, L. F. (2017). *How emotions are made: The secret life of the brain.* New York: Houghton Mifflin Harcourt.

(2020). *Seven and a half lessons about the brain.* New York: Houghton Mifflin Harcourt.

Barsalou, L. W. (1999). Perceptual symbol systems. *Behavioral and Brain Sciences, 22,* 577–609.

(2003). Situated simulation in the human conceptual system. *Language and Cognitive Processes, 18,* 513–562.

(2008). Grounded cognition. *Annual Review of Psychology, 59,* 617–645.

Barsalou, L. W., and Wiemer-Hastings, K. (2005). Situating abstract concepts. In Pecher, D. and Zwaan, R., eds., *Grounding cognition: The role of perception and action in memory, language, and thought.* Cambridge: Cambridge University Press, pp. 129–163. Available at: www.psychology.emory.edu/cognition/barsalou/papers/Barsalou_Wiemer-Hastings_chap_2005_abstract_concepts.pdf.

Bateson, P. (2005). The role of play in the evolution of great apes and humans. In Pellegrini, A. D. and Smith, P. K., eds., *The nature of play: Great apes and humans.* New York: Guilford Press, pp. 13–26.

Baumeister, R. F., and Masicampo, E. J. (2010). Conscious thought is for facilitating social and cultural interactions: How mental simulations serve the animal–culture interface. *Psychological Review*, *117*, 945–971.

Bechara, A., Damasio, H., Tranel, D., and Damasio, A. R. (2005). The Iowa Gambling Task and the somatic marker hypothesis: Some questions and answers. *Trends in Cognitive Sciences*, *9*, 159–162. https://doi.org/10.1016.

Bem, D. J. (1972). Self-perception theory. In Berkowitz, L., ed., *Advances in experimental social psychology*, vol. 6. New York: Academic Press, pp. 1–62.

Beniger, J. R. (1983). Does television enhance the shared symbolic environment? Trends in labeling of editorial cartoons, 1948–1980. *American Sociological Review*, *48*, 103–111.

Bergen, B., and Wheeler, K. (2005). Sentence understanding engages motor processes. In *Proceedings of the Twenty-Seventh Annual Conference of the Cognitive Science Society*. Mahwah, NJ: Lawrence Erlbaum Associates

  (2010). Grammatical aspect and mental simulation. *Brain & Language*, *112*, 150–158.

Bergen, B. K. (2012). *Louder than words: The new science of how the mind makes meaning*. New York: Basic Books.

Berger, C. R. (1979). Beyond initial interaction: Uncertainty, understanding, and the development of interpersonal relationships. In Giles, H. and St. Clair, N., eds., *Language and social psychology*. Oxford: Basil Blackwell, pp. 122–144.

Berger, C. R., and Calabrese, R. J. (1975). Some explorations in initial interaction and beyond: Toward a developmental theory of interpersonal communication. *Human Communication Research*, *1*, 99–112.

Berger, P. L. (1979). *The heretical imperative: Contemporary possibilities of religious affirmation*. Garden City, NY: Doubleday.

Berger, P. L., and Luckmann, T. (1966). *The social construction of reality: A treatise in the sociology of knowledge*. New York: Doubleday.

Bickerton, D. (2009). *Adam's tongue: How humans made language, how language made humans*. New York: Hill & Wang.

Billig, M. (2005). *Laughter and ridicule: Towards a social critique of humor*. London: Sage.

Birdwhistell, R. (1970). *Kinesics and context: Essays on body motion communication*. Philadelphia: University of Pennsylvania Press.

Blow, C. M. (2021). History can be erased. It often has been. *New York Times* (on-line), May 19. www.nytimes.com/2021/05/19/opinion/capitol-riot-tulsa-massacre.html.

Borghi, A. M., Glenberg, A. M., and Kaschak, M. P. (2004). Putting words in perspective. *Memory and Cognition*, *32*, 863–873.

Boroditsky, L., and Prinz, J. (2008). What thoughts are made of. In Semin, G. R. and Smith, E. R., eds., *Embodied grounding: Social, cognitive, affective, and neuroscientific approaches*. Cambridge: Cambridge University Press, pp. 98–115.

Boroditsky, L., and Ramscar, M. (2003). Guilt by association: Gleaning meaning from contextual co-occurrence. *Proceedings of the 25th Annual Meeting of the Cognitive Science Society*, Boston, MA.

Borregine, K. L., and Kaschak, M. P. (2006). The action-sentence compatibility effect: It's all in the timing. *Cognitive Science*, *30*, 1097–1112.

Boulenger, V., Hauk, O., and Pulvermüller, F. (2009). Grasping ideas with the motor system: Semantic somototopy in idiom comprehension. *Cerebral Cortex*, *19*, 1905–1914.

Bro, H. H. (1971). *High play: Turning on without drugs.* New York: Paperback Library.
Brône, G., and Feyaerts, K. (2004). Assessing the SSTH and GTVH: A view from cognitive linguistics. *Humor – International Journal of Humor Research, 17*, 361–372.
Brown, P., and Levinson, S. C. (1987). *Politeness.* Cambridge: Cambridge University Press.
Bruner, J. (1983). *Child's talk: Learning to use language.* New York: Norton.
  (2002). *Making stories: Law, literature, life.* New York: Farrar, Straus, and Giroux.
Brunvand, J. H. (1981). *The vanishing hitchhiker: American urban legends and their meanings.* New York: Norton.
Buck, R. (1984). *The communication of emotion.* New York: Guilford.
Burgoon, J. K., Guerrero, L. K., and Floyd, K. (2016). *Nonverbal communication.* New York: Routledge.
Burgoon, J. K., and Hale, J. L. (1984). The fundamental topoi of relational communication. *Communication Monographs, 51*, 193–214.
Cabeza, R., Prince, S. E., Daselaar, S. M., Greenberg, D. L., Budde, M., Dolcos, F., and Rubin, D. C. (2004). Brain activity during episodic retrieval of autobiographical and laboratory events: An fMRI study using a novel photo paradigm. *Journal of Cognitive Neuroscience, 16*(9), 1583–1594.
Cacioppo, J. T., and Petty, R. E. (1982). The need for cognition. *Journal of Personality and Social Psychology, 42*(1), 116–131.
Cacioppo, J. T., Priester, J. R., and Berntson, G. G. (1993). Rudimentary determinants of attitudes: II. Arm flexion and extension have differential effects on attitudes. *Journal of Personality and Social Psychology, 65*, 5–17. www.dx.doi.org/10.1037/0022-3514.65.1.5
Callaway, E. (2014). Homo erectus made world's oldest doodle 500,000 years ago. *Nature News.* doi:10.1038/nature.2014.16477. S2CID 164153158.
Calvert, G. A., and Campbell, R. (2003). Reading speech from still and moving faces: The neural substrates of visible speech. *Journal of Cognitive Neuroscience, 15*, 57–70.
Cameron, L. J. (2003). *Metaphor in educational discourse.* London: Continuum.
  Principal Investigator (2006). Procedure for metaphor analysis. *The metaphor analysis project.* Milton Keynes, UK: Open University.
  (2007). Patterns of metaphor use in reconciliation talk. *Discourse and Society, 18*, 197–222.
Cameron, L. J., and Deignan, A. (2003). Using large and small corpora to investigate tuning devices around metaphor in spoken discourse. *Metaphor and Symbol, 18*, 149–160.
Cameron, L., and Maslen, R. eds. (2010). *Metaphor analysis: Research practice in applied linguistics, social sciences and the humanities.* London: Eqinox, pp. 161–179.
Cameron, L., Maslen, R., and Low, G. (2010). Finding systematicity in metaphor use. In Cameron, L. and Maslen, R., eds., *Metaphor analysis: Research practice in applied linguistics, social sciences and the humanities.* London: Eqinox, pp. 116–146.
Cantor, J. R., Bryant, J., and Zillmann, D. (1974). Enhancement of humor appreciation by transferred excitation. *Journal of Personality and Social Psychology, 30*, 812–821.

Cantor, J. R., and Zillmann, D. (1973). The effect of affective state and emotional arousal on music appreciation. *Journal of General Psychology, 89*, 97–108.

Cantor, J. R., Zillmann, D., and Bryant, J. (1975). Enhancement of experienced sexual arousal in response to erotic stimuli through mis attribution of unrelated residual excitation. *Journal of Personality and Social Psychology, 32*, 69–75.

Cappella, J. N. (1993). The facial feedback hypothesis in human interaction: Review and speculation. *Journal of Language and Social Psychology, 12*, 13–29.

Carroll, L. (1871). "Jabberwocky." From *Through the looking-glass, and what Alice found there.*

Carter, R. (2004). *Language and creativity: The art of common talk.* New York: Routledge.

Casasanto, D., and Boroditsky, L. (2008). Time in the mind: Using space to think about time. *Cognition, 106*, 579–593.

Casasanto, D., and Gijssels, T. (2015). What makes a metaphor an embodied metaphor? *Quellenangabe: Linguistics Vanguard.* ISSN (Online) 2199-174X, doi: 10.1515/lingvan-2014-1015, January 2015.

Chafe, W. (1994). *Discourse, consciousness, and time: The flow and displacement of conscious experience in speaking and writing.* Chicago, IL: University of Chicago Press.

(2012). From thoughts to sounds. In Gee, J. P. and Handford, M. (eds.), *The Routledge handbook of discourse analysis.* New York: Routledge, pp. 356–368.

Chaiken, S. (1979). Communicator physical attractiveness and persuasion. *Journal of Personality and Social Psychology, 3*, 1387–1397.

Cheney, D. L., and Seyfarth, R. M. (1985). Vervet monkey alarm calls: Manipulation through shared information? *Behaviour, 94*, 150–166.

Chiappe, D. L., and Kennedy, J. M. (2001). Literal bases for metaphor and simile. *Metaphor and Symbol, 16*, 249–276.

Cienki, A., and Müller, C. (2008). *Metaphor and gesture.* Amsterdam: John Benjamins.

Clark, A. (1997). *Being there: Putting brain, body, and world together again.* Cambridge, MA: MIT Press.

Clark, H. H. (1996). *Using language.* Cambridge: Cambridge University Press.

Clay, Z., and Zuberbuhler, K. (2014). Vocal communication and social awareness in chimpanzees and bonobos. In Dor, D., Knight, C. and Lewis, J., eds., *The social origins of language.* Oxford: Oxford University Press, pp. 105–125.

Coates, J. (2007). Talk in a play frame: More on laughter and intimacy. *Journal of Pragmatics, 39*, 29–49.

Colombetti, G. (2014). *The feeling body: Affective science meets the enactive mind.* Cambridge, MA: MIT.

Cook, G. (2000). *Language play, language learning.* Oxford: Oxford University Press.

Cook, R., Bird, G., Catmur, C., Press, C., and Heyes, C. (2014). Mirror neurons: From origin to function. *Behavioral and Brain Sciences,* 37(2), 177–192. doi: 10.1017/S0140525X13000903

Cooper, L. A., and Shepard, R. N. (1973). Chronometric studies of the rotation of mental images. In Chase, W. G., ed., *Visual information processing.* New York: Academic Press.

Corballis, M. C. (2004). The origins of modernity: Was autonomous speech the critical factor? *Psychological Review, 111*, 543–552.

Coulson, S (2001). *Semantic leaps: Frame-shifting and conceptual blending in meaning construction*. Cambridge: Cambridge University Press.
Crivelli, C., and Fridlund, A. J. (2018). Facial displays are tools of social influence. *Trends in Cognitive Sciences*, *22*, 388–399.
Csikszentmihalyi, M. (1980). *Flow: The psychology of optimal experience*. New York: Harper & Row.
Culpeper, J. (1996). Towards an anatomy of impoliteness. *Journal of Pragmatics*, *25*, 349–367.
  (2011). *Impoliteness: Using language to cause offence*. Cambridge: Cambridge University Press.
Culpeper, J., Bousfield, D., and Wichmann, A. (2003). Impoliteness revisited: With special reference to dynamic and prosodic features. *Journal of Pragmatics*, *35*(10/11), 1545–1579.
Curtis, M. E., and Bharucha, J. J. (2010). The minor third communicates sadness in speech, mirroring its use in music. *Emotion*, *10*(3), 335–348. www.doi-org.proxy.lib.pdx.edu/10.1037/a0017928.
Damasio, A. R. (1996). The somatic marker hypothesis and the possible functions of the prefrontal cortex. *Philosophical Transactions of the Royal Society of London. Series B: Biological Sciences*, 351(1346), 1413–1420. www.doi.org/10.1098/rstb.1996.0125.
  (1999). *The feeling of what happens: Body and emotion in the making of consciousness*. New York: Harcourt Brace & Co.
Damasio, A. (2018). *The strange order of things*. New York: Pantheon.
Davis, J. I., Senghas, A., Brandt, F., & Ochsner, K. N. (2010). The effects of BOTOX injections on emotional experience. *Emotion*, *10*, 433–440. doi: 10.1037/a0018690
Dawkins, R. (1976). *The selfish gene*. Oxford: Oxford University Press.
Dediu, D., and Levinson, S. C. (2014). The time frame of the emergence of modern language and its implications. In Dor, D., Knight, C. and Lewis, J., eds., *The social origins of language*. Oxford: Oxford University Press, pp. 105–125.
Demjén, Z. (2016). Laughing at cancer: Humour, empowerment, solidarity and coping online. *Journal of Pragmatics*, *101*, 18–30.
  (2018). Complexity theory and conversational humour: Tracing the birth and decline of a running joke in an online cancer support community. *Journal of Pragmatics*, *133*, 93–104.
Dennett, D. C. (2017). *From bacteria to Bach and back: The evolution of minds*. New York: Norton.
DeRuiter, J. P., Mitterer, H., and Enfield, N. J. (2006). Projecting the end of a speaker's turn: A cognitive cornerstone of conversation. *Language*, *82*, 515–535.
Desai, R. H., Binder, J. R., Conant, L. L., Mano, Q., R., and Seidenberg, M. S. (2012). The neural career of sensorimotor metaphors. *Journal of Cognitive Neuroscience*, *23*, 2376–2386.
Dessalles, J-L. (2014). Why talk? In Dor, D., Knight, C. and Lewis, J., eds., *The social origins of language*. Oxford: Oxford University Press, pp. 284–296.
Di Paolo, E. A., Rohde, M., and De Jaegher, H. (2010). Horizons for the enactive mind: Values, social interaction, and play. In Stewart, J., Gapenne, O. and Di Paolo, E. A., eds., *Enaction: Toward a new paradigm for cognitive science*. Cambridge, MA: MIT, pp. 33–87.

References

di Pellegrino, G., Fadiga, L., Fogassi, L., Gallese, V., and Rizzolatti, G. (1992). Understanding motor events: A neurophysiological study. *Experimental Brain Research*, 91(1), 176–180.

Dor, D. (2014). The instruction of imagination: Language and its evolution as a communication technology. In Dor, D., Knight, C. and Lewis, J., eds., *The social origins of language*. Oxford: Oxford University Press, pp. 105–125.

(2014). The instruction of imagination: Language and its evolution as a communication technology. In Dor, D., Knight, C. and Lewis, J., eds., *The social origins of language*. Oxford: Oxford University Press, pp. 318–324.

Douthat, R. (2017). Who are we? *New York Times*, Feb. 4. www.nytimes.com/2017/02/04/opinion/who-are-we.html.

Dunbar, R. (1996). *Grooming, gossip, and the evolution of language*. Cambridge, MA: Harvard University Press.

(2003). The social brain: Mind, language, and society in evolutionary perspective. *Annual Review of Anthropology*, 32, 163–181.

(2014). *Human evolution*. London: Pelican Books.

Dunn, B. D., Dalgleish, T., and Lawrence, A. D. (2006). The somatic marker hypothesis: A critical evaluation. *Neuroscience & Biobehavioral Reviews*, 30, 239–271.

Dutton, D., and Aron, A. (1974). Some evidence for heightened sexual attraction under conditions of high anxiety. *Journal of Personality and Social Psychology*, 30, 510–517.

DuVernay, A. (2014). *Selma*. Paramount Pictures.

Ehrsson, H. H., Geyer, S., and Naito, E. (2003). Imagery of voluntary movement of fingers, toes, and tongue activates corresponding body-part-specific motor representations. *Journal of Neurophysiology*, 90, 3304–3316.

Eibl-Eibesfeldt, I. (1970). *Ethology: The biology of behavior*. New York: Holt, Rinehart & Winston.

Eisenstein, E. (1980). *The printing press as an agent of change*. Cambridge: Cambridge University Press.

Ekman, P. (1993). Facial expression and emotion. *American Psychologist*, 48, 384–392.

Ekman, P., and Cordaro, D. T. (2011). What is meant by calling emotions basic? *Emotion Review*, 3, 364–370.

Ekman, P., and Friesen, W. V. (1971). Constants across cultures in the face and emotion. *Journal of Personality and Social Psychology*, 17, 124–129.

Enfield, N. J. (2017). *How we talk: The inner workings of conversation*. New York: Basic Books.

Enfield, N. J., and Sidnell, J. (2014). Language presupposes an enchronic infrastructure for social interaction. In Dor, D., Knight, C. and Lewis, J., eds., *The social origins of language*. Oxford: Oxford University Press, pp. 92–104.

Enticott, P. G., Johnston, P. J., Herring, S. E., Hoy, K. E., and Fitzgerald, P. B. (2008). Mirror neuron activation is associated with facial emotion processing. *Neuropsychologia*, 46, 2851–2854.

Epstein, R. H. (2018). *Aroused: The history of hormones and how they control just about everything*. New York: W. W. Norton & Company.

Esmaeili, P., Akhavan, B., and Amjad, F. A. (2015). Metaphorically speaking: Embodied conceptualization and emotion language in Tim O'Brien's *The things*

they carried. International Journal of Applied Linguistics & English Literature, *4*, 137–146.
Everett, D. L. (2017). *How language began: The story of humanity's greatest invention.* New York: Liveright.
Everts, E. (2003). Identifying a particular family humor style: A sociolinguistic discourse analysis. *Humor: International Journal of Humor Studies*, *16*, 369–412.
Fagen, R. (1995). Animal play, games of angels, biology, and Brian. In Pellegrini, A. D., ed., *The future of play theory: A multidisciplinary inquiry into the contributions of Brian Sutton-Smith.* Albany: State University of New York Press, pp. 23–44.
Farr, R. M., and Moscovici, S. (1984). *Social representations.* Cambridge: Cambridge University Press.
Fauconnier, G., and Turner, M. (2002). *The way we think: Conceptual blending and the mind's hidden complexities.* New York: Basic Books.
Fausey, C. M., and Boroditsky, L. (2010). Subtle linguistic cues influence perceived blame and financial liability. *Psychonomic Bulletin & Review*, *17*, 644–650.
  (2011). Who dunnit? Cross-linguistic differences in eye-witness memory. *Psychonomic Bulletin & Review*, *18*, 157.
Feirstein, B. (1982). *Real men don't eat quiche.* New York: Pocket Books.
Feldman, J. A. (2006). *From molecule to metaphor: A neural theory of language.* Cambridge, MA: MIT Press.
Fine, G. A., and DeSoucey, M. (2005). Joking cultures: Humor themes as social regulation in group life. *Humor*, *18–1*(2005), 1–22.
Fitzpatrick, M. A., and Ritchie, L. D. (1994). Communication schemata within the family: Multiple perspectives on family interaction. *Human Communication Research*, *20*(3), March, 275–301.
Fitzpatrick, M. A., Vance, L., and Witterman, H. (1984). Interpersonal communication in the casual interaction of marital partner. *Journal of Language and Social Psychology*, *3*, 81095.
Fodor, J. (1975). *The language of thought.* Cambridge, MA: Harvard University Press.
Ford, T. E., Richardson, K., and Petit, W. E. (2015). Disparagement humor and prejudice: Contemporary theory and research. *Humor*, *28*, 171–186.
Förster, J., and Strack, F. (1997). Motor actions in retrieval of valenced information: A motor congruence effect. *Perceptual and Motor Skills*, *85*, 1419–1427. www.doi.org/10.2466/pms.1997.85.3f.1419.
French Jr., J. R. P., and Raven, B. (1959). The bases of social power. In Cartwright, D., ed., *Studies in social power.* Ann Arbor, MI: Institute for Social Research, pp. 150–167.
Fuller, R. B. (1961). Tensegrity. *Portfolio and Art News Annual* (4), 112–127, 144, 148.
  (1982) [1975]. *Synergetics: Explorations in the geometry of thinking. I.* Macmillan. ISBN 978-0-02-065320-2.
Furley, P., Memmert, D., and Heller, C. (2010). The dark side of visual awareness in sport: Inattentional blindness in a real-world basketball task. *Attention, Perception, & Psychophysics*, *72*, 1327–1337. www.doi-org.proxy.lib.pdx.edu/10.3758/APP.72.5.1327.
Galati, D., Scherer, K. R., and Ricci-Bitti, P. E. (1997). Voluntary facial expression of emotion: Comparing congenitally blind with normally sighted encoders. *Journal*

of Personality and Social Psychology, 73(6), 1363–1379. www.doi.org/10.1037/0022-3514.73.6.1363.
Gallese, V., Fadiga, L., Fogassi, L., and Rizzolatti, G. (1996). Action recognition in the premotor cortex. *Brain*, 119(Pt 2), 593–609.
Gallese, V., and Goldman, A. (1998). Mirror neurons and the simulation theory of mind-reading. *Trends in Cognitive Sciences*, 2, 493–501.
Gamson, W. (1992). *Talking politics*. New York: Cambridge University Press.
Gendron, M., Roberson, D., van der Vyver, J. M., and Barrett, L. F. (2014). Perceptions of emotion from facial expressions are not culturally universal: Evidence from a remote culture. *Emotion*, 14(2), 251–262. www.doi-org.proxy.lib.pdx.edu/10.1037/a0036052.
Gentner, D., and Bowdle, B. F. (2001). Convention, form, and figurative language processing. *Metaphor and Symbol*, 16, 223–247.
Gerrig, R. J. (1993). *Experiencing narrative worlds: On the psychological activities of reading*. New Haven, CT: Yale University Press.
Giapraki, M., Moraitou, D., Pezirkianidis, C., and Stalikas, A. (2020). Humor in aging: Is it able to enhance wellbeing in community dwelling older adults? *Psychology: The Journal of the Hellenic Psychological Society*, 25, 128–150.
Gibbs Jr., R. W. (2000). Irony in talk among friends. *Metaphor and Symbol*, 15, 5–27.
  (2006). Metaphor interpretation as embodied simulation. *Mind and Language*, 21, 434–458.
  (2008). Metaphor and thought: The state of the art. In Gibbs Jr., R. W., ed., *The Cambridge handbook of metaphor and thought*. Cambridge: Cambridge University Press, pp. 3–16.
  (2011). The allegorical impulse. *Metaphor and Symbol*, 26, 121–130.
Gibbs Jr., R. W., and Boers, E. (2005). Metaphoric processing of allegorical poetry. In Maalej, Z., ed., *Metaphor and culture*. Tunis, Tunisia: University of Manouba Press.
Gibbs, R., Gould, J., and Andric, M. (2005–2006). Imagining metaphorical actions: Embodied simulations make the impossible plausible. *Imagination, Cognition, and Personality*, 25, 221–238.
Gibbs Jr., R. W., and Izett, C. D. (2005). Irony as persuasive communication. In Colston, H. L. and Katz, A. N., eds., *Figurative language comprehension: Social and cultural influences*. Mahwah, NJ: Lawrence Erlbaum, pp. 131–152.
Gibbs Jr., R. W., and Matlock, T. (2008). Metaphor, imagination, and simulation: Psycholinguistic evidence. In Gibbs Jr., R. W., ed., *The Cambridge handbook of metaphor and thought*. Cambridge: Cambridge University Press, pp. 161–176.
Ginsburg, S., and Jablonka, E. (2014). Memory, imagination, and the evolution of modern language. In Dor, D., Knight, C. and Lewis, J., eds., *The social origins of language*. Oxford: Oxford University Press, pp. 105–125.
Giora, R. (2003). *On our mind: Salience, context, and figurative language*. Oxford: Oxford University Press.
Giora, R., Balaban, N., Fein, O., and Alkabets, I. (2004). Negation as positivity in disguise. In Colston, H. L. and Katz, A., eds., *Figurative language comprehension: Social and cultural influences*. Mahwah, NJ: Erlbaum, pp. 233–258.
Glenberg, A. M. (2010). Embodiment as a unifying perspective for psychology. *Wiley Interdisciplinary Reviews: Cognitive Science*, 1, 586–596. www.doi.org/10.1002/wcs.55

Glenberg, A. M., and Kaschak, M. P. (2002). Grounding language in action. *Psychonomic Bulletin & Review*, *9*, 558–565.

Glenberg, A. M., Sato, M., Cattaneo, L., Palumbo, D., and Buccini, G. (2008). Processing abstract language modulates motor system activity. *Quarterly Journal of Experimental Psychology*, *61*, 905–919.

Glucksberg, S. (2001). *Understanding figurative language*. Oxford: Oxford University Press.

Goatly A. P. (2007). *Washing the brain: Metaphor and hidden ideology*. Amsterdam: Benjamins.

Godfrey-Smith, P. (2018). Primates, cephalopods, and the evolution of communication. In Seyfarth, R. M. and Cheney, D. L., eds., *The social origins of language*. Princeton, NJ: Princeton University Press, pp. 102–120.

Goffman, E. (1963). *Stigma: Notes on the management of spoiled identity*. New York: Touchstone.

Goffman, E. (1967). *Interaction ritual: Essays on face-to-face behavior*. New York: Anchor Books.

Greene, J. D. (2014). Beyond point-and-shoot morality: Why cognitive (Neuro)science matters for ethics. *Ethics*, *124*(4), 695–726.

Green, M. C. (2004). Transportation into narrative worlds: The role of prior knowledge and perceived realism. *Discourse Processes*, *38*, 247–266.

Grice, H. P. (1975). Logic and conversation. In Cole, P., ed., *Syntax and semantics* (vol. 9)*: Pragmatics*. New York: Academic Press.

Griffiths, P., and Scarantino, A. (2009). Emotions in the wild: The situated perspective on emotion. In Robbins, P. and Aydede, M., eds., *The Cambridge handbook of situated cognition*. Cambridge: Cambridge University Press, pp. 437–453.

Gruner, C. W. (1997). *The game of humor: A comprehensive theory of why we laugh*. London: Transaction.

Haidt, J. (2001). The emotional dog and its rational tail: A social intuitionist approach to moral judgment. *Psychological Review*, *108*, 814–834.

Halliday, M. A. K. (1998). Things and relations: Regrammaticising experience as technical knowledge. In Martin, J. R. and Veel, R., eds., *Reading science: Critical and functional perspectives on discourses of science*. London/New York: Routledge, pp. 185–237.

Halliday, M. A. K., and Matthiessen, C. M. I. M. (1999). *Construing experience through meaning: A language-based approach to cognition*. London and New York: Cassel.

Halpern, A. R., and Zatorre, R. J. (1999). When that tune runs through your head: a PET investigation of auditory imagery for familiar melodies. *Cerebral Cortex*, *9*, 697–704.

Havas, D. A., Glenberg, A. M., Gutowski, K. A., Lucarelli, M. J., and Davidson, R. J. (2010). Cosmetic use of botulinum toxin-A affects processing of emotional language. *Psychological Science*, *21*(7), 895–900. www.doi.org/10.1177/0956797610374742.

Hawkins, J. (2021): *A thousand brains: A new theory of intelligence*. New York: Basic Books.

Heyes, C., Bang, D., Shea, N., Frith, C. D., and Fleming, S. M. (2020). Knowing ourselves together: The cultural origins of metacognition. *Trends in Cognitive Sciences*, *24*, 349–362. www.doi.org/10.1016/j.tics.2020.02.007.

References

Hoey, M. (2005). *Lexical priming: A new theory of words and language.* London: Routledge.
Holmes, J., and Marra, M. (2002). Over the edge? Subversive humor between colleagues and friends. *Humor: International Journal of Humor Research, 15,* 65–87.
Hogan, P. C. (2003). *The mind and its stories.* Cambridge: Cambridge University Press.
Horgan, J. (1998). *The end of science.* London: Abacus.
Huizinga, J. (1955). *Homo Ludens; A study of the play-element in culture.* Boston, MA: Beacon Press.
Hurley, M. M., Dennett, D. C., and Adams Jr., R. B. (2011). *Inside jokes: Using humor to reverse-engineer the mind.* Cambridge, MA: MIT Press.
Hutchby, I. (1996). *Confrontation talk. Arguments, asymmetries and power on talk radio.* Hillsdale, NJ: Erlbaum.
Hutchins, E. (1994). *Cognition in the Wild.* Cambridge, MA: MIT Press.
Ijzerman, H., and Semin, G. R. (2009). The thermometer of social relations mapping social proximity on temperature. *Psychological Science,* 20(10), 1214–1220.
Iyengar, S. (1991). *Is anyone responsible? How television frames political issues.* Chicago: University of Chicago Press.
Jacobs, J. (1961). *Death and life of great American cities.* New York: Random House.
James, W. (1890/1981). *The principles of psychology.* Cambridge, MA: Harvard University Press.
Jamrozik, A., McQuire, M., Cardillo, E. R., and Chatterjee, A. (2016). Metaphor: Bridging embodiment to abstraction. *Psychonomic Bulletin & Review, 23,* 1080–1089. www.doi.org/10.3758/s13423-015-0861-0.
Jones, R. S. (1982). *Physics as metaphor.* New York: New American Library.
Kahneman, D., and Tversky, A. (1982). The simulation heuristic. In Kahneman, D., Slovic, P. and Tversky, A., eds., *Judgment under uncertainty: Heuristics and biases.* Cambridge: Cambridge University Press, pp. 201–208.
Kaschak, M. P., and Borregine, K. L. (2008). Is long-term structural priming affected by patterns of experience with individual verbs? *Journal of Memory and Language, 58,* 862–878.
Kaup, B., Lüdtke, J., and Zwaan, R. A. (2006). Processing negated sentences with contradictory predicates: Is a door that is open mentally closed? *Journal of Pragmatics, 38,* 1033–1050.
Kaup, B., Yaxley, R. H., Madden, C. J., Zwaan, R. A., and Lüdtke, J. (2007). Experiential simlations of negated tyext information. *Quarterly Journal of Experimental Psychology, 60,* 976–990.
Kendon, A. (2014). The 'poly-modalic' nature of utterances and its relevance for inquiring into language origins. In Dor, D., Knight, C. and Lewis, J., eds., *The social origins of language.* Oxford: Oxford University Press, pp. 67–76.
Kendrick, K. H., and Torreira, F. (2015). The timing and construction of preference: A quantitative study. *Discourse Processes, 52,* 255–289.
Keysar, B., Lin, S., and Barr, D. J. (2003). Limits on theory of mind use in adults. *Cognition,* 89(1), 25–41.
Kintsch, W. (1998). *Comprehension: A paradigm for cognition.* Cambridge: Cambridge University Press.
  (2000). Metaphor comprehension: A computational theory. *Psychonomic Bulletin and Review, 7,* 257–266.

(2008). How the mind computes the meaning of metaphor: A simulation based on LSA. In Gibbs Jr., R. W., ed., *The Cambridge handbook of metaphor and thought*. Cambridge: Cambridge University Press, pp. 129–142.

Knight, C., and Lewis, J. (2014). Vocal deception, laughter, and the linguistic significance of reverse dominance. In Dor, D., Knight, C. and Lewis, J., eds., *The social origins of language*. Oxford: Oxford University Press, pp. 105–125.

Koch, C. (2019). *The feeling of life itself: Why consciousness is widespread but can't be computed*. Cambridge, MA: MIT Press.

Koestler, A. (1964). *The act of creation*. London: Hutchinson.

Kohn, A. (1986). *No contest: The case against competition*. Boston: Houghton Mifflin.

Krippendorff, K. (2017). Three concepts to retire, *Annals of the International Communication Association*, 41(1), 92–99, doi: 10.1080/23808985.2017.1291281

Krout, M. H. (1954a). An experimental attempt to determine the significance of unconscious manual symbolic movements. *The Journal of General Psychology*, *51*, 121–152. doi: 10.1080/00221309.1954.9920210.

(1954b). An experimental attempt to produce unconscious manual symbolic movements. *The Journal of General Psychology*, *51*, 93–120. doi: 10.1080/00221309.1954.9920209.

Krzeszowski, T. P. (2020). Metaphors we communicate by. *Discourses on Culture*, *13*, 25–50. www.dyskursy.san.edu.pl/docs/dyskursy13.pdf#page=25.

Kuhn, D. (1991). *The skills of argument*. Cambridge: Cambridge University Press.

Kunda, Z. (1990). The case for motivated reasoning. *Psychological Bulletin*, *108*(3), 480–498.

Labov, W. (2013). *The language of life and death: The transformation of experience in oral narrative*. Cambridge: Cambridge University Press.

Labov, W., and Waletsky, J. (1967). Narrative analysis. In Helm, J., ed., *Essays on the verbal and visual arts*. Seattle: University of Washington Press, pp. 12–44.

Lakoff, G. (1996). *Moral politics: What conservatives know that liberals don't*. Chicago, IL: University of Chicago Press.

(2008). *The political mind*. New York, NY: Penguin.

(2014). Mapping the brain's metaphor circuitry: Metaphorical thought in everyday reason. *Frontiers of Human Neuroscience*, 16 December.

Lakoff, G., and Johnson, M. (1980). *Metaphors we live by*. Chicago, IL: University of Chicago Press.

(1999). *Philosophy in the flesh: The embodied mind and its challenge to western thought*. New York: Basic Books.

Lakoff, G., and Kövecses, Z. (1987). The cognitive model of anger inherent in American English. In Holland, D. and Quinn, N., eds., *Cultural models in language and thought*. Cambridge: Cambridge University Press, pp. 195–221.

Lakoff, G., and Nuñez, R. E. (2000). *Where mathematics comes from: How the embodied mind brings mathematics into being*. New York: Basic Books.

LaMarre, H. L., Landreville, K. D., and Beam, M. A. (2009). The irony of satire: Political ideology and the motivation to see what you want to see in *The Colbert Report*. *The International Journal of Press/Politics*, *14*, 212–231.

Lampert, M. D., & Ervin-Tripp, S. M. (2006). Risky laughter: Teasing and self-directed joking among male and female friends. *Journal of Pragmatics*, *38*, 51–72.

Landau, M. J., Meier, B. P., and Keefer, L. A. (2010). A metaphor-enriched social cognition. *Psychological Bulletin*, *136*(6), 1045–1067. doi: 10.1037/a0020970

Landauer, T. K., and Dumais, S. T. (1997). A solution to Plato's problem: The latent semantic analysis theory of acquisition induction, and representation of knowledge. *Psychological Review*, *104*, 211–240.

Lear, E. (1871). The owl and the pussycat. In *Nonsense Songs, Stories, Botany, and Alphabets*. In the public domain; original publication data not available.

LeDoux, J. (2012). Rethinking the emotional brain. *Neuron*, *73*, 653–676.

Lee, D. (1986). *Language, children & society: An introduction to linguistics & language development*. New York: New York University Press.

Leech, G. N. (1983). *Principles of pragmatics*. Harlow: Longman.

(2005). Politeness: Is there an East–West Divide? *Journal of Foreign Languages*, 6, 1–30.

Lehmann-Willenbrock, N., and Allen, J. A. (2014). How fun are your meetings? Investigating the relationship between humor patterns in team interactions and team performance. *Journal of Applied Psychology*, *99*, 1278–1287.

Lepper, M. R., Greene, D., and Nisbett, R. E. (1973). Undermining children's intrinsic interest with extrinsic reward: A test of the "overjustification" hypothesis. *Journal of Personality and Social Psychology*, *28*(1), 129–137.

Level, W. J. M. (1989). *Speaking: From intention to articulation*. Cambridge, MA: MIT Press.

Lewis, J. (2014). BaYaka Pygmy multi-modal and mimetic communication traditions. In Dor, D., Knight, C. and Lewis, J., eds., *The social origins of language*. Oxford: Oxford University Press, pp. 77–91.

Linder, S. B. (1970). *The harried leisure class*. New York: Columbia University Press.

Lindquist, K. A., Wager, T. D., Kober, H., Bliss-Moreau, E., and Barrett, L. F. (2012). The brain basis of emotion: A meta-analytic review. *Behavioral and Brain Sciences*, *35*, 121–202. doi:10.1017/S0140525X11000446.

Littlemore, J. (2019). *Metaphors in the mind: Sources of variation in embodied metaphor*. Cambridge: Cambridge University Press.

Lubin, A. (Director, 1941). *In the Navy*. Hollywood, CA: Universal Pictures.

Lucariello, J. M., Durand, T. M., and Yarnell, L. (2007). Social versus intrapersonal ToM: Social ToM is a cognitive strength for low-and middle-SES children. *Journal of Applied Developmental Psychology*, *28*(4), 285–297.

Lyons, J. (1977). *Semantics*. Cambridge: Cambridge University Press.

Malaby, T. (2006). Parlaying value: Capital in and beyond virtual worlds. *Games and Culture*, *1*, 141–162.

(2007). Beyond play: A new approach to games. *Social Science Research Network*, id922456.

Mao, F. (2010). *On cognition and function of grammatical metaphor*. A dissertation presented for the degree Doctor of Philosophy. Shanghai International Studies University.

Marshall, G. D., and Zimbardo, P. G. (1979). Affective consequences of inadequately explained physiological arousal. *Journal of Personality and Social Psychology*, *37*(6), 970–988.

Martin, R. A. (2007). *The psychology of humor: An integrative approach*. Amsterdam, The Netherlands: Elsevier.

Maslow, A. H. (1943). A theory of human motivation. *Psychological Review*, 50(4), 370–396.

Matlock, T. (2004). Fictive motion as cognitive simulation. *Memory and Cognition, 32*, 1389–1400.
Maturana, H. R., and Varela, F. J. (1980). Autopoiesis: The organization of living. In Maturana, H. R. and Varela, F. J., eds., *Autopoiesis and cognition*. Dordrecht: Reidel, pp. 73–155.
McNeill, D. (2000). *Language and gesture*. Cambridge: Cambridge University Press.
McNeill, D. (2005). *Gesture and thought*. Chicago, IL: University of Chicago Press.
  (2012). *How language began: Gesture and speech in human evolution*. Cambridge: Cambridge University Press.
McWhorter, J. (2018). Linguistics and pragmatics. In Seyfarth, R. M. and Cheney, D. L., eds., *The social origins of language*. Princeton, NJ: Princeton University Press, pp. 37–45.
Mead, G. H. (1934). *Mind, self, and society*. Chicago, IL: University of Chicago Press.
Meier, B. P., and Dionne, S. (2009). Downright sexy: Verticality, implicit power, and perceived physical attractiveness. *Social Cognition, 27*(6), 883–892.
Mezzacappa, E. S., Katkin, E. S., and Palmer, S. N. (1999). Epinephrine, arousal, and emotion: A new look at two-factor theory. *Cognition and Emotion, 13*, 181–199.
Miller, D. T. and McFarland, C. (1991). When social comparison goes awry: The case of pluralistic ignorance. In Suls, J. and Wills, T. A., eds., *Social comparison: Contemporary theory and research*. Hillsdale, NJ: Lawrence Erlbaum Associates, Inc, pp. 287–313.
Montpare, J. M. (1995). The impact of variations in height on young children's impressions of men and women. *Journal of Nonverbal Behavior, 19*, 31–47.
Moscovici, S. (1961). *La psychanalyse: Son image et son public*. Paris: Presses Universitaires de France.
Moyer-Gusé, E. (2008). Toward a theory of entertainment persuasion: Explaining the persuasive effects of entertainment-education messages. *Communication Theory, 18*, 407–425.
Müller, C., and Cienki, A. (2009). Words, gestures, and beyond: Forms of multimodal metaphor in the use of spoken language. In Forceville, C. J. and Urios-Aparisi, E., eds., *Multi-modal metaphor*. Berlin and New York: Mouton de Gruyter, pp. 297–328.
Muntigl, P., and Turnbull, W. (1998). Conversational structure and facework in arguing. *Journal of Pragmatics, 29*, 225–256.
Musolff, A. (2004). *Metaphor and political discourse. Analogical reasoning in debates about Europe*. Basingstoke: Palgrave-Macmillan.
  (2006). Metaphor scenarios in public discourse. *Metaphor and Symbol, 21*, 23–38.
Mutz, D. (2016). Harry Potter and the Deathly Donald. *PS: Political Science & Politics, 49*(4), 722–729. doi:10.1017/S1049096516001633
Mutz, D. C. (2007). Effects of "In-Your-Face" television discourse on perceptions of a legitimate opposition. *American Political Science Review, 101*(4), 621–635.
Mutz, D. C., and Reeves, B. (2005). The new videomalaise: Effects of televised incivility on political trust. *American Political Science Review, 99*(1), 1–15.
Nabi, R. L., Moyer-Gusé, E., and Byrne, S. (2007). All joking aside: A serious investigation into the persuasive effect of funny social issue messages. *Communication Monographs, 74*, 29–54.
Neal, D. T., and Chartrand, T. L. (2011). Embodied emotion perception: Amplifying and dampening facial feedback modulates emotion perception accuracy. *Social*

Psychological and Personality Science, 2(6), 673–678. www.doi.org/10.1177/1948550611406138.

Newcomb, T. M. (1968). Interpersonal balance. In Abelson, R. P., et al., eds., *Theories of cognitive consistency: A sourcebook*. Chicago: Rand McNally, pp. 28–51.

Norrick, N. R. (1993). *Conversational joking: Humor in everyday talk*. Bloomington: Indiana University Press.

(1997). Twice-told tales: Collaborative narration of familiar stories. *Language in Society*, 26, 199–220.

(2003). Issues in conversational joking. *Journal of Pragmatics*, 35, 1333–1359.

(2010). *Conversational narrative: Storytelling in everyday talk*. Amsterdam: Benjamins.

Norrick, N. R., and Spitz, A. (2010). The interplay of humor and conflict in conversation and scripted humorous performance. *Humor*, 23, 83–111.

Obama, B. (2008). A more perfect union. Constitution Center, Philadelphia, PA, March 18, 2008.

(2013). Remarks by the President on climate change at Georgetown University. www.whitehouse.gov.

Oberman, L. M., Winkielman, P., and Vilayanur, S. (2007). Face to face: Blocking facial mimicry can selectively impair recognition of emotional expressions. *Social Neuroscience*, 2, 167–178.

O'Brien, T. (1990). *The things they carried*. New York: Broadway Books.

Ong, W. (2002). *Orality and literacy: The technologizing of the word*. London: Routledge.

Pei, M. (1965). *The story of language* (2nd ed.). Philadelphia: Lippincourt.

Pepperberg, I. M. (2006). Cognitive and communicative abilities of grey parrots. *Applied Animal Behaviour Science*, 100, 77–86.

Perlmutter, D. D. (2002). On incongruities and logical inconsistencies in humor: The delicate balance. *Humor: International Journal of Humor Research*, 15, 155–168.

Perner, J., and Wimmer, H. (1985). "John thinks that Mary thinks that . . ." attribution of second-order beliefs by 5- to 10-year-old children. *Journal of Experimental Child Psychology*, 39(3), 437–471.

Petri, A. (2020). Relax and do not panic. Donald Trump is in charge. *Washington Post* (on-line), September 11, 2020. www.washingtonpost.com/opinions/2020/09/11/relax-do-not-panic-donald-trump-is-charge/. Accessed September 12, 2020.

Petty, R. E., and Cacioppo, J. T. (1981). *Attitudes and persuasion – classic and contemporary approaches*. Dubuque, IA: W. C. Brown.

Piaget, J., and Inhelder, B. (1967). *The child's conception of space*. New York: Norton. (Original work published 1948).

Plester, J. A., and Sayers, J. (2007). "Taking the piss": Functions of banter in the IT industry. *Humor*, 20, 157–187.

Pragglejaz Group (2007). MIP: A method for identifying metaphorically used words in discourse. *Metaphor and Symbol*, 22, 1–39.

Premack, D., and Woodruff, G. (1978). Does the chimpanzee have a theory of mind? *Behavioral and Brain Sciences*, 1(4), 515–526.

Price, V. (1992). *Public opinion*. Beverly Hills, CA: Sage.

Price, V., Tewksbury, D., and Powers, E. (1997). Switching trains of thought: The impact of news frames on reader's cognitive responses. *Communication Research*, 24, 481.

Prinz, J. J. (2007). *The emotional construction of morals.* Oxford: Oxford University Press.
Progovac, J. E. (2018). Fluency effects in human language. In Seyfarth, R. M. and Cheney, D. L., eds., *The social origins of language.* Princeton, NJ: Princeton University Press, pp. 46–61.
Pulvermüller, F. (1999). Words in the brain's language. Behavioral and Brain Sciences, *22*(2), 253–279. DOI: www.doi.org/10.1017/S0140525X9900182X.
Raskin, V. (1985). *Semantic mechanisms of humor.* Boston, MA: D. Reidel.
Raskin, J. D., & Attardo, S. (1994). Non-literalness and non-bona-fide in language: An approach to formal and computational treatments of humor. *Pragmatics & Cognition*, *2*(1), 31–69.
Raymond, G. (2003). Grammar and social organization: Yes/no interrogatives and the structure of responding. *American Sociological Review*, *68*, 939–967.
Reddy, M. J. (1993). The conduit metaphor: A case of frame conflict in our language about language. In Ortony, A., ed., *Metaphor and thought* (2nd ed.). Cambridge: Cambridge University Press, pp. 164–201.
Reps, P. (1957). *Zen flesh, Zen bones: A collection of Zen and pre-Zen writings.* New York: Doubleday Anchor.
Rinn, W. E. (1991). Neuropsychology of facial expression. In Feldman, R. S. and Rimé, B., eds., *Fundamentals of non-verbal communication.* Cambridge: Cambridge University Press, pp. 3–30.
Ritchie, L. D. (1986). Shannon - and Weaver: Unravelling the paradox of information. *Communication Research*, *13*(2), 278–298.
  (1991). *Communication concepts 2: Information.* Beverly Hills, CA: Sage.
  (2003a). Categories and similarities: A note on circularity. *Metaphor and Symbol*, *18*, 49–53.
  (2003b). "ARGUMENT IS WAR" – Or is it a game of chess? Multiple meanings in the analysis of implicit metaphors. *Metaphor and Symbol*, *18*, 125–146.
  (2003c). Uncertainty and the fragmentation of knowledge. In Dervin, B. and Chaffee, S., eds., *Communication: A different kind of horse race. Essays honoring Richard F. Carter.* Cresskill, NJ: Hampton Press.
  (2003d). Statistical probability as a metaphor for epistemological probability. *Metaphor and Symbol*, *18*, 1–12.
  (2004) Lost in "*Conceptual Space*": Metaphors of conceptual integration. *Metaphor and Symbol*, *19*, 31–50.
  (2005). Frame-shifting in humor and irony. *Metaphor and Symbol*, *20*, 275–294.
  (2006). *Context and connection in metaphor.* Basingstoke: Palgrave Macmillan Ltd.
  (2008). Gateshead revisited: The integrative function of ambiguous metaphors in a tricky political situation. *Metaphor and Symbol*, *23*, 24–49.
  (2009a). Relevance and simulation in metaphor. *Metaphor and Symbol*, *24*, 249–262.
  (2009b). Distributed cognition and play in the quest for the double helix. Ch. 11. In Pishwa, H., ed., *Language and social cognition: Expression of the social mind.* Berlin: Mouton de Gruyter, pp. 289–323.
  (2010). "*Everybody goes down*": Metaphors, stories, and simulations in conversations. *Metaphor and Symbol*, *25*, 123–143.
  (2011a). "*Justice is blind*": A model for analyzing metaphor transformations and narratives in actual discourse. *Metaphor and the Social World*, *1*, 70–89.

(2011b). Why the block is *the block*: Reinforcing community through casual conversation. *Metaphor and the Social World*, *1*, 240–261.

(2011c). "You're lying to Jesus!" Humor and play in a discussion about homelessness. *Humor*, *24*, 481–511.

(2012). Metaphor and stories in discourse about personal and social change. In Wagoner, B., Jensen, E. and Oldmeadow, J., eds., *Culture and social change: Transforming society through the power of ideas*. London: Information Age Publishing.

(2013). *Metaphor*. Cambridge: Cambridge University Press.

(2014). "*Born on third base*": Stories, simulations, and metaphor comprehension. Presented at the annual conference of Researching and Analyzing Metaphor, Cagliari, Italy.

(2017). *Metaphorical stories in discourse*. Cambridge: Cambridge University Press.

(2019). Reclaiming a unified American Narrative: Lexical, grammatical, and story metaphors in a discussion of polarized identities. *Metaphor and the Social World*, 9, 242–262.

(2021a). The "thinking meme" meme: Person and organism metaphors in Daniel Dennett's theory of cultural evolution. *Metaphor and the Social World*, 11(1), 122–144. ISSN 2210-4070 | E-ISSN 2210-4097.

(2021b). The "glass ceiling" of CMT: Homeostasis, codes, and metaphor. Unpublished ms., submitted.

Ritchie, L. D., and Cameron, L. (2014). Open hearts or smoke and mirrors: Metaphorical framing and frame conflicts in a public meeting. *Metaphor and Symbol*, *29*, 204-223.

Ritchie, L. D. and Dyhouse, V. (2008). FINE AS FROG'S HAIR: Three models for the development of meaning in figurative language. *Metaphor and Symbol*, 23, 85–107.

Ritchie, L. D., Feliciano, A., and Sparks, A. (2018). Rhetorical confinement, contrasting metaphors, and cultural polarities: "Yes we can" meets "Carnage in the cities." *Metaphor and the Social World*, *8*(2), 248–267.

Ritchie, L. D., and Fitzpatrick, M. A. (1990). Family communication patterns: Measuring intra-personal perceptions of inter-personal relationships. *Communication Research*, *17*(4), 523–544.

Ritchie, L. D., and Negrea-Busuioc, E. (2014). "*Now everyone knows I'm a serial killer*." Spontaneous intentionality in conversational metaphor and storytelling. *Metaphor and The Social World*, 4, 171–195.

Ritchie, L. D., and Schell, C. (2009). "*The ivory tower*" on an "*unstable foundation*": Playful language, humor, and metaphor in the negotiation of scientists' identities. *Metaphor and Symbol*, *24*, 90–104.

Ritchie, L. D., and Thomas, M. (2015). A "*glowing marble*": "*brushed with clouds*" or "*parched, scorched, and washed away*"? Obama's use of contrasting metaphors and stories in framing climate change. *Metaphor and the Social World*, 5, 1–19.

Ritchie, L. D., and Zhu, M. (2015). "Nixon stonewalled the investigation": Potential contributions of grammatical metaphor to conceptual metaphor theory and analysis. *Metaphor and Symbol*, *30*, 118–136.

Rizzolatti, G., and Arbib, M. (1998). Language within our grasp. *Trends in Neurosciences*, *21*, 188–194.

Rosch, E. H. (1973). Natural categories. *Cognitive Psychology*, *4*(3), 328–350.
  (1975). Cognitive representation of semantic categories. *Journal of Experimental Psychology*, *104*(3), 192–233.
Rozin, p., Lowery, L., Imada, S., and Haidt, J. (1999). The CAD triad hypothesis: A mapping between three moral emotions (contempt, anger, disgust) and three moral codes (community, autonomy, divinity). *Journal of Personality and Social Psychology*, *76*, 574–586.
Rutlede, L. L., and Hupka, R. B. (1985). The facial feedback hypothesis: Methodological concerns and new supporting evidence. *Motivation and Emotion*, *9*, 219–240.
Sampson, G. (2005). *The 'Language Instinct' debate*. New York: Continuum.
Sato, M., Schafer, A. J., and Bergen, B. K. (2015). Metaphor priming in sentence production: Concrete pictures affect abstract language production. *Acta Psychologica*, *156*, 136–142. www.doi.org/10.1016/j.actpsy.2014.09.010.
Sauter, D. A., Eisner, F., Ekman, P., and Scott, S. K. (2015). Emotional vocalizations are recognized across cultures regardless of the valence of distractors. *Psychological Science*, *26*, 354–356.
Schachter, S., and Singer, J. (1962). Cognitive, social, and physiological determinants of emotional state. *Psychological Review*, *69*, 379–399.
Schank, R. C., and Abelson, R. P. (1995). Knowledge and memory: The real story. In Wyer Jr., R. S., ed., *Knowledge and memory: The real story. Advances in Social Cognition,* Vol. VIII. Hillsdale, NJ: Lawrence Erlbaum Associates, pp. 1–86.
Schank, R. C., and Berman, T. R. (2002). The pervasive role of stories in knowledge and action. In Green, M. C., Strange, J. J. & Brock, T. C., eds., *Narrative impact: Social and cognitive foundations*. Mahwah, NJ: Lawrence Erlbaum Associates, pp. 287–314.
Schegloff, E. A., Jefferson, G., and Sacks, H. (1977). The preference for self-correction in the organization of repair in conversation. *Language*, *53*, 361–382.
Schiffrin, D. (1985). Everyday argument: The organisation of diversity in talk. In Van Dijk, T. A., ed., *Handbook of discourse analysis*. London: Academic Press, vol. 3, pp. 35–46.
Schilperoord, J., and Maes, A. (2009). Visual metaphoric conceptualization in editorial cartoons. In Forceville, C. J. and Urios-Aparisi, E., eds., *Multi-modal metaphor*. Berlin and New York: Mouton de Gruyter, pp. 213–240.
Schnurr, S., and Chan, A. (2011). When laughter is not enough. Responding to teasing and self-denigrating humour at work. *Journal of Pragmatics*, *43*, 20–35.
Schön, D. (1993). Generative metaphor: A perspective on problem solving in social policy. In Ortony, A., ed., *Metaphor and thought*. Cambridge: Cambridge University Press.
Schubert, T. W., Waldzus, S., and Seibt, B. (2008). The embodiment of power and communalism in space and bodily contact. In Semin, G. R. and Smith, E. R., eds., *Embodied grounding: Social, cognitive, affective, and neuroscientific approaches*. Cambridge: Cambridge University Press, pp. 160–183.
Scott, J. C. (2017). *Against the grain: A deep history of the earliest states*. New Haven, Connecticut: Yale University Press. Kindle Edition.
Searle, J. R. (1995). *The construction of social reality*. New York, London: Free Press.
Seligman, M. E. P., Railton, P., Baumeister, R. F., and Sripada, C. (2016). *Homo prospectus*. Oxford: Oxford University Press.

References

Seyfarth, R. M., and Cheney, D. L. (2018). The social origins of language. In Seyfarth, R. M. and Cheney, D. L., eds., *The social origins of language*. Princeton, NJ: Princeton University Press, pp. 9–33.

Shannon, C. (1948, July & October). The mathematical theory of communication. *Bell System Technical Journal*, *27*, 379–423, 623–656.

  (1956). The bandwagon. *IRE Transactions on Information Theory*, *2*, 3.

Shannon, C., and Weaver, W. (1949). *The mathematical theory of communication*. Urbana: University of Illinois Press.

Shanton, K., and Goldman, A. (2010). Simulation theory. *Wiley Interdisciplinary Reviews: Cognitive Science*, *1*(4), 527–538.

Shepard, R. N., and Metzler, J. (1971). Mental rotation of three-dimensional objects. *Science*, *171*, 701–703.

Sherzer, J. (2002). *Speech play and verbal art*. Austin: University of Texas Press.

Smith, C. (2021). We mourn for all we do not know. *The Atlantic Monthly*, *327*(2), 28–41.

Sperber, D. (2000). An objection to the memetic approach to culture. In Aunger, R., ed., *Darwinizing culture: The status of memetics as a science*. Oxford: Oxford University Press, pp. 163–174.

Sperber, D., and Wilson, D. (1986, 1995). *Relevance: Communication and cognition*. Cambridge, MA: Harvard University Press.

Spivey, M. J., and Geng, J. J. (2001). Oculomotor mechanisms activated by imagery and memory: Eye movements to absent objets. *Psychological Research*, *65*, 235–241.

Stanfield, R. A., & Zwaan, R. A. (2001). The effect of implied orientation derived from verbal context on picture recognition. *Psychological Science*, *12*, 153–156.

Steen, G. (2015). Developing, testing and interpreting Deliberate Metaphor Theory. *Journal of Pragmatics*. dx.doi.org/10.1016/j.pragma.2015.03.013.

Steen, G. S., Reijnierse, W. G., and Burgers, C. (2013). When do natural language metaphors influence reasoning? A follow-up study to Thibodeau and Boroditsky. *PLOS One*. www.plosone.org/article/info%3Adoi%2F10.1371%2Fjournal.pone.0113536.

Stivers, T. (2010). An overview of the question-response system in American English conversation. *Journal of Pragmatics*, *41*, 2772–2781. DOI:10.106/j.pragma.2010.04.0111.

Stohr, K. (2017). THE STONE: Our new age of contempt. *New York Times on-line*, Jan. 23. www.nytimes.com/2017/01/23/opinion/our-new-age-of-contempt.html.

Strack, F., Martin, L. L., & Stepper, S. (1985). The facial feedback hypothesis: Methodological concerns and new supporting evidence. *Motivation and Emotion*, *9*, 219–240.

  (1988). Inhibiting and facilitating conditions of the human smile: A nonobtrusive test of the facial feedback hypothesis. *Journal of Personality and Social Psychology*, *54*(5), 768–777. www.dx.doi.org/10.1037/0022-3514.54.5.768.

Sutton-Smith, B. (1995). Conclusion: The persuasive rhetorics of play. In Pellegrini, A. D., ed., *The future of play theory: A multidisciplinary inquiry into the contributions of Brian Sutton-Smith*. Albany: State University of New York Press, pp. 275–296.

Tabossi, P. (1989). What's in a context? In Gorfein, D. S., ed., *Resolving semantic ambiguity*. Berlin: Springer Verlag, pp. 25–39.

Tannen, D. (1984). *Conversational style: Analyzing talk among friends.* Norwood, NJ: Ablex.
  (1991). What's in a frame? Surface evidence for underlying expectations. In Tannen, D., ed., 1993. *Framing in discourse.* Oxford: Oxford University Press, Ch. 1, pp. 14–56.
Tassinary, L. G., and Cacioppo, J. T. (1992). Unobservable facial actions and emotion. *Psychological Science, 3*, 28–33.
Teng, N. (2009). Image alignment in multimodal metaphor. In Forceville, C. J. and Urios-Aparisi, E., eds., *Multi-modal metaphor.* Berlin and New York: Mouton de Gruyter, pp. 197–212.
Terrion, J. L., and Ashforth, B. E. (2002). From 'I' to 'we': The role of putdown humor and identity in the development of a temporary group. *Human Relations, 55*, 55–88.
Thagard, P. (2011). The brain is wider than the sky: Analogy, emotion, and allegory. *Metaphor and Symbol, 26*, 131–142.
Thagard, P., and Aubie, B. (2008). Emotional consciousness: A neural model of how cognitive appraisal and somatic perception interact to produce qualitative experience. *Consciousness and Cognition, 17*, 811–834.
Thagard, P., and Stewart, T. C. (2011). The AHA! Experience: Creativity through emergent binding in neural networks. *Cognitive Science, 35*, 1–33.
Thibodeau, P. H., and Boroditsky, L. (2011). Metaphors we think with: The role of metaphor in reasoning. *PLoS ONE, 6*(2), Feb 2011, ArtID e16782.
  (2015). Measuring effects of metaphor in a dynamic opinion landscape. *PLoS ONE*, Jul 28, *10*(7), e0133939.
Thibodeau, P. H., Iyiewuare, P. O., and Boroditsky, L. (2016). Metaphors we think with: The role of metaphor in reasoning. *PLoS ONE, 6*(2), Feb 2011, ArtID e16782.
Thorson, E., Wicks, R., and Leshner, G. (2012). Experimental methodology in journalism and mass communication research. *Journalism & Mass Communication Quarterly, 89*(1), 112–124. www.doi.org/10.1177/1077699011430066.
Tom, G., Ramil, E., Zapanta, I., Demir, K., and Lopez, S. (2006). The role of overt head movement and attention in persuasion. *The Journal of Psychology, 140*(3), 247–253. www.doi.org/10.3200/JRLP.140.3.247-253.
Tomasello, M. (2008). *Origins of human communication.* Cambridge, MA: MIT Press.
Topolinski, S., Lindner, S., and Freudenberg, A. (2014). Popcorn in the cinema: Oral interference sabotages advertising effects. *Journal of Consumer Psychology, 24*(2), 169–176. www.doi.org/10.1016/j.jcps.2013.09.008.
Tourangeau, R., and Rips, L. (1991). Interpreting and evaluating metaphors. *Journal of Memory and Language, 30*, 452–472.
Tracy, K. (1997). Interactional trouble in emergency service requests: A problem of frames. *Research on language and social interaction, 30*, 315–343.
Tseng, M., and Bergen, B. (2005). Lexical processing drives motor simulation. In *Proceedings of the Twenty-Seventh Annual Conference of the Cognitive Science Society.*
Valedesolo, P., and DeSten, D. (2016). Manipulations of emotional context shape moral judgment. *Psychological Science, 16*, 476–477.

References

Varela, F. J., Thompson, E., and Rosch, E. (1991). *The embodied mind: Cognitive science and human experience*. Cambridge, MA: MIT Press.

Veblen, T. (1973). *The theory of the leisure class. With an introduction by John Kenneth Galbraith*. Boston, MA: Houghton Mifflin.

Vidmar, N., and Rokeach, M. (1974). Archie Bunker's bigotry: A study in selective perception and exposure. *Journal of Communication*, 24, 36–47.

Watson, J. D. (1968). *The double helix*. New York: Penguin.

Watzlawick, P., Beavin (Bavelas), J., and Jackson, D. D. (1967/2011). *A study of interactional patterns, pathologies, and paradoxes*. New York: Norton.

Weaver, W. (1949). Recent contributions to the mathematical theory of communication. In Shannon, C. and Weaver, W., eds., *The mathematical theory of communication*. Urbana: University of Illinois Press, pp. 1–28.

Wellman, H. M., Fang, F., and Peterson, C. C. (2011). Sequential progressions in a theory-of-mind scale: Longitudinal perspectives. *Child Development*, 82(3), 780–792.

Wells, G. L., and Petty, R. E. (1980). The effects of over head movements on persuasion: Compatibility and incompatibility of responses. *Basic and Applied Social Psychology*, 1(3), 219–230. www.doi.org/10.1207/s15324834basp0103_2.

Westby, C., and Robinson, L. (2014). A developmental perspective for promoting theory of mind. *Topics in Language Disorders*, 34(4), 362–382.

Wheatley, T., and Haidt, J. (2005). Hypnotic disgust makes moral judgments more severe. *Psychological Science*, 16, 780–784.

Wheeler, M. E., Petersen, S. E., and Buckner, R. L. (2000). Memory's echo: Vivid remembering reactivates sensory-specific cortex. In *Proceedings of the National Academy of Sciences. (USA)*, 97, 11125–11129.

Whitehead, C. (2014). Why humans and not apes: The social preconditions for the emergence of language. In Dor, D., Knight, C. and Lewis, J., eds., *The social origins of language*. Oxford: Oxford University Press, pp. 105–125.

Whiten, A. (2021). The burgeoning reach of animal culture. *Science*, 372(6537), eabe6514. doi: 10.1126/science.abe6514.

Williams, L. E., and Bargh, J. A. (2008). Experiencing physical warmth influences interpersonal warmth. *Science*, 322, 606–607.

Wilson, A. E., and Ross, M. (2001). From chump to champ: People's appraisals of their earlier and present selves. *Journal of Personality and Social Psychology*, 80(4), 572.

Wilson, D., and Sperber, D. (2004). Relevance theory. Chapter 27. In Horn, L. R. and Ward, G., eds., *The handbook of pragmatics*. Oxford: Blackwell Publishing, pp. 607–632.

Wilson, E. O. (2017). *The origins of creativity*. New York: Liveright.

Wilson, P. R. (1968). Perceptual distortion of height as a function of ascribed academic status. *The Journal of Social Psychology*, 74(1), 97–102. DOI: 10.1080/00224545.1968.9919806

Winograd, T., and Flores, F. (1986). *Understanding computers and cognition*. Norwood, NJ: Ablex.

Yaxley, R. H., and Zwaan, R. A. (2007). Simulating visibility during language comprehension. *Cognition*, 150, 229–236.

Zajonc, R. B., Murphy, S. T., and Englehart, M. (1989). Feeling and facial efference: Implications of the vascular theory of emotion. *Psychological Review*, 96, 395–416.

Zbikowski, L. M. (2009). Music, language, and multimodal metaphor. In Forceville, C. J. and Urios-Aparisi, E., eds., *Multi-modal metaphor*. Berlin and New York: Mouton de Gruyter, pp. 359–381.

Zhong, C.-B., and Leonardelli, G. J. (2008). Cold and lonely: Does social exclusion literally feel cold? *Psychological Science*, *19*, 838–842.

Zhong, C. B., and Liljenquist, K. (2006). Washing away your sins: Threatened morality and physical cleansing. *Science*, *313*, 1451–1452.

Zillmann, D., and Cantor, J. R. (1976). A disposition theory of humor and mirth. In Chapman, T. and Foot, H., eds.), *Humor and laughter: Theory, research, and applications*. London: Wiley, pp. 93–115.

Zillmann, D., Hoyt, J. L., and Day, K. D. (1974). Strength and duration of the effect of aggressive, violent, and erotic communications on subsequent aggressive behavior. *Communication Research*, *1*, 286–306.

Zwaan, R. A. (2014). Embodiment and language comprehension: Reframing the discussion. *Trends in cognitive sciences*, 18(5), 229-234.

  (2015). Situation models, mental simulations, and abstract concepts in discourse comprehension. *Pscychonomic Bulletin Review*. DOI: 10.3758/s13423–015-0864-x.

Zwaan, R. A., Madden, C. J., Yaxley, R. H., and Aveyard, M. E. (2004). Moving words: Dynamic mental representations in language comprehension. *Cognitive Science*, *28*, 611–619.

Zwaan, R. A., and Radvansky, G. A. (1998). Situation models in language comprehension and memory. *Psychological Bulletin*, 123(2), 162–185. www.dx.doi.org/10.1037/0033-2909.123.2.162.

Zwaan, R. A., Stanfield, R. A., and Yaxley, R. H. (2002). Language comprehenders mentally represent the shapes of objects. *Psychological Science*, *13*, 168–171.

Zwaan, R. A., and Taylor, L. J. (2006). Seeing, acting, understanding: Motor resonance in language comprehension. *Journal of Experimental Psychology: General*, *135*, 1–11.

Index

Abbott, H. P., 266–267
Abelson, R. P., 267
abstract symbols, 11, 27, 70, 99
Action Units, facial, 102–103
action-sequence compatibility effect, 91
ad hoc signals, 143–144
Adams, R. B. Jr., 44n155, 183n644, 208, 216, 250
adrenaline, 44, 165
affect, 101, 114–116
affective valence, 117, 156
  interoceptive experience and, 107, 109, 115, 119
  relationships and, 156
affiliation, signals of, 142
affordance, 125, 279
  of tools, 54, 56
aggression
  aggression theory, 248
  avoidance systems and, 109
  coercive power and, 175–176
  communication relationships and, 163–164
  coping with, 51
  homeostasis and, 174, 246
  humor and, 174, 207, 247–249
  mating and, 39
  playful language and, 207
  sexual, 61, 69
  signals of, 61
  survival circuits and, 106
agon (competition), 211
Akhavan, B., 230
alea (games of chance), 211
Allen, J. A., 255
ambiguity
  communication and, 7
  joke resolution and, 252
  of language, 50, 72, 98, 134, 149
  metaphor and, 240
  signals and, 143
Amjad, F. A., 230
analogy, 241–244

animal communication, 53, 242–244
Arbib, M. A., 221
argumentation
  communication and, 185
  conflict talk and, 203
  conversation and, 204–206
  layering and, 202
  play and, 214
  silent, 205
Aron, A., 107
arousal
  action and, 308
  neurons and, 39
  physiological, 111, 117, 121, 140
  sensory input and, 109
  survival circuits and, 39, 108
arousal, emotion and, 96, 107, 114–116, 119
Arundale, R. B., 187–188, 190
Attardo, S., 249–250
attribution, 107, 129
audience, 151–153, 284–287
auditory metaphor, 236
autonomy, perceived, 161, 167
autopoesis, 2, 21
avoidance systems, 109
awareness, phenomenal, 36
axons, 23

back-channel signals, 139
background knowledge, 50, 191, 226
Baldwin effect, 34, 43
Bargh, J. A., 243
Baron-Cohen, S., 16, 181
Barrett, L. F.
  basic emotions, 105
  body budget, 106
  emotion and communication, 104, 106n446
  emotion specificity, 112
  interoception, 119
  language and emotion, 114–115
  layers and, 202

333

334   Index

Barsalou, L. W.
  computational processing, 22n93
  conceptual thought, 87
  introspection, 37
  perceptual simulations, 2, 11, 86, 93, 242
Basic Emotion Theory, 112
Baumeister, R. F., 83–84
Beam, M. A., 262
Beavin (Bavelas), J., 13, 128
Bem, D. J., 83
Bergen, B. K., 90
Berman, T. R., 264
bitter humor, 261
Blow, C. M., 296
bonding, interpersonal, 15, 49, 207
Borghi, A. M., 90
Boroditsky, L.
  cognitive science origins, 85
  frames, 95
  human conceptual system, 97
  perceptual simulations, 92–93
  symbol relations, 97
Bowdle, B. F., 242
brain, 22–23. *See also* forward projection
  computer model of, 6, 8, 27, 29
  consciousness and, 37
  dual-mode, 171
  embodiment perspective and, 22–23, 30–31
  emotion and, 102, 106
  hemispheric specialization of, 38–39
  homeostasis and, 302, 308
  meme theory and, 75–79
  mentalese and, 1, 27, 86
  mind and, 15
  simulation and, 146
  social relationships and, 303
  structure of, 30–31
brain-body connection, 30
Broca's area, 33, 38, 68, 132
Bruner, J., 221, 264
Brunvand, J. H., 273
Bryant, G., 225, 232
Bryant, J., 108
Buck, R., 109n458

Cacioppo, J. T., 7n47, 98, 104, 171n602, 184, 242
Cameron, L. J., 151, 224, 228, 244
Cantor, J. R., 108, 247
Cappella, J. N., 109
cellphone, 286–287
central nervous system, 22–23, 29
cerebral cortex, 11, 55
Chafe, W., 100, 138
Chaffee, S. H., 6

Chan, A., 256
character types in story, 266–268
Cheney, D. L., 60, 62, 64
Chomsky, N., 85
Civil War, US, 293–298
civility schema, 168
Clark, A., 216
Clark, H. H., 149–151, 182, 201, 268
Clinton, H., 152, 227
Coates, J., 217, 272
code metaphor, 70, 187, 190, 282n1013
cognition. *See also* computer model of cognition; metacognition
  defined, 280
  embodied, 1, 11, 19
  evolution of, 47–63
  extended, 281, 288
  feelings as dimension of, 55
  homeostasis and, 51, 55
  humor and, 250–251
  language and, 81–100
  need for, 184
  signaling and, 302–304
  theory of, 28
cognitive context, 147–149, 158. *See also* cognitive environment
  affective valence and, 156
  common ground and, 147
  cues and, 153
  culture and, 158–160
  discourse context and, 153–154
  face and, 160
  frames and, 156–158
  homeostasis and, 161
  multiple, 252
  mutual cognitive environment and, 148
  participants as part of, 151
  perceived autonomy and, 161
  personal identity and, 148
  relationships and, 154–156
  relevance and, 148–149
  schemas and, 147, 151
  scripts and, 147, 154
  types of conversation, 152–153
cognitive environment. *See also* mutual cognitive environment
  cognitive context and, 147–148, 151, 154
  common ground and, 147
  defined, 148
  face and, 161
  forward projection and, 161
  impoliteness and, 161
  representation and, 178
Cognitive-Affective Model, 241–242
Colbert, S., 262

Index

collaborative story, 270–271, 273, 278
Colombetti, G., 112–113, 120
common ground
  cognitive context and, 147
  communication and, 146
  conversation and, 192
  establishing, 149–150
  maintaining, 161
  mutual cognitive environment and, 147, 161
  relationships and, 161
  representation and, 178
  theory of mind and, 60–61, 67
communication. *See also* metacommunication; metaphor, computer; signals; technology, communication
  aggression and, 163–164
  animal, 52–55
  biological basis of, 7–9, 12
  brain and, 22–23, 30–31
  central nervous system and, 22–23
  cognition and, 11–12
  communication media, 279
  concepts of, 13–15
  conceptual perspective, 7
  consciousness and, 84
  cultural, 7, 12–13
  defined, 13, 128
  embodiment perspective, 6, 20
  emotion and, 106, 120–121
  facework and, 181
  functions of, 146
  homeostasis and, 6, 15–44, 166, 301–311
  indirect, 223
  instruction and, 203
  intentionality and, 57, 125–131
  invention and, 17
  language development and, 63–65
  metaphorical terms for, 13–15
  metaphors of communication and, 9–11
  mutual cognitive environment and, 147
  nonverbal/nonlexical, 118, 130, 142
  paratelic communication, 80, 164, 186
  physical environment and, 146
  physiology of, 30–31, 40–43
  process of, 1, 146
  relevance and, 148–149
  representation and, 15–18
  reproductive fitness and, 57
  reward systems and, 43–44
  social, 6, 12
  social environment and, 146
  social perspective, 6–7
  symbolic, 64
  telic, 185–186
  theory of, 1, 4, 7
  theory of mind and, 59
communicative context, 43, 91, 145
competition
  games and, 208
  play and, 211–212
  relationships and, 164
  social interaction and, 174
  status, 61
comprehension, semantic association models of, 225–226
computer model of cognition
  coding and, 27
  communication and, 8–9
  communication signals and, 28
  digital mind, the, 85–86
  embodiment perspective and, 27–30
  inadequacy of, 29
  model of the brain, 27–30
  neurons and, 27, 29
  problem-solving and, 88
computer/internet, 286
Conceptual Metaphor Theory, 2, 11, 121, 228
conceptual metaphors, 226–234
  abstract concepts and, 93, 120, 234, 244
  analogy and, 242–244
  complex concepts and, 215
  generic, 244
  interpretation of, 233
  language development and, 70
  simulations and, 70
  system of, 121
conflict talk, 203–205
Conjoint Co-Constituting Model of Communication, 187–191
consciousness, 81–85. *See also* mind
  awareness and, 2
  brain and, 37
  communication and, 84
  development of, 71
  messages and, 2
  representation and, 15, 84
  role of, 83–85
  self-awareness and, 16
contested identity story, 272
context, 146–161. *See also* cognitive context; social context
  common ground and, 149–150
  culture and, 158–160
  discourse, 153
  elements of, 146
  framing and, 156–158
  homeostasis and, 161
  interpretation and, 115, 149–150, 241
  physical environment and, 158

context (cont.)
    politeness and, 160–161
    relationship and, 155–156
    relevance and, 147–149
    social setting and, 150–153
    story and, 265
Context-Limited Simulation Theory, 97–100, 244
conversation, 182–206
    argumentation and, 204–206
    beginnings of, 192
    broader discourse and, 155
    code metaphor and, 190
    common ground and, 192
    communication media and, 279–300
    comprehension and, 2
    conflict talk and, 203–204
    Conjoint Co-Constituting Model of Communication and, 187–191
    contextual knowledge and, 147
    culture and, 178–180
    defined, 289
    delay in, 196–197, 275, 286
    deliberation and, 127
    evolution of, 46–47, 62
    face and, 186, 197
    fine structure of, 187–191
    flow of language in, 139
    forward projection and, 184–186, 195–196
    frames and, 158, 192–193
    functions of, 186
    genres of, 202–206
    grooming and, 164, 182
    homeostasis and, 161, 182–206
    impoliteness and, 185
    intentionality and, 127
    language and, 46–47, 304–306
    layers and, 201
    logic and, 204–206
    mediated context, 152–153
    narrative skills and, 183
    paratelic communication and, 186
    participants in, 151
    personhood and, 304–306
    physical environment and, 158
    play frames and, 203
    play in, 216–220
    politeness and, 160–161
    positive response preference in, 198, 275
    power and, 174–177, 193
    public discourse vs., 289–292
    purposes of, 154
    readiness for, 191
    recursion in, 200–202
    relationships and, 180–181
    relevance and, 160–161
    repairs and, 200
    sequence of utterances in, 189
    settings for, 150–153, 202–206
    signals and, 132, 138–140, 306
    social dominance and, 183
    speaker support in, 140
    status and, 174–177, 193
    storytelling in, 138, 268–276
    structure of, 65, 186–200
    telic communication and, 185–186
    termination of, 192
    topic changes and, 192–193
    turn-taking and, 139, 193–200
conversation machine, the, 185, 193
conversational delay, 196–197, 286
convolution, 241–242
Cook, G., 211, 215
cooperation, 302
coordination, 40, 49, 71
Corballis, M. C., 63
cortisol, 44, 165
creativity, 58, 215, 242, 263, 278
Crivelli, C., 112
Csikszentmihalyi, M., 210
cues
    affective, 106
    affordances and, 126
    emotional, 104, 117–119
    face and, 306
    framing and, 157, 160
    intentionality and, 177
    nonverbal, 124
    patterns and, 128–130
    vs. signals, 14
    social, 94
    speaker support and, 140
    turn-taking and, 194, 272
Culpeper, J., 169
cultural communication, 12–13
cultural construction model of emotion, 109
cultural development, 5, 16, 49, 69
cultural practice, 62, 73–75, 78
cultural processes, 62, 78
culture
    abstract concepts and, 227
    adaptation and, 287
    cognitive context and, 158–160
    control and, 174
    culture wars, 276
    defined, 158
    development of, 280
    dimensions of, 159
    display rules and, 113
    emotion categories and, 115

Index

expectations and, 179, 186
gestures and, 135
group, 166
homeostasis and, 164–165
joking, 218, 255–257
master-plots and, 267
meme propagation and, 181
representation and, 179, 248
reproductive fitness and, 12
signals and, 141
social settings and, 150
curiosity, 17, 68, 208, 213

Damasio, A.
  computational processing, 22n93
  computer metaphor, 9
  cross-excitation, on, 23
  emotion, 2, 96, 116
  forward projection, 26, 114, 149
  homeostasis, 4, 21, 107
  perception, 22, 86
  representation, 55, 148
  representation and, 51
  somatic marker hypothesis, 116
  survival circuits, 39
Dawkins, R., 7, 20n85, 73–74
De Jaegher, H., 22n93
Dediu, D., 47
delay, conversational, 196–197, 286
deliberate metaphor, 240
deliberation, 127, 205
Demjén, Z., 257
dendrites, 23
Dennett, D. C.
  cultural evolution model, 75
  fitness of memes, the, 78
  homeostasis, 165n583
  humor, 44n155, 183n644, 208, 216, 250
  meme evolution, 76
  meme propagation, 181
  memes, 7, 74–75, 78
DeRuiter, J. P., 194
DeSoucey, M., 218, 255
Dessalles, J. L.
  friendship, 176, 216
  language play, 221
  relationships, 278
  social functions of language, 51, 55, 183–184
Di Paolo, E. A., 22n93
digital code model, 43, 134, 142–143
discourse
  development of, 306
  fragmentation of, 299
  gossip and, 306

  public, 206
  society, of, 288
  technology, communication and, 280, 299
discourse context, 153, 155, 189
displacement, 56, 81
display, emotional, 101, 140–141
DNA, 23
dominance, social, 183
dopamine, 25, 44
Dor, D., 28n108, 49
Douthat, R., 276, 291, 293–294, 297–298
drift, language, 72
dualism, mind-body, 1
Dumais, S. T., 72, 96, 225
Dunbar, R.
  cognition and language, 55
  friendship, 168
  gossip/grooming, 6, 12
  grooming, 182, 184
  social functions of language, 51, 72, 123
  social structure, 71
  social themes, 267
Dutton, D., 107
DuVernay, A., 298
Dyhouse, V., 238

Ekman, P.
  basic emotions, 106, 110, 113–114
  emotion categories, 103
  expression matching, 118
  facial Action Units, 103
  research procedures, 104
Elaboration Likelihood Model, 7n47, 77, 98
electronic media, 285–287
emblems, 135–136
embodiment perspective, 1
  action, coordinating, 40
  brain and, 22–23, 30–31
  central nervous system and, 22–23
  cognition and, 19
  communication and, 6–9
  computer model of cognition and, 27–30
  evolution and, 20–21
  experience and, 37
  hemispheric specialization and, 38–39
  homeostasis and, 21–22
  memory and, 37–38
  metaphors of communication and, 9–11
  mind and, 20
  perception and, 34–37
  physiology and, 40–43
  representations, coordinating, 40
  reward systems and, 43–44
  social communication and, 2–18
  survival circuits and, 39–40

emotion, 101–122. *See also* emotion, arousal and
  affect and, 114–116
  basic, 101–103, 140
  Basic Emotion Theory, 112
  biological basis of, 115
  bodily effect of, 113
  categories of, 103–104, 106, 115, 119–120, 150
  communicating, 117–121
  complex social organization and, 116
  core affect and, 101
  cues and, 117–119
  cultural construction of, 106–109, 115
  enactive view of, 112–114
  entrained, 112
  excitation transfer and, 107–109
  expressions of, 120
  facial Action Units and, 102
  facial feedback effect and, 109
  homeostasis and, 99, 109–112, 307–308
  interoception and, 96, 119
  methodological issues in the study of, 104–105
  mirror neurons and, 111
  natural kind theory of, 137
  nonverbal expression of, 101
  perceptual simulation and, 95–96
  physiology of, 106
  psychological constructionist theory of, 101
  reason and, 116–117
  self-attribution of, 107
  signals and, 117–119
  simulation of, 120
  social emotions, 105, 112
  strategic signaling and, 111–112
  survival circuits and, 105–106, 108, 110
  symbols and, 111
  volition and, 131
emotion, arousal, and, 114–116
  emotion categories and, 115
  excitation transfer and, 107
  induced, 107
  interoception and, 119, 145
  perceptual simulations and, 96
empathy, 16, 67, 181, 300
endorphins
  bonds and, 15
  grooming and, 44, 210, 212
  humor and, 253
  pleasure circuits and, 210
  positive affect and, 114
  relationships and, 165
  reward systems and, 109, 167, 213
  social behavior and, 44

Enfield, N. J.
  conversation machine, the, 185, 193
  question phrasing, 198
  sound particles, 132
  turn-taking, 194–196
environment, 21n88, 22n80, 22. *See also* cognitive environment
ephapsis, 29
Esmaeili, P., 229–230
Everett, D. L.
  abstract concepts, 68
  computer metaphor, 28n108
  evolution of human intelligence, 71
  gesture and language development, 67
  language, purpose of, 49
  language and physiology, 40
  language development, 50, 62
  language patterns, 47
  sign progression theory, 56
Everts, E., 217
evidence, 205
evolution
  brain and, 308
  cognition and, 47–51
  creationist account of, 10
  cultural, 5, 7, 75
  embodiment perspective and, 6
  evolutionary pressures, 57
  fitness and, 20
  genetic, 43, 73, 287
  human intelligence and, 71
  humor and, 250–251
  language development and, 47–51, 71, 79
  neural systems, of, 22
  process of, 61
  reward systems, of, 43
  signaling and, 65, 131
  social organization and, 161
  stimulus-response systems and, 131
  storytelling and, 264
  vocabulary and, 65
excitation transfer, 107–109
expectations, 179, 186, 190
experience, conversation and, 37, 49
exteroception, 15, 22, 34, 119

face. *See also* face-threatening act; face-work
  grooming and, 187, 193
  homeostasis and, 110, 169
  impoliteness and, 166–174, 185
  lying and, 172
  negative, 160, 166, 168–169, 212
  play and, 212
  politeness and, 160, 185

Index

positive, 160, 166–168, 212
privacy and, 172
reactance and, 168
relationships and, 156, 160
sexual morality and, 172
turn-taking and, 197
face-threatening act. *See also* face; face-work
civility and, 168
cognitive environment and, 161
conversation and, 186
defined, 161
effects of, 167
homeostasis and, 169–171, 173
humor and, 256
impoliteness and, 170
irony and, 260
morality and, 173
repairs and, 200
social control and, 173
status and, 193
strategic impoliteness and, 170
facework. *See also* face; face-threatening act
defined, 17
development of, 71
exchange and, 168
forward projection and, 190
homeostasis and, 171–173
relationships and, 160, 164, 166–174
representation and, 170
theory of mind and, 71
facial efference, 109
facts, 205, 287, 291–292
fake news, 298–299
feelings, 19–44, 55
fiction, 284
Fine, G. A., 218, 255
flow, 210–211
flow of language, 71, 138–139
forward projection
alternative realities and, 221
brain and, 26, 114, 195, 221
cognitive context and, 149
cognitive environment and, 161
conversation and, 184–186
decision-making and, 305
facework and, 190, 304
group, 307–308
homeostasis and, 21, 99, 110
interoception and, 119
interpersonal relations and, 178
logic and, 185
social context and, 111
social status and, 174
storytelling and, 79, 221
turn-taking and, 195–196

frames, 94–95
attentional, 58
Civil War and, 293
conflict in, 293
cues and, 160
defined, 156–158
humor and, 249–251, 258
incongruity and, 249
play and, 203, 208, 217, 222, 248, 262
recipient design principle, 190
scripts and, 158
topic changes and, 192–193
wordplay and, 214
French, J. R. P. Jr, 175
Frenkel, N., 225
Fridlund, A. J., 112
Friesen, W. B., 103–104

Galati, D., 103
Gamson, W., 249, 254
gaps, experiential, 49
Gendron, M., 104
genes
detrimental, 20n73
DNA and, 23
evolution and, 43
forward-looking behavior and, 22
reproductive fitness and, 20n85, 73
the selfish, 73
genres, conversational, 186, 202–206
Gentner, D., 242
gestures
coded, 135–136, 192
culture-specific, 135
development of, 67
gesture language, 53
imitation of, 64
language and, 63
nonsymbolic, 48
social status and, 141
speech and, 139
turn-taking and, 194
as words, 47
Gettysburg, Battle of, 295
Gibbs, R., 87, 259–262
Giora, R., 92, 251
glass ceiling, 225, 227, 232–233
Glenberg, A. M., 91
glia, 23, 29
Goatly, A. P., 28n108
Godfrey-Smith, S., 60, 62
Goethe, J. W., 284
Goffman, E., 156, 160, 167
gossip, 12
cultural frames and, 260

gossip (cont.)
  discourse and, 306
  exchanging news as, 3
  homeostasis and, 16
  relationships and, 72, 182
  secondary surveillance, as, 79
  surveillance function of, 16
Graded Salience Theory, 251
grammar, 62, 68
grammatical metaphor, 234–235
Greene, J. D., 3, 171
Grice, H. P., 161
Griffiths, P., 111, 117, 119
grooming
  bonding, interpersonal, 15
  cell-phones and, 286
  conversation and, 164, 182
  endorphins and, 44, 210, 212
  face and, 187, 193
  as function of language, 6
  language and, 72, 304
  play and, 221
  politeness and, 169, 185
  protolanguage and, 64
  relationships and, 3, 12, 166, 176
  signals and, 53, 67
group homeostasis. *See also* homeostasis
  bitter humor and, 246
  degrees of, 302
  early hominids and, 51
  emotions and, 308
  facework and, 171
  impoliteness and, 171, 185
  individual and, 150
  interactions and, 182, 303
  language and, 280
  maintenance of, 164
  narrative and, 292
  relationships and, 164–166
  social control and, 173–174
  social emotions and, 105
  sweet humor and, 247
  threats to, 174, 232
group identity
  defined, 289
  status and, 177
  story and, 274, 276, 278, 289
  wordplay and, 213
Gruner, C. W., 247–248

Halliday, M. A. K., 69, 234
Hawkins, J., 95
hearing, 30, 36, 305
hemispheric specialization, 38–39

heuristics, moral, 3
Heyes, C., 62, 75n311, 106n446, 121
Hogan, P. C., 267
homeostasis, 2, 15–44. *See also* group homeostasis
  aggression and, 174, 246
  brain and, 99, 302
  cognitive context and, 161
  communication and, 6, 301–311
  conversation and, 182–206
  defined, 301
  emotion and, 107, 109–112, 307–308
  expanded groups and, 307
  face and, 110, 169–172
  face-threatening acts and, 169–171, 173
  feelings and, 19–44
  forward projection and, 21, 99, 110
  gossip and, 16
  humor and, 246–247, 261
  individual vs. group, 166
  language and, 79–80
  mind and, 125
  morality and, 173
  narrative, 292
  nervous system and, 15
  perception and, 19–44
  play and, 213, 220–221
  politeness and, 169
  process of, 21, 99, 295
  relationships and, 164–166, 177
  representation and, 99
  reproductive fitness and, 65, 123
  signaling and, 19–44, 61
  survival circuits and, 39–40
  vocabulary and, 64
Homo erectus, 33, 43
hormones, 39, 44, 109
humor, 246–263. *See also* humor, incongruity and
  aggression and, 174, 207, 247–249
  ambiguity and, 252
  bitter, 246, 261, 263
  cognition and, 250–251
  cognitive context, 250
  conflict talk and, 204
  coping mechanism, as, 257–259
  endorphins and, 253
  evolution and, 250–251
  face threats and, 256
  frames and, 249–251, 258
  Graded Salience Theory and, 251
  groups and, 255
  homeostasis and, 246–247, 261
  humor cultures, 255–257
  informativeness and, 251

Index

irony and, 246–263
play frames and, 203, 248, 262
playful, 253–254
political, 261
relevance and, 251–253
Relevance Theory and, 252
schemas and, 252
social interaction and, 254–257
stringing a line, 220
sweet, 246, 263
teasing and, 254
theories of, 247–257
humor, incongruity and, 183n644, 247, 249–250, 254, 257–258
Hurley, M. M., 44n155, 183n644, 208, 216, 250

identity. *See also* group identity
accents and, 142
collective, 46
contested, 272
homeostasis and, 295
metaphor and, 243–245
national, 277
the self and, 82–83
stories and, 276–277
theory of mind and, 60
ilinx, 211
illusion, perceptual, 5
illustrators, 136–137
images, visual, 281–282
imitation
cues and, 118
memes and, 76, 106
play and, 58
totemic, 67–68
vocabulary and, 64
impoliteness
cognitive environment and, 161
face and, 169–170, 185
group homeostasis and, 171, 185
intentional, 66
morality and, 172–173
strategic, 170, 172–173, 185n650
theory, 169–170
incivility, 170
incongruity. *See also* humor, incongruity and
deep, 250
frames and, 249
irony and, 222
metaphor and, 227
perceptual simulations and, 250
play and, 208, 221–222, 253
recognition, 221
resolution of, 44n155, 263

indexes, 57
information theory, 51, 51n181
informativeness, humor and, 251–252
instruction, 5, 12, 64, 78, 203
intentionality
communication and, 57
deliberate, 127
genes and, 73
nonconscious/nondeliberate, 127
nonverbal communication and, 130
signals and, 125–131
theory of mind and, 62–63
interoception
emotion and, 96, 119
forward projection and, 119
internal environment and, 22
nervous system and, 15
perception and, 34
phenomenal awareness and, 36
representation and, 30
simulations and, 87
survival circuits and, 105
interpersonal bonding, 49
interpretation
context and, 115, 149–150, 241
history and, 294
intended, 237
recipient design principle, 190
representations and, 287
sequential interpretation principle, 189
intonation unit, 138, 282
introspection
emotion and, 96
introspective awareness, 34, 82
metacognition and, 37, 87, 119
meta-simulation and, 68
perception and, 115
invention, communication and, 17
irony
face-threatening acts and, 260
humor and, 246–263
incongruity and, 222
metaphor and, 235
Izett, C. D., 260, 262

Jackson, D. D., 13, 128
Johnson, M.
analogy, 242
conceptual metaphors, 11, 93, 215, 228, 234
metaphor, 69n284
juvenile play, 209–210

Kahneman, D., 3
Kaschak, M. P., 91
Kaup, B., 92

Kintsch, W., 97, 226n802
Koch, C., 69n278
Kohn, A., 208
Kövecses, Z., 230
Krippendorff, K., 10
Krzeszowski, T. P., 9, 15
Kuhn, D., 3

Labov, W., 264, 266, 269, 277
Lakoff, G.
  analogy, 242
  conceptual metaphors, 11–12, 93, 215, 228, 230, 234–235
  metaphor, 69n284
  perceptual simulations, 93
LaMarre, H. L., 262
Landauer, T. K., 72, 96, 225
Landreville, K. D., 262
language. *See also* non-verbal/non-lexical communication
  ambiguity of, 50, 72, 98
  animal communication and, 52–55
  cognition and, 81–100
  components of, 49–50
  contemporary, 72–73
  coordinating action and, 71–72
  defined, 47–51
  development of, 63–65
  digital code, as, 134
  drift of, 72
  early, 48
  embedded, 201
  emblems and, 135–136
  embodied simulation, 87
  emotion and, 115
  evolution of, 15–16, 46–63, 79
  figurative uses of, 133
  flow of, 139
  framing and, 156–158
  gestures and, 53, 63
  grooming and, 72, 304
  homeostasis and, 79–80
  memes and, 73–79
  natural, 27–28, 28n109, 93, 96–97, 99
  origins of, 46, 49, 221–222
  perceptual simulations and, 88
  personhood and, 304–306
  representation and, 50
  role of, 8
  sign languages, 131
  sign progression theory and, 56
  signals and, 65–67, 125–132, 305
  social bonding and, 305
  social interaction and, 161, 183
  social tool, as, 55–58
  surveillance function of, 279
  syntax and, 68–71
  telic uses of, 66–67
  theory of mind and, 304
  turn-taking and, 139
  uses of, 48, 85–88
  vocabulary and, 67–68
  word form and, 134–135
  written language, 282–283
language play. *See* play
larynx, 42
Latent Semantic Analysis, 96
layering, 201–202, 268
LeDoux, J.
  emotions, 110
  negative affect, 114
  survival circuits, 39, 99, 105, 117, 119
Leech, G. N., 161
Lehman-Willenbrock, N., 255
Leonardelli, G. J., 243
Lepper, M. R., 208, 210
Levinson, S. C., 47
lexical priming, 97
lexicon, 47, 49
logic, formal, 3, 185, 204–206
logic indicators, 68
Luckmann, T., 280
Lüdtke, J., 92
lying, 172

Mao, F., 234
mapping, metaphors and, 228, 241
Marshall, G. D., 107
Masicampo, E. J., 83
master-plots, 266–268
Maturana, Humberto R., 2, 21
McNeill, D., 67
McWhorter, J., 68
meaning, private intentional, 50
media
  audience and, 284–287
  communication and, 17, 279
  electronic, 285–287
  misinformation and, 298
  print, 283–284
  role of, 280
  social, 292, 298
  technologies, 297
  visual images, 281–282
  written language, 282–283
memes
  competence without comprehension, 78
  cultural practice and, 73–75
  defined, 74
  development of, 76

Index

evolution of, 75–76, 75n311, 78
fitness of, 78
imitation and, 76, 106
logic as, 185
memeplex, 61, 74–75
pernicious, 5
play and, 213
print media and, 284
reproductive fitness and, 76
social interaction and, 17
social media and, 287
spread of, 74
suicide meme, 44, 76–77
symbolic behaviors as, 61
theory of, 75–79
ways, as, 74
memory
declarative, 38
dynamic nature of, 84–85
embodiment perspective and, 37–38
episodic, 38, 85
implicit, 37–38
semantic, 38
situational, 65
story and, 267
types of, 37–38
mentalese, 1, 27, 28n108, 86
metacognition, 16, 37, 65, 84, 87. *See also* cognition
metacommunication, 16, 66. *See also* communication
metaphor, 223–245. *See also* Conceptual Metaphor Theory; conceptual metaphors
ambiguity and, 240
analogy and, 242–244
auditory, 236
background knowledge and, 226
code, 14, 70
Cognitive-Affective Model and, 242
communication and, 9–11
computer, 8, 14, 19, 23, 27–30
container/conduit metaphor, 9
convolution, 242
creativity and, 58
dead/sleeping, 224
defined, 69n284, 224
deliberate, 240
development of, 69
emotion and, 115, 229
figurative language, as, 133
generic, 229
gestures and, 136–137
grammatical, 234–235
identity and, 243–245
incongruity and, 227
indirect communication, as, 223
interpretation and, 233, 241
lexical, 223–225
mappings and, 228, 241
metaphorical terms, 5–6
multimodal, 235–236
perceptual simulations and, 93–94, 98, 226, 240, 242
personal identity and, 243–245
playful, 238–240
schemas and, 69
self-perception and, 243
semantic association model, 225–226
semantic connections and, 240
simulations and, 215, 240–241
social structure and, 243–245
story and, 236–240, 270–271
thematic, 244
transcategorization, 234
visual, 235
word origins and, 305
meta-simulation, 68
metonymy, 223–225
mimicry, 69, 211
mind, 1–2, 15, 19–20, 81–83. *See also* theory of mind; consciousness
mind-wandering, 82
mirror neurons, 54, 64, 111
mirror systems, 68
morality, 171–172
emotion and, 96
face-threatening acts and, 173
frameworks for, 96
homeostasis and, 173
moral judgment, 170–171
reasoning and, 96, 171
sexual, 172
strategic impoliteness and, 172–173
morphemes, 134
morphology, 48, 134–135. *See also* word form
Moscovici, S., 165
motivated reasoning, 3, 3n31, 5, 205, 262, 298
multimodal metaphor, 235–236
muscular activity, 40, 91–92
music, 113, 285
mutual cognitive environment. *See also* cognitive environment
common ground and, 147–148
communication and, 98, 144, 149
establishment of, 149
humor and, 190, 251
physical environment and, 158
relationships and, 161
signals and, 309

Mutz, D. C., 170
myelin, 23

narrative. *See also* story
  chronological sequence in, 266
  conflicting, 294–298
  defined, 264–266
  foundational, 297
  frame conflict and, 293
  hero in, 292
  homeostasis and, 292
  incongruity and, 222
  national, 276–277, 291
  skills, 183
  societal, 292–298
national identity, 277
natural language, 27–28, 28n109, 93, 96–97, 99
neocortex, 25, 27
nervous system, 15, 22–23, 29
neural functioning, 23–27
neural processes, 4, 83, 112
neural system
  consciousness and, 69n278
  evolution of, 43
  homeostasis and, 125
  language and, 280
  perceptual simulations and, 86
  signaling and, 302
  triggering event and, 112
neural transmission, 23, 25, 27, 29
neurons, 23
  arousal and, 39
  computer metaphor and, 27, 29
  mirror, 64, 111
  pyramidal, 37
nonverbal/nonlexical communication, 101, 118, 124, 130
nonverbal/nonlexical communication and signals
  ambiguity of, 142
  functions of, 12, 47, 144
  meaning and, 64
  representation and, 124
  written language and, 283
norepinephrine, 44
Norrick, N. R., 203, 219, 234, 249, 269, 277
Nuñez, R. E., 93

Obama, B., 224, 228, 234–235, 238, 241

parasocial relationships, 67, 76, 284–285
paratelic communication
  conversation and, 186, 222
  power and, 193
participants, categories of conversational, 151

Pei, M., 42
perception, 34
  embodiment perspective and, 34–37
  expectation and, 35
  homeostasis and, 19–44, 99
  interoception and, 34
  introspection and, 115
  perceptual world, the, 128
  selective, 298
perceptual neural system, 87
perceptual simulations. *See also* simulations
  abstract concepts and, 11
  activation of, 88, 99
  concept association and, 87
  defined, 2
  embodied, 87, 146
  emotion and, 95–96
  evidence for, 88–89
  expressive language and, 215
  homeostasis and, 22
  incongruity and, 250
  muscular experience and, 91–92
  neural system and, 86
  partial nature of, 90
  play and, 215
  scenarios and, 94
  schemas and, 94
  scripts and, 94
  syntax and, 90
  theories of, 93
  visual, 89–91
  words and, 72, 133
perceptual simulations and metaphor, 93–94, 240–241
  activation of, 94, 226, 240
  context and, 98
  novel metaphors, 92
  processing of, 242
perceptual symbols, 86–88, 92–93
perceptual systems, 22, 135, 146
personal identity, 148, 243–245, 276–277, 304–306
Petri, A., 261
Petty, R. E., 7n47, 98, 171n602, 184, 242
phenomenal awareness, 36
phonemes, 47, 134
phonemic clause, 138
phonetics, 48
phonology, 48
physical environment, 158
  communication and, 146
physiology. *See* brain; neural system
Plato, 2, 282
play, 58, 207–222
  adult, 211–214

Index

aggression and, 207
argumentation and, 214
categories of, 211
cognitive evolution and, 213
competition and, 208, 211–212
in conversation, 216–220
creativity and, 213
curiosity and, 17, 208
endorphins and, 210
face and, 212
flow and, 210
grooming and, 221
group identity and, 213
homeostasis and, 213, 220–221
humor and, 253–254
imitation and, 58
incongruity and, 208, 222
joking culture and, 218
juvenile, 209–210
language origins and, 221–222
language play, 214–216
memes and, 213
metaphor and, 238–240
mimicry and, 211
nature of, 207–209
object, 208
pattern completion and, 216
poetry and, 214
pretend play, 68
rehearsal function of, 209
role play, 212, 221
simulations and, 215
social functions of, 208, 254–257
subversion of reality in, 214
wordplay, 212
play and frames
conflict talk and, 204
establishment of, 203
humor and, 217, 262
reframing, 208
teasing and, 248
termination of, 222
poetry, 214
politeness
cognitive context and, 148
conversation and, 185
face and, 71, 166–174, 185
grooming and, 185
homeostasis and, 169
maxims, 161
norms of, 197
relevance and, 160–161
signaling and, 66
theory, 160–161, 169
theory of mind and, 71

political humor, 261
power
bases of, 175–176
coercive, 176
conversation and, 193
paratelic communication and, 193
referent, 176
relationships and, 174–177
signals of, 141, 175
status and, 193
Powers, E., 95
pragmatics, 48, 63
prediction, 26, 37, 99–100
Premack, D., 58
pretend play, 68
Price, V., 95
print media, 283–284, 291
Prinz, J., 85, 92–94, 97
privacy, 172
Progovac, L., 60, 62
prosody, 50, 195
public discourse, 289–292
defined, 289
fake news, 298–299
fragmentation and, 299
narrative and, 292–298
topic-focused, 289
US Civil War and, 293–298
punishment imperative, 16

radio, 285–286
Ramscar, M., 97
Raskin, V., 249
Raven, B., 175
Raymond, G., 190
reactance, 168, 232
readiness, signals of, 191
reasoning
abstract, 119
communication and, 48
emotion and, 116–117
inductive/deductive, 205
language play and, 214
mathematical, 93
moral, 96, 171
reasoning, motivated, 3, 3n31, 5, 205, 262, 298
recall, 57, 153
recipient design principle, 190
recursion in conversation, 200–202
Reddy, Michael, 9
reference, displaced, 51
relationship maintenance, 154
relationships
affective valence and, 156

relationships (cont.)
  basic human, 163–164
  cellphones and, 287
  cognitive context and, 155–156
  common ground and, 161
  competition and, 164
  culture and, 178–180
  dimensions of, 180–181
  equal status, 177–178
  expectations and, 179
  facework and, 16, 166–174
  gossip and, 72, 182
  grooming and, 166, 176
  groups and, 163–181
  homeostasis and, 164–166, 169
  impoliteness and, 169–170
  maintenance of, 154
  narrative themes and, 267
  norms and, 179
  parasocial, 284–285
  power and, 174–177
  representation and, 178–180
  reproductive fitness and, 174
  sexual, 163, 178
  signals and, 142, 180
  social, 3, 6
  social control and, 173–174
  social distance and, 176–177
  status and, 174–177
relevance
  assumption of maximal, 189
  cognitive context and, 149, 160–161
  communication and, 148
  context and, 147–149
  discourse context and, 189
  humor and, 251–253
  intentionality and, 126
Relevance Theory, 98, 161, 252
repairs, conversational, 200
representation, 15–18
  brain and, 110
  cognitive, 15, 55
  common ground and, 178
  consciousness and, 15
  creativity and, 242
  culture and, 179
  embodiment perspective and, 40
  homeostasis and, 23, 99
  predictive, 37
  shared, 204, 223, 290
  social, 165
  tools, of, 54
reproductive fitness
  communication and, 57
  culture and, 12, 78, 280

  defined, 20–21
  embodied cognition and, 20
  environment and, 21n88, 22n92
  genes and, 20n85, 44, 73
  homeostasis and, 4, 65, 123, 301
  language and, 31
  memes and, 76
  nervous system and, 15
  relationships and, 174
  signals and, 61, 167
reward systems, 43–44, 109, 167, 213
Rinn, W. E., 103
Ritchie, L. D., 51n181, 238, 271
Rohde, M., 22n93
Rokeach, M., 262
role play, 212, 215–216, 221
Rosch, E., 2, 21
Ross, M., 244

salience. *See* Graded Salience Theory
Sauter, D., 104
Scarantino, A., 111, 117, 119
scenarios, 94
scent, 36
Schachter, S., 107
Schank, R. C., 264, 267
schemas. *See also* scripts
  civility, 168
  cognitive context and, 147, 151
  humor and, 252
  knowledge and, 38, 94
  metaphors and, 69
  scripts and, 94
  shared, 151
  word activation and, 225
  word meaning and, 133
Schnurr, S., 256
Schubert, T. W., 243
scripts, 94, 147, 151, 154, 157–158. *See also* schemas
Seibt, B., 243
selective perception, 298
self
  identity and, 82–83
  the Other and, 165
  private, 83
  representation of, 82
  self-perception, 83, 107, 243
  sense of, 71, 82–83
  social, 83
semantics
  connections, 96–97, 240
  language and, 48, 50
  Latent Semantic Analysis, 96
  semantic association model, 225–226

Index 347

semantic priming, 92
semantic web, 49
sensory perception
  exteroceptive senses, 15, 22, 34
  hearing, 36
  intentional objects and, 113
  interoceptive senses, 34, 36
  introspective awareness, 34
  processing, 22, 30, 34–37
  scent, 36
  sensory experience, 113
  taste, 48
  touch, 36
  transparent objects and, 113
  vision, 34–35
serotonin, 25
setting, 150–153, 202–206, 266–268
sexuality, 141–142, 172, 174, 178
Seyfarth, R. M., 60, 62, 64
Shannon, C., 85, 216, 282n1013
Shepard, R. N., 88–89
sign languages, 33, 47, 131
signals, 123–145
  abstract, 66
  ad hoc, 143–144
  affiliation, of, 142
  ambiguity and, 149
  animals and, 53
  back-channel, 139
  behavior and, 10, 12
  brain and, 33
  cognition and, 303
  conversation and, 306
  cue-based, 65
  vs. cues, 14, 126
  culture-specific, 141
  defined, 128, 130, 303
  digital vs. analog, 142–143
  ecological, 65
  elaboration of, 65–67
  emblems as, 135–136
  emotional, 117–119, 140–141
  expressive, 140–142
  framing and, 192–193
  grooming and, 53, 67
  homeostasis and, 19–44, 61, 302
  illustrators and, 136–137
  information theory and, 51n181
  intentionality and, 125–132
  language and, 132, 305
  play and, 203
  politeness and, 66
  power and, 141, 175
  relational, 142, 180
  reproductive fitness and, 61, 167

  response and, 67
  sexual, 141–142
  sign progression theory, 56
  signal stream, 57
  vs signs, 14
  simulations and, 71
  social status, 141
  strategic, and emotion, 111–112
  symbolic communication, as, 64
  symbols and, 57
  systems, 4–5
  theory of mind and, 58–59, 62
  volitional, 131
  word meaning and, 132–134
signals, communicative
  codes, as, 145
  common ground and, 67
  computer model and, 28
  cues and, 64
  emotion and, 118
  intentionality and, 130
  needs and, 21
  rules and, 159
  theory of mind and, 59
signals, nonverbal/nonlexical, 12, 48, 66, 130,
    142, 144
signs vs. signals, 14
simulation-activation process, 70
simulations. See perceptual simulations
Singer, J., 107
social context, 111–112, 120, 178
social environment
  communication and, 146
  embodied cognition and, 20
  emotion and, 308
  forward projection and, 22
  representation and, 165
  reproductive fitness and, 4, 20n87
social interactions
  biologically evolved processes of, 4
  bonding, 17, 305
  communication, 12
  determinants of, 174
  dominance, 183
  facework and, 17, 164
  homeostasis and, 303
  humor and, 254–257
  inner dialogue and, 71
  knowledge and, 60–63
  language acquisition and, 50
  perception and, 128
  play and, 207
  representation and, 165
  signals and, 53
  social contagion, 111

social interactions (cont.)
  social control, 70, 173–174, 305
  social distance, 176–177
  social emotions and, 105
  social groups, 5, 288
  social realities, 280, 288
social media, 287, 292, 298
social organization, 116, 302, 309
social realities, 280, 287–301
social settings, 146, 150–153
social status, 174–178, 193
  ceremonial conversations and, 154
  gestures and, 141
  sense of self and, 304
  signals of, 141
somatic marker hypothesis, 116
speaker support, 140
speech, inner, 66, 71
Sperber, D.
  ambiguity of language, 149
  cognitive context, 147
  cognitive environment, 148, 190
  intentionality, 144
  relevance, 98, 148, 189, 251
Spitz, A., 203, 219, 234
Spivey, M. J., 89
status
  competition and, 61
  equal, 177–178
  face-threatening acts and, 193
  group identity and, 177
  power and, 174–177, 193
  relationships and, 174–177
Steen, G., 240
Stewart, T. C., 242
stimuli, 39, 111, 117, 129, 131
Stivers, T., 198
story, 264–278. *See also* narrative
  character types and, 266–268
  cognition and, 23
  defined, 264–266
  as evidence, 205
  identity and, 272, 274, 276–277, 289
  layering and, 201, 268
  master-plots and, 266–268
  memory and, 267
  metaphor and, 236–241, 270
  moral of the, 237
  national, 276
  setting and, 266–268
  story index, 265
  story world, 267, 275
  tellability of, 274
  time sequence in, 266
  types of, 268

storytelling
  collaborative, 270–271, 273
  collective, 297
  context and, 155, 265
  conversation and, 268–276
  conversational, 268–276
  forward projection and, 221
  group norms and, 173
  incongruity and, 222
  jazz performance metaphor, 272
  norms of, 269
  representation and, 79
Strack, F., 109
strategic impoliteness, 172–173, 185n650
survival circuits, 105–106
  arousal and, 39, 108
  emotion and, 108
  homeostasis and, 39–40, 110
  interoception and, 105
  prediction and, 99
  reflexive responses and, 109
  stimuli and, 117
sweet humor, 246, 253, 263
symbols
  abstract, 11, 52, 70, 99
  communication and, 64
  emotion and, 111
  Homo erectus and, 34
  modal, 11
  perceptual, 86–88, 92–93, 100
  semantic web and, 49
  signals and, 57
  social, 65
  symbolic reference, 64
  theory of mind and, 61
  utterances and, 50
synapses, 23, 26, 29
syntax
  development of, 65, 68–69
  elaboration of, 68–71
  language and, 47
  patterns and, 47
  perceptual simulations and, 90
  signals and, 132

Tassinary, L. G., 104
teasing, 212, 248, 254, 257, 271
technology, communication
  audience fragmentation and, 292
  discourse and, 280, 299
  effects of, 279
  forward projection and, 308
  group homeostasis and, 307
  misinformation and, 299
  narrative and, 297

Index

television, 285–286, 291
telic communication, 185–186
  functions of, 186, 202
  theories of language and, 72
  topic changes and, 192–193
  uses of language, 66–67
termination, conversational, 192
Tewksbury, D., 95
Thagard, P., 241–242
thematic metaphors, 244
theory of mind. *See also* mind
  abstract signaling and, 66
  common ground and, 61, 67
  concepts of time and, 68
  early hominids and, 16
  empathy and, 16
  face and, 167
  first order, 59, 82
  group-bonding rituals and, 221
  intentionality and, 63
  language use and, 304
  moral judgment and, 170–171
  natural events and, 67
  religion and, 307
  second order, 59, 61–64, 82
  signaling and, 58–59, 62
  third order, 66, 82
Thompson, E., 2
tools, 56
topic changes, conversational, 192–193
touch, 36
Tracy, K., 95
transcategorization, 234
triggering event, 112
Trump, D., 170, 172, 185n650, 261–262, 276, 287
turn-taking, 139, 193–200
  conversation and, 65
  cues and, 194
  face and, 197, 306
  gestures and, 194
Tversky, A., 3
Twitter, 287, 299

utterances, 50, 137–138, 155
utterances, sequence of, 189–190

values, 307–308
Varela, F. J., 2, 21
Vidmar, N., 262
vision, 34
visual experience, simulating, 89–91
visual images, 281–282
vocabulary
  curiosity and, 68
  development of, 67–68
  homeostasis and, 64
  imitation and, 64
  introspective, 68
  language play and, 17
  limited, problem of, 61
  signals and, 132
  size of, 62
vocalics, 61, 137
volition, signals, and, 131

Waldzus, S., 243
Waletsky, J., 266
Watzlawick, P., 13, 128
Weaver, W., 85
Wernicke's area, 33, 38, 68, 132
Williams, L. E., 243
Wilson, A. E., 244
Wilson, D.
  ambiguity of language, 149
  cognitive context, 147
  cognitive environment and, 128n496, 148, 190
  intentionality, 144
  relevance, 98, 148, 189, 251
Woodruff, G., 58
word form, 134–135
word meaning, 132–134, 225
wordplay, 212–214
written language, 70, 214, 282–284, 309

Yaxley, R. H., 91

Zhong, C. B., 243
Zillmann, D., 108, 247
Zimbardo, P. G., 107
Zwaan, R. A.
  language use, 99
  simulations, 89–92
  symbols, 11, 93

Printed in the United States
by Baker & Taylor Publisher Services